# The Struggle
# and the Urban South

# The Struggle
# and the Urban South

CONFRONTING JIM CROW IN BALTIMORE
BEFORE THE MOVEMENT

**David Taft Terry**

The University of Georgia Press

ATHENS

© 2019 by the University of Georgia Press
Athens, Georgia 30602
www.ugapress.org
All rights reserved
Set in 10.25/13.5 Minion Pro by Graphic Composition, Inc. Bogart, GA.

Most University of Georgia Press titles are
available from popular e-book vendors.

Printed digitally

Library of Congress Cataloging-in-Publication Data

Names: Terry, David Taft, author.
Title: The struggle and the urban South : confronting Jim Crow in Baltimore before the
    movement / David Taft Terry.
Other titles: Politics and culture in the twentieth-century South.
Description: Athens : The University of Georgia Press, [2019] | Series: Politics and culture in
    the twentieth-century South | Includes bibliographical references and index.
Identifiers: LCCN 2018049584| ISBN 9780820355078 (hardcover : alk. paper) |
    ISBN 9780820355085 (ebook)
Subjects: LCSH: African Americans—Segregation—Maryland—Baltimore. | Baltimore
    (Md.)—Race relations—History—20th century. | African Americans—Civil rights—
    Maryland—Baltimore—History—20th century. | Civil rights movements—Maryland—
    Baltimore—History—20th century.
Classification: LCC F189.B19 N478 2019 | DDC 323.1196/073075260904—dc23
    LC record available at https://lccn.loc.gov/2018049584

For you, Pop—
In my dreams I can see your face again

# CONTENTS

# TABLES

# ACKNOWLEDGMENTS

This work draws from a doctoral dissertation completed at Howard University in 2002. Between its completion as a dissertation and the moment I decided to return to academia and prepare this for publication were more than a dozen rewarding years spent professionally at archives and museums, working in public history capacities. During those years, I never lost the passion that brought me to the topic in graduate school. And surely, as I spent many semesters as a part-time adjunct at colleges and universities while supporting a growing family at home, the material represented herein found its way into lectures and justified my continued curiosity, research trips, and presentation of papers. I have truly lived with this work and am honored to share it now. That said, I remain indebted to all of those who gave their time, energy, and consideration to this project in all of its iterations along the way, and I mention only a few here whose efforts on my behalf I will not forget.

My colleagues at Morgan State University have been consistently supportive and encouraging. Particular thanks are extended to the chair of the Department of History and Geography, Annette Palmer, for allowing the time and latitude needed to complete this work. Also at Morgan, I single out these colleagues for particular thanks for their contributions: Glenn O. Phillips, Debra Newman Ham, Brandi C. Brimmer, Takkara Brunson, Frances Dube, and Natanya Duncan. Morgan colleagues Rosalyn Terborg-Penn, Susan Ellery Chapelle, Jeremiah Dibua, Brett Berliner, and Larry Peskin have offered support and feedback on presentations of parts of the chapters herein.

At former posts, colleagues have been aware of my research interest and allowed me to explore them whenever appropriate to the scope of my duties. As such, to Edward C. Papenfuse and the staff of the Maryland State Archives—with special gratitude for Chris Haley and Robert Schoeberlein—I say thank you. Likewise, my thanks go to my former colleagues in the Department of Collections and Exhibitions at the Reginald F. Lewis Museum of Maryland African American History and Culture—Kathryn Coney, Christina Batipps, and Margaret Hutto. Some of the interpretive positions I take up in this book began life as conversations at the museum about exhibit scripts and collection priorities concerning Baltimore civil rights history.

The staffs of several institutions and research facilities made solid contributions to my work, and I wish to acknowledge them here: the Western High School (Baltimore City) Alumni Association; the Library and Special Collections staffs at the Maryland Historical Society; the Baltimore City Archives; the African-American Department and the Maryland Room at Enoch Pratt Free Library, Baltimore; the Manuscripts Division, Library of Congress; the Manuscript Division of the Moorland-Spingarn Research Center, Howard University; King Center Library and Archives; the Beulah M. Davis Special Collections Room, Morgan State University; the Special Collections Department, University of Maryland at College Park; and the *Afro American Newspapers* Archives and Research Center, Baltimore.

Special thanks to all of the wonderful individuals who shared parts of their fascinating life stories with me to help me see Baltimore as they did: Anastatia Phillips Benton, Leroy Carroll, Carl Clark, Carolyn A. Collins, Aubrey Edwards, Natalie Forrest, Gene A. Giles, Lynda Hall Gowie, Delores Richburg Harried, Garry Harried, Rosalie Carter Hillman, Donna Tyler Hollie, Ann Todd Jealous, Clarence Logan, Michael May, Jamie McClellan, Judy Bernstein Miller, Keiffer J. Mitchell, Thelma Koger Parker, Nathaniel Redd, Carol St. Clair, Doug Sands, Judith Spintman, Calla Smorodin, Mamie Bland Todd, McAllister Tyler, and Patricia Logan Welsh.

Formal and informal feedback from historians in the field and subject experts has also been useful and welcome, and so I thank Larry S. Gibson, Sherrilyn Ifill, Matthew Crenson, Garrett Power, Susan Carle, Bob Brugger, Prudence Cumberbatch, Lewis Diuguid, Eli Pousson, Andor Skotnes, Howell Baum, Vivian Fisher, Helena Hicks, John Oliver, Frances Murphy, and Sam Lacy.

To friends and colleagues whose conversations over the years helped me to see the material more clearly, I say thanks. Your kindnesses will not be forgotten. These include Joy L. Bailey, Jabari Asim, Wil Haygood, Judi M. Latta, Sonja Williams, Jana Long, John Gartrell, Leslie Gartrell, Tamara L. Brown, Jelani Cobb, and Ida Jones.

I am also deeply indebted to Walter Biggins and the editorial staff of the University of Georgia Press. Because of their patience and professionalism, the publishing process has been a wonderful experience for me.

Finally, I wish to thank my wonderful family for supporting me and understanding what has been a journey of sorts. To my wife and partner, Alisia, and to our beautiful, inspiring children, David and Grace, I say thank you for your love, which means the world to me.

# ABBREVIATIONS

| | |
|---|---|
| ADA | Americans for Democratic Action |
| AFL | American Federation of Labor |
| BASR | Baltimore Association for States' Rights |
| BCHD | Baltimore Committee for Homefront Democracy |
| BCSDA | Baltimore City Chapter, Students for Democratic Action |
| BHA | Baltimore Housing Authority |
| BIC | Baltimore Inter-racial Conference |
| BIF | Baltimore Interracial Fellowship |
| BPC Minutes BCA | Board of Park Commissioners Meeting Minutes, Records of the Department of Recreation and Parks, 1865–Present, RG 51, Baltimore City Archives |
| BSC Minutes BCA | Minutes of the Board of School Commissioners for Baltimore City (Executive Committee), Records of the Department of Education, Baltimore City Archives |
| BTC | Baltimore Transit Company |
| BUDA | Baltimore Union for Democratic Action |
| C&P | Chesapeake and Potomac Telephone Company |
| CCCU | Coordinating Council for Civic Unity |
| CCJ | Citizens' Committee for Justice |
| CCPA | Coordinated Committee on Poly Admission |
| CIC | Commission on Interracial Cooperation |
| CIG | Civic Interest Group |
| CIO | Congress of Industrial Organizations |
| CORE | Congress of Racial Equality |
| CPHA | Citizens' Planning and Housing Association |
| CWDCC | Colored Women's Democratic Campaign Committee of Maryland |
| FBI | Federal Bureau of Investigation |
| FEPC | Fair Employment Practices Commission |
| FOR | Fellowship of Reconciliation |
| Forum | City-Wide Young People's Forum |
| FPHA | Federal Public Housing Authority |
| HBLA | Homemakers' Building and Loan Association |

| | |
|---|---|
| HUAC | House Un-American Activities Committee |
| JHUSDA | Johns Hopkins University, Students for Democratic Action |
| MIC | Maryland Interracial Commission |
| MNM | Maryland Niagara Movement |
| MPC | Maryland Petition Committee |
| NAACP | National Association for the Advancement of Colored People |
| NAAWP | National Association for the Advancement of White People |
| NANA | New Area Neighborhood Association |
| NBA | National Bar Association |
| NNA | New Negro Alliance |
| NOI | Nation of Islam |
| NUL | National Urban League (National League on Urban Conditions among Negroes) |
| PBEA | Point Breeze Employees Association |
| PCA | Progressive Citizens of America |
| SAC | Social Action Committee |
| SDA | Students for Democratic Action |
| SLM | Suffrage League of Maryland |
| TWEC | Total War Employment Committee |
| UCCHR | United Citizens Committee for Human Rights |
| UDA | Union for Democratic Action |
| UNIA | United Negro Improvement Association and African Communities League |
| USES | United States Employment Service |
| WB&A | Washington, Baltimore, and Annapolis Electric Railway Line |
| WLB | War Labor Board |
| WMC | War Manpower Commission |

**The Struggle
and the Urban South**

# An Enduring Black Struggle for Equality in Baltimore

Toward the close of the nineteenth century, a full generation before southern blacks began coming North in search of new urban lives, black southerners made the big cities of the South even bigger. Even in antebellum years, southern blacks associated urban life with opportunities for greater community and greater agency. Within only a generation of slavery's demise, the memory of these truths drew blacks to the cities without yet leaving the South.

Many of the younger blacks, especially, arrived in the city with optimism, competitive skill sets, and a willingness to contribute to the broader good as well as to compete for opportunities the future would surely bring. White southerners responded to the new, urban black with the construction of formalized systems of racial segregation that came to be known en masse as Jim Crow. Jim Crow's rise, at the close of the nineteenth century, represented the codification of mounting white backlash against black mobility—physical, social, economic, and political. Indeed, Jim Crow emerged as a signature component of law and custom across the urban South, including Baltimore. From this beginning, blacks would respond.

Situating the historical contexts of the emergence of racial segregation, *The Struggle and the Urban South: Confronting Jim Crow in Baltimore before the Movement* explores the nature of that response—an enduring black struggle for equality—as it evolved from the 1890s through the 1950s. At the turn of the century, southern white commitments to white supremacy appeared intractable and enjoyed the broad support of government and other institutions. Through the example of Baltimore, urban South blacks will be seen pursuing greater capacities for self-determination through community building and "equalization" protest. The point of equalization was not social proximity with whites or any obsequious desire to win white approval and acceptance.

Rather, the point of early struggle and its equalization goal was for blacks to attain the greatest capacity for self-determined, if largely separate, urban life in the South.

With each passing decade following Jim Crow's construction, segregation imposed an interdependency on the many elements of urban black life in the South. This, in turn, cultivated nationalist instincts, and blacks responded to their common situation by building communities to serve their common goals. Indeed, in the urban environment by the turn of the twentieth century, if not sooner, the characteristic differences between the interdependent coalitions that made up southern black life—middle class and working class, sanctified and worldly, native and newcomer—were de-emphasized. Blacks gained advantage in their struggle for equality due to the sheer size of the communities they were amassing. These coalitions would not stand in perpetuity, of course. But, for the time, to borrow historian Earl Lewis's phrasing, "segregation became congregation" in the urban South.[1]

An important transformation in the historical arc of the enduring black struggle occurred during the 1930s. White solidarity on segregation began to falter—or the lengths to which some whites were willing to go to preserve segregation grew shorter. To varying degrees this apparent shift was notable in the emergent movement attempting to organize urban southern workers, in the transformation of urban politics with the rise of the welfare state under FDR's New Deal, and in a range of local, regional, and national institutions as they responded to economic crisis and looming war. Sensing an opportunity to affect struggles traditionally beyond their control, urban South blacks in places like Baltimore pushed against the limits of the day. They pushed harder, still, for equalization under Jim Crow, and, when that proved impossible, for circumstantial desegregation as its surrogate. "If separate, then equal," was the demand.[2]

*The Struggle and the Urban South* has been written as something of a historical narrative, seeking to balance analysis with information. Despite what historian George Callcott noted as Baltimore's "characteristic anonymity" within the national, southern, and African American historical narratives, scholarship on race in Baltimore during the nineteenth and twentieth centuries has benefited from a number of important books in the last decade or so—Andor Skotnes's *A New Deal for All?*, Rhonda Williams's *The Politics of Public Housing*, Kenneth Durr's *Behind the Backlash*, and Howell S. Baum's *"Brown" in Baltimore* all come to mind.[3]

From these and earlier books, a standard timeline of the Baltimore struggle has emerged around the following assertions: that the economic boycotts of the 1930s primarily sought integration; that lynching in rural Maryland was a cause for the struggle of Baltimore blacks; that the most impactful activism before 1960 was conducted by the Baltimore NAACP and the rise of Lillie Jackson's leadership (and that the branch was moribund until 1935); and that school desegregation in 1954 was the sole turning point because "integrationism" best frames the strategic orientation of Baltimore civil rights from its start. This selection of ideas, however, is not so well established that analysis alone suffices. The opposite may be truer. With this book I hope to contribute to a broader, more nuanced understanding of the black struggle for equality in Baltimore. The analysis herein suggests different interpretive views, and the narrative details reveal a depth of struggle across a longer periodization than has been interrogated by other scholarship.

The book is arranged into two parts and six chapters. Part 1 consists of chapters 1–3. These are driven by chronological progress, with each chapter advancing an explanation of how black Baltimore conceived, structured, and organized its resistance to Jim Crow. Briefly, chapter 1 chronicles the rise and proliferation of formal, de jure racial segregation from the 1890s to the 1910s and analyzes the perspectives of black Baltimoreans at the time within a broader historical framework of black urbanicity in the South during those years.

Chapter 2 examines the 1910s to the 1930s, as Baltimore's black population reconceptualized older traditions of community-based protest. Ultimately guided in resistance by a pragmatic, black nationalist strategy for "equalization"—even if within the segregated system—black activists responded to the specific circumstances of Baltimore by affiliating with national social justice entities. This allowed black Baltimoreans to pull more resources to local resistance projects.

The final chapter of part 1 considers the impacts of the late 1930s and the war years of the 1940s on Baltimore's enduring black struggle for equality. These years mark an era of transformation, as allies beyond the black community were recruited (or instigated) into service of the struggle. White leftist radicals, for example, were especially active. And a true opportunity developed in the courts, when the first judicial critiques—though not yet full repudiations—of the "separate but equal" standard were handed down.

The chapters of part 2 investigate the overlapping narratives of the 1940s and 1950s. These chapters consider postwar transformations in the black struggle, which battled racist inequality concurrently across multiple social spaces. As anticommunist hysteria in these years depleted leftist ranks, new interest in antiracist activism remade liberal politics in Baltimore, creating fresh opportunities for African Americans to instigate antisegregation interventions by white-controlled entities.

As such, chapter 4 analyzes activism in Baltimore housing and recreation facilities into the postwar years. Where the advent of public housing pushed old questions of who would live where, causing politicians to waffle, developments in the private market proved dramatic. Transformations flowing from victories against racism in housing encouraged blacks to remap the city and to press against the inequality of Jim Crow culture from multiple points, including the use of recreational spaces.

Similarly, the struggle for access to public accommodations and public spaces downtown during the postwar 1940s and 1950s is the subject of chapter 5. By the force of the insistence of black Baltimoreans under everyday circumstance pressing against inequity, a new antiracist liberal program by white-led entities entered the struggle. Jim Crow began to fall in Baltimore's public spaces.

The final chapter explores student activism in the postwar city, including direct-action campaigns and efforts to desegregate schools. All of this struggle and accomplishment was completed before the end of the 1950s, before the "movement" begins.

### The Black Vernacular Ethos of Urbanicity in the South

Scholarly studies of Jim Crow from the perspectives of African American southerners have generally subscribed to a range of tropes drawn from the broader southern historical discourse. Albeit unintended, a number of these often lead to interpretations that marginalize or exclude black perspectives and deemphasize black self-determination and agency. Perhaps the most ubiquitous of these tropes posits that only rural and small-town locales of the former Confederacy constitute the *true* South. Four years of secession and its impacts for whites, rather than four centuries of slavery and segregation for blacks, are held up as the region's defining historical considerations. Other attributes are seen somehow as less illuminating of the South and thus less authentically southern. Toward these ends, in most scholarship, the historical perspectives and actions of white rural southerners are primary. As a result, Border South states like Maryland (because it did not secede) and big cities like Baltimore are marginalized if not defined completely out of the true South. To my view, not only is the history of urbanization in the postbellum South hidden, but also the Border South lens wholly distorts black perceptions and definitions of their region.

In this book, I define the South as southern blacks of antebellum and Jim Crow eras understood it. From historical African American vantages, legacies of slavery (not simply the Confederacy) defined the South. The South was where slavery had remained law until destroyed by the Civil War; the South included the "loyal" slave states as well as the rebels. The South was where sometime after Emancipation, despite the destruction of slavery and the granting of citizenship, white privilege *as a fact of law* continued and was enforced by the state until destroyed by a coalition led by black southerners themselves in the mid-twentieth century. And, in the historical black imagination since the antebellum era, the South included urban life, particularly as it involved self-determination and agency.

Therefore, in place of the Border South lens, I begin instead with a broad if underappreciated truth: in the South, urbanization has long been an important shaper of African American life. The consequences of living in the city, and of urban life—urbanicity—carried specific meaning in the black vernacular traditions of the South. Urbanicity for southern blacks encouraged an ethos of empowerment and self-determination, often in pointed contrast with the vulnerabilities and dependencies of rurality. Indeed, scholars have grasped the cultural import of urban life for blacks in southern history as they have described relationships of "separate cities" and "communities of identity and fellowship" in seeing black communities within broader circumscribing white orders.[4]

This black vernacular ethos of urbanicity in the South grew up in the antebellum nineteenth century, on the rural slave quarters. There, firsthand and secondhand tales of black life in the burgeoning big cities were heard. This was Frederick Douglass's experience, for example. As a boy in rural Maryland, Douglass heard of Baltimore—of black life, of black community, of greater black autonomy—from older boys who worked as part of enslaved crews transporting goods back and forth across the Chesapeake Bay. "These [boys] were esteemed very highly by the other slaves, and looked upon as the privileged ones of the plantation," Douglass wrote in 1845. Talk of urban life in Douglass's rural quarter left him and many others with "the strongest desire to see Baltimore." Indeed, news that his owner was transferring him away from the only home he had ever known was tempered by the fact that he was going to Baltimore. Though he would still be enslaved there, Douglass confessed, "I left without a regret, and with the highest hopes of future happiness."[5]

Similarly, the number of southern black fugitives from slavery seeking asylum in the region's cities likely surpassed those seeking to cross into the celebrated promised land above the Mason-Dixon line. Big cities in the antebellum South, historian Richard C. Wade reminds us, "always attracted more fugitives than they lost." Rather than risk immediate long-distance treks, runaways from rural bondage often fled toward the more nearby but sufficiently inconspicuous protections of community and kinship available in the large urban centers within the South. There they "quickly lost themselves in the congestion, protected as much by the anonymity of urban life as [by] the collusion of other Negroes." Many likely remained in the South's cities among that community and kin as fugitives at large. Others used urban community and kinship as the central resource for eventual flight out of the South altogether. Even those gaining legal freedom through manumission often resettled in the nearest large urban area of the South. From these bases, physical proximity with kinfolk still enslaved could be maintained. Not surprisingly, once Emancipation came, urbanicity maintained its association with greater opportunities for community, resistance, and agency, and migration to cities continued into the mid-twentieth century. Urbanicity was self-determination. Southern cities like Baltimore—where native black populations were already considerable—grew exponentially larger.[6]

This book is particularly concerned with Baltimore's Westside neighborhoods, where a transformation into the city's most populous black enclave tracked the rise of Jim Crow. A combination of white racist compulsion and blacks' sense of dignity derived from their own capacities for self-respect and self-determination saw blacks respond to Jim Crow by ordering a world for themselves in West Baltimore. To be clear, West Baltimore was no utopia. No community under Jim Crow could be. Racism's disproportionate empowerment of whites barred urban blacks from most desirable occupations and employment. Likewise, white prerogatives in housing, education, and access to public space also enjoyed broad hegemony. However, migrating blacks did not judge the quality of urban life simply against what white counterparts enjoyed. Rather, the black vernacular ethos determined the value of urbanicity largely against what had been left behind in the equally iniquitous but more brutal rural South. Rurality versus urbanicity was the comparison of consequence.

Hundreds of thousands of southern blacks believed that urbanicity presented the greatest platform for community, resistance, and agency. The meaning black southerners ascribed to this view cannot be overstated. Whatever white folk and their coercive Jim Crow structures sought to deny southern blacks, urbanicity as ethos suggested more was attainable if blacks only stuck together. If most southerners still lived rurally at this time, the irrepressible demographic momentum in the South, as elsewhere, was toward cities. Everywhere in the nation, from the late nineteenth through the mid-twentieth century, cities grew, most because rural Americans relocated to them. Representing not just evidence of the region's continuing political recovery and physical reconstruction after the devastations of war, expansive urbanization in the late nineteenth-century South, historian Edward Ayers notes, "was as great as in other American cities." If late nineteenth-century southern cities were not equal in size, economic diversity, or ethnic mixture to the nation's largest, Ayers writes, "compared with the South of 1860 or 1870, the region had undergone an important transformation." Not only were blacks part of this phenomenon, but also perhaps no native-born subset of the population embraced urbanization during this era more than blacks did. And, as a majority of African Americans still resided in the fifteen former slave states (plus Washington, D.C.) as late as 1970, compared with places outside of the region, the South's cities had a tremendous head start on black urbanization.[7]

In only three decades, 1880 to 1910, urban residency among black southerners more than doubled, from 8.1 percent of the black population living in the region's cities to 18.8 percent.[8] In the biggest cities of the South, blacks maintained a higher proportion of the total population than in the urban North. This fact remained throughout the century, even as several urban black populations in the North greatly surpassed southern ones. With the period of great urbanization before the Great Migration, the new century's first decade found more blacks in Louisville than in Detroit, more in Memphis than Chicago, and more in Baltimore than Harlem (see table 1). By 1920, when the full impact of World War I migration had registered, a number of southern cities mirrored the black populations of the faster-growing urban industrial North and Midwest. While Cleveland had 34,451 black residents, Nashville had 35,633. Pittsburgh and Detroit, respectively, had 37,725 and 40,838 black residents, but Richmond had 54,041, and St. Louis had 69,854. Harlem's 109,133 blacks in 1920 were fewer than the 109,966 blacks populating Washington, D.C. And, while Baltimore had nearly two million fewer total residents than Chicago, the black populations of the cities were practically identical (108,322 and 109,458 respectively).[9]

The scope and scale of urban life in the South made deep impressions on migrating rural blacks. The presence and diversity of black businesses, black professionals, black organizations, and black institutions contributed to these impressions. Then too there was the sheer size and concentration of the urban black world—"more blacks than they had ever seen in their lives," David Goldfield notes. And, while "numbers and institutions did not necessarily afford safety," Goldfield continues, migrating blacks "did respond to new possibilities while creating other new possibilities of their own." Just as important was the interracial element. Having left behind the social requirements of rural and small-town community life, which continued to exact from blacks the demoralizing racial performance of dependency, obeisance, and sycophancy, urban blacks—even in the South—enjoyed a relative neglect of such mores, largely due to less frequent, often impersonal interactions with whites. In this

**TABLE 1.** Ten Largest Black Populations in U.S. Cities, 1890–1950: Two Views

**BY SIZE OF BLACK POPULATION**

| | 1890 | | | 1910 | | | 1930 | | | 1950 | | |
|---|---|---|---|---|---|---|---|---|---|---|---|---|
| City | Blacks | % of total | City | Blacks | % of total | City | Blacks | % of total | City | Blacks | % of total |
| Washington | 75,572 | 32.8 | Washington | 94,446 | 28.5 | New York | 327,706 | 4.7 | New York | 775,516 | 9.8 |
| Baltimore | 67,104 | 15.4 | New York | 91,709 | 1.9 | Chicago | 233,903 | 6.9 | Chicago | 509,437 | 14.1 |
| New Orleans | 64,691 | 26.7 | New Orleans | 89,262 | 26.3 | Philadelphia | 219,599 | 11.3 | Philadelphia | 378,968 | 18.3 |
| Philadelphia | 39,371 | 3.8 | Baltimore | 84,749 | 15.2 | Baltimore | 142,106 | 17.7 | Detroit | 303,721 | 16.4 |
| New York | 39,371 | 1.6 | Philadelphia | 84,459 | 5.5 | Washington | 132,068 | 27.1 | Washington | 284,313 | 35.4 |
| Richmond | 36,620 | 39.7 | Memphis | 52,441 | 40.0 | New Orleans | 129,632 | 28.3 | Baltimore | 226,053 | 23.8 |
| Charleston | 30,970 | 56.4 | Birmingham | 52,305 | 39.4 | Detroit | 120,066 | 7.7 | Los Angeles | 211,585 | 10.7 |
| Nashville | 29,382 | 38.6 | Atlanta | 51,902 | 33.5 | Birmingham | 99,077 | 38.2 | New Orleans | 182,631 | 32.0 |
| Memphis | 28,706 | 44.5 | Richmond | 46,733 | 36.6 | Memphis | 96,550 | 38.1 | St. Louis | 154,448 | 18.0 |
| Louisville | 28,651 | 1.8 | Chicago | 44,103 | 2.0 | St. Louis | 93,580 | 11.4 | Cleveland | 149,544 | 15.6 |

**BY PROPORTIONALITY OF BLACK POPULATION**

| | 1890 | | | 1910 | | | 1930 | | | 1950 | | |
|---|---|---|---|---|---|---|---|---|---|---|---|---|
| City | Blacks | % of total | City | Blacks | % of total | City | Blacks | % of total | City | Blacks | % of total |
| Charleston | 30,970 | 56.4 | Memphis | 52,441 | 40.0 | Birmingham | 99,077 | 38.2 | Washington | 284,313 | 35.4 |
| Memphis | 28,706 | 44.5 | Birmingham | 52,305 | 39.4 | Memphis | 96,550 | 38.1 | New Orleans | 182,631 | 32.0 |
| Richmond | 36,620 | 39.7 | Richmond | 46,733 | 36.6 | New Orleans | 129,632 | 28.3 | Baltimore | 226,053 | 23.8 |
| Nashville | 29,382 | 38.6 | Atlanta | 51,902 | 33.5 | Washington | 132,068 | 27.1 | Philadelphia | 378,968 | 18.3 |
| Washington | 75,572 | 32.8 | Washington | 94,446 | 28.5 | Baltimore | 142,106 | 17.7 | St Louis | 154,448 | 18.0 |
| New Orleans | 64,691 | 26.7 | New Orleans | 89,262 | 26.3 | St Louis | 93,580 | 11.4 | Detroit | 303,721 | 16.4 |
| Baltimore | 67,104 | 15.4 | Baltimore | 84,749 | 15.2 | Philadelphia | 219,599 | 11.3 | Cleveland | 149,544 | 15.6 |
| Philadelphia | 39,371 | 3.8 | Philadelphia | 84,459 | 5.5 | Detroit | 120,066 | 7.7 | Chicago | 509,437 | 14.1 |
| Louisville | 28,651 | 1.8 | Chicago | 44,103 | 2.0 | Chicago | 233,903 | 6.9 | Los Angeles | 211,585 | 10.7 |
| New York | 39,371 | 1.6 | New York | 91,709 | 1.9 | New York | 327,706 | 4.7 | New York | 775,516 | 9.8 |

Calculated from U.S. Census figures as cited in Hollis R. Lynch, *The Black Urban Condition: A Documentary History, 1866–1971* (New York: Thomas Y. Crowell, 1973), appendix A.

broad context, therefore, more and more rural blacks arrived in southern cities like Baltimore during the late nineteenth and early twentieth centuries.[10]

## The Urban South Nature of Jim Crow

Many rural blacks migrating to cities like Baltimore arrived with ambitions, vibrancy, and energy, if not always clear prospects. Among them were those most likely to "look out for new opportunities, resist indignities, [and] join new organizations," in the words of Edward Ayers, "creating an uneasiness in whites who watched from a distance." To late nineteenth-century white eyes, however, urban South blacks were more self-assertive than their rural kin. Particularly among the young, black middle-class strivers met white presumptions with impudence. And the lower classes demonstrated a readiness to respond to white violence (even police violence) with black violence. All in all, urban southern blacks seemed impatient with white expectations and showed little willingness to remain in their historical places.[11]

The threat of blacks assuming postures as equal citizens was unacceptable to the white masses. As the activist-scholar W. E. B. Du Bois observed, "there was one thing that the white South feared more than Negro dishonesty, ignorance, and incompetency, and that was Negro honesty, knowledge, and efficiency." Thus, if New South modes of urbanization signaled a modernization of the region, white supremacy's survival of that transformation was imperative for most white southerners girding against urban black threats. The need for new systems of "coercion and control" were urgent. "Driven by fears about the consequences if blacks were not 'kept in their place'," Howard Rabinowitz concludes, "whites had helped establish a new pattern of race relations in the urban South by 1890."[12]

Defining more than a general environment of racism and discrimination, whites created Jim Crow segregation during the closing years of the nineteenth century to effect, within the bounds of the U.S. Constitution, a lived and practical inequality between whites and blacks. Specifically, Jim Crow mandated for whites privileged access to the socially competitive spaces of citizenship. In this way, Jim Crow was decidedly urban, reflecting transformations overtaking the South at the end of the nineteenth century more so than what had come before. It was intended as decidedly modern, Ayers reminds us. "The newer a Southern city, the more likely it was to be consistently segregated by race; the faster a Southern city grew, the faster it became segregated." Segregation sought to institutionalize racism and inequality in the urban space where large numbers of blacks and larger numbers of whites competed for hegemony.

Hard and fast lines delimited which jobs were and were not "black jobs." Space to live in the city proved an early and constant problem, as racists attempted to choke black residential expansion. And "ugliness" in public settings pervaded, especially downtown, where, as one black southern urbanite recalled, "white people delighted in shunting their dirt and misery on you." Indeed, a primary intent of segregation's corollary, electoral disfranchisement, was to protect white racists' prerogatives in urban public space by removing black influence from the political discourse. Pervasive and durable throughout the region, Jim Crow enjoyed awesome power thanks to the coercive might of state sanction and enforcement.[13]

Surprisingly, perhaps, much of the white political will toward racial segregation in the urban South emerged as liberal reform, not conservative reaction. Jim Crow was the work of turn-of-the-century Progressivism characterized by scientific racism embraced by whites of all political persuasions. Classic studies of the institutionalization of white supremacy find that Jim Crow affected "the very foundation of southern progressivism." In their effort to bring order and orthodoxy to the region's urbanizing masses, southern whites advocating Progressive reform and those advocating segregation were often identical. Further, the Progressive reformer ranks drew from the well-educated and comparatively moderate white urban elites. Their constituencies, however, drew mainly from the southern white working and lower classes that held skeptical and even cynical views of much of the Progressive program. Yet, if differences over many Progressive agenda items often put whites at odds with each other, the segregation of blacks met only wide acceptance among the cross section of whites.[14]

A broad and near-unanimous sympathy across the white urban South supported racial segregation. Protecting southern cities from the racial pogroms sure to accompany black-white competition for space—in the factory, neighborhood, and school, for example—southern Progressives pursued racial separation by legal mandate. Added to this, Don Doyle reminds us, was the ascendance of public health planning informed by both "germ theory" and older proclivities for anti-black scientific racism. The result justified physical quarantine of blacks away from non-black citizens as rational public policy.[15]

## The Black Struggle in the Urban South: Themes and Chronologies

If the history of late nineteenth-century urbanization in the South was in large part shaped by segregation culture, belief in the empowering nature of big-city life—that black vernacular ethos of urbanicity—also continued. Into the twentieth century, this served as a foundation upon which urban southern blacks established a protest tradition, an enduring struggle for equality, to meet Jim Crow as it emerged and proliferated over the first half of the century. Yet, directly or indirectly, most scholarship on the subject has privileged a periodization that pivots on the 1960s. Despite the far-reaching chronologies associated with the "long civil rights movement," the 1960s have remained an interpretive centerline. Somehow that single decade anchors our perceptions of black resistance to racism in America, as if all else presents approach or decline. Such interpretations have led to vigorous debate among recent scholars.[16]

My perception of this history, however, is ordered by an admittedly simplistic semantic distinction between the respective concepts of "struggles" and "movements." The civil rights movement was just that, a movement—a social, political, and cultural phenomenon with a discernible beginning and a discernible end. If its beginnings owed to many things, white media coverage (print and broadcast) of southern sit-in campaigns after February 1, 1960, was a catalyst. From there, the role of white media came to overdetermine the civil rights movement in some ways. By logic of this definition, the white media's increasing disenchantment with the "race beat" between 1965 (and the passage of the Voting Rights Act) and 1968 (when disillusion over the subsequent course of things peaked with Martin King's assassination) represented the movement's culmination.

If movements have beginnings and ends, struggles continue, often bridging generations. Thus I appropriate "struggle" for this book's title, *The Struggle and the Urban South*. "Struggle" captures my sense that urban southern blacks cultivated opportunities to mount sustained, complex, and productive resistance to codified white supremacy, from the 1890s through the 1950s. The goal of equality remained constant throughout this time. Black perspectives informing resistance strategies and tactics would evolve and adjust as new possibilities arose.

I explore the enduring black struggle for equality across three themes: the struggle's counter-narrative functionality; its promotion of creative, intragroup tensions; and its instigation of antisegregation interventions by white-controlled entities. Taken together, these themes broadly track the chronological progression of black resistance during the Jim Crow years in the urban South. In an example of the earliest of the chronological themes, blacks in Baltimore responded to Jim Crow's affront by rejecting its underpinning false narratives about black life and black people. Those false narratives emerged from amalgamations of white supremacy and scientific racism ascribing "innate inability" to blacks. From the closing decades of the nineteenth century into the early decades of the twentieth, an anti-black diatribe spewed forth pseudoscientific claims about biological determinism, ostensible black moral deficiency, and cultural bankruptcy traceable to African ancestry and blackness. Thus, from the earliest years, the black resistance struggle projected ideas of self-dignity, as blacks undertook their own "symbolic production of race" (to borrow Michelle Alexander's useful phrasing). We find blacks in the urban South performing a community life concerned with building a counter-narrative to Jim Crow doctrine.[17]

Blacks understood themselves denied but deserving in every way the rights and privileges they demanded. White supremacy was their enemy. Thus, by demonstrating commitment to communal institutions and notions of black achievement, race betterment, self-determination, and self-reliance, blacks and the vitality and fullness of their lives served as counter-narrative to Jim Crow's aspersions. Because it seemed especially possible in the urban South, given the proportional scale, complexity, and diversity of black life there, this counter-narrative successfully confronted the imposed stigmas of being black.

In the course of its function, this counter-narrative promoted education against charges of ignorance, counseled dignity and determination to meet presumptions of obeisance and servility, and celebrated achievement as demonstrations of competence and ability. This black counter-narrative held out community in response to individual identity, respectability to meet accusations of immorality, and self-respect and independent initiatives to answer presumptions of dependency. Sometimes the counter-narrative was articulated simply by protest—the willingness to speak truths to power and to not let white lies and white injustices go unnamed. Similarly, the counter-narrative was institutionalized and put into action in a range of ways. Black schools, churches, humor, song, organizations, and foodways are examples. The black press too under Jim Crow served this counter-narrative. The complexity of political discourse and sociocultural critique (including self-criticism) evident in the pages of the black press in the urban South touted the authenticity of black worldviews. "Get the *Afro* . . . this is your paper . . . it's your spokesman," local NAACP president Lillie Jackson often advised Baltimore audiences, "let's keep it strong and free." The counter-narrative would not allow the black world to be invisible or anything but central to black people.[18]

A second theme in the rough chronology of the enduring black struggle for equality concerns the centrality of intragroup relations. By the second decade of the twentieth century, blacks in the urban South had organized, allied, and collectively structured resistance programs of regional and national reach. This entailed long-term strengthening of local organizations through national affiliation without surrendering local agency or self-determination. Blacks in cities like Baltimore pursued (and were pursued by) a number of strategic national programs and organizations that promised to assist local resistance agendas in return for support of regional and national ones. This included the establishment of local branches of national social justice organizations. Contrary to what is often portrayed, these were not intrinsically top-down affairs, with the national headquarters always dictating to the local branch. The resulting creative tension between branches and national offices regularly saw Baltimore set aside broad organizational philosophy for more pragmatic approaches to the pursuit of equality.[19]

This creative tension proved mutually beneficial. Insisting on a national program tailored to local needs ensured local enthusiasm and support—and membership dollars—that benefited the national organization. Those organizations proving most durable and effective on the ground in the urban South were those for which ideology and national policy could be kneaded into the pragmatism of local branch work. This was most readily apparent, for example, with the national NAACP and its urban southern branches. The Baltimore NAACP was most effective by the 1930s after its leaders had worked to make it more of a mass membership organization locally than it had been earlier, when membership was mainly culled from the black elite. Shifting the nature of its basic program, the organization engaged in a number of direct-action campaigns, addressing the likes of employment discrimination and lynching. Throughout this phase, the Baltimore NAACP often clashed ideologically, strategically, and in terms of personalities with the national headquarters. Concessions from both sides, however, ultimately kept the intraorganizational peace. Meanwhile, the branch collaborated regularly with other local social justice organizations and emergent labor groups to mobilize large segments of the black community. Commitment by the local black press to publicizing the Baltimore NAACP's messages and promoting its visibility contributed greatly to mobilization efforts.[20]

A number of other tensions also shaped intragroup relations in the struggle in Baltimore and many southern cities. These tensions appeared within single organizations, pitting traditional "respectability" politics against what Clarence Lang identified among black working-class activists of 1930s St. Louis as an emergent politics of self-respect. Here Lang brought to the fore an aspect of the black working-class identity easily visible in the urban South—one anchored in a self-determined social politics "autonomous from both white approval and black middle-class assent." Later, tensions also emerged between organizations situated fully within black Baltimore—and thus dominated by black voices—and those groups led by antiracist/interracialist Baltimore whites with little or no organizational footing in the black community. The Baltimore Interracial Fellowship, which had organized by the early 1940s, is an example of the latter.

Yet, like those governing local and national tensions, these tensions too ultimately proved to be assets to the enduring black struggle.[21]

The final chronological theme in the progression of the enduring black struggle entails blacks' ability to instigate anti–Jim Crow interventions by white entities. Black resisters had always attempted to appeal to whites and to at least coax from them an acknowledgment of Jim Crow injustice, regionally and nationally. However, not until the decade after World War II were blacks evidently heard. With a suddenness indicating transformation in whites, these years marked an unprecedented degree of remedial acknowledgment of the black struggle. Previously, for example, with regard to white engagement, the interwar years saw an antifascist Popular Front strategy confront Jim Crow. White communists and other leftists attempted to organize southern workers across traditional divisions, including race. However, black support required an appeal for economic rights articulated in the language of antiracist equality and interracialism. The white-controlled criminal justice system and the lynching of blacks by white mobs combined to become a keynote cause. Communists were among the first whites to stand up for Euel Lee in Maryland and the "Scottsboro Boys" in Alabama. But the radical discourses of the interwar years attracted only a tiny minority of rank-and-file white southerners, even in the cities, and growing repression quickly made even this unsustainable. Nonetheless, the moment suggested that forces outside of the black community could, in fact, be instigated to support the black struggle.[22]

Meanwhile, transformations in the postwar liberal agenda brought opportunities for still-broader audiences, if only, as Glenda Gilmore argues, at the cost of a narrower and less radical argument for equality. In the first postwar decade, successful federal suits instigated by blacks themselves signaled the delegitimization of southern Jim Crow in the eyes of many whites outside the region. The postwar decade saw the ascension of anticommunist liberalism, which moved to wrench "the strategic value of civil rights reform" from leftist radicals who had allied with the black struggle since at least the 1930s. As such, urban southern blacks worked to force confrontations between white racist transgressors and white federal authorities. Along with litigation, black demand instigated U.S. presidents into action, including the establishment of Harry Truman's President's Committee on Civil Rights, and Dwight Eisenhower's reluctant aid to the Little Rock Nine. Even Congress, where white segregationists held their greatest influence in national affairs, produced at least tepid civil rights acts in 1957 and 1960.[23]

Similarly, white social justice organizations of various ideological moorings first approached the black struggle in these years. The Baltimore branch of Americans for Democratic Action, for example, worked mainly as a liberal political lobby—"little more than a refuge for anti-Communist liberals," writes historian Doug Rossinow. The white political and economic elites of ADA advocated for civil rights reform as a rhetorical mainstay and necessary pillar of forward-looking national policy. Meanwhile, demonstrations of interracialism and nonviolent direct-action tactics distinguished radical outfits like the Baltimore branch of the Congress of Racial Equality, and these became targets of antiradical hysteria and increasingly ostracized.[24]

Increasing sensitivity to issues concerning the urban southern black voter drove postwar federal interventions in employment, housing, education, and access to public spaces. Favorable federal court rulings validated electoral reform, and, according to Goldfield, 85 percent of the South's registered black voters by 1950 lived in cities. Black Baltimore modeled voter registration activism for the region, demonstrating black capacities as a viable voting bloc.[25]

The shift toward desegregation represented a notable turn. To that point, with few allies in positions of influence, blacks had lacked the political tools to force their nation to rid itself of Jim Crow via policy or legislation. Instead, blacks battled in the courts for some semblance of equity and equalization within the segregated system. Meanwhile, among whites, new liberal mantras of antiracism arose after 1945 in service of America's Cold War propaganda needs. Outside of the South at least, more white politicians and white citizens called for an end to Jim Crow. Thus, while blacks could not force desegregation before these new circumstances, they also could not be satisfied with equalization now that much more seemed possible. This is not to privilege desegregation over equalization as strategy but rather to encourage us to respect historical actors for their perceptions of the possibilities available to them in their own historical moments. Insisting upon the authenticity of the decades before the 1960s, therefore, *The Struggle and the Urban South* argues that the conditions and forces of both segregation and the struggle against it reflected specific political, social, and cultural economies.

This nuanced interpretation of the Jim Crow decades reveals a record of commitment to reform activism and reform culture: organization and institution building; litigation, legislative lobbying, and electoral strategies; an uplift agenda; direct-action campaigns; and the collective impact of everyday black folk seeking more than white racism said they should have. Large and diverse black communities within the formally segregated environment existed only in Baltimore and the other big cities in the South (e.g., Washington, Richmond, Atlanta, New Orleans, Memphis, Louisville, and St. Louis). An enduring black struggle confronted Jim Crow in Baltimore and elsewhere in the urban South long before it inspired the rest of the nation toward a brief if spectacular civil rights movement in the 1960s. Despite legacies of the nineteenth century, or perhaps because of the same forward-looking pragmatism that allowed blacks to survive them, black Baltimoreans worked toward and through the Jim Crow twentieth century, building pathways they hoped would lead them to equality and dignity in the future. That's what this book is about.

# PART I

The rise of Jim Crow in Baltimore was met by a black commitment to struggle. Two key strategic characteristics would mark the struggle for nearly four decades thereafter. First, as Jim Crow was couched in the expansive false narratives of white supremacy—narratives that cast blacks as "lesser than," with inherent cultural shortcomings, chronic intellectual incapacity, and broad moral insufficiency— blacks developed counter-narratives of independence, agency, and self-respect. The second characteristic of the black struggle that emerged through the first four decades of the twentieth century saw southern blacks establish regional and national intragroup alliances, particularly within the structures of nonpartisan social justice entities. National organizations moved to establish branches and commence work in the region, building a black nation of resistance.

# CHAPTER 1

# Jim Crowed

## Baltimore, 1890s–1910s

The Baltimore *American* ran a small headline on page six of its June 1, 1889, edition: "Thirty-Three New Lawyers." The night before in Ford's Opera House, the University of Maryland School of Law had held commencement. Though a violent rainstorm raged outside, "the night was not too bad for a good audience to be present." Charles W. Johnson and Harry Sythe Cummings, third and tenth in the class respectively, stood among the graduates. Both men had completed the three-year program in only two years. Both men were black, and each had several well-wishers in the audience celebrating their achievement.

Days before the commencement, the community had fêted Johnson and Cummings at the Madison Avenue Presbyterian Church, with Everett J. Waring, the first black admitted to the bar in Baltimore, providing a keynote. "Let our young people have full and free access to . . . literary, industrial, and professional training," he told those gathered, "[and] remove all hindrance to their entrance into any and all professions or callings and pursuits." "Grant us this," he said with assurance, "[and then] turn on the full blaze of the judgment and discriminations of this great age. . . . We cheerfully and confidently will abide the result." Southern blacks in big cities like Baltimore were not afraid of the modernizing future. They embraced it. They pursued it.[1]

If back in 1887, when Johnson and Cummings first entered law school, their matriculation had met with at least mild protest, their subsequent overall experience had been one of inclusion, they argued—as "gentlemen associating with gentlemen." Faculty and fellow students treated them without apparent racial prejudice, and this atmosphere continued through to the rainy graduation night at Ford's. As a contemporary observer noted, "Good judgment and tact . . . prevented any color discrimination in seating the guests at the graduation exercises." Before an audience of faculty, alumni, family, and friends—a gathering that included not only common folk, black and white, but also "some of the most aristocratic families of the South," according to the *New York Times*—Cummings and Johnson were awarded their degrees without incident or special circumstance.[2]

In the fall of 1889, the semester after the graduation of Cummings and Johnson, two more blacks enrolled at the University of Maryland School of Law. One, John L. Dozier, had graduated from Johnson and Cummings's alma mater, Lincoln College of Pennsylvania. The other new law student, W. Ashbie Hawkins, was an alumnus of Baltimore's Centenary Biblical Institute (renamed Morgan College in 1890). They arrived at law school as prepared for its rigors as any other member of that first-year class. They also had reason to be encouraged about the prospects for a career after graduation, as both Johnson and Cummings were putting their degrees to appropriate use—together, for example, they had successfully defended a young black man falsely accused of assaulting a white girl, before an all-white jury, no less.

Quickly, however, things began to change at the law school—and in the city. Suddenly, it seemed, the ascendance of the likes of Johnson and Cummings represented a threat to the spaces and prerogatives of whiteness in Baltimore. White citizens raised the specter of "Negro domination" and began to demand statutory and other institutionalized restrictions on black opportunity. At the law school, this developed into a movement of white students and faculty alike who wanted not only for the university to cease admitting blacks but also for Dozier and Hawkins to be ousted before they finished the program. While both men ultimately finished their training at Howard University's law school, nearly half a century would elapse before another of their color entered the University of Maryland.

Black Baltimoreans could feel their world changing around them. By the century's close, whites had begun to curtail black access to public spaces or close them to blacks altogether. Things began to grow tighter, blatantly unequal, and more personal, with more derogatory language used to describe and address blacks. In the course of but a generation, to appropriate C. Vann Woodward's famous phrasing, a comprehensive "capitulation to racism" had transpired. Jim Crow spread like a virus in the urban South, moving state to state, infecting education, housing, and employment. "The civil rights and privileges which the colored citizens have been enjoying for years have been gradually retrenched until now they are merely nominal," the black press observed in 1890. Testament to the newness of these snubs was the apparent newsworthiness of their increasingly frequent incidence.[3]

Familiar public spaces, like parks and other places of outdoor recreation, became off-limits to blacks. A number of private concerns closed to blacks altogether, and those that continued to offer service (e.g., theaters, retailers, eateries) did so in separate and inferior ways or established dual pricing policies that charged black patrons a premium for the privilege of giving white businessmen their money. Even white Republicans—theretofore, since Emancipation, "friends of the Negro" whose gatherings in Baltimore had traditionally operated on the basis of interracialism—began to "Jim Crow" blacks to the balcony at party functions. By the 1890s in Baltimore, one of the South's most populous cities, "prejudice . . . against Afro-Americans began at the street lemonade vendor," one observer noted, "and like infinite series in mathematics continued without end." Claiming to be "cast down but not dismayed," Baltimore blacks were truly disappointed over being "Jim Crowed," as they phrased it, and at "the great extent of the backsliding in moral conscience of the white people of Maryland." No doubt searching for ways to salve wounded dignity, the black press editorialized that the moment offered "the opportunity of our lives," the chance for blacks to react with unity, poise, and courage in meeting segregation's challenge.[4]

In the eyes of black Americans and others, Jim Crow marked the whole of the South, as slavery had before, with a broad regional identity. This identity legally mandated white supremacy, and this was underpinned by narratives of anti-black racism. If there was nuance to urban blacks' view, it perceived their capacity to resist Jim Crow in the South, marking their struggles in the South as functionally unlike those of their rural counterparts. Histories of Jim Crow must confront this. Blacks in the urban South—in communities like Baltimore—nurtured their capacities to resist in fundamentally different ways than did rural and small-town blacks. Consolidating their communities, they produced defiant counter-narratives to white supremacy, challenging the legitimacy of Jim Crow from the first moments of its rise at the end of the nineteenth century. These counter-narratives were executed in black professional and academic achievement, in entrepreneurial pursuits (large and small), and in their personal comportment. Indeed, from the "respectability politics" of strivers and elites to the demand from the lower and working classes for recognition of their personal dignity and self-respect, urban blacks in the South resisted the limiting presumptions of white citizens and authority figures alike, even at the cost of rebuke and sometimes physical violence. In the end, theirs proved to be an enduring black struggle for equality. Decades later, it inspired a civil rights movement, which demanded activism and the attention of broad segments of American life. For now, however, at the turn of the twentieth century, blacks struggled largely on their own.[5]

## Building a More Human Life

At the start of the Jim Crow era, the Baltimore experience represented a broad historical framework of black urbanicity in the South. The ethos of urbanicity that had been an element of southern black vernacular consciousness since slavery continued to draw blacks to Baltimore and other cities in the region. As was the case in most of the urban South then, no central or single neighborhood of blacks existed in Baltimore. Both established and newly arriving black residents were spread in all quadrants of the city. Blacks constituted 10 percent or more of the total population in fifteen of the city's twenty wards as late as 1880. They comprised no more than one-third of the residents of any single Baltimore ward, living in patchwork clusters across the city. If some residential blocks were all-black or all-white, many others were mixed—black and white living in close physical proximity.[6]

Annexation of land from Baltimore County, to the north and west of the city, nearly tripled Baltimore City's size in 1888. Well-to-do whites moved farther from center city. What they left behind constituted the secondhand residences of an emerging black enclave. This development accommodated a consolidation of blacks. Blacks had lived in all parts of Baltimore before, but West Baltimore became prominent as a black enclave soon after the push and pull of emerging Jim Crow culture in the city. For decades West Baltimore received thousands of migrants annually—from the Maryland countryside, from the rural regions of other southern states, and even from other points within Baltimore itself.

Jim Crow descended with the rise of West Baltimore, and blacks met circumscription by building community, which became the key resource of resistance. To borrow Ronald Takaki's useful description of American Chinatowns, West Baltimore early in the Jim Crow era promised to be for blacks "places where they could live a warmer, freer, and more human life among their relatives and friends than among [hostile] strangers." Aspects of culture and identity that would be rebuked or received as threatening to empowered white prerogative elsewhere in the city could be expressed in these black spaces of the urban South without fear. For those blacks migrating to Baltimore from rural areas, a familiar southernness was discernable—an approach to urban life influenced by long-standing rural migration and inflected with rural sensibilities and mores. Tensions between black natives and black newcomers were evident, but high rates of in-migration to southern cities beginning in the late nineteenth century made newcomers ubiquitous. Quoting Angela Davis, Luther Adams has noted this quality of southernness as "Home" in his study of segregation-era blacks in Louisville. Early in the Jim

Crow era, the southern black ethos of urbanicity nurtured an illusion that the black world was the whole world—that it could be made to sustain blacks and perhaps even allow them to thrive.[7]

West Baltimore's rise as a black enclave came in stages, but these took place quickly. In little more than a generation, a fully diverse black population lived there: newcomers to the city (and even the state) and natives of Baltimore who had relocated across town to be where increasingly everyone wanted to be. Black households came to be tucked into the alleys and service ways along lower Pennsylvania Avenue and adjacent streets, which were some of the first to turn from white to black residency. From there they "push[ed] from the narrower streets to the wider ones," according to historian Sherry Olson, "[moving] uphill, block by block." Newcomers and natives from other parts of the city began to arrive, settling into clustered webs of structures that sat in the shadows of more substantial and fashionable homes. Some of the earliest West Baltimore arrivals were African American domestic workers employed by well-to-do whites. They lived in the neighborhood's modest homes in smaller streets and alleys. Soon thereafter, with increasing flight of the white affluent population farther from center city, came a quiet arrival of Baltimore's nebulous but emerging black middle class—service workers, teachers and other professionals, and strivers of all stripes. These took up occupancy, if not always ownership, of the neighborhood's three-story row homes of exceptional quality. By the 1910s a great proportion of the "colored" schools' faculties in the city lived amid the tree-lined splendor of upper Druid Hill Avenue and its fashionable cross streets. Soon working-class blacks too found the means to move deeper into West Baltimore, especially to the smaller streets but also along the grander streets where landlords divided some single-family homes into apartments for rent. Older neighborhoods around the city also attracted black migrants in sizeable numbers—Hughes Street District and Pigtown, for example—but these numbered far fewer than West Baltimore.[8]

Baltimore's black population grew by 63.3 percent between 1880 and 1910. This population expansion outpaced the residential space available to blacks, however, and a harmful population density came to characterize West Baltimore. A typical neighborhood in this way was the 500 block of Biddle Alley. By the turn of the twentieth century, this single block contained fifty-six residences. The alley was cramped, spanning just twenty feet. By comparison, major streets nearby stretched at least three times as wide. Zoning was not in evidence, and six animal stables existed there, connected to carpenter shops, a firehouse, and blacksmithing shops. A 1907 study found only ten bathtubs on an entire similarly situated block: "One bathtub was evidently permanently devoted to the storage of old clothes, another served as a kitchen sink of a second-story apartment, a third had no water connection, and a fourth was used as a bed." None had running water but instead accessed a hydrant in the courtyard, and "all used in common an exceedingly filthy and dilapidated privy with an overflowing vault." Surface drainage oozed into the cellars of the homes. As worn-out and unhealthy environments of alleys and small streets spilled onto the main streets, blacks with the means to do so moved out along a northwest axis, expanding the black footprint of West Baltimore.[9]

Facing Jim Crow, Baltimore blacks built their institutions toward self-sufficiency and self-determination. Churches have long been acknowledged as symbolic and functional cornerstones of community development, but schools too were highly desired. Indeed, sometimes blacks perceived white educational privilege with great emotion. As a boy, for example, Baltimore native E. Franklin Frazier walked to school from his home on St. Paul Street, and his daily route took him past Johns Hopkins University (its original campus sat at the entrance to West Baltimore). Born in 1894 as segregation was beginning to remap the city, Frazier had come to realize that he would never enter Hopkins, no matter how well he did as a student. Hopkins would never allow him to compete with the best and brightest, because he was not white. As he walked, to get the distaste of frustration out of his mouth, he sometimes spat on the walls of the university as he passed them. Though it changed nothing about his material existence, he later recorded that he felt better, at least for the rest of his walk to school.[10]

Beyond their personal meanings to individuals, schools often functioned as markers of status, political clout, potential, and competence for the black community in the early Jim Crow urban South. Access to public education and control of it comprised an important signifier of urbanicity. Schools met present needs but were also foundations of resistance and possibility. From Emancipation through the end of the century, Bettye Thomas notes, "the education of black children remained the focal point of black protest in Baltimore." On the whole, Baltimore's public school system was inadequate for the masses. However, whites of means and ability did have access to educations at Baltimore Polytechnic High School, Baltimore City College (a high school), and Eastern and Western High Schools, which were more than adequate and offered college prep science and tech programs. But blacks, no matter their means and ability, were not afforded the opportunity to attend them—for no reason other than the color of their skin.[11]

The task of building schools and educational infrastructure represented a first-order priority as the West Baltimore black enclave began to grow by the 1880s. Prior to 1888, only one public school in West Baltimore admitted black children, School No. 4, on Biddle Street near Pennsylvania Avenue, just a few steps into the emerging community. The twelve remaining "colored" schools in Baltimore were scattered across the city's older black neighborhoods. At first the paltry public education in West Baltimore was supplemented through a networking program arranged by concerned blacks. Several unemployed teachers converted spaces in their homes into classrooms. Churches and other community institutions also opened their facilities for this purpose. Rev. William Moncure Alexander, of the Mutual United Brotherhood of Liberty (MUBL), for example, opened his Patterson Avenue Baptist Church as a neighborhood school. The MUBL was a local social justice organization formed in 1885. Over three hundred students at a time were taught by just three teachers in Alexander's makeshift school. One of the chief items of the MUBL's protest agenda was educational equity, even within the city's segregated structure. In 1883 the Colored High School opened in West Baltimore. It featured only a two-year curriculum at its start, however, and was crammed into a dilapidated and hazardous building already overcrowded as a grammar school. Inspired or embarrassed to action, the city began construction of a new school for blacks at Carrollton Avenue and Riggs Street by 1888, which would be known as School No. 9.[12]

As the twentieth century loomed, blacks might have argued that in their persistence they seemed to be building something from nothing. In 1892 the school board inaugurated the Colored Polytechnic Institute, a manual training school for black boys, similar to one that existed for whites. By 1901 the programs of Colored High School and Colored Polytechnic were consolidated into one building on Pennsylvania Avenue at Dolphin Street in West Baltimore. The high school curriculum was finally expanded to four years and made identical to that of white high school students. Still, the schools were far from equal. White officials touted the allocation of facilities as fair, yet no schools for black children were built between 1898 and 1915, a period of considerable population expansion especially in West Baltimore neighborhoods. All facilities available for black classroom use were hand-me-downs from whites.[13]

The development of black institutions and other community achievements supported the production of a narrative that countered white presumptions about black abilities. In the urban South, schools were critical in this. Concomitant with opportunities for their children to attend school, black parents and the black community at large understood that they needed to control their own schools, with their culture and long-term goals in mind. Schools functioned as cultural bedrock in a community. They developed future leaders and offered employment that in turn helped pay membership dues and tithings to other vital organizations and institutions. But when Baltimore's public education system first accommodated black students back in 1867, with segregated schools for them, it had barred blacks as teachers and administrators, exercising its racist monopoly to protect white teachers' access to jobs. Adding insult to injury, the city had nonetheless acknowledged the qualifications of potential black teachers by issuing certificates of their eligibility for service in the city schools. Of all the "colored" schools at the close of the century, only school No. 9 had an all-black staff (including teachers and administrators).[14]

The traditional monopoly of white teachers in black schools prevented the schools from having as positive an impact as they might have had with black teachers. Blacks saw white teachers as antagonistic and harmful to their children and ultimately their community. The U.S. Supreme Court saw it differently, sanctioning such "separate but equal" segregation with its *Plessy v. Ferguson* decision in 1896.

The push for access to schools and control of them was part of the black response to Jim Crow. "If we are to have separate schools, and we are perfectly satisfied and contented to have them," black activists declared defiantly, "they ought to be wholly so." For blacks, it was a matter of inequality and inconsistency. Blacks noted that whites were willing to violate the color line when it suited them, as in the pursuit of money from teaching in purportedly black-only schools. After all, the presence of white teachers and administrators meant that blacks schools were in effect "mixed schools." "Having great respect for our white women," one activist mocked, "the School Board ought not to force them to mix in a social way in a colored school." If such reciprocity as blacks being allowed on the faculties of white schools was "regarded as an outrage and a humiliation of Anglo-Saxon blood," then whites must understand that blacks felt the same. "Why should one class of citizens enjoy more privileges in this matter than other citizens?"[15]

After the white press brought light to the matter, the school board finessed the situation. In the case of black schools, it agreed to replace retiring or resigning white teachers with temporarily appointed black teachers. Eventually, when any given black school was staffed fully by such temporary appointees, the black faculty would become permanent employees. When the city finally dropped the bar against employment of black teachers in black schools, the transition came quickly. In 1902 just over half of the black schools had all-black staffs. That rose to 75 percent by 1904, and by 1907 all-black staffs ran all of the black schools in Baltimore. High school graduates meeting a performance standard were certified to teach in city schools and black teachers won guarantees of salaries equal to those of white teachers with similar experience and training. Moreover, by 1910 the school board hierarchy had added black supervisors for the "colored schools." In Baltimore and other southern cities, blacks forged their schools into resources for identity and employment, camaraderie and status, and opportunity and progress. With this platform, in some black minds, equality might be achievable.[16]

## Faith with the Common People

Blacks in the urban South understood that their disadvantage under segregation went hand in hand with the powerful and prolific narrative of white supremacy. This narrative was invented as part of the "Lost Cause" mythology, as Grace Elizabeth Hale and others have described, which looked back favorably to a supposedly less complicated time, a time of black slavery. Now, as Hale explains, at the end of the nineteenth century, with the Reconstruction behind them, adherents of Jim Crow demanded of blacks a "performance of inferiority." Young blacks—the "new generation"—Leon Litwack writes, were particularly scrutinized in the white supremacy narrative, which perceived them for their ambitions as "a subversive and potentially dangerous force capable of plunging the entire section into racial warfare."[17]

Recognizing the apparently unanimous agreement among whites over this narrative of their supremacy, blacks citizens pursued what they perceived as fairness and what they believed was attainable, because more did not seem possible. Seeking to expand their capacity through community development, blacks intended the organizations and institutions they built for themselves under Jim Crow as counter-narrative. This psychology marginalized the practical importance of white people. Indeed, "it would be incorrect to conclude," Earl Lewis found with another urban South black community, that blacks "merely reacted to white racism." According to Lewis, in the urban South, if blacks under Jim Crow were "always cognizant of racism, they were never all-consumed by its presence." The whites of the everyday black world were obstacles and guardians of white privilege—exploiting employers, fascist police officers, usurious merchants, and contemptible public officials.[18]

Likely the most accurate generalization that can be made about the closing decade of the nineteenth century in terms of black access to jobs and professions in Baltimore is that they could only get what whites did not want. If they strove for something more, they were confined to a clientele of their own people, in their own neighborhoods. Sherry Olson has demonstrated that the final decade and a half of the nineteenth century saw black employment opportunities in Baltimore curbed to satisfy white appetites. In the mid-1880s, for example, blacks were pushed out of the railroad and waterfront industries upon an influx of white immigrants from Europe and other U.S. cities. Thanks to what one called "trade union ostracism," even during times of emergency and need for labor, skilled blacks were unable to ply their trades. The Great Baltimore Fire of February 1904 leveled the entire business district surrounding the harbor, but all blacks could garner was a few jobs hauling away debris. They were frozen out of trade union membership by white racist protectionism, and only union shops were receiving lucrative business in the cleanup and rebuilding effort.[19]

In this way, perhaps, black entrepreneurialism under Jim Crow can also be understood as serving the counter-narrative. By the close of the century in their emerging enclave, black Baltimoreans could boast of a large number of enterprises. Mom-and-pop shops, five and dimes, grocers, caterers, funeral parlors, financial institutions, insurance providers, medical facilities, hauling operations, barbershops, salons, and saloons were all to be found in the various neighborhoods and blocks. Indeed, the veritable entry gate to black West Baltimore at the turn of the century, Druid Hill Avenue and West Biddle Street, came to be known as "the busy corner" for its bustling din of black commercial, institutional, and residential life. Not least a part of this busyness was the black press, which represented black entrepreneurialism but also acknowledged its leading role in the struggle for social justice. The same source of wealth that would later support the editorial independence of black newspapers in New York, Chicago, and Detroit—the "concentrated consumer power of tens of thousands of wage-earning black families"—also buttressed black papers in the urban South, especially Baltimore.[20]

Representing a competitive entrepreneurial space in the late nineteenth and early twentieth centuries, numerous black-edited publications appeared in Baltimore. Most were short lived. A political action group called the Committee of Sixty, for example, organized the *Vindicator*, edited by Rev. C. W. Fitzhugh and later William Murrill, to educate the (male) black voter as to his responsibilities and prerogatives. The *Dawn*, a monthly publication edited by E. W. Scott, made its appearance in Baltimore during 1887. Concurrently another newspaper, The *Director*, was also published by and for blacks in the city. Wesley Adams is reported to have published a daily black newspaper for a time, the *Public Ledger*, as late as 1890. Joseph Dorsey edited The *Crusader* for several years beginning in the 1890s. Everett J. Waring, the first attorney admitted to the Maryland bar (in 1888) threw himself into the fray by publishing the *Star*. Another attorney, W. Ashbie Hawkins (who had ignobly been ousted from the University of Maryland in 1891 by emerging Jim Crow there), edited the *Baltimore Spokesman* during the mid-1890s. George Wellington Bryant published the short-lived *Race-Standard*—billed as a national newspaper and carrying the motto "Equal and Exact Justice." The best of these, however, the *Afro-American*, simultaneously claimed race and citizenship and spoke at once for the city's optimistic black newcomers and impatient black natives. Two newcomers to Baltimore—Rev. William M. Alexander and Rev. George Freeman Bragg—and one native, John H. Murphy Sr., brought the *Afro-American* (or "*Afro*," for short, as it quickly became known) to life and forged its crusading edge at the very moment whites completed Jim Crow's construction in the city.[21]

As a migrant and activist, Alexander possessed dynamic characteristics that made him stand out among blacks of the emerging Westside. He was one of the throng of blacks who migrated to the city (in his case from Virginia) in the closing decades of the nineteenth century. Also, Alexander had been activated to serve social justice causes by the rise of the anti-black Jim Crow culture in the city. He joined the Mutual United Brotherhood of Liberty, an organization of activist clergy that pursued legal redress of racial discrimination. In August 1892 Alexander launched the *Afro-American*.[22]

George Bragg was one of Alexander's most visible contemporaries in Baltimore. A North Carolinian by birth, Bragg had come to Baltimore by way of Petersburg, Virginia, in 1891, as the new rector of St. James First African Church. Rev. Bragg lived as a "race man" in the parlance of the day. Time and again, from the moment of his arrival, he set the example for his new community, championing social causes and joining the fraternity of activist clergy already at work in the city. Almost immediately, Rev. Bragg began publishing for religious as well as secular readers, including the socially conscious weekly *Ledger*.[23]

One of Bragg's early acquaintances in Baltimore seems to have been John Murphy, a native, a freedman, and a Civil War veteran. Murphy had begun to learn the printing business by the 1880s. With $200 borrowed from his wife, the fifty-six-year-old Murphy purchased the *Afro-American* in 1897 (Alexander had sold the paper two years earlier). After a short hiatus, the *Afro-American* resumed publication, listing "J. H. Murphy" as manager. In 1900 Murphy and Bragg became business partners, merging their newspapers into the *Afro-American Ledger* (as the masthead read until January 1916, when it reverted to *Afro-American*). Many black Baltimoreans held shares of stock in the new company. This exclusive black ownership, writes Hayward Farrar, "facilitated its crusades for racial advancement by keeping it free from white control."[24]

Black newspapers in the urban South were charged with keeping "faith with the common people," as John Murphy would later recall, "whether [they have] no other goal except to see that their liberties are preserved and their future assured." The black press helped sustain positive self-perspective against the disfiguring aesthetic of racism, and it gave valuable leadership, vision, and encouragement to those creating the cultural norms in the black community. The black press in the era of Jim Crow promoted self-determined uplift, and in the biggest southern cities, like Baltimore, even became a booster of sorts, enticing blacks to come, holding up high all that was right, promising, and possible when blacks did things for themselves.[25]

At the other end of the entrepreneurial spectrum from newspapermen like those of the *Afro-American*, the ubiquitous black laundress worked near-invisibly and without plaudit. Still, not only did these women stretch their meager, hard-earned incomes to support themselves and their families, but their support was also the sustaining economic bedrock of community institutions and the black social justice struggle. Indeed, the entrepreneurial impulse as counter-narrative to Jim Crow's affront revealed itself even among those of fewer skills and resources. Every day, laundresses determined to feed, clothe, and shelter themselves and their families, all the while contributing, however meagerly, to the organizations and institutions in their communities that served the broader good and brighter future. Their work may be classified as menial and "survivalist," and what they did seemed only to be what whites would *not* do—"Negro work." Yet the black women took what they might from this circumstance and when necessary even protected their turf.[26]

Washing laundry represented "the single most onerous chore" in late nineteenth and early twentieth-century women's lives. Middle-class and professional-class households in modernizing America looked to relieve their women of the drudgery of that work. Laundry represented "the first chore [women] would hire someone else to perform whenever the slightest bit of discretionary income was available." An early 1920s study of Baltimore found 7,716 black women in the unincorporated sole proprietor laundry service business. This number did not include the 733 black women employed as "laundry operatives" by institutionalized commercial laundries (see table 2).

Blocked from participation and open competition in the broader economy by Jim Crow, as Tera Hunter, Elizabeth Clark-Lewis, and others have demonstrated, black women found spaces they could exploit to the best advantage of themselves and their families. Working-class black families relied on women's wages as much as men's. For these reasons, Hunter explains, "laundry work was the optimal choice." And, while these "survivalist entrepreneurs" as Robert Boyd frames them, clearly chose self-employment "in response to a desperate need to find an independent means of livelihood," it is also true that the self-determined nature of it seemed equally attractive.[27]

Meager returns notwithstanding, independent laundry work afforded some freedom and flexibility, a desirable feature since these women were often married with children. Independent laundresses tended to be older than women

**TABLE 2.** Black Occupational Profile (Selected): Baltimore, 1923

| Category | Occupation | Total blacks | Black men | Black women |
|---|---|---|---|---|
| Domestic and personal service | Laundresses (Not in laundry) | 7,716 | 0 | 7,716 |
| Unskilled workers | Building (general) | 4,879 | 4,879 | 0 |
| Unskilled workers (transport) | Stevedores | 3,151 | 3,151 | 0 |
| Domestic and personal service | Waiters and waitresses | 2,222 | 1,476 | 746 |
| Domestic and personal service | Chauffeurs | 1,831 | 1,831 | 0 |
| Unskilled workers (transport) | Teamsters and drayman | 1,712 | 1,712 | 0 |
| Domestic and personal service | Porters and helpers in stores | 1,602 | 1,602 | 0 |
| Unskilled workers (transport) | Road and street building, etc. | 1,412 | 1,412 | 0 |
| Domestic and personal service | Porters (except in stores) | 1,299 | 1,299 | 0 |
| Domestic and personal service | Janitors and sextons | 1,082 | 884 | 198 |
| Unskilled workers | Blast furnaces and steel rolling mill workers | 1,024 | 1,024 | 0 |
| Unskilled workers | Ship and boat builders | 1,008 | 1,008 | 0 |
| Unskilled workers | Fertilizer factories | 919 | 919 | 0 |
| Domestic and personal service | Laundry operatives | 850 | 117 | 733 |
| Unskilled workers (transport) | Deliverymen | 819 | 819 | 0 |
| Unskilled workers (transport) | Steam railroad workers | 721 | 721 | 0 |
| Skilled workers | Dressmakers and seamstresses | 661 | 0 | 661 |
| Entrepreneurs | Retail dealers | 597 | 519 | 78 |
| Skilled workers | Firemen (except locomotive and fire dept.) | 545 | 545 | 0 |
| Domestic and personal service | Barbers, hairdressers, manicurists | 515 | 291 | 224 |
| Public service | Laborers | 491 | 491 | 0 |
| Professional service | Teachers | 449 | 53 | 396 |
| Semi-skilled workers (manufacturing) | Shirt, collar, and cuff makers | 449 | 22 | 427 |
| Semi-skilled workers (manufacturing) | Suit and coat makers, etc. | 363 | 119 | 244 |
| Clerical workers | Clerks (except in stores) | 361 | 282 | 79 |
| Unskilled workers | All other occupations | 314 | 0 | 314 |
| Semi-skilled workers (manufacturing) | Ship and boat builders | 262 | 262 | 0 |
| Professional service | Clergymen | 187 | 187 | 0 |
| Entrepreneurs | Restaurant, cafe, and lunchroom workers | 181 | 91 | 90 |
| Skilled workers | Tailors | 130 | 130 | 0 |
| Skilled workers | Mechanics | 122 | 122 | 0 |
| Clerical workers | Salesmen and saleswomen | 121 | 81 | 40 |
| Skilled workers | Machinists | 109 | 109 | 0 |
| Professional service | Physicians and surgeons | 107 | 107 | 0 |
| Clerical workers | Clerks in stores | 102 | 76 | 26 |

Compiled from Charles S. Johnson, "Negroes at Work in Baltimore, Md.: A Summary of the Report on the Industrial Survey of the Negro Population," *Opportunity: A Journal of Negro Life* (June 1923), 13–14.

who worked as live-in domestic servants. Lastly, the growing white middle class brought a high demand for laundry work in the late nineteenth and early twentieth centuries. Indeed, the "black woman who wanted to create a life of her own" saw more than mere survival in choosing laundry work. The coins and small notes of laundresses filled the coffers of churches, supported the small shops of neighborhoods, purchased the goods of vendors and hawkers, and allowed the promising students among their children to attend college or at least take night classes at local normal schools.[28]

Providing a client-based service, black women laundresses managed their own labor and maintained their economic and social autonomy. As such, they might expand or restrict operations as they determined, based on their personal resources or the needs of their families and children. Between pickup and delivery, women performed the actual work (washing) in their own homes or at some public facility, often together with other laundry entrepreneurs. Such community nurtured solidarity and even fueled protest action and labor organizing in some places, though nearly all such events were ultimately unsuccessful.[29]

Given that laundering represented most of the little economic terrain staked out by black women in the urban South, surely the appearance of Chinese laundrymen caused concern. Perceiving black women's ability to defend their interests reveals a capacity largely hidden in traditional interpretations of black life under Jim Crow. Chinese immigrants had become somewhat conspicuous in Baltimore by 1890, if only due to their complete absence in the years previous. The black population had increased 24 percent over the preceding decade, counting fifteen out of every hundred people in the city. But the population of Chinese (and to a lesser degree Chinese Americans) had relatively exploded. Where census takers had only enumerated 4 there a decade earlier, now they counted 170 (a 4,450 percent increase). They must have seemed to have come out of thin air, and they first appeared as small entrepreneurs. For blacks feeling the pinch and prod of Jim Crow toward what seemed at first a doom of social and economic marginalization, anti-Chinese sentiments fed their sense of outrage. "[Even] the Chinese enjoy privileges here that far exceed the Negroes," one black observer of Baltimore concluded as Jim Crow emerged.[30]

Examining the relations of blacks in the urban South with a nonwhite ethnoracial group helps debunk the notion that whites and whiteness were omnipresent in the southern black purview. It also allows an interpretation of poor and working-class black women in entrepreneurial modes—rejecting the pejorative "survivalist" tag other scholars have affixed to such menial activity. Poor though they were, and tenuous as were their circumstances, black women at the center of this scene competed independently and ably against the economic encroachment of Chinese laundries for market share and clientele.[31]

The conditions and responses out of which Chinatowns emerged reveal the broader implications of segregation culture, as "color in America operated within an economic context." Employers encouraged antagonism along any number of lines—racial, cultural, native versus stranger—designed to keep overall wages low. White workers by and large responded by demanding, in the language of racism, exclusive access to a range of fields and industries (and thus occupation-derived social status). "Pushed out of competition for employment by racial discrimination and white working-class hostility," as one scholar demonstrates, "many Asian immigrants became shopkeepers, merchants, and small business [operators]." Still, the southern cities with Chinatowns—Baltimore, St. Louis, Washington, and New Orleans—had only small to middling ones, where populations ranged from several hundred to a few thousand through the early decades of the twentieth century.[32]

With the advent of Baltimore's Chinatown, Chinese Americans sought what they would be allowed to do and built out from that position. In spite of having existed largely as rural and agricultural workers before coming to the big city, "they *became* shopkeepers and ethnic enterprisers" as empowered white racists excluded them, along with other nonwhites, from most employment and other economic opportunity. "As a means of survival [and] a response to racial discrimination and exclusion in the labor market," Takaki writes, entrepreneurialism came to be the predominant or determinative trait "peculiar to strangers." Chinese laundries—"one of the few things they could do"—emerged in the biggest southern cities because of the economic opportunities there. Their appearance there between the 1890s and 1930s coincides with the period Joan Wang identifies as "interim" in their evolution in the northeastern United States. At least 130 Chinese laundries operated in Baltimore by 1901, representing approximately 69 percent of all commercial laundries listed. Twenty years later that market share held.[33]

If these first Chinese American enterprises in Baltimore (along with restaurants) emerged on the fringes of the business district, they would soon be found in nearly every section of the city. In fact, many significant proprietors in the field owned laundries in a number of locations around town. Still, the growth of Chinese laundries in the urban South proved slower than in other U.S. cities, owing mainly to the efforts of black women laundresses who competed ably. According to a 1923 study, laundresses in Baltimore represented 29.05 percent of the 26,565 employed black women surveyed. Only black women as domestic servants numbered greater, and together the two occupations represented nearly nine out of every ten black women employed in Baltimore during the early 1920s. As noted in Wang's study, black women laundresses' ability to protect their entrepreneurial turf in the urban South even held off the spread of mechanized, better-financed commercial operations for a time. Thus, if never wealthy—indeed, most struggled constantly against the throes of abject poverty—these women ran businesses: they canvassed and advertised for clientele, and they exercised personal and professional discretion when developing clienteles and menus of service and when setting fees with a mind to competitors. They also used the home labor of their families, especially adolescent children, as their businesses demanded.[34]

## To Be Humiliated in This Manner

The strictures of Jim Crow were profound because they impacted the essential, if ordinary, issues of where to live and play, how to earn money, and what to do about the need for children's education. More than simply exclusion from competition with whites, Jim Crow entailed circumscription of black aspiration as a matter of public policy. Formal, organized resistance would begin at home. The everyday nature of segregation's affront explains why the core black community institution of the urban South, the church, often represented the frontline response. Reliant on the activism of community building, Baltimore churchgoers set their institutions and their clergy at the center of their resistance to Jim Crow as it emerged. Indeed, without breaking from their responsibility for the sacred needs of life, many clergymen contributed to a grand vision of secular resistance to racial injustice in the city, representing perhaps the most remarkable aspect of protest traditions established during the early Jim Crow era. Methodologies of clergy-led resistance varied from advocacy to community organization to political lobbying to economic boycott and litigation.

Local clergy also embraced the black press as essential to indigenous social justice advocacy. As noted above, Baptist minister William Alexander founded the *Afro-American*, and one of his successors there, George Bragg, a Methodist, would be the paper's most strident editorial voice into the 1910s. In the way of lobbying, the efforts to establish schools for black children in West Baltimore and place black teachers in all of the city's black schools also resulted from minister-led organizing of constituents and community pressure on school officials. Similarly, when the directors of the Baltimore and Ohio Railroad suddenly imposed Jim Crow policies on passenger accommodations in the Camden Yards station, black consumers insisted that they "did not propose to be humiliated in this manner." They successfully mobilized opposition and were supported by their clergy.[35]

Clergy even led boycotts. Savvy activists knew that the collective economic strength of a poor but sizable black community could at least force concessions from Jim Crow. Such was the case with the so-called "excursion" industry. Church groups and other social entities organized day-trip excursions for the everyday folk of black Baltimore to celebrate special occasions or simply escape the summer heat for a while. Pooling their money, they boarded trains or other means of transport and spent a day picnicking along the shores of the Patapsco River and the Chesapeake Bay. By the early twentieth century, the market was so lucrative that many white-owned transport firms offered rebates to black church groups for volume business.[36]

In 1904 the state pushed through Jim Crow laws that impinged on the dignity of such day-trippers. Some blacks defiantly ignored the new laws and were arrested. Others responded with pledges of economic boycott where possible, especially against those "passive and indifferent in the presence of our mortification and pain." So intimidated were the white-owned transport companies that they made demonstrative public apologies for being compelled to comply with segregation. "This company did what it could to prevent the passage of what is called the Jim Crow law," the Baltimore and Annapolis Short Line implored in a newspaper ad. "Now that the law is on the statute books it must be obeyed like any other law." Hoping to assure the continuance of its lucrative business taking blacks to Round Bay Resort, the proprietors promised that the new law "made little difference" in the high-quality customer service that black patrons would receive.[37]

Before this development, however, very early on, as segregation was formalized into law throughout the South, indigenous social justice organizers responded with litigation as the primary tool of resistance, and Jim Crow transportation was an early target. Rev. Harvey Johnson of Union Baptist Church was a leader in this. As early as the 1880s, Johnson encouraged his parishioners to fight emerging Jim Crow in the courts. Four members of Union Baptist—the Stewart sisters: Martha, Lucy, Winnie, and Mary—brought suit against a steamer line that had suddenly changed its policies, forcing them to sleep in filthy "colored" accommodations rather than the first-class rooms they had paid for (and had enjoyed previously). Johnson had earlier had a similar experience of his own on a different carrier and was also seeking relief from the courts. The Stewarts won their case, and garnered damages, but the cresting Jim Crow era would not be turned back.[38]

The success of the Stewarts' suit (against the company owning the steamer ironically named *Sue*) showed that the courts were a viable path of resistance. Although able white lawyers had represented the plaintiffs, going forward Johnson came to believe that black lawyers had to be brought to this fight. Through the Mutual United Brotherhood of Liberty, pledged "to use all legal means within our power to procure and maintain our rights as citizens of this our common country," Johnson spearheaded the push to admit blacks to the Maryland bar and then, once admitted, have black lawyers lead anti–Jim Crow litigation. By the fall of 1885, Johnson and his colleagues had lured to Baltimore a fresh graduate from Howard University School of Law, Everett J. Waring. Waring applied to the Baltimore bar and on October 10, 1885, was admitted. Waring was but the first, as several other black lawyers were admitted to the bar in quick succession.[39]

Another example of anti–Jim Crow litigation in the urban South during this era challenged municipal residential segregation laws. Reacting to a black lawyer's purchase of a long-vacant West Baltimore home in a middle-class white neighborhood as an investment property (which he rented to a black lawyer colleague), the Baltimore City Council enacted the nation's first law designating city blocks on the basis of race. Blacks rejected the law's white supremacist presumptions that blacks chose residence solely on the basis of close proximity to whites. Social contact with whites was "a thing colored men who have pride in themselves and race detest," the *Afro* opined. Indeed, George W. F. McMechen, the attorney whose residential choice whites cast as an "invasion" of their peace, remarked that "association with [whites] would be just as distasteful to us as it would be to them."[40]

Blacks did not concede to whites the authority to dictate who should live where in the city. While such laws were quickly imitated elsewhere in the South and in cities across the nation, so too were modes of resistance. Without ever being truly coordinated, legal tactics began to be copied from one city to the next. The fight against residential segregation ordinances became intraregional and ultimately national, setting the example for others organizing against segregation in the very near future.[41]

In truth, Baltimore's first residential segregation ordinance did very little to curb the types of real estate transaction it was designed to deter. Blacks continued to meet their need for homes wherever someone would sell to them. The ordinance also failed to withstand judicial scrutiny: multiple revisions appeared between 1910 and 1917, each subsequently thrown out by the Maryland courts. Notably, however, the fourth version of the residential segregation law had reached the Maryland Court of Appeals when the U.S. Supreme Court decided *Buchanan v. Warley* (1917), a case originating in Louisville, where the residential segregation ordinance was based on Baltimore's original 1910 law.

When the Louisville law was ruled unconstitutional, it marked the first time that the U.S. Supreme Court had decided against segregation. With precedent established, the Maryland Court of Appeals overturned Baltimore's fourth segregation law in 1917. Not long after, it bears noting, in the 1920s, Baltimore mayor Howard Jackson created a committee on segregation "and charged it with the protection of white neighborhoods from Negro invasion."[42]

Coming when they did, residential segregation ordinances represented the final components of the construction of Jim Crow in Baltimore. Despite the ultimate declaration of their unconstitutionality, the effect of state-enforced residential segregation was more than ably continued by restrictive covenant agreements. These agreements, between private property holders, not to sell to blacks (or any other group designated undesirable) would be enforced by the courts and withstand constitutional challenges into the post–World War II years.

## Police Lynchings

On Christmas Day 1911, Baltimoreans awoke to more evidence that the violent brand of racial reaction known to the rural South had come close to their city. After more than a decade of struggling for access to public accommodations and pushing for equal education opportunities for black children, it seemed to Baltimore blacks that now perhaps even their very lives were threatened. Just beyond the southern boundary of the city, some black and white "laboring class" men had spent Christmas Eve gambling together in a saloon. Among the everyday folk especially, mixed-race social settings were never as rare or distasteful as portrayed by politicians (or historians). Alcohol inspired bravado in the winners and exacerbated hard feelings in the losers. Late in the evening, arguments and then a fistfight began. King Johnson, an African American, tussled with a white man he knew, Frank Schwab. The two were employees at the Rasin Monumental Company, a nearby fertilizer manufacturing plant. Ultimately Johnson shot and killed Schwab, then claimed self-defense. Local law enforcement arrested and jailed Johnson, and within hours a mob of local whites stood at the jailhouse door.[43]

This southern scenario was grimly familiar. Authorities arranged for Johnson to be transported to Annapolis later that day "for safe keeping," but, as the mob called, he had yet to be moved. At two in the morning, with no deputies on duty, "persons unknown" broke into the jail and into Johnson's cell. They attempted to hang him by a noose there, but Johnson fought back. The mob cornered him, overwhelmed Johnson with their number, beat him to unconsciousness, and then dragged him down the jailhouse stairwell and out the front door. Then the mob carried him some two hundred yards into the night to exact retribution.

King Johnson died from multiple gunshots to the head and chest. No one identified the perpetrators—not the other prisoner in the jail that night, who was reportedly terrorized into silence; not the policeman reportedly asleep in his home, which sat next door to the jailhouse. Earlier that year Rev. Bragg in the *Afro-American* had been prophetic when he opined, "The lynching fever seems to have broken out again, . . . [but with liberal whites] they hardly excite surprise and indignation any longer." During the decades of Jim Crow's rise, 1890 to 1910, Johnson was the eighteenth black Marylander lynched and one of nearly two thousand blacks murdered by lynching in the United States during this time.[44]

The site of King Johnson's murder in Anne Arundel County, Maryland, lay barely three miles from Baltimore City Hall. Insofar as the record reveals, this is as physically close as the Jim Crow lynching scourge came to Baltimore's city limits. Still, state-sanctioned violence underpinned Jim Crow across the South. In the rural south (like Anne Arundel County) it was lynching. In the urban south, however, the police served this function through more routine, institutionalized forms. Police and policing of urban South blacks approximated the terroristic impact of lynching. And, while Baltimore blacks vigorously embraced the anti-lynching campaign emerging across black America after the 1920s, it was local campaigns against police brutality that proved to be ubiquitous for nearly the duration of the Jim Crow era. As such, these efforts stand as more relevant examples of urban southern activism against racist terrorism than anti-lynching campaigns.[45]

Professionalized policing toward the end of the nineteenth century evolved as an expression of an urban reform movement known as Progressivism. In the urban South, this was the same movement that produced Jim Crow. Even though Progressivism left a legacy that was beneficent in countless ways, its role as the ideological foundation of Jim Crow segregation cannot be overlooked. In the South, state by state, a powerful and primary Progressive impulse sought to construct and formalize a "modern" and "efficient" society ordered to the expressed and exclusive benefit of white people. "As reformers redefined early 20th century law-enforcement making local policemen 'crime fighters' and as the rule of law gradually supplanted popular justice," Jeffrey Adler writes, "patrolman and detectives . . . blended older notions of rough justice with newer methods of policing." "They believed that their mandate to preserve social order entailed both fighting crime and safeguarding the racial hierarchy, especially as lynching and other forms of violent racial control waned." In the urban South, the rarity of large-scale, overly public anti-black violence by white civilians was a key component to maintaining what David L. Chappell refers to as "the respectability of segregation." As such, if night riders and vigilante mobs can be understood for their roles in preventing black ambition from challenging white prerogatives in the rural areas, "professional" and "modern" police forces under the guise of law and order but guided by white supremacy enjoyed broad permission to do the same with the teeming black populace in the cities of the South.[46]

Like their hooded rural kin, police in the urban South before and after the turn of the twentieth century were committed not to justice for blacks but only to the maintenance of white supremacy. As Litwack observes in his study of Jim Crow, "White officers assumed primary responsibility for maintaining the color line and detecting any breaches or suspicious black behavior." Armed and authorized, the systematic and routine brutality of white police officers against black citizens served this end.[47]

The white privilege-keeping aspect was clear enough given the frequency with which black strivers—those Du Bois counted as his "Talented Tenth"— were victimized. Such was the case in West Baltimore when a white city policeman jumped upon the running board of a moving car in 1925. Inside there appeared to be a middle-class black man driving and a white woman passenger. Forcing the driver to stop, the cop learned that the occupants were not only man and wife but also both African Americans. Rather than apologize for the mistake, the officer handled the black man roughly and arrested him. "With all of these colored chauffeurs and their white female employers . . . ?," an incredulous *Afro* asked. Indiscriminate harassment, arrests, and fining had plagued black citizens in West Baltimore—for no more than "stop[ping] . . . for a conversation" with friends on Pennsylvania Avenue, the *Afro* reported— since they had begun arriving there in significant numbers around the turn of the century.[48]

Relatedly, the police in the urban South functioned at the service of white business interests and private citizens to curb black self-protection and self-defense. The black press in turn-of-the-century Atlanta, for example, described the local police force as "a [mean] set of lowdown cutthroats, scrapes, and murderers." The police—"the state"—ejected, corrected, and punished black transgressors for violations of "store policy" (segregation), giving privatized Jim Crow customs the force of public law. Police officers also regularly stood by as white citizens committed atrocities with impunity upon black people's bodies and dignity for allegedly disturbing the peace of "race relations" and white privilege in urban public spaces.[49]

As in rural areas, urban police and policing worked to tamp down black political aspirations and participation, understanding that these were the citizens' most effective weapons against abuse. Even where many urban blacks in the South had retained some voting rights during the onslaught of disfranchisement in the early twentieth century, including Baltimore, intimidating and widespread police presence at polling places and preemptive arrests systematically blunted urban black political and electoral objectives.

The most unwitting and chance encounters with police on the streets of a southern city frequently resulted in violence for some imagined transgression against racist social etiquette. Baltimore native Joe Gans, for example, recalls being accosted and nearly brutalized by a police officer sometime between 1902 and 1910 as he sat quietly waiting for a trolley. The patrolman—a much larger man than Gans, who at the time was the lightweight boxing champion of the world—asked rhetorically what Gans was doing sitting at the trolley stop. Perhaps Gans's demeanor was not deferential enough, since the officer struck him with a nightstick soon after demanding, "Get up nigger! Stand up when you talk to me." Despite his main profession, boxing (he had parlayed his prize winnings into a range of entrepreneurial concerns by this time), Gans was known for a calm, disarming demeanor. After Gans became the toast of the Baltimore sporting scene when he bested a white competitor for the lightweight title in 1902, whites somehow had to come to terms with his confounding racial identity. That he was a black man was undeniable. At the same time, white supremacy demanded exercises in racist disbelief, and so, for many, Gans became "the whitest nigger I ever seen" or "white [at] the core." Yet this "gentlemanly" Baltimorean whom whites called "a credit to his race" barely missed being brutalized by the racist police officer at the trolley stop, for the offense of happening to be there. Only the intervention of another officer—a boxing fan who recognized the champ and wanted to meet Gans—saved him. Countless other blacks in the Jim Crow urban South were not so fortunate.[50]

In another event involving a black boxing champion near the turn of the century, perhaps a metaphor for the race war many anticipated during the Jim Crow era, white Baltimore police officers brutalized a crowd of celebratory blacks. On Independence Day 1910 in Nevada, the heavyweight champion of the world, black Texan Jack Johnson, had just completed an unqualified destruction of "Great White Hope" Jim Jeffries. As news spread, relayed from Reno by wire and barked into a megaphone to a breathless crowd amassed in front of the *Baltimore News* building downtown, blacks danced in the streets. White cops exacted some measure of racist revenge by arresting seventy blacks on the Westside and elsewhere in the city for "disorderly celebration," according to the *New York Times*, half of them women. Similar scenes unfolded across the nation, some brutally violent. In this way, urban southern blacks perceived police brutality in ways very similar to their rural counter-parts' view of lynching. The rural racial ethic of black and white informed the urban racial ethic of black and blue.[51]

In service to racism, African Americans were beaten indiscriminately and without provocation, arrested unjustly, and prosecuted unfairly—often as much on public display as with a lynching in a small-town square. The spectacle of it seemed necessary for white supremacy; public shaming was its intention. Indeed, notable symmetry was evident between the rural and urban variants of this white prerogative (the former by plain-clothed white citizens in mobs, the latter by whites in uniform and wearing badges). The urban routine of anti-black harassment, hostility, and brutality by law enforcement was periodically punctuated by "murderous" encounters—what *Afro* columnist Ralph Matthews came to call "police lynchings." Sometimes the excessive force came in otherwise legitimate police confrontations with criminality. Too often, however, blacks were accosted for real or imagined transgressions against racist demands of interpersonal deference. "Sassing" was ubiquitous as justification for violence by white police against black citizens. In this way, we can understand the persistence of "sassing" as a form of the black counter-narrative to Jim Crow's presumption and a refutation of the stereotype of black cowardice and obeisance to white and masculine authority.[52]

As such, for "sassing," police officer Patrick McDonald bludgeoned Daniel Brown across his head before shooting him in the back in 1875, killing a man known to be "industrious and sober, quite intelligent and strong in urging his own way," in his own home while his wife watched in horror. Likewise, officer F. L. Kruse killed John Wesley Green in July 1884. Kruse was exonerated despite a police commissioner's finding that "the officer did not see Green commit any offense and he did not have a warrant of law to arrest him." Beyond the countless recorded and unrecorded incidents of harassment and brutality, killings of Baltimore African Americans by city police occurred frequently during Jim Crow's rise. Just for example, Fulton Smith was killed by officer Charles Weaver on September 27, 1898; Charles Harris was killed by officer James Hamilton on September 19, 1906; James Williams was killed by officer Philip Hanson on August 30, 1912; Robert Stevender was killed by officer James Coles on June 1, 1918.[53]

With the urban police, as with the rural lynch mob, whites generally accepted police violence against blacks as necessary, and it was intended that blacks feel helpless to prevent it. John Henry Parker was killed by officer John C. Henry in August 1924. The following month, officer Charles Davis killed John Williams. In 1926 Ernest Gamble was killed by patrolman Charles Schinbarr. Also in 1926 officer Webster Schuman killed Vannie Lee. In 1927 Barney Richardson was killed by Officer Charles Bruff. Officer Otis Bradley killed Joseph Lyons in October 1928, days before his colleague Howard Singer killed Shady Polite. In nearly all incidents, the policemen were exonerated (and sometimes they received commendation).[54]

Meanwhile, police and police culture created the criminalized identity of the black person, giving moral comfort to those justifying what might otherwise be considered un-American treatment of them. Almost assuring the efficacy of urban white privilege-keeping, police culture was equally evident in attempts to devalue and debase blacks' own urban spaces, what Du Bois once described in Atlanta as that "crowded and unpoliced gloom." Police departments in the urban South notoriously ignored crime—even murder—within black communities until it affected white employers. John Dittmer identifies a useful example of this in Atlanta, where during a time of particularly heinous crime in the black community, police acted only begrudgingly and not until black domestics hesitated to be out at night for fear of attack, leaving well-to-do white society ladies helpless in their kitchens.[55]

Such an approach was pervasive across the urban South, where all-white police forces approached black communities and individuals therein with suspicion, contempt, and little enthusiasm for meeting their duty. Given this penchant for neglect, coupled with racist housing practices that saw especially poor and working-class blacks in every southern city stacked on top of one another, crime rates stayed disproportionately high. As a result, blacks viewed white police with resentment more than respecting police authority. Richmond's blacks regarded city police with "distress bordering on hatred," according to Litwack, who noted that police officers felt the same about black citizens, only "with compound interest." Blacks needing assistance in even the most serious situations seldom saw police as a resource. This proved chronically problematic, for example, with black women who, when faced with domestic violence, feared calling in the police because white police officers often made bad situations worse.[56]

From the beginning of the Jim Crow era, policing in urban black southern communities like West Baltimore always seemed less about protection than occupation. If a broader Progressive Era white supremacy drove this penchant for quarantine and persecution of black life, police and policing culture facilitated it. By the 1910s, while racist social science had at least begrudgingly acknowledged blacks as members of the human family, new grounds for marginalization remained plentiful. The black community and black culture still represented the "other" and still amounted to "less than" in white estimation. What is more, theories of inherent criminality abounded, and from these, police in the Jim Crow urban South moved as they always had, presuming black ill intent and guilt.

The all-white police force in the Jim Crow urban South moved as an occupying force in black neighborhoods. Police officers not only brutalized blacks in full view of others, showing no respect for black witnesses, but also discharged their firearms sometimes with disregard for innocents nearby. Indeed, there seems to have been a presumption of guilt by mere fact of skin tone. The *Afro* observed early in the Jim Crow era that the main business and cultural thoroughfare of West Baltimore seemed peremptorily "indicted" as criminal by the city's white racist police culture.[57]

Blacks perceived the racist policing as unique to their urban situation and due to the growth of their numbers. Indeed they viewed police harassment as an attempt to keep them in their place, to push back against blacks emboldened with a sense of possibilities now that they were in the city instead of the rural South. According to the *Afro-American*, around the turn of the century, as blacks were completing their relocation to the Pennsylvania Avenue corridor, police routinely made indiscriminate arrests, harassing black citizens who "happened to stop even for a conversation."[58]

Police brutality in the urban South was an expression of white supremacy and served the Jim Crow order. Therefore, the brutality was not simply in the physical abuse but also in the emotional abuse inherent in treating the average black person as a criminal. Grievances blacks lodged against police encompassed more than just beatings, rough handling, and shootings. Blacks protested the common police practices of warrantless entry and searches of black homes, use of "third-degree" interrogation to coerce confessions, and bald-faced lying to secure convictions and ensure overly long sentences for black defendants.

In the West Baltimore black enclave, many people refused to be passive when confronted by brutal cops. There were always those willing to push back. Routinely newspapers reported city blacks' violence against police in self-defense or to protect kin being abused by police. Even those who did not physically engage officers often refused to cooperate with them, even when police were not being abusive. Animosity and distrust of the police pervaded the Jim Crow urban South.[59]

In a number of instances, black individuals or their representative organizations and institutions protested police abuse by reporting incidents to administrative and political authorities, though seldom were they satisfied with outcomes. In the largest cities of the South, however, sometimes the police violence against black citizens, whether suspected of some crime or apparently random—proved so egregious, so gratuitous and arbitrary, that *whites* lodged complaints with authorities, usually with no more effect than when blacks protested. As with most other instances calling for police reprimand, these almost always were dismissed as justifiable behavior, often citing an officer's need for self-defense against a black threat.[60]

One aspect of police brutality against blacks that received almost constant protest was the interrogation tactic called the third degree—ritualized torture to extract confessions from crime suspects. The *Afro-American* reported in 1918 on a suspect subjected to this. He was forced to drink a pint of whiskey, knocked down, not allowed council, had a loaded gun pointed behind his ear, and told emphatically to "confess or die." As Jeffrey Adler explains, after the professionalization movement in law enforcement at the turn of the century, replete with its "scientific crime detection" methodologies, older forms like the third degree were nonetheless retained—and racialized. Adler notes in his study of early Jim Crow New Orleans that while police brutality had been previously confined to on-the-street engagement between cops and citizens—"where local law enforcement harassed, bludgeoned, and occasionally shot suspects usually while apprehending them"—these same tactics had become in-precinct tools of interrogation for blacks in the urban South by the early Jim Crow decades. Students at Baltimore's Colored High School, which sat at the corner of Dolphin Street and Pennsylvania Avenue, directly across from the Northwest District Police Station, could hear through open windows police administering third degree interrogations: "We could hear police in there beating the hell out of people," one recalled. This shift toward a racialized third degree interrogation occurred "as part of a larger transformation in criminal justice," Adler explains. Whites "increasingly relied on legal institutions rather than popular justice as tools of racial control."[61]

"Detectives embraced this strategy, aggressively pursued African American suspects, and worked zealously to secure convictions," Adler notes, "often employing violent coercive interrogation practices to extract confessions." Forced confessions were made all the more reprehensible by the racial disparity in sentencing. This development created further animosity between law enforcement and black communities in the urban South. Around the turn of the century, police magistrates like "King" Bill Garland, for example, were being criticized for their penchant for oversentencing black Baltimoreans. In an editorial endorsing Theodore Roosevelt's 1904 presidential bid, for example, George Bragg of the *Afro-American* editorialized that Roosevelt stood opposite "Disfranchisement," "Jimcrow," "King Bill," and the "Nigger domination" crowd. "The average Police Magistrate is about as fit to administer justice . . . as a mule is to dance a hornpipe," the *Afro* later observed. "Just stop in one of those Police Stations some morning and you will be convinced that if what you see is justice, justice has the wrong name."[62]

Thus, after the turn of the twentieth century, police through neglect, brutality, and unaccountability sought to check the promise of black urbanization underway across the South. Confrontation of this racist policing and efforts to reverse its impact represent an underappreciated aspect of the enduring black struggle for equality. If reform of police and policing culture never appeared on the national civil rights agenda, it nonetheless remained consistently near the center of discourse everywhere in the big cities of the South, including Baltimore.

◎ ◎ ◎

Meanwhile, in the party politics of racism, the close of the century entailed Republican silence and Democrat demagoguery. Maryland Republicans experienced unexpected electoral victories between 1895 and 1898, winning on "bland [and] uncontroversial" platforms that made no overt appeal to black voters. This break with tradition disillusioned black party members, who protested aloud that they had been "treated as a set of 'niggers'," disregarded in spite of competency and service to the party. A contingent of them even broke away, fielding an unsuccessful all-black ticket in the 1897 Baltimore mayoral and city council races.[63] Responding to this brief Republican ascendancy, Maryland Democrats reclaiming office after 1900 raised the banner of white supremacy higher than ever. They vociferously claimed Baltimore as "a white man's city" and pledged to "preserve in every conservative and constitutional way the political ascendancy of our race." They spent the next decade attempting to disfranchise blacks.[64]

Between 1890 and 1910, eleven other southern states disfranchised blacks. In Maryland, white Democrats first changed laws to make voting more difficult for citizens who were illiterate—which meant a large proportion of black voters in the state. This brought only limited success, however. More dramatically, Democrats sought to revise the Maryland constitution in what one historian called "surely the most lengthy and complex disfranchising plan ever seriously considered in the United States." A "grandfather" clause would allow voting by anyone previously registered. Otherwise a voter was required to pass a literacy test, have two years' worth of tax receipts for five hundred dollars of real or personal property, and complete a form that required one's name, age, date and place of birth, residence for up to two years prior, names of employers, jurisdiction in which the person had last cast a ballot, the full names of the president of the United States, the governor of Maryland, a U.S.

Supreme Court justice, a Maryland Court of Appeals justice, the mayor of Baltimore, and the commissioner of his county. The *Afro-American* dubbed it "the Negro Humiliation Act," noting that, if approved, the result would be "wholesale disfranchisement."[65]

Baltimore blacks organized the Suffrage League of Maryland (SLM) in January 1904, as soon as the Maryland legislature began constitutional disfranchisement discussions. Headed by Rev. Alexander, the SLM responded not only to disfranchisement efforts but also to a concurrent and equally obnoxious Jim Crow transportation bill that was soon to be passed by the General Assembly. Much of the leadership comprised social activist clergy like Alexander. Local organization by blacks had seldom before adopted such a mass protest philosophy in Baltimore. The formation of the SLM portended things to come as it urged churches, the press, and anyone else with a public platform in the black community to rally the masses. Claiming to represent hundreds of blacks from all walks of Baltimore life—"ministers, lawyers, doctors, newspaper men, waiters, porters, and businessmen, all interested in the outcome of what appears to be one of the greatest disasters that the colored people of this state have experienced since the days of slavery"—the SLM invited branch affiliates to organize in every county of Maryland.[66]

Baltimoreans' efforts mirrored those of activists elsewhere protesting the black political neutering. For example, the National Negro Suffrage League (organized in 1903) was an organization whose leaders pledged to marshal black political capital—an asset they readily acknowledged "is fast passing from us"—to stave off disfranchisement and "save our people." Despite the similarity in purpose, it was not affiliated with the Suffrage League of Maryland. The National Negro Suffrage League, a national political lobby, hoped to coax federal intervention against anti-black disfranchisement in individual states. The body worked strategically to secure liberal white northern political support. Not a mass organization, its regional leaders were simultaneously affiliated with other efforts, including those of the Afro-American Council, a pioneering (if short-lived) civil rights organization that was national in scope.[67]

Many members of National Negro Suffrage League called upon the clout of the "Tuskegee Machine," the informal organization of conservative and moderate black leaders under Alabama educator Booker Taliaferro Washington who crafted considerable influence with white politicians and philanthropists from the late nineteenth through early twentieth centuries. In this way Baltimore's Harry Sythe Cummings connected Maryland to the national effort. After Cummings's graduation from the University of Maryland School of Law in 1889—the school would draw the color line the next year—his public career had gotten off to a successful start. In 1890 he had been the first black elected to the Baltimore City Council, and he would go on to serve several nonconsecutive terms. Cummings also launched a productive legal career, becoming something of a race man in the eyes of local blacks for his advocacy of equal rights. By the end of 1904, as Maryland's disfranchisement referendum was being readied, Cummings had been validated as a player in national race politics and he delivered a seconding speech at the Republican Party's national convention. With Theodore Roosevelt's reelection, Cummings looked to spend whatever political capital he had accumulated. He participated, for example, in a small committee that called on Roosevelt at the White House in December 1904 to discuss "Negro disfranchisement," hoping to gain support for a plan to penalize offending southern states by reducing their congressional representation. However, as Booker Washington—unofficial gatekeeper on matters of race for the Roosevelt administration—had not endorsed this strategy, Roosevelt gave Cummings and his colleagues the cold shoulder that day.[68]

Tactical philosophy aside, Booker Washington recognized the Maryland situation as a "desperate battle." Using his Committee of Twelve for the Advancement of the Interests of the Negro Race, a think tank and ideological brokerage between black causes and white philanthropy, Washington set to work against disfranchisement in Maryland—behind the scenes, as was his way. Interestingly, this represented the only instance that the Committee of Twelve "act[ed] in a way that promised the advancement of blacks," his biographer, Louis Harlan, concluded, as it functioned as "largely a paper organization . . . [whose] work consisted almost entirely of a succession of pamphlets." When the Committee of Twelve met in early August 1905, on Washington's motion, the body determined to "furnish such assistance as it may find practicable" to the Suffrage League of Maryland's efforts to defeat whites' disfranchisement amendment. Washington would even advocate on behalf of the Maryland cause to at least one other activist group of national ambition, the biracial Constitution League.[69]

Disfranchisement by constitutional amendment required statewide voter approval through a referendum. Resistance was strongest in Baltimore (home to more than 43 percent of the state's population in 1910). In addition to the well-organized and consistent black opposition, white Republicans were opposed, acknowledging that black disfranchisement would harm their party's electoral prospects irreparably. Likewise organizations representing the considerable populations of foreign-born and second-generation immigrant whites in Baltimore also resisted, similarly stymied by literacy tests and the other hurdles. Meanwhile, the Committee of Twelve met privately with the Marylanders and offered strategic advice and ultimately financial resources.

The committee also, as Harlan noted, supplied thousands of copies of pamphlets on voting rights, including *Why Disfranchisement Is Bad* (authored by Archibald Grimké), *Voting Instructions to Maryland Voters*, and *To the Colored Men of Voting Age in the Southern States: What a Colored Man Should Do to Vote*.

In the end, three separate referenda efforts failed—in 1905, 1909, and 1911—each time most resoundingly in Baltimore. Washington and those working against Maryland disfranchisement efforts from afar played valuable roles in the defeats of all three referenda. By the 1910s, for the defeat of Maryland disfranchisement and for Baltimore's national leadership in the defeat of residential segregation laws in the courts, the city's place within an emergent national black resistance had been acknowledged. Yet, as Doug McAdam has observed of efforts to expand Jim Crow in the federal government under the Wilson administration, "that most of these [efforts] failed to obtain the support needed for passage hardly diminishes the significance of the trend." Besides residential segregation—not to mention successfully enacted Jim Crow laws—there was a message in even the failed attempt at disfranchisement.[70]

Despite retaining the franchise, Baltimore blacks had sound reason to question the stand-alone efficacy of electoral politics to resist Jim Crow. Thereafter they exercised little political power because their numbers never approached more than a sizeable minority. If they perhaps single-handedly kept the Republican Party in their state from going the way of its counterpart in the former Confederacy, little else resulted. Bourbon Democrats (as the national party's conservative southern members were pejoratively known) in rural southern Maryland and the Eastern Shore vied for power with the machine politicians of Baltimore. As noted, occasionally—thanks to Democratic infighting and the consistent loyalty of black voters—Republicans took a statewide or Baltimore seat of significance. But when Republicans did gain power for a term or two, they showed themselves to be white men first and members of the biracial Republican Party of Maryland last. Black Republicans gained little for their loyalty.[71]

Indeed, after 1900 white supremacy was practically nonpartisan. Thus, as Susan Carle and others have demonstrated, so too became the black response to Jim Crow as "the first generation of national non-partisan organizations" emerged. Meanwhile, if the construction of racial segregation had come as a profound disappointment to black Baltimore, some argued that it should not have been a surprise. Society had never fully opened to blacks, and important public and private institutions had always excluded them (as in the case of schools). Still, during the first decade of the new century, Maryland's white supremacist legislature enacted more Jim Crow laws than any previous or subsequent era in the state's history. The *Afro-American* was blunt: blacks had seen this coming and still were not prepared to meet it. "There are hundreds of old conservative Negroes who could not be persuaded that such a thing was among the possibilities for Maryland," George Bragg chided. "And yet it is now a fact and not a theory." Though continuing to acknowledge the useful if limited role whites could play in the black struggle, blacks in the urban South embraced the belief that the most effective response to Jim Crow had to be indigenous, had to emanate from their community. "We cannot and should not depend on white men to do for us what we have the opportunity to do for ourselves." During the first three decades of the twentieth century, political party alliances with local white allies—if never fully discarded—would be devalued. In their place, blacks sought ones based in a racial nationalism, across the South and nationwide.[72]

# CHAPTER 2

# National Struggle, Local Agenda

## Community against Jim Crow, 1900–1936

During the initial decades of the Jim Crow era, Baltimore's black population expanded by 212 percent, adding 75,002 residents between 1890 (67,104) and 1930 (142,106). This phenomenon continued a tradition of black southerners seeking greater freedom in the region's cities, a tradition that dated back to before the Civil War. If they no longer fled slavery on plantations in the rural South, they nonetheless came to the region's cities thinking that urbanicity brought greater community and perhaps personal agency. In the cities, black southerners believed, they might protect and defend themselves in ways unavailable to them in rural isolation or the small towns most of them had known before. With their greater numbers in the cities, they enjoyed more organizations and stronger institutions. Black children had better educational opportunities in cities, and even the modest prospect of menial and low-skilled industrial work there outshone the near-certainty of rural peonage and poverty.

A critical mass of some of the most dynamic elements of black Baltimore coalesced on the Westside after 1900. Individuals, institutions, culture, and lifestyles came together there as black citizens organized to meet emergent Jim Crow and its economic, political, and physical brutality. Organizing was a grassroots affair, but it owed much to the proliferation of the black press and the continuing influx of rural black southerners. National social justice and welfare programs set to work in the city too, and these would succeed or fail according to their adaptability to local people and their needs. With its tradition of community-based organization, black Baltimore provided an example to the rest of the black South of the Jim Crow era.

With the influx of national groups, Baltimore's social justice scene became highly contested. From the 1910s through the 1930s, as national organizations moved to establish branch affiliates in Baltimore, a number of local individuals facilitated this work. Among those with the most lasting influence was Carl James Murphy, the young academic turned publisher of the *Afro-American* (and son of John H. Murphy). Like many of his peers in the black press across the urban South, Murphy took up the black struggle for equality as a social justice crusade, viewing regional and national alliances as indispensable. However, neither Murphy nor Baltimore was looking for leadership from outside. Local communities insisted upon exercising self-determination in planning programs and establishing priorities, even while availing themselves of the benefits of national affiliation. A powerful creative tension resulted from social justice alliances between black southern communities in cities such as Baltimore and the emerging black protest movement nationally.

## The Black Nation's Baltimore Branch

Among the first truly national civil rights organizations, the all-black National Afro-American Council, which formed in 1898, never successfully established a branch in Baltimore. The council protested mob violence and advocated litigation against segregation, focusing on constitutionality. Yet, immutable perception of Booker Washington's influence on the group made many doubt its sincerity. Baltimore was not anti-"Bookerite," of course. A branch of Washington's National Negro Business League established itself in the city in 1900. But organizational problems hampered the National Afro-American Council. In its bid to recruit Baltimore, the council held its 1907 annual conference in the city. Serendipitously, perhaps, that conference would be the council's last.[1] Many black Baltimore activists considered Washington's Tuskegee Machine just as they had all other nonlocal entities through at least the turn of the century: they sought help, not leadership or agenda setting. Washington's behind-the-scenes role with the Suffrage League of Maryland to combat the state's disfranchisement campaign (see chapter 1) had been welcome, but the Tuskegee Machine sought to build nothing politically on the ground in the city. Other national black activist organizations competed to establish branch offices in Baltimore, each with its particular perspective and counter-narrative. Among social justice organizations challenging Jim Crow in Baltimore just after the turn of the century, at least three orientations are visible: separatist black nationalist, reform interracialist, and pragmatist black nationalist.[2]

Generally, in southern history to that point, black separatism as a response to racism involved strategies of emigration to another country or to delineated locations within the United States (for example, the post-Reconstruction movement to establish all-black towns).[3] As an iteration of the black counter-narrative drawing from nineteenth-century traditions more than it anticipated what was to come in the twentieth century, separatist black nationalism experienced a revival of sorts. It supported the cultural production of new racial meaning that revealed whiteness as a corrupting influence on black life. This allowed, for example, rational middle-class blacks to respond favorably to calls for cultural distinctions, black over white, as grounds for separatism. The activist clergyman Harvey Johnson arrived at this remedy only after having long advocated for racial integration. Johnson had recruited black lawyers to Maryland and led the effort that saw them admitted to the bar to protect and assert black citizenship rights. His primary modi operandi: lobbying and litigation.[4]

But Johnson was continually disillusioned by the persistence of white supremacy, and he came to see the separatist black nationalist pivot as corrective. "I would declare the white man's color to be a disease, or a strange freak of nature," Johnson reported to the city's Monumental Literary and Scientific Association by the early 1890s. His pronouncements represented examples of what Mia Bay identifies as the "nonscientific" black critique of white supremacy that experienced "renewed vitality" during the early 1900s. Johnson published essays melding earlier black self-perspective with defiant plain language, pressing themes of racial essentialism in "The Question of Race" (1891) and "The White Man's Failure in Government" (1900). Similarly, he advocated for black separatism in the Baptist church.[5]

Cynical about the prospect of a just future for blacks in white supremacist America, Johnson and his separatist nationalism ultimately evolved into his National Texas Purchase Movement Association. "The inordinate, extravagant, and unreasonable conduct of the government towards its colored citizens called forth indignation and resentment among us," the constitution of the association stated when it organized in 1910. Johnson now saw the best course as a course apart. "No alternative is left us but the formation of a republic, or our continual humiliation by this government." "We are told that we are burdensome to the government," Johnson said, and so he envisioned political lobbying to affect a transfer of the state of Texas from the United States to a newly established independent black republic. The project was to be financed by the federal government, which would "sell" Texas to African Americans on favorable terms repayable over the course of a century.[6]

While it is difficult to gauge everyday black folks' reception of the Texas Purchase Movement, Johnson no doubt remained widely respected in Baltimore until his death in 1923. Within a decade of the Texas Purchase Movement's appearance, Marcus Garvey and his United Negro Improvement Association and African Communities League (UNIA) made a bid to establish its brand of separatist black nationalism in Baltimore. As with other separatist black nationalist efforts before it, historian Mary Rolinson notes that "very little of the Garvey ideology was original." Still, while Garvey's message borrowed from older forms—nineteenth-century constructs—black folks in the interwar twentieth century responded to it with no small enthusiasm.[7]

In mid-December 1918, Garvey took the stage at the Regent Theatre on Pennsylvania Avenue to introduce his UNIA program to Baltimore. "A new and radical movement" was establishing itself in the city, the *Afro* reported, one that "comprehend[s] all colored peoples, Americans, West Indians, Africans, and Indians in its membership." From the stage, Garvey shared a vision of an empowered African Diaspora. Employing the "rhetoric of redemptionism," drawn from older black nationalist thought, Garvey spoke of his vision of a strong and independent Africa. His "Africa for the Africans" included a role for those blacks sitting in that West Baltimore audience. Nearly one hundred joined the UNIA on the spot. John Bowles, a "colored informant" planted in the crowd that night by the Bureau of Investigation, later reported ominously, "There is more in the wind than you think."[8]

While membership totals are difficult to recover, the UNIA claimed a number of "divisions" in the state by the mid-1920s, according to historian Tony Martin. The Baltimore division operated from 1918 through 1923, and organizing Baltimore was clearly a priority during those first years. Garvey was in and out of Baltimore on a number of occasions. A single week in 1919, for example, found him speaking to sizeable Baltimore crowds at three churches, Bethel AME, Macedonia Baptist, and John Wesley Methodist, respectively. After one of those talks, Garvey returned to New York for daytime business the next day before traveling back to Baltimore that night. His editorials for his newspaper, the *Negro World*, occasionally carried a Baltimore dateline.[9]

In the course of Baltimore UNIA operations, four different presidents led the division to different degrees of success in building a membership base in the city. Garvey himself maintained visibility in Baltimore (as he likely did also for UNIA divisions in Atlanta, New Orleans, Memphis, Norfolk, and elsewhere in the urban South). This complicates the popular view that his was a northern urban movement with only a secondary imprint on the South.

The first two presidents of the Baltimore UNIA, William D. Rankin and Universal Ethiopian Church pastor Joseph Josiah "J. J." Cranston, were seemingly charged with setting up shop and putting the division into motion. Rankin opened the Baltimore UNIA's first division headquarters at 1900 Pennsylvania Avenue in 1918, before moving on. His successor, Cranston, who would have the shortest tenure of all Baltimore UNIA presidents, was reassigned not long after arriving in the city. Leadership and organizational structure imported from outside the community marked a distinction between the UNIA and other national entities organizing in Baltimore, which responded best to hometown talent. Neither Cranston nor Rankin had been in Baltimore prior to their appointments there. The third president of the division, however, was a native Marylander and a Baltimore resident prior to taking up UNIA duties. Indeed, Rev. James Robert Lincoln "J. R. L." Diggs was also easily the most credentialed of the division's members during the tenure of the UNIA in the city. Diggs hailed originally from Upper Marlboro, a rural hamlet in Prince George's County. Highly educated, he had become only the ninth African American in the nation to take a PhD, which he earned at Illinois Wesleyan University in 1906. Perhaps most importantly, Rev. Diggs was well connected in radical circles. Prior to beginning his leadership of the Baltimore UNIA in October 1921, Diggs had been one of the founding members of W. E. B. Du Bois's Niagara Movement (a militant black rights advocacy organization), and he had also been a member (along with Garvey) of Monroe Trotter's National Equal Rights League.[10]

Diggs's appointment represented an important development in the UNIA effort to gain footing in Baltimore, connecting it with one of the city's leading churches, Diggs's prestigious Trinity Baptist, whose leaders had a tradition of social justice activism. (Diggs's predecessor at Trinity, G. R. Waller, had been a founding Niagarite too.) As Rolinson notes, Garvey's *Negro World* newspaper, his charismatic leadership, and his ability to attract the support of clergy in the South allowed him to present "comprehensive strategy for racial uplift to the masses." If former Baltimore UNIA presidents Rankin and Cranston had been pulled away from Baltimore for other duties in the association, Rev. Diggs saw his role expand within the larger organization without surrender of his Baltimore base (probably due to his Trinity connection). He ultimately became chaplin-general of the national UNIA. In July 1922 he presided over the marriage of Marcus Garvey and his second wife, Amy Jacques Garvey, an event that took place in Baltimore. Tragically, not long thereafter, Diggs's life was cut short by cancer in 1923. That same year the Baltimore UNIA filed petition for receivership in Baltimore Circuit Court. Reconstituting itself by 1924, the division pressed on, turning its reins over to Hattie Johnson, the first woman to lead the Baltimore UNIA and one of at least three women to lead UNIA divisions in the South.[11]

On the ground in Baltimore, the UNIA division enjoyed early success in terms of public reception and membership development. Indeed, black Baltimore responded so robustly that UNIA meetings regularly filled some of the largest Westside venues. The rural roots of many urban blacks in the South of the 1920s made them particularly receptive to the UNIA message. Garvey's "genius," Rolinson contends, allowed him to understand that he had to "appeal to the ideals and instincts of men and women only one or two generations removed from slavery . . . [and] he came to understand the typical, not the exceptional, black American experience and molded his philosophy to have maximum resonance." The UNIA held its weekly public meetings at Laurens Street Baptist Church, around the corner from its Pennsylvania Avenue division offices. On nights when Garvey himself made appearances in Baltimore, larger venues were secured. The first such venue was Bethel AME Church on Druid Hill Avenue. Cranston realized near-immediate success in building membership. He took command of a division of only 130 members around May 1920, brought it to 300 by July, and claimed 500 members in August. Despite his success, Cranston's tenure would be the briefest of Baltimore division presidents. By the end of summer, he left Baltimore to take up UNIA work in Pittsburgh.[12]

The membership numbers Cranston built up did not hold, and the division seemed challenged to sustain community buy-in. Early in his work to organize Baltimore, Garvey signaled his recognition that the UNIA had to work at the grass roots, engaging the community at its nerve center—the black church. Regardless, Garvey's local organization failed to sustain alliances with powerful black churches. There was early association with Bethel, but that was not continued. The appointment of Rev. Diggs of Trinity Baptist was important and promising but cut short by his untimely death.[13]

Ordinary Baltimore blacks warmly received Garvey's message, but Garvey's brand of separatist black nationalism had rivals. For example, a chapter of the African Blood Brotherhood for African Liberation and Redemption (ABB) appeared by the early 1920s in Baltimore. Little is known about the Baltimore operations of this smallish rival outfit. In these years, however, Tony Martin notes, members of the ABB moved among Baltimore's black working class and also sought alliances with white communists and the labor Left. Against such a backdrop, and despite much attention and effort from Garvey himself, the UNIA program in Baltimore never had a great impact.[14]

Meanwhile, coming as it did in the wake of the division's stint in receivership and following Marcus Garvey's 1923 conviction on a mail fraud charge, Hattie Johnson's tenure as president coincided with the decline of the local UNIA. Johnson was in charge of a Baltimore UNIA that had, by the time of her appointment, lost "a very large number of members." She would even meet resistance from Baltimore pastors, a group that had been generally supportive of the local UNIA. Still, Johnson's Baltimore appointment was in line with those in other southern UNIA divisions and chapters, where women played

"significant role[s]" as senior leaders after 1920, appointed as local organization presidents or secretaries. Unfortunately, prospects for Johnson's success
suffered from factors beyond her control. Regarding the parent organization,
for example, the black press had turned on Garvey by the mid-1920s. "Public sentiment backs the Federal courts, which are showing Mr. Garvey the
door," the *Afro-American* wrote about the UNIA leader's 1925 legal appeals.[15]
Black newspaper coverage of the Baltimore UNIA cast it as an outfit of violent
thugs.[16]

Lamenting the local organization's circumstances, President Johnson expressed concern over the migration of favorable public sentiment and energy to the Baltimore UNIA's chief in-town rivals, principally the Baltimore
NAACP. As they shifted allegiance, however, informal UNIA supporters and
full-fledged former Garveyites alike would pressure the local NAACP to employ strategies that would appeal to the masses. Before long, for example,
the local NAACP offered a well-publicized (if ultimately fruitless) campaign
against police brutality. By the mid-1930s, the local NAACP—and most other
local social justice organizations—would discover "the masses," Wilson Jeremiah Moses demonstrates in *The Golden Age of Black Nationalism, 1850–1925*.
Owing much to the example of UNIA organizing on the ground in the South,
these groups by this time "seem[ed] to be drawing upon the power of the folk,
rather than imposing order from above."[17]

By the mid-1920s, Garvey's Baltimore program was neither well developed
nor effectively executed. Garvey's charisma had comprised the near totality of
the program—"Garvey, in person!" the ads in the *Afro* had announced—and
Garvey was able to tap what Moses calls early twentieth century blacks' "urban mass consciousness." Otherwise, though, the Baltimore UNIA had trouble
consistently identifying an appealing program and offered no commitment
to community services, social advocacy, or litigation. Furthermore, the public face of the larger UNIA agenda, Garvey's troubled back-to-Africa venture,
remained constantly vulnerable to its many detractors.[18]

At the same time that separatist black nationalists were active, reform interracialists also began to organize the South. Reform interracialists were
not integrationists; they hoped only to perfect segregation, not do away with
it. As Morton Sosna and others observe, the reform interracialist ranks absorbed many of the South's turn-of-the-century racial liberals, whose dissent had since been tempered by the repression of the First Red Scare after
World War I.[19]

Reform interracialists tended to focus more on social welfare than on social justice. White reform interracialists hoped to assist blacks in amassing the

tools necessary for their development, albeit appropriately behind whites, in ways that served the modernizing regional needs. If they hoped to effect some measure of fairness—perhaps even promote "Negro advancement"—they were also well seated in the ideas of white supremacy and therefore accepted Jim Crow as necessary.[20]

In their organizations, they were happy to welcome black voices, though never black leadership. The reform interracialists dominated race relations in the South from the early decades of Jim Crow until at least the 1940s, when the rise of racial liberalism outside of the South had the effect of polarizing positions in the region, to the point where even reform interracialism among whites became untenable.

Across the South, state-sponsored "interracial" bodies engaged in this social welfare work. Authorized by an act of the legislature, for example, Maryland's conservative Democrat governor Albert C. Ritchie appointed the first members of the Maryland Interracial Commission (MIC) in 1924. As its initial activity, the MIC undertook a two-year study of conditions in the state and then submitted a formal report (with annual reporting thereafter). The MIC's report put forth wide-ranging recommendations regarding Jim Crow laws, economic and educational disparities, policing and the judiciary, and housing. Decades into its existence, however, the state's interracial commissions had accomplished little beyond reporting.[21]

Private organizations also emerged. The Commission on Interracial Cooperation (CIC) took the lead in the South upon its organization in Atlanta in 1919. As in interracialist organizations that followed, educated middle-class whites dominated the CIC, and their focus was not social justice but "the Negro problem." Black membership in CIC affiliates across the South was only token, meant to "lend an aura of black support for the Commission's activities." The CIC acknowledged only certain modes of black grievance as legitimate (e.g., patient appeal to white political patrons who would lobby for change on blacks' behalf in language that did not challenge presumptions of white supremacy or Jim Crow's legitimacy) as fear of black militancy grew in the biggest cities of the South, where urban black populations expanded rapidly in these years.[22]

Reform interracialist culture came to Baltimore organizationally by 1920, when two whites, Rev. Peter Ainslie of the Calhoun Street Christian Church and John R. Carey of Provident Savings Bank, launched the Baltimore Interracial Conference (BIC). In the mold of the CIC, the BIC hoped to address the "Negro problem" through economic opportunity. One of its most visible accomplishments, for example, the Homemakers' Building and Loan Association (HBLA), was aimed at alleviating housing congestion. Rather than challenge the government-supported business practices that kept the housing stocks available to blacks artificially restricted and low, the HBLA helped blacks buy and build where they were welcomed. In the often patronizing language of reform interracialism, under this program blacks purportedly learned "how to use their money to help their race."[23]

The commission sought allies in the black community to aid its work and connected with the National League on Urban Conditions among Negroes, or National Urban League (NUL). In its early years, the NUL served black citizens as a bridge to white-controlled opportunities without fundamentally questioning white supremacy. Still, a 1922 NUL industrial study of Baltimore commissioned by the BIC found that white discrimination excluded blacks categorically from most industries. As a result, half of all employed blacks worked in domestic services. "No [rational] standard appears to be observed, no objective basis for selecting a labor supply seems to exist," the report concluded—no standard beyond whiteness, of course. The National Urban League organized the Baltimore Urban League (BUL) in 1924, absorbing the older Baltimore Interracial Conference. Baltimore became one of eight Urban League affiliates organized in the interwar South—along with Richmond (1918), St. Louis (1918), Atlanta (1920), Louisville (1921), Memphis (1932), Washington, D.C. (1938), and New Orleans (1938). In these places, both de jure and de facto segregation complicated the organization's work.[24]

Through these years, the vast majority of whites remained in favor of the economic and political status quo, including segregation, and defended perceived attacks on it, sometimes with anti-black violence largely committed with impunity. White reform interracialists supposed themselves morally above white racist firebrands, but they too sought to save segregation—racial egalitarianism seemed unconscionable to them. As white "friends" and foes alike agreed on the rationality of segregation, most southern blacks sought equality, even if under segregation. By the 1920s, then, segregation had evolved for whites and blacks into a common mean toward different ends. Soberly, early twentieth-century blacks in the urban South worked to protect against the ugly insult of Jim Crow by building and promoting community as a nation within a nation.

While not frequently entailing separatist ideology (as at the basis of Harvey Johnson's Texas Purchase Movement or Marcus Garvey's UNIA), nationalist responses to Jim Crow were common among urban blacks in the South. More offended by the belittling presumptions of whites than fearful or doubtful about their own ability to meet segregation's challenges, black activists and everyday folks alike assumed pragmatic black nationalist stances. Self-assured nationalist visions emerged in spite of Jim Crow. "If they must have one, let them create a Negro district," opined the *Afro-American* around this time, "[and] in that district let us have a police station, with a colored captain, colored police and a colored magistrate . . . colored men on the public works, colored stores wholly, . . . and colored men in the legislature . . . in fact, have everything colored, as the district would be ours, and ours only." As long as blacks believed in this vision of self-sufficiency, that separate might be forced to yield equal, they need not suffer the petty indignities of white people.[25]

Blacks concurred with W. E. B. Du Bois when he declared, "We will build black homes and schools and churches; but when in these homes and schools and churches of our own the white South steps with a new demand for segregation, we absolutely refuse to permit it." Self-reliance and self-respect governed the perspectives of everyday blacks. They rejected segregation's premise, pursuing all avenues to undercut its supposed legitimacy. But they also put sincere effort in developing their segregated institutions and sacrificed much to insure the durability of those black institutions. The facts of their lives in the segregated urban South left little choice.[26]

Black Baltimore made its way between the doctrinal extremes of Booker Washington's accommodations to racism and the agitation of Du Bois, Trotter, and others. The city's black press labeled this dichotomy as one of "submissionists" versus "resisters." If black Baltimoreans recognized the importance of national alliance ("men scattered throughout the country is the real solution of the problem"), what they built showed ideological dexterity and strategic flexibility. According to the *Afro*, "All are 'Submissionists' and all are 'Resisters.'" In the real, day-to-day navigation of Jim Crow, blacks could acknowledge that, despite all the ideological discourse and theoretical suppositions to the contrary, "most of us find it very convenient to submit when there seems to be nothing else in sight . . . [but] none of us are slow to resist when we are persuaded that we can win." Progress was both a daily concern and a long-term strategy. Neither was sacrificed for the other. "It is no fun in kicking just to be kicking," the *Afro* averred. "When you come to a doorway which is awfully low, stoop and so refrain from butting out your brains."[27]

The arrival of the Niagara Movement (1905) and its Maryland branch (1906) illustrates resistance more than stooping. A few years earlier, in December 1903, Du Bois had spoken at Sharp Street Methodist Church in West Baltimore, having published *Souls of Black Folk* only months earlier. Impressive as speaker and writer, Du Bois developed a reputation in Baltimore as elsewhere as a defiant voice. After Du Bois issued a call to meet at Niagara Falls in 1905 to organize resistance to segregation, Rev. Garnett R. Waller of Baltimore's Trinity Baptist Church was one of only twenty-nine men to respond and to attend the meeting (future Garveyite J. R. L. Diggs, referenced above, was another). Waller would serve as the first president of the Maryland branch of the Niagara Movement, which, despite its name, was exclusively a Baltimore endeavor.[28]

The Maryland Niagara Movement (MNM) was not a mass membership organization but a concern of activists among the black middle class. As the *Afro-American* described it, Maryland Niagara served the concerns of "a considerable number of interested and cultured people of the city." Soon after its organization, the MNM counted among its members several pastors across a range of Protestant denominations and a number of black physicians, attorneys, and educators. Those attending its meetings spoke and heard words of inspiration, sacred and secular music selections, and topical oratory. In February 1908, for example, guest speaker Prof. L. M. Hershaw of Washington, D.C., spoke at length on "Agitation and Progress."[29]

The *Afro* asserted, "We believe in the Niagara Movement and we want to see it succeed . . . we expect the men in this movement to be bolder than Dr. Washington," but Baltimoreans for the most part took no side in the ideological match. Rather, opinion makers like George Bragg, editor of the *Afro*, advocated a middle course, which drew from the best of both approaches. After Du Bois discussed the Niagara Movement when he was in Baltimore again in early 1906, the *Afro* concluded, "The real objective of the Niagara Movement is not in conflict with Dr. Washington." Indeed, many Baltimoreans appreciated Booker Washington's quiet approach but also had an appetite for what one called the "gospel of agitation and war" against racist discrimination in America. Harry T. Pratt, for example, presided over the conservative and "Bookerite" Negro Business League of Baltimore but saw no contradiction or duplicity in his simultaneous membership in the politically militant Maryland Niagara Movement. Black Baltimoreans assumed the pragmatist black nationalist approach more than doctrinal radical or conservative commitments to defeat Jim Crow, but, as the *Afro* noted, "There is but one aim although different methods are employed."[30]

Professing to "stand unselfishly and uncompromisingly for the development of the race in every conceivable way," the message of Niagara came to Baltimore in the heat of local African American battles for public space, residential space, and space at the ballot box. During its years in the city, 1906–1911, MNM—like the national body—functioned as a forum for protest more than a platform for activism. As with Harry Pratt, most social justice activists in that era, including those of MNM, maintained multiple organizational affiliations simultaneously. Maryland Niagarites involved in antisegregation action did so under the auspices of other groups. The Suffrage League of Maryland (see chapter 1), for example, counted several local Niagarites in its ranks.[31]

When the national group ended its operations, members of Maryland Niagara formed the nucleus of the local branch of a new social justice organization, the National Association for the Advancement of Colored People (NAACP), organized in New York in 1909. Maryland Niagara veterans made the Baltimore branch of the NAACP their new organizational home. Three years after the NAACP founding, the *Afro* got its name wrong, imploring its readers in early spring 1912 to attend a "big meeting" at Harvey Johnson's Union Baptist to hear Du Bois talk about the new "Maryland Branch of the Association for the Advancement of the Negro." Notwithstanding, the *Afro* became a willing partner in pursuit of the NAACP's goals, and its editors did as much as any to shape the local branch's consistent pragmatist black nationalist approach.[32]

Like Maryland Niagara, like every other NAACP branch that would be organized in the South in those decades, but quite *unlike* the national organization, the Baltimore NAACP was an all-black entity. Its national leaders drew support from whites as well as blacks, and the national NAACP ideologically rejected all but an integrationist future. However, if the national headquarters in New York was the organization's face, it was not its strength or its soul—at least not in the black communities. The NAACP's critical strength in its first decades was on the ground, at the grass roots in the South, where pragmatist black nationalism was the ideology of consequence. The NAACP's all-black southern branches concerned themselves especially with the pursuit of self-determination—equality by the vehicle that delivered it the soonest. Despite an inaugural call billed as a "mass meeting," the Baltimore NAACP (formally chartered in April 1912), like its Niagara predecessor, did not begin as a mass organization. Despite some early success, this limited engagement with the community would need to be addressed. Meanwhile, two years after the Baltimore branch launched, two thousand people attended the national NAACP's annual convention at the city's Lyric Theatre, the most to attend an annual convention in the young organization's history to that point. Before closing its session, the NAACP's executive committee adopted a resolution "wish[ing] for the Negro press an increase in prosperity and influence for the future and invit[ing] its cooperation in the war which is now on." By "war" the NAACP meant the enduring black struggle for equality in America.[33]

The pragmatist black nationalist Baltimore NAACP and the reform interracialist Baltimore Urban League emerged as the two most impactful local branches of national affiliation by the interwar years. While they largely shared a membership base, with black Baltimoreans and their homegrown institutions broadly supporting both, each organization's leaders nonetheless understood the strategic and tactical space that separated their programs. The Baltimore NAACP was concerned primarily with greater self-determination for blacks. The NAACP was concerned about legislation and was litigious in its approach—Baltimore NAACP attorneys had been credited with much of the success against residential segregation during the 1910s (see chapter 1). Altogether the NAACP protested white supremacy, encouraging blacks to beat against the Jim Crow wall while also nurturing (and relying on) an all-black community. The national NAACP's board of directors featured powerful, highly visible whites, but NAACP branches in the South were black. In the local branches like Baltimore's, membership dues produced most of the organization's revenues, and local folks set their own agendas. Conversely, the authority of the BUL, like its parent National Urban League, resonated with dominant white voices. Despite the fact that black executive directors led most local Urban Leagues in the South, (again like the parent entity) white-dominated local boards of directors controlled their agendas and set funding priorities. While assessment of the Baltimore NAACP program came from the black churches, black schools, black professional organizations, and the black press, the BUL had to respond to the sources of its funding: liberal white philanthropists and those with reform interracialist sensibilities.

## The Education of Carl James Murphy

The social justice scene in Baltimore just after World War I owed more to local circumstances than to anything brought to town from elsewhere. National social justice organizations at work in the city were everywhere in evidence via local branches, but those branches—their programs and people—reflected local perspectives more than national ones. The pragmatist black nationalist approach, focusing on local agendas, had its most able caretaker during these years in the person of Carl James Murphy, who came of age during the century's early decades. Murphy's broad leadership became ever more influential in the Baltimore struggle, and his pragmatist black nationalism would continue for at least a generation beyond. Aggressive in his pursuit of equality, he nonetheless understood the import of context.

Murphy had at his disposal economic independence thanks to the considerable financial success of the *Afro-American*, the Murphy family business since the mid-1890s. As late as the 1910s the *Afro* was one of several newspapers published in black Baltimore, but as the others began to fold, the *Afro* continued to thrive ultimately under Carl's leadership. It became the best and most profitable black newspaper in Baltimore and one of the leaders in circulation and editorial impact nationally. As publisher and president, Carl Murphy expanded the paper's footprint in the South and along the Eastern Seaboard by the 1930s. At its height, the *Afro* produced editions not only in Baltimore but also in Washington, Philadelphia, Newark, and Richmond, and there was also a national edition.

Economic success as a newspaper publisher, even through the Great Depression, afforded Murphy considerable civic influence, which he also exercised through the National Association for the Advancement of Colored People. He became a national board member in 1931, but his most regular and passionate service to the organization came through the local branch, with which he became affiliated in the 1910s. As with the *Afro* and other black papers in Baltimore, the local NAACP was one of many organizations in the black struggle competing for hegemony when Murphy arrived there. His leadership of the Baltimore NAACP was less direct than at the *Afro*, and his impact was certainly less forceful than at the paper. But during Murphy's tenure as chair of the branch executive committee and leader of its committee on legal redress and legislation, his pragmatist black nationalist approach came to the fore.

Carl Murphy was one of a generation of black southern strivers, some of whom, like Murphy, were aristocrats distinguished by formal education, personal achievement, and service. In the biggest cities of the South and later those outside of the region, their relationship to whites was not the same as that of their ambitious forbears. These blacks—the first generation to write about themselves as "New Negroes" (not as artists but rather to describe a self-perspective, an identity, and an approach to life in the South)—saw Jim Crow as an affront aimed at them personally and at the competition they seemed to pose. These were the "race men" and "race women" who comprised the black response to segregation during the interwar years and beyond.

Carl James Murphy was born January 17, 1889, the son of John H. Murphy Sr. and Martha Howard Murphy. John Murphy took ownership of the *Afro-American* newspaper in 1897 (see chapter 1). Upon Carl's graduation from high school—a school whose principal, Mason A. Hawkins, was then an active member of the Niagara Movement—he went off to Howard University in Washington, D.C. Finishing Howard in 1911, Carl next completed a graduate degree from Harvard (1913) before accepting a position in the German Department at Howard, ultimately becoming its chair. He soon married one of his students, Vashti Turley, who had cofounded Delta Sigma Theta Sorority (1913), and he settled into his life as an academic.[34]

Carl Murphy's academic career would be short lived since he soon answered his father's call to join the family business. Working in printing, editorial, and distribution roles at the paper, young Carl witnessed his father and his father's business partner, George Bragg, wield the *Afro* as a weapon in the fight for black social justice. One example of this was the paper's coverage and advocacy of Baltimoreans' protest and litigation against Jim Crow transportation between 1902 and 1918. The pragmatist black nationalist tack was to address an immediate case of inequality instead of launching an frontal attack on segregation's constitutionality.

By definition, pragmatist black nationalists were not doctrinaire or ideological radicals. In the Jim Crow urban South they pushed insistently for the most immediate improvements in black material circumstances ("equalization"), quite consciously working within the structure of segregation. At the same time, however, they worked continually toward eroding both the moral and constitutional moorings of segregation. Indeed, from the first, Carl Murphy looked for opportunities to pick fights with Jim Crow, to force confrontations. Such was the case in 1914 when Murphy, then twenty-five, set out to study in Germany for a summer. Upon boarding the German ship *Königin Luise*, Murphy learned that he would be refused a seat in the main dining room. *Königin Luise* would be steaming out of Baltimore, Jim Crow land, so he was told that he would have to take his meals in the smoking room. It is likely that Murphy knew of the *Königin Luise*'s policies before boarding, wishing to publicly make a protest, and he reported on the ordeal prominently in the *Afro*. Point made, Murphy returned his *Königin Luise* ticket and purchased passage aboard the *Bremen*, which sailed from New York City a month later without Jim Crow on the passenger list.[35]

He would seize other opportunities as well. In August 1918 Murphy inserted himself into a developing legal action against the Washington, Baltimore, and Annapolis Electric Railway Line (WB&A), which one of Murphy's contemporaries noted with certainty "ha[d] no great love for colored folk." More than a decade earlier, as the first test of a "Jim Crow Car" law the Maryland legislature had passed in 1904, a black Howard University professor, William Henry Harrison Hart, sued. He had traveled by rail from Pennsylvania to Washington, D.C., neither of which required racial segregation on trains. Maryland, however, expected Hart to be Jim Crowed en route, as he passed through the state. In *Hart v. State* (1905), the Maryland Court of Appeals ruled the 1904 law requiring separate cars for white and black interstate passengers unconstitutional, as an infringement on interstate commerce. The court suggested that only journeys that began and ended in the state could be governed by Maryland law, as only the U.S. Congress regulated interstate matters. In the intervening years, as David Bogen rightly argued, "although the state could not require the segregation of interstate passengers, it might enforce the decisions of the railroad with respect to such passengers." A subsequent case, *State v. Jenkins* (1914), affirmed the interstate nature of the Baltimore–Washington route and thus the illegality of enforcing Jim Crow on the WB&A. Yet enforcement of Jim Crow by WB&A employees continued unabated on its high-volume Baltimore–Washington route, by the mere prerogative of white passengers and sheer strength of white police officers. Carl Murphy too found himself arrested and charged with disorderly conduct for his refusal to be "Jim Crowed." And, like Hart and several others, Murphy sued. The *Afro* called Murphy's suit an action against "illegal Jim Crow." While its outcome is unclear from the record, what is known is that by 1921 a Washingtonian, William Waller, had won a judgment against the WB&A. In 1923 the D.C. Court of Appeals upheld a lower court's ruling in the case. A decade later, although news reports confirm that intrastate traffic on the WB&A was still legally Jim Crow in Maryland, "no Jim Crow [was enforced] on the company's trains between Baltimore and Washington."[36]

Despite this, through the first decades of the century transportation segregation became more and more normative in the opinions of the courts. Realizing this, "rather than seeking integration directly," pragmatist black nationalists like Murphy pressed the letter of Jim Crow law, focusing on "the conditions of segregated cars," Bogen observes. First, as the 1904 statute in Maryland required Jim Crow but prohibited discrimination in the quality of accommodation—separate but equal—the pragmatist black nationalist strategy hoped to reveal mandated equalization as so financially and operationally burdensome that all but segregation's most ardent supporters would abandon it for want of efficiency if nothing else. Second, as the Supreme Court had disallowed Jim Crow on interstate lines, such as that from Baltimore to D.C., pragmatist black nationalists pushed back against illegal expansions of Jim Crow. The struggle on this front would continue. As much as suffrage or residential segregation, Jim Crow transportation remained a field of battle.[37]

Many of the early legal actions challenging the form and function of Jim Crow in Baltimore were taken up by attorneys associated with the fledgling Baltimore branch of the NAACP—namely William Ashbie Hawkins and Warner T. McGuinn. Carl Murphy's faith in the legal course of action began in these years, and his rise to the ranks of social justice leadership in Baltimore was significant. Within five years of Carl's formally joining his father's staff at the *Afro-American*, the elder Murphy died. Thus, in 1922, at thirty-three, Carl became publisher and president of the paper. Under his leadership the *Afro* continued "in the interest of the race," the mission its founders had developed and pursued for more than a generation.

Beyond what he might accomplish with his paper, Carl looked for more personal ways to serve the cause, taking up the mantle of crusading race man, facilitator, and social justice kingmaker. Coming into this role, Carl Murphy believed that the most effective weapons against Jim Crow's deprivations were the law—the courts—and one's voice. Murphy's visions for self-determination and desegregation were not contradictory but rather mirrored black community-building of the early twentieth century. Murphy came to see the power of place, the value of efficient organization, and the virtue of an impatient pragmatism.

Murphy lamented that the once-flourishing Baltimore NAACP branch had fallen into inactivity and invisibility in the community despite the need for its services. Whereas the branch only a few years earlier had been hailed as a champion for its hand in the defeat of the city's residential segregation ordinances, now in the early 1920s, it seemed to have mismanaged its momentum.[38]

For Murphy, organized, vigilant, legalistic agitation by the young NAACP seemed a promising way forward for blacks. Black strength—comprising strong black citizenship, institutions, and organizations—was the only way to defeat Jim Crow and for blacks to win access to opportunities equal to those afforded other U.S. citizens. Murphy was not ideological in his prescriptions for the struggle. Rather, he offered a consistent, steady, pragmatic message. He was impatient for equality but not impetuous. "Run as fast as you can," he counseled, "without falling." Thus Murphy would push and prod the local NAACP branch to meet its potential.[39]

His dedication to the struggle was obvious. The national office repeatedly sought Murphy's advice on matters relating to the Baltimore branch, many times requesting that Murphy intervene on behalf of the national office in matters concerning the administration and operation of the local branch. The admiration was no doubt mutual, since Murphy clearly pursued the relationship. In 1930 the national office made its first of several attempts to convince Murphy that he himself should lead the branch—"[Baltimore could be one of] our strongest branches if we could get you to accept the presidency." He declined, citing duties with the *Afro*. Desperate—scheming even—to link Murphy more closely to the day-to-day operations of the branch, the NAACP national director of branches, Robert Bagnall, took a less direct route. On the advice of mutual acquaintance George Bragg, who advised Bagnall to seek "a brainy and energetic woman" for the branch presidency, Bagnall approached Murphy's wife, Vashti. Though Vashti was capable in her own right, Bagnall nonetheless all but admitted his well-intended duplicity: "If Baltimore had many persons like Carl Murphy, the [racial] situation would be different." Like her husband, however, Vashti Murphy declined the offer. Though not interested in the branch presidency, Carl Murphy by 1931 had nonetheless agreed to an appointment to the NAACP's national board of directors.[40]

In his new capacity as board member, Murphy attended the 1932 annual conference of the NAACP, held in Washington, D.C. He stood proudly with his new colleagues for a group portrait snapped by famed photographer Addison Scurlock to memorialize the event. But Murphy would remember the Washington meeting for other reasons as well. While much of what he heard during the conference deeply impressed him with the possibilities of effective social justice advocacy generally and the work of the association in particular, two sessions would resonate most fully, presaging the decades of activism that lay ahead Carl Murphy.

The first session was a presentation by W. E. B. Du Bois. It may be instructive here to consider the collegial relationship Carl J. Murphy would develop with Du Bois during the 1930s and 1940s. Du Bois became something of a resource, if not a full-on confidante, as Murphy looked to reconceptualize the Baltimore struggle in these years. The late 1930s would not only see Du Bois move to Baltimore but also to Murphy's neighborhood, Morgan Park, where the two became friends. Also, this was the era when Du Bois completed his highly visible journey toward the radical Left. In the spring of 1932, just before the NAACP conference in Washington (and years before his relocation to Baltimore), Du Bois had published in the NAACP's *Crisis* one of a number of articles through which he explored the potential application of communist doctrine to the problems of race in America. For one piece, "Negro Editors on Communism," Du Bois invited Murphy's participation. Setting aside ideology and doctrine, Murphy approached the topic pragmatically, readily acknowledging that among whites it was communists in particular who demonstrably advocated social justice for black people. As Du Bois biographer David Levering Lewis put it, Murphy's "qualified indulgence of communism" was motivated by the pragmatist needs of the black struggle.[41]

Only weeks after the *Crisis* article was published, Murphy and the other NAACP conventioneers in Washington sat to listen to Du Bois's address with these thoughts "fresh in their minds."[42] It was certainly not a pep talk. Du Bois asked, "What is wrong with NAACP?" And then he answered the question by advocating for a new grounding of the NAACP in the needs of the black masses instead of the black elite. "The N.A.A.C.P. has not faced this decision in the past," he granted, as "there has been hitherto in the Negro race no sufficient division of economic interests to make the decision necessary."[43]

To accomplish this vital turn to "increasingly enlist the co-operation of masses of colored people," Du Bois pointed to the need for a strengthened branch program. To that point in the organization's history, Du Bois observed, the practice had been top-heavy discipline, with the national office working to "send life down" to the branches. "The NAACP as a mass-based organization could never become a reality," Du Bois declared, "so long as the attitude was to work 'for the black masses but not with them.'" The national office would work best, he said, if it worked in support of people on the ground in their branches, which would operate as "living cells of activity and ideals." Corollary to his call for branches to be at the center of the organization's most important work and thus connect with the masses of black people, Du Bois also called for the stimulation of more vigorous youth programs as sources for fresh perspectives and renewed energy for the NAACP.[44]

It is doubtful that Walter F. White, the recently installed executive secretary of the national NAACP agreed with his colleague-adversary Du Bois fully on these fronts. Despite Du Bois's admonitions, at the national headquarters in New York in the coming years White would aspire to maintain stricter organizational discipline over his branches—and his attempt at paternalism would be frustrated. Especially with the larger branches, the NAACP had never worked that way. Traditions of localism in the biggest cities still held fast regarding programmatic agenda. In fact, despite the ebb and flow of branch activity, urban blacks in the South saw themselves as partners, not wards—as on the vanguard, not in the backwater. They had good reason for this and for their sense of themselves. The NAACP's operating funds came from members, and this was money literally raised on the streets, by black folk in the communities, through the churches, and by door-to-door efforts.

If Du Bois's remarks on the importance of branches and youth work rang true for Murphy, a second 1932 conference session, one held on Friday morning, May 20, spurred him to nearly immediate action. The theme was "Legal Defense," and the audience heard presentations from a range of expert attorneys, including Louis L. Redding of Delaware, Jesse S. Heslip of Ohio, William Hastie of Washington, D.C., Nathan Margold of New York, and Charles Hamilton Houston, also of Washington, D.C. Back in New York at the national NAACP's office before trekking to Washington for the conference, Margold had produced for the organization what would become a landmark report blueprinting a legal strategy against educational segregation. Margold was one of several fresh legal minds coming into the NAACP fold. Another was Houston, dean of law at Howard University. At the urging of the university's indomitable president, Mordecai Wyatt Johnson (the first African American to hold that post), Houston was in the midst of remaking the law school into a civil rights litigator's training ground.[45]

Presented at the "Legal Defense" session of the NAACP conference, the

"Margold Report" reenvisioned antisegregation efforts but kept within the equalization tradition of pragmatist black nationalist resistance, at least strategically. It recognized that the climate would not support direct challenges to the constitutionality of racial segregation, as that seemed by a number of Supreme Court decisions since the 1920s to be settled law. The approach Margold proposed, as Skotnes points out, "was an *offensive* . . . attack against the racist regime" and so broke with what had been a history of "defensive actions attempting to limit or reverse a racist intrusion." Margold reasoned that it would be simpler to prove that, as practiced, segregation separated races but never provided equality. In its perpetually narrow interpretations of *Plessy v. Ferguson* since 1896, the U.S. Supreme Court had never given an opinion on such a scenario as separate yet unequal. Since then, with but a nod to *Plessy* and equality, southern courts, legislators, law enforcement officials, and white southerners generally had made a mockery of black citizens' Fourteenth Amendment protections. Margold therefore suggested that the NAACP make efforts toward court-ordered equalization of opportunities and conditions. In terms of goal, however, it was clear that the outcome of Margold's approach would be more than mere equalization. Because of the impossibility of separate but equal, Jim Crow would be unsustainable, and desegregation would be the result. Whatever else the 1932 NAACP conference did for Carl Murphy, what he heard that Friday morning as he sat and listened to Margold and Houston would stay with him and embolden him.[46]

Coming away from the conference, Murphy conceived an agenda for the leaderless Baltimore NAACP. At the same time, there was a feeling of desperation at the national office about the prospect of revitalizing its most promising branches, many of which languished like Baltimore's. In truth, the entire association was hurting under the Depression. Whether anyone at the national office acknowledged the truth or not, the NAACP in the early 1930s was only as strong as its branches. And the strength of the branches reflected the mood of black communities across the nation. Black purses and wallets, large and small, contributed the lion's share of NAACP revenue to that point, and the association's economic struggle reflected that of its members. In fact, as Murphy began to imagine a future implementation of Margold's basic ideas, the national NAACP owed thousands of dollars to creditors and had cash on hand of mere hundreds. Still, though they could not yet know it, the NAACP was on to something in Margold's idea. A new and historic path had been found, and the first steps would be taken in Baltimore. As Murphy told Walter White in December 1932, "One of the first things we plan to do is to attack the University of Maryland . . . [which] excludes Negroes by force rather than by law."[47]

### Seeking Equality

On a sweltering August afternoon in 1934, just before Labor Day weekend, a group of fifty-nine attorneys from across the nation posed for the *Afro-American*'s photographer on the steps of the Baltimore City Courthouse. All were members of the National Bar Association (NBA), a body of black attorneys begun several years earlier, since the American Bar Association had a whites-only membership policy. They had just left a reception in their honor in the chambers of a sitting Baltimore judge, Eugene O'Dunne.[48]

Earlier, in remarks to the gathering, O'Dunne, who was white, singled out the venerable W. Ashbie Hawkins for praise. Since before the turn of the century Hawkins had defended black rights with energy and intelligence. As noted earlier, Hawkins had the ignominy of being one the last two blacks to attend the University of Maryland before newly constructed Jim Crow forced his ouster in 1891. He had finished his legal education at Howard University and returned to Baltimore to battle Jim Crow. Though Hawkins had since the 1920s retreated somewhat to private practice, he was still recognized by many as the first great civil rights lawyer in the city.[49]

Also in the photo snapped that hot August day was another Howard Law alumnus peering into the camera from the fringes of the group. Standing tall, with the staid gaze of a young professional wishing to be taken seriously, Thurgood Marshall—one of the city's newest lawyers—was largely responsible for the group's meeting with O'Dunne that day. Since passing the bar in June 1933, Marshall had worked to coddle a "positive relationship" with O'Dunne, Larry Gibson notes, from whom he came to believe blacks might at least get a fair hearing. His beliefs would soon be put to a test.[50]

The Depression years presented opportunities for transformation of the black struggle in the urban South. Baltimore's black activists formed a critical component of the considerable and highly visible emerging black activist nation. In addition to their connection with the wider movement across the country, pragmatist black nationalist activists in Baltimore found kinship with the rising radical white labor movement, with which they threatened for a time to erase the color line in the name of class unity. The black struggle for equality and the forces for industrial unionism worked toward common goals in the city, developing "a complex web of interrelationships" during the 1930s. "They allied, sometimes they interpenetrated," writes Skotnes, "[and] always they influenced each other." But there were limits, and these most often were defined by the distance between the sincere rhetoric of labor leaders and the unwillingness of urban South whites to surrender historical prerogatives on the shop floor for the sake of union with blacks. Meanwhile, the era's young black adults were moving aggressively to connect local agendas with national struggles and to find synergies between the black equality agenda and the white liberal effort for greater democracy. By these means, black resistance at the community level in West Baltimore embraced mass mobilization.[51]

In 1931 Juanita E. Jackson, daughter of Lillie Jackson, launched an activist organization of mainly local twentysomethings, the City-Wide Young People's Forum (the Forum). Smart and driven, Jackson and the Forum sparked Baltimore's black activist scene and, as Prudence Cumberbatch argues, "creat[ed] a distinct youth political culture [that] engag[ed] in a transformative dialogue with the larger black community." The impact of the Forum was considerable. While providing a valued social outlet for its core constituency, the Forum raised political consciousness and "infused [the] community with a revitalizing excitement" about the course of the black struggle. Information provision and dialogue were key programmatic tools. From 1931 through 1938, every Friday night, the City-Wide Young People's Forum engaged the community in meaningful conversation with experts, politicians, and opinion makers— black and white—from across Baltimore and throughout the country.[52]

The Forum embraced all of the earlier forms of the black struggle for equality but pushed to "increasingly [channel] its energy into the neighborhood and public spheres." In this way, its most fortuitous collaboration came early on in support of an economic boycott of Pennsylvania Avenue merchants. Doing business in the commercial and cultural heart of black West Baltimore, white merchants refused to hire black employees. The boycott represented a collaboration between the Forum and a small committee led by self-described faith healer, "Prophet" Kiowa Costonie. They dubbed the effort "Buy Where You Can Work."[53]

Corporate leaders of a chief target of the earliest protests, an A&P grocery store, ultimately proposed an all-black staff at the Pennsylvania Avenue location. Activists rejoiced. Notably, the fact that the store staff would be all-black did not resonate as a moral wrong (nor did the fact that white workers would be fired to make room for blacks to be hired). Some protesters even carried signs on the picket lines complaining, "This Store Does Not Employ *All* Colored." They wanted equalization, not integration. Just as in white neighborhoods the staffs were all-white, they wanted an all-black staff for the black neighborhood's A&P.[54]

Black owners of mom-and-pop groceries in West Baltimore criticized this temporary boycott of white-owned businesses, however. Of the 210 grocers in West Baltimore in 1934 (including a few national chain stores like A&P) only 16, or 7.08 percent, were black-owned. Writing to the *Afro*, the Negro Grocers' Association warned that, in exchange for a few jobs, a successful but temporary boycott would ultimately hurt black-owned stores in the neighborhood. This group suggested a permanent boycott. In a rhetorical "buy black" statement sent as a letter to the *Afro-American* they asked, "Is it right to annoy, beg, and boycott white stores to employ us or is it best to boost *our enterprise* so [we] will expand and hire [our] own race?" Commenting on this, the *Afro*'s pragmatist perspective shone through: "Do both," it urged. "The corner grocery has a mission as well as the chain store . . . we need both and can support both."[55]

From a broader vantage point, "Buy Where You Can Work" can be seen as a community protest similar to others elsewhere in Depression America. Not only did it draw from older traditions of economic activism, it also reflected a contemporary strategy. Two years earlier, for example, in 1931, Carl Murphy had argued that blacks too often failed to use the coercive might of their collective purchasing power. Surveying the employment opportunities and capacity of West Baltimore in the professional, service, and retail sectors, Murphy had implored readers to press for "a campaign to have these neighborhood stores employ colored girls and boys." He had even given his proposed campaign a name: "Don't Spend Your Money Where You Can't Work."[56]

Meanwhile, throughout the fall of 1933, immediately prior to the Costonie/Forum boycott campaign in West Baltimore, the *Afro-American* carried extensive news of a boycott in black Washington, D.C. A group of young activists there, the New Negro Alliance (NNA), distinguished their efforts—and seemed to respond to Carl Murphy's criticism in 1931—by employing mass protest and direct action. Indeed, for the young Baltimore activists of the Forum too, mass mobilization and direct action were key. "Solutions to the problems of the black community," Cumberbatch points out, "demanded a confrontation." Still, the confrontation sought pragmatist black nationalist outcomes, insisting that black consumer dollars remain in the black community through salaries paid to black store employees.[57]

Despite the success of the A&P boycott, a coterie of white small business owners secured a permanent injunction against future picketing. Nevertheless, having followed the Forum's progress from New York, W. E. B. Du Bois recommended restructuring of national youth activism, urging that the Baltimore example be used as a model. This was ultimately achieved by attracting Juanita Jackson herself to the NAACP's national staff for a time, further illustrating the importance of branch-level activism and effecting a national legacy for the work of the City-Wide Young People's Forum.[58]

As the "Buy Where You Can Work" campaign was underway, from the rural Eastern Shore region of Maryland came news of the state's second lynching in less than two years. George Armwood, a black man in his early twenties, was taken from the local jail in the hamlet of Princess Anne, Maryland (population 975 in 1930), where he was being held on suspicion of attempted assault of a local white woman. A large mob of whites sadistically tortured Armwood before murdering him and then made public spectacle of the desecration of his corpse. Two years earlier, in 1931, in Salisbury, Maryland (population 10,997 in 1930), about a dozen miles north of where Armwood would be slain, a mob of local whites lynched Matthew Williams. In a macabre carnival, more than two thousand whites participated in the ritualistic murder—torture and brutalization, hanging, desecration of the corpse, and post mortem public exhibition—of the black man, Williams, who was suspected of killing a white man. State officials had recognized the potential for each of these outcomes beforehand and taken some preventive steps, but clearly the political will for more than this was absent. In fact, after Williams's murder but before Armwood's, in the fall of 1933, many contended that the State of Maryland itself had conducted a "legal lynching" when it had executed Euel Lee, another Eastern Shore black man, from Berlin, Maryland (population 1,480 in 1930). Lee had originally been arrested as a murder suspect in October 1931, but the appeals process, local whites believed, had been needlessly drawn out.[59]

The Williams lynching, the Armwood lynching, and the Euel Lee trials would each be something of a local cause célèbre with the social justice scene in Maryland's largest city, Baltimore (population 804,874 in 1930). The national office of the NAACP had been lobbying for federal anti-lynching legislation since the horrors of 1919's "Red Summer," a period marked by dozens of race riots and hundreds of resultant deaths across the United States. Despite nearly annual congressional inaction on the issue, the arrival of the new Democratic regime under Franklin Roosevelt renewed hopes for legislative action (only for them to be frustrated yet again). To be sure, the fact of lynching brought Maryland into infamous company with the rest of the South and inspired Marylanders to see their struggle in a national light. Likewise the Euel Lee case showed symmetry with the most notorious attempted "legal lynching" of the era, the "Scottsboro Boys" case in Alabama. Yet the principal similarity of these local travesties to national examples was the subsequent involvement of the white radical Left, which mobilized mass support and coordinated legal defenses.[60]

As Andor Skotnes reveals, the leftist embrace of black social justice in Maryland was part of its broader commitment toward elevating the class struggle above the race struggle as the basis for restructuring America. Yet, as the white Left principally engaged in a doctrinal contest against capitalism, it quite often bumped clumsily against the real-life pragmatism of the black struggle on the ground in the urban South. Most often, these were minor incidents, which Skotnes rightly advises should not be exaggerated or over-stated in their individual and incidental impacts. However, collectively, they reminded blacks of the validity of their historical distrust of white people. For instance, many in West Baltimore took umbrage when the white Left demeaned rural blacks as cowardly in the face of a lynch mob. Likewise, suspicions that the Left was interested in no more than a crass political appropriation of the black struggle were confirmed in the minds of many when it was learned that white leftists intended to take Euel Lee's corpse to New York for display as propaganda at an anti-lynching rally. Until sustained experience proved otherwise, it was hard for everyday black folk in the 1930s to trust white people—leftists or not.[61]

West Baltimore blacks, writes Skotnes, "were not about to let those allies set the agenda or define the character of the black community." Blacks insisted on stating the grounds for alliance and never relinquishing the authority or agency for their movement's strategizing and goal setting. For blacks this was not about integration or interracial struggle. This was about the attainment of equality. Black Baltimore would hold to its pragmatist black nationalist position. "I have urged Negroes to arm themselves to fight," the *Afro*'s Ralph Matthews confessed in 1933, "[and] I have told men to die for the cause of racial advancement, knowing all the while that most of it was pure bunk, impractical and illogical." "A program which fails to temper indignation and zeal for reform with common sense," he clarified, "is worse than no program at all."[62]

The protest and mass mobilization agenda of the City-Wide Young People's Forum in the early 1930s—anti-lynching efforts, boycotts, public information, and educational programming—revealed the potential for mass mobilization as a true opportunity of the struggle. Even as that struggle maintained a commitment to equalization litigation, the 1930s represented a significant shift insofar as mass mobilization was strategically built atop legal activism. In this way, equalization became a platform to strategically transform the local struggle toward desegregation and multifront activism. The signal development of the decade came in 1935, when local activists sued to open the state's public law school to black students. Jim Crow had separated legal education but provided blacks with no equal opportunities. The Baltimore NAACP played a central role—and reaped the benefits in terms of prestige and community standing. Still, through its transformation, the Baltimore struggle maintained its pragmatist black nationalist orientation. The transformation of the Baltimore struggle was accomplished only through a willingness to set aside lines of organizational demarcation in pursuit of collaborative, community-wide efforts. This is a historical attribute of the pragmatism of local activists. Many of them supported and maintained multiple organizational affiliations concurrently and used this to promote collaboration.

For its role in this broad-based struggle, the Baltimore NAACP had to re-envision itself. It had been a small coterie whose agenda and productivity centered on a strong president and single-issue activism, reliant on lobbying and litigation. Despite early success, by the close of the 1920s the branch experienced difficulty identifying suitable causes and suffered under a string of presidents unable to give the branch the singular focus of their attention that it required. Having failed to convince Carl Murphy (or his wife, Vashti Murphy) to assume the branch presidency, the Baltimore NAACP ultimately installed Rev. Charles Young Trigg, pastor of the Metropolitan Methodist Episcopal Church, in the role. Activist clergy had been effective leaders of the Baltimore struggle since the late nineteenth century. Indeed, pastors had arguably launched the struggle in the 1880s (see chapter 1). Trigg entered office in January 1933, and while he proved not to be a long-term president, during his administration the branch developed what would be its sustaining strategic focus. "Local N.A.A.C.P. to Start Fight on Color Bar in State Supported Institutions," the *Afro* announced. This new direction flowed from a pledge Carl Murphy had made to Walter White at the end of 1932, to "attack the University of Maryland."[63]

In reaction to this declaration of war, the Board of Regents of the University of Maryland successfully pressed the Maryland General Assembly to authorize a new and ostensibly reparative scholarship fund for black students. Known commonly as the "Out-of-State Scholarships Program," the program putatively offset Jim Crow's imposition on blacks hoping to attend the university. The state operated no four-year liberal arts college open to blacks and no graduate or professional schools that would admit them (save for teacher training). However, if black students sought admission to the University of Maryland, the program funds could be used to pay tuition to any comparable out-of-state college that would have them. The program also supported students who chose to attend Maryland's only four-year liberal arts school open to blacks, Baltimore's Morgan College, run by the Methodist Church. Predictably, as Jim Crow was intended to preserve white supremacy, not provide equality for blacks, no funds were actually allocated for the scholarships at the time the law creating the program passed. It was a ruse, the sort of Jim Crow wink and nod that had always protected "separate" for whites without ever quite providing "equal" to blacks.[64]

Carl Murphy had been visualizing the dimensions of the attack of Jim Crow in publically funded institutions since his experiences at the 1932 NAACP conference. Murphy understood what Nathan Margold and Charles Hamilton

Houston had laid out at the conference: that *Plessy* presented an opportunity. Through litigation blacks might attempt to compel the courts to hold *Plessy* to its word, separate *and* equal. But when such a standard was not met, Murphy believed, available remedies skewed in favor of desegregation. The presence of reasonable, if not liberal, judges in the lower courts of the urban South could be useful in this regard, but otherwise careful case selection and management might lead to the Supreme Court, where segregation might be found unconstitutional because it rendered inequality.

Murphy benefited from Charles Houston's interest in testing his theory. By 1933 Houston was preparing to take a leave of absence from Howard University to go to New York as lead special council of the NAACP. Houston's protégé at Howard Law, Thurgood Marshall, had just completed the program and returned to his native Baltimore, a freshly minted attorney. Marshall began working on civil rights cases for the Baltimore NAACP by the fall of 1933. Murphy was aware of young Marshall since the Murphy and Marshall families had enjoyed multiple social connections through the years. In 1927, when Thurgood Marshall went off to Lincoln College in Pennsylvania, his roommate was a fellow Baltimorean, James Murphy—Carl's nephew. Likewise, Marshall's maternal uncle, Fearless M. Williams, in whose Division Street home young Thurgood and his parents had lived for a time, was a fellow member of the Baltimore NAACP's executive committee along with Murphy. Uncle Fearless would have told Carl about the talented young lawyer who had just graduated top of the class at Howard and was trying to establish himself in the middle of the Depression. At any rate, familiarity and personal interest may combine to explain why Thurgood's unfolding collegiate career garnered more than just an occasional mention in the *Afro*.[65]

Giving Murphy's growing cadre more confidence, attorneys Houston and Marshall had satisfied themselves that the out-of-state scholarship program would likely not withstand constitutional scrutiny. Further, while Maryland had a long list of statutes requiring segregation, no law mandated Jim Crow at the University of Maryland, and no language in the school's charter required it. Exclusion had simply been a tradition expressing the preference of whites running the school since 1891, when W. Ashbie Hawkins was summarily dismissed. Arrogant presumption ever since had made university racists so secure that they had never even bothered with formalities like charter amendments.

Owing to the involvement of the City-Wide Young People's Forum in the early stages of test-case planning in the Baltimore NAACP suit against the University of Maryland School of Law, the branch began to build broad-based grassroots support for the first time. By 1933, as the Forum's more public work involved support for anti-lynching legislation and the "Buy Where You Can Work" campaign, Forum head Juanita Jackson and others in the organization helped Murphy and the NAACP branch canvas for potential plaintiffs. It is noteworthy that support of this work brought the Forum into the realm of older resistance forms and into partnership with established entities like the Baltimore NAACP. And it is equally notable that the latter, not the former, would change as a result. The local NAACP would emerge from the 1930s with the Forum's personnel and its tactics of mass mobilization largely incorporated into its own new profile.

Jackson and the Forum led the effort to expose the scholarships law for what it was. First they tested whether or not qualified blacks would actually be barred from the University of Maryland's professional schools. At best, they concluded, the university would be desegregated, and blacks would have access to training on par with whites. At worst, the NAACP would take its battle into the courtrooms. This effort also began a sustained connection between students at Morgan and the broader local black struggle for equality. There was formal if likely unofficial cooperation from Morgan College for the NAACP's desegregation campaign. John Haywood Jr., on the faculty at Morgan and a member of the Baltimore NAACP branch's executive committee, took it upon himself to get Morgan's students involved in the campaign.[66]

At Jackson's direction, at least nine blacks applied to the University of Maryland. A form letter in response from university president Raymond A. Pearson stated frankly that blacks, regardless of qualification, were not considered for admission, and Pearson suggested applying for the out-of-state-study scholarships. When the black students did this, however, they were first told that the committee empowered to award such scholarships had not yet been appointed. Next they were told that the law providing the scholarships had been passed "without any special appropriation of funds for carrying out the law." The facts of the boondoggle having been documented, Jackson next directed the students to forward all correspondence with the university to the NAACP's Charles Houston.[67]

Students from Morgan College helped demonstrate the chicanery underlying Jim Crow at the University of Maryland School of Law, but the plaintiff settled on by the legal team was not a Morganite. Ultimately a suit was brought against the university in the name of Donald Gaines Murray, a native Baltimorean and recent Amherst College graduate who had returned to Baltimore after completing his undergraduate education. Murray likely did not require much cajoling since his grandparents had raised him in the traditions of the struggle. His grandfather, Rev. Abraham Lincoln "A. L." Gaines, who died in 1931, had been a vocal opponent of Jim Crow since the turn of the century and active in both the Maryland Niagara Movement and the NAACP. His grandmother, Minnie L. Gaines, was active too, having served as a leader of the Maryland Federation of Women's Clubs and on the founding executive committee of the Baltimore NAACP when it organized in 1912. Donald Murray himself had been active with the City-Wide Young People's Forum upon his return to Baltimore. Murray applied to the University of Maryland School of Law in 1935 expecting to be rejected on the basis of race, which he was. He received a form letter identical to the one other blacks had been receiving for two years from the school. Subsequently the Baltimore branch of the NAACP filed a suit on his behalf. Marshall would do the research, while Houston did the in-court arguments.[68]

The case would be heard by Eugene O'Dunne, the judge who had hosted a reception in his chambers for Marshall and members of the National Bar Association in August 1934. O'Dunne was not an interracialist but held moderate views on race. As legal historian Michael Klarman argues, white moderates often proved as intransigent as their hard-line racist cohorts on the most important points—"the difference between white moderates and extremists was in the costs they were prepared to bear to maintain segregation, not in their preference for it." Moderate jurists like O'Dunne (Larry Gibson characterizes him, perhaps more accurately, as "non-conformist") drew the line at the letter of the law. Judge O'Dunne had long given clues to his fairness regarding race. He had been, for example, one of the few voices on the Baltimore bench consistent about reprimanding police officers who brutalized black citizens for the social offense of insolence. No one could be sure how he would rule in the law school suit, however. Donald Murray's lawyers pointedly asked O'Dunne to uphold *Plessy v. Ferguson*, to insist on its mandate as dual: separate *and* equal. If accomplished, this would make segregation untenable, as Charles Houston intended: "su[ing] Jim Crow out of the South."[69]

On the day Judge O'Dunne heard *Donald G. Murray vs. Raymond A. Pearson, et al., the University of Maryland* in his courtroom, Lillie Jackson, who earlier that year had replaced Rev. Trigg as NAACP branch president, ensured that the courtroom was "packed with well-dressed black citizens" to show the dignity of the city's working-class and middle-class blacks. Thurgood Marshall's parents, Will and Norma, sat proudly among them. While their son performed ably in what became his first big day in court, the Marshalls and others more significantly witnessed Charles Houston's dismantling of the university's justification for keeping Donald Murray out of his state's law school. Interrogating witnesses in succession, Houston upbraided the racist logic of university president Raymond Pearson and then Roger Howell, the law school's dean. At one point, making an analogy to disparities in railroad service, Houston got the dean to say that he believed oxcarts for blacks could be made "as good as" train cars for whites if preservation of Jim Crow were at stake.[70]

Such biases laid bare, Houston and Marshall masterfully demonstrated that black taxpayers like Will and Norma Marshall, the family of Donald Murray, and those seated all around them had supported the educations of whites at the University of Maryland for generations. There was no separate and equal. Witnesses for the defense betrayed that maintenance of segregation was their main aim, not equal protection under law, supposedly guaranteed by the Fourteenth Amendment.

O'Dunne was fair minded and certainly had not predetermined his ruling. At times, however, he seemed amused by the audacity of the university's position, but at a number of points in the proceedings he lost patience with the university's lead counsel, Charles LeViness, for his minimizing of ugly facts. On June 18, 1935, with arguments complete and without even leaving the bench to deliberate, O'Dunne—an alumnus of Maryland Law—declared that the wink and nod would suffice no more. Out-of-state scholarships did not satisfy the state's Fourteenth Amendment obligation to provide for blacks as it did for whites. No black law school existed, and none could or should be hastily organized. Equal opportunity had to be afforded, said *Plessy*. If these opportunities could not be had equally in separation, then they could not be had separately. O'Dunne issued a writ of mandamus ordering the University of Maryland to admit Donald Murray to the school in time for the upcoming fall term.

If, as Juanita Jackson would recall, "the colored people were on fire . . . they were euphoric with victory," a sober Charles Houston was quick to advise the jubilant public that "victory in the University of Maryland test case does not mean the battle for educational equality for Negroes is over." "Maybe the next generation will be able to take time out to rest, but we have too far to go and too much work to do," he assured them. "Shout if you want, but don't shout too soon." Segregators certainly had not lost hope. The exposed "equal" loophole could be closed, they believed, if the state developed a black university equivalent to the University of Maryland.[71]

Even the sober Houston had to be hopeful, though. *Murray* saw Jim Crow in Baltimore pass through a doorway of no return. Houston's caution notwithstanding, *Murray* proved to be galvanizing, and many black folks in the city did find reason to shout. O'Dunne's ruling said to them that at least some well-placed whites were willing to acknowledge the facts. Further, O'Dunne had called separate but not equal what it was: illegal. *Murray* suggested that separation was no longer automatically the white prerogative and asserted that equality could no longer be simply promised—even if actually intended—

without its being delivered. This was a first. The case validated for many others besides Donald Murray the pragmatist black nationalist perspective that Jim Crow could be made to collapse under his own weight.

Thus invigorated, NAACP branch lawyers like Thurgood Marshall assured that there was more to come. "This is but the beginning of our campaign in this state," Marshall told a well-wisher in 1936. And so it was. *Murray* had a great impact on the push for access to greater educational opportunities not just in Maryland but also throughout the entire nation. The NAACP took a nearly identical case against the University of Missouri School of Law all the way to the U.S. Supreme Court and won less than two years later. For Baltimoreans the *Murray* victory also fostered fresh enthusiasm to press for equalization in access to other areas of public life. Blacks pressed *Murray* for all it could give them.[72]

◎  ◎  ◎

At the time the Maryland State Assembly legislated its out of state-scholarships boondoggle, Morgan College had been in existence for nearly seventy years. Located for years in Methodist church buildings, the school by the 1930s was nestled in a bucolic campus in a part of Baltimore annexed into the city limits in 1918. If Morgan's environs were accommodating, its neighbors often were not. When the first buildings for the new campus went up in 1919, surrounded largely by rural countryside, whites in the nearby hamlet of Lauraville protested. And, as Baltimore's sprawl eventually caught up to the campus, newcomer whites had the nerve to erect a wall—dubbed the "Wall of Shame" by Carl Murphy's *Afro*—to protect themselves from the progressive black school.

Meanwhile, a push in the city for a black public liberal arts college had begun but went almost undetected. "We hope that the next General Assembly of Maryland will grant our people a state university," the Baltimore-based Colored Citizens League of Maryland announced in 1929, "like they have in many other states." At the time, a state commission reported, not only did Maryland not support a public liberal arts college open to blacks, but also the annual aid it gave Morgan, a private college—the only liberal arts college in the state open to blacks—barely approached half of what the state gave its whites-only private schools like Goucher College and Johns Hopkins. As the Depression deepened, Morgan suffered considerably. With little additional support available from the Methodist Church, Morgan's trustees cut faculty salaries by 10 percent. Then came *Murray*. In the edition of the *Afro* trumpeting victory in the case, Carl Murphy featured a photo of the entrance to the

University of Maryland's undergraduate campus in College Park. The caption read: "Applications are expected to enter this department next."[73]

The university comprised several campuses. The law school, which *Murray* impacted directly, and most of the university's other professional schools were in Baltimore proper. Its graduate and undergraduate programs were based in a modern and expansive campus thirty miles away in College Park, a suburb to the northeast of Washington, D.C. Having followed through on his promise to open the University of Maryland School of Law, Murphy's threat to desegregate College Park was not taken lightly, and those wishing to protect segregation grew nervous. Chief among these was Harry Clifton "Curley" Byrd, new president of the University of Maryland. Byrd championed the maintenance of segregation with a mind to his political aspirations—in Maryland white supremacy and Democrats were bedfellows. *Murray* concerned Byrd. Though the law school may have been lost, it was not the entire university. Blacks would have to sue to gain access to the other professional programs, and Byrd drew a hard line around the College Park campus, the undergraduate campus—"where our white women are," he would later say. If separate had proven unequal in legal education, so it likely would prove in graduate programs—and even in undergraduate programs. White taxpayers got the publicly supported University of Maryland. Black taxpayers got nothing. Now, however, College Park and its white women seemed vulnerable, or so segregationists posited. Carl Murphy, for one, had given fair warning years before that the push against separate but not equal was coming.

Therefore, almost immediately after NAACP attorneys began their suit on behalf of Donald Murray in 1935, everything suddenly began to change. Quickly the state legislature created a Maryland Commission on Higher Education of Negroes. Rumors surfaced that the intent of the body was to turn Morgan into a state college for blacks just as the University of Maryland was for whites— with undergraduate, graduate, and professional schools. Curley Byrd, a member of this commission, later admitted that his intention was to ensure that "segregation could be properly maintained."[74]

The issue was hotly debated. Morgan trustee Albert J. Mitchell feared there was much to lose. He argued that the importance of the college as the sole private institution for blacks statewide should not be underestimated. Regardless of whether or not Morgan became a state institution, he argued, Maryland had to develop a black college. If the state took over the reins of Morgan, there was no assurance that it would not neglect the school, as it had neglected its other black schools (a teachers college and a vocational college). Mitchell believed that Morgan's autonomy was indispensable as the best hope for legitimate black higher education in the state. Then there was the matter of whites potentially appointing Morgan's leaders. "Very ordinary men," he warned, "would dictate its course and determine its policy and select its officers and faculty with no regard to the efficiency of the institution."[75]

The Maryland Commission on Higher Education of Negroes published its final report in January 1937. Indisputably identifying the state's neglect of black higher education, the commission spelled out a remedy, calling a state takeover of Morgan College essential. The proposed state-owned school was to be named Morgan University, and the commission recommended that the state make Morgan equal to the University of Maryland in function.[76]

In addition to graduate and professional schools to be developed in "the not distant future," the commission recommended that Morgan University consist of the existing college in Baltimore as the main campus and that satellite campuses be established at another location in the city, in Prince George County (the same suburban county that was home to the University of Maryland), and at a site in Baltimore County. This plan could be implemented, the commission suggested, at a moderate start-up cost of $1.5 million and with "reasonable" maintenance allotments. Alternative plans were also spelled out in the event that Morgan refused to capitulate, but the lasting effect, the commission said, would be decline in Morgan's function due to a likely discontinuance of all state aid. One of the black commissioners, Carl Murphy, favored Morgan as a public college but only in conjunction with complete desegregation of the University of Maryland. That recommendation was not included in the commission's report, which Murphy—alone among the eleven commissioners—ultimately refused to sign. Meanwhile, accepting the report and recommendations, the state pressed forward with negotiations to purchase Morgan College from the Methodist Church.[77]

Morgan trustees struggled with what to do. After a number of attempts over the summer months of 1939 the board finally voted to approve the sale. Many finally cast a favorable vote with heavy heart, given that the new Morgan State College (not "Morgan University," after all) came with no assurances of black student access to graduate and professional training. As he voted in favor of turning Morgan over to the state, Mitchell asked that he be put on record as "at least one colored man on the Board who feels that Morgan College is merely saving the State of Maryland from an embarrassing situation rather than meeting the real needs of the colored people." Mitchell gave voice to what all surely understood: the state's segregationists only wanted Morgan in order to save Jim Crow at College Park. Anything good that came from Morgan as a state college would not come easily from segregationists overseeing state government. Curley Byrd's dominion over the state's colleges, and increasingly its politics, was unparalleled in these years. He was not a race-baiting demagogue in the mold of Mississippi governor Theodore Bilbo or South Carolina politician "Cotton Ed" Smith, but he was a slick racist southern white Democrat all the same. Still, blacks reasoned, he was only a politician. In the end, the state paid $225,000 to complete the deal, which was executed on November 20, 1939. When the news of Morgan's sale was received in the community, reactions were mixed. Many saw the potential for funding increases as extremely favorable. Yet the state's history of neglect of its black citizens and their institutions made others skeptical. Several mocked the price paid as far too low, and one of the key figures initiating the process, former governor Harry Nice, smugly noted that Morgan had been "sold . . . for a song."[78]

Morgan State College directly resulted from the equalization strategies pursued by pragmatist black nationalists. To continue their struggle and community building, they reasoned that they needed a full-fledged public college now. The precedent of *Murray* might open the undergraduate and graduate programs at College Park as Carl Murphy portended back in 1932. But no one knew how long that might take. Morgan's future had to be assured against all threats, the most immediate being the economic challenge of the Great Depression.

As noted, Carl Murphy would not endorse the plan to turn Morgan into a public college if that was only meant to prevent desegregation and to perpetuate separate but unequal. That said, black institutions remained a part of Murphy's vision of a desegregated future. He believed that schools like Morgan would find fair funding and equitable budgeting through desegregation. As with the importance of the black church and the black press, he saw the need of black schools like Morgan continuing beyond the death of Jim Crow. Desegregation would strengthen those institutions that served blacks under Jim Crow. For these reasons, he fully embraced Morgan once it became a state college in 1939. Beyond his *Afro-American* newspaper and the NAACP, no other entity for the remainder of Murphy's life would receive the benefit of his work, wisdom, and wealth than would Morgan State College.

CHAPTER 3

# "We Have to Fight Segregation before We Can Get to Hitler"

## Transformation in Depression and War, 1936–1945

"The only people who want peace," observed Carl Murphy in September 1939, "are those who are satisfied with the world as it is." Germany had just loosed its blitzkrieg on Poland. Not voicing approval for Hitler's aggression, Murphy hoped rather that *Afro* readers would see the wider opportunity presenting itself. A new war brought a new chance to truly remake the South in ways that had failed to materialize following the peace in the last global conflict. Murphy also well understood by this time that he had a voice and a responsibility to use it. Despite the devastation of the Great Depression, Carl Murphy brought the *Afro* out of the 1930s stronger than it had been when the decade began. Now he published not just the Baltimore edition but also ones in Philadelphia, Newark, Richmond, and Washington D.C.[1]

Murphy's role as an opinion shaper was considerable. Rather than shrink from the moment, Murphy used the *Afro* to keep the pressure on for equality throughout the war years. When the United States entered World War II, he sent correspondents to the front, his daughter among them. Black newspapers across the nation provided readers with valuable black perspectives, otherwise absent from mainstream coverage. Carl Murphy kept the war and his people's sacrifice to it fresh in their hearts and minds. Once victory approached, Murphy published a master volume of his paper's coverage in *This Is Our War*, capturing his long-range view and his strategy for the postwar 1940s. "Share the war, share the peace," he would say.[2]

Murphy's candid approach often drew ire. A Baltimore woman writing to national columnist and radio personality Walter Winchell in August 1942, for example, identifying herself only as "not a colored person," suggested that someone should teach Murphy "what it mean[s] to be American." Winchell, in turn, passed the concern along to J. Edgar Hoover, director of the Federal

Bureau of Investigation. Hoover's FBI monitored the writings and activities of the black press generally but gave special attention to the *Afro-American*. Coordinating efforts with Baltimore FBI field officers, Hoover demanded and received detailed synopses of the contents of every edition of the *Afro* in each city in which it published from 1941 to 1944. Characterizing most of what he found there as "seditious," Hoover pressed Assistant Attorney General Wendell Berge to determine whether or not Murphy's actions violated the Sedition Act. For Hoover and the FBI, Murphy's penchant "towards the development of racial hate and a persecution complex among the colored people . . . designed to increase the tendency to 'flare-up' in the least responsible elements of the population" were matters of "internal security" for the duration of the war. However, by December 1944, the attorney general had determined that, while outspoken, Murphy and the *Afro* had committed no crimes.[3]

Meanwhile, Murphy worked to ensure that the boon of war mobilization would benefit blacks. It seemed logical to focus on increasing access to vocational and other skilled training in black high schools to guarantee black participation in the job market. Access to higher-pay war-related employment, Murphy knew, would mean greater purchasing power of the black masses, who would spend a fair chunk of their earnings with black retailers, professionals, and service providers, thus benefiting the entire black community.

The Baltimore Board of School Commissioners had previously authorized vocational training for white youth geared toward war industries. Blacks had received no such opportunities. In response, Murphy and others organized a citizens' committee to press for equalization in wartime defense industry training programs and employment opportunities. This required a new vocational school for blacks and expansion of vocational course offerings. In addition, the committee called for curricular improvements at the black high schools and the creation of a new city office: assistant superintendent in charge of colored schools.[4]

The school board responded by insisting that no demand for skilled blacks existed among private employers in the defense industries. Training for such employment was unnecessary, board members said, if not downright counterproductive. Murphy suggested to the board that such a policy violated the Fourteenth Amendment, but the board disagreed. However, in what Murphy characterized as an empty gesture, the board offered one training program in auto mechanics to black boys.

Murphy pushed for training opportunities covering a much wider range: sheet metallurgy, brick masonry, roofing, damp proofing, cement finishing, carpentry, tractor operation, plastering, et cetera. With negotiations at a stalemate, Thurgood Marshall, now NAACP special counsel, suggested that federal court intervention might be necessary. If qualified blacks applied to white vocational schools for courses not offered at black high schools and were refused (as expected), the students should reapply directly to the city superintendent, who would also turn them away. At this point, Marshall believed, the students could hold the Baltimore superintendent of schools personally liable for their inability to access public vocational training.

By this time however, early 1941, news began to spread of Asa Phillip Randolph's proposed March on Washington to force federal government intervention concerning the anti-black posture of the defense industries. Resolved to wait and see the effect of Randolph's work, Murphy decided not to follow Marshall's advice on federal court action. However, as Murphy's cohort Juanita Jackson Mitchell later recalled, after Randolph called off the March on Washington in the summer of 1941 following a perceived concession from President Roosevelt in the form of Executive Order 8802, which purported to ensure black access to defense jobs and training, a degenerating police situation in Baltimore led to a different march, not in Washington but in Annapolis.[5]

## Instead of Rioting

During the spring Carl Murphy liked to end long days at the office with an announcement: "I'm going home to my garden—to my flowers—to restore my soul." Over the years he had shared thousands of his flowers with hundreds of his friends around town. One Saturday in May 1941, as he tended to his garden, two police officers appeared at his home on Overland Street in the Morgan Park neighborhood with questions about an auto accident. Within moments it seemed, the diminutive fifty-two-year-old newspaper publisher found himself manhandled into the backseat of a patrol car. He did not even have a chance to call out to his daughter, who was working inside the house.[6]

Murphy had not been involved in the accident in question and had not been a witness to it, yet the officers, knowing this, arrested him anyway. They had come to Five Elms, the Murphy home, looking for Carl's wife Vashti, who had been a party in the accident the evening before. One of the officers, Horace Heinze, had already been at the Murphy home, spoken with Vashti, and issued her a summons for traffic court. Requesting time to contact an attorney, on her husband's advice Mrs. Murphy had declined to speak further on the matter. Later Heinze had come back, Vashti had not been at home, and now Carl was heading to jail because he, a black man—a wealthy one, at that—had "sassed" a white cop.

Murphy was booked for "undue interference with a police officer in lawful execution of his duty" and placed in a cell with others for a time. The charges were quickly thrown out—though Baltimore police commissioner Robert Stanton refused to censure Heinze. Believing the time had come for "a fight to make police more careful of the rights of colored citizens," Murphy filed a $25,000 suit in civil court against Heinze. He would ultimately be awarded twenty-five dollars. From the broadest perspective, of course, Murphy's run-in with Horace Heinze was uneventful. Yet he was also fortunate, since Baltimore's white cops thought nothing of hurting black people. Still, even though Murphy's ordeal was relatively mild, his treatment as a criminal—his unjust arrest and humiliation on his own property—spoke loudly. In a city that empowered white racists, Heinze made clear that to him Carl Murphy was black and black only.[7]

In Baltimore, the police and policing made Jim Crow work. Laws and their enforcement "assumed a pivotal role," writes Litwack, in the maintenance of white supremacy and the transformation of white privilege-keeping into public policy. Writing of another large southern city during roughly the same time period, New Orleans, Adam Fairclough concluded that "police violence against blacks was so routine that it caused a little comment outside of the pages of the Negro press." Police brutality came to function as a control—as an expression of the outsized power racism afforded the white community and that community's desire to see its vision of the racial norm maintained.[8]

To this end, white patrolmen in black neighborhoods during the Jim Crow era often assumed the mantle of an occupying force, deploying terroristic methods meant to demoralize black citizens, demean the value of black citizenship, and in the words of Litwack, "remind blacks at every opportunity of their vulnerability and helplessness." In this way, white police officers brought the presumptions of whiteness in the Jim Crow South to bear on their daily encounters with black citizens. These were not simply presumptions of inherent black criminality but more an abiding moral authority of white over black in all manner of interaction. In the rural and small-town South, where lower population densities left blacks isolated and individually vulnerable, the at-large white citizenry had a long tradition of policing their black citizen counterparts. One manifestation of this was an obligation of interpersonal deference from black to white in all public encounters. In big southern cities, however, with densely populated black enclaves numbering in the hundreds of thousands, a white citizen's demand for deference from a black counterpart in public was often met with contempt, mockery, and even violent threat. White police officers, however, could and did demand interpersonal deference. Thus, in the South's big cities, the obligation of deference when it came to black and white was transferred largely to exchanges between black and blue. "Wealth, status, and education afforded no protection," notes Fairclough. "Some policemen delighted in humiliating blacks whom they perceived to be climbing above their proper station."[9]

Encounters with police brutality remained a scourge in West Baltimore as they had been in previous decades. Police regularly harassed and threatened ordinary law-abiding blacks with no provocation, usually for nothing more than refusal of deference. Since the rise of Jim Crow and black urbanization in the South, brutal punishment for "not moving fast enough when commanded to move" was rampant. In 1927, for example, policemen assaulted Henry Simuels, a working-class black electrician employed by the gas company, for stopping to talk with a friend on the street. Simuels had not moved fast enough when ordered—for no apparent reason—to move on. Despite formal complaints nothing was done.[10]

Urban southern police forces often drew their recruits from the ranks of poor rural whites or European immigrants. These groups were willing "to accept low-wage status in exchange for the personal power their position conferred," Michael Honey writes. "Their sense of white skin privilege did nothing to shore up wages but provided many of them with a more visceral incentive to serve as defenders of white supremacy."[11]

This seemed to be the case throughout the urban South. In New Orleans, for example, brutality went unchecked, and "every year two or three blacks were shot dead in dubious circumstances." So it was elsewhere, including Baltimore. In March 1930 Baltimore policeman Herman Trautner killed Roosevelt Yates. The following year, William Johnson died from injuries sustained after patrolman Harry Holley clubbed him viciously for allegedly lying in response to the officer's inquiries. Similarly, in August 1932, Jefferson Mackey was beaten to death with the blackjack of Officer John Erdman for picketing a former employer following an unjust firing. Not only was Erdman exonerated, he also received a commendation from his captain. While fleeing in a stolen car on March 11, 1939, a twenty-five-year-old black Baltimorean received fatal shots to the back from the pistol of Officer Edwin Humphreys, who went unpunished. In a September 1939 incident known as the "School Yard slayings," two black teenagers, Eugene Duvall and Laurence Harvey, were killed by multiple gunshots from several officers. In February 1940 Officer Edward Bender fatally shot Charles Parker, a black man.[12]

Blacks protested beating, rough handling, and indiscriminate shooting, and they protested warrantless searches of black houses, use of third-degree interrogation to extract confessions, and lying by officers in order to secure convictions. As part of a cresting equalization agenda of the late 1930s black movement in the urban South, therefore, activists pushed for a black presence on police oversight boards and for appointment of black police magistrates. These would come, but only later.

More immediately, however, as police brutality and lack of accountability threatened to become an issue in election campaigns, the black press and black citizens demanded the hiring of black police officers to patrol their neighborhoods, if nothing else. After petition campaigns and public forums increased the pressure, a few of the larger southern cities—Baltimore among them—hired African American police officers for the first time. Unlike the white concession in hiring black teachers for the black public schools two generations earlier (see chapter 1), after which Jim Crow black schools quickly had all-black faculties and staffs, no serious consideration was ever given to all-black police precincts in all-black neighborhoods.

Black police hires were limited and tokenistic for at least the first few decades. Nonetheless, in late 1937, the Baltimore Police Department hired Violet Hill Whyte as its first black police officer. The *Afro*'s Clarence Mitchell called on the entire black community to help ensure that the "experiment" represented by Whyte's hiring was a success. "One slip on her part would indict all others to come after her," Mitchell warned, "and anything constructive on her part will be a boost for those yet unnamed." The following year (followed by a similar admonition), four black men were hired to the force: J. Hiram Butler Jr., Walter T. Eubanks Jr., Milton Gardner, and Harry S. Scott.[13]

The experience of these first token black officers in Baltimore and elsewhere in the urban South would be frustrating. They were met with persistent racism from the white public and even more so from their white fellow officers. In the first instance, and to their consternation, blacks got exactly and *only* what they wanted: in nearly every southern instance, black officers were restricted to patrolling black neighborhoods. Even when it was otherwise, during the earliest years black officers in the urban South could not arrest white suspects. Baltimore's first black officers were not even issued uniforms. They patrolled in street clothes. In other cities, if black officers wore uniforms on their beats, they could not wear their uniforms home (unlike their white colleagues) or even in court while making official testimony. Many black police officers in the urban South during the Jim Crow years were restricted to walking their beats. They were not allowed patrol cars even after use of patrol cars became widespread after 1950.

White officers often failed to support black police in making arrests, sometimes endangering their lives, and commonly defamed them or made false statements about their performance. During these years, black officers would categorically not be promoted or given seniority consideration. Such deep restrictions further degraded black citizens' view of police in the Jim Crow urban South.[14]

It is difficult to see what, if anything, black police officers in southern cities like Baltimore accomplished during Jim Crow. Their token numbers were always inadequate, and neglect, insufficient service, and poor quality service continued as before. Brutality by white officers went on almost unabated. Even when historic concerns were voiced by black officers themselves, problems persisted, as police chiefs and other leaders proved insincere and ineffective. The black public continued to see the police as unaccountable to them.

Just as southern whites knew about the anti-black "justice" of the rural lynch mob since lynchings often took place in town squares as public spectacle, most whites in the urban South were aware of police treatment of blacks. They shared with police the presumption that blacks were criminals. Indeed, as the Jim Crow era wore on, whites called for *increased* police occupation of black communities. The indiscriminate brutalization of African Americans, with little if any provocation and often in full view of the black public, was intended as an exhibition of white supremacy. In Baltimore, for example, Officer John Barry dragged Frank James from his home, knocked him to the ground with his nightstick, and kicked him as he lay on the ground. Likewise, Henry Simuels (mentioned above) was clubbed so viciously that he lost several teeth. And all of this was done in broad daylight with impunity despite several black witnesses.[15]

The popular responses to police brutality ranged from nervous compliance with all police orders to self-defense and even retaliation. Black West Baltimore was the site of nearly routine retaliatory violence. As the police became increasingly brutal, the incidents of retaliation did too. Observing blacks reacting to "murderous cops" during these years, Carl Murphy found violent self-defense and perhaps even retaliation to be natural, and thus the police misconduct amounted to dangerous instigation. Confronted with verbal abuse and police harassment, "men and women are usually willing to be arrested," the *Afro* allowed, "but not clubbed."[16]

The racist culture underpinning police brutality could also not be denied. Writing about New Orleans, Fairclough notes that in many instances "policemen simply picked on blacks, in a more or less arbitrary fashion," to ensure that "patterns of deference" remained intact.[17] One observer of Baltimore insisted that even when dealing with criminals and ne'er-do-wells—to say nothing of the average innocent citizen—"if police can be gentlemen in [white working-class] southeast Baltimore, they can be gentlemen in the [predominantly black] northwestern part of the city." The problem was not with black citizens—even black criminals. The problem was the fundamental influence of white supremacy in the city police force and policing culture, which promoted a biased and brutalizing perspective on law enforcement in black communities: "shoot first, investigate, and explain later."[18]

Since before the turn of the century, the organized Baltimore struggle had protested racist policing. Yet the successes or even the visibility of this protest are difficult to discern. One difficulty for activists, we can surmise, is that instances of police brutality sometimes involved blacks who were not as upstanding as Carl and Vashti Murphy. Some victims of police brutality were folks carousing at night on Pennsylvania Avenue and drinking in public, and others were people involved in petty crime (like prostitution and small-scale burglary). Some were even violent and dangerous offenders who posed threats to other black people. Regardless, the long-standing black complaint against police brutality was that it was an outsized and inappropriate expression of legitimate policing, driven by a white supremacist disregard for blacks no matter what their class. Thus the absence of all but token black beat cops and the complete lack of black police administrators and magistrates were problematic. Black self-policing—the presence of black officers in place of hostile white racist ones—would alleviate brutality and make for better police-community relations, or so blacks during the Jim Crow era believed.

Historians often present the Baltimore Branch of the NAACP in the 1920s and early 1930s as do-nothing or dysfunctional, in large part driven by the national office's complaint against the branch's underperforming membership programs. Baltimore NAACP branch efforts against police brutality, however, had been gaining since the earliest days of the local struggle, and the branch protested and made note of nearly every example of police brutality. Since police brutality was seen as an inherently local issue, branches worked largely without national office support. In anti-lynching activism the national office's role was critical since federal legislation was the sought-after remedy. But of the national black social justice organizations, only the recently emerged National Negro Congress (NNC) had a pronounced national anti-police-brutality campaign in these years. NNC was composed largely of antiracist black labor activists. The local Baltimore council of the NNC, organized in 1936, largely concerned itself with labor issues, however, especially those entailing steel workers.[19]

During the interwar period, the Baltimore NAACP called for punishment of offending officers, removal of accommodating police leaders, and for the addition of blacks to oversight commissions. The anti-brutality advocacy of one branch president, Linwood G. Koger, ultimately led him to fear reprisals against his family. He cited this among other reasons when he stepped back from the presidency in 1930 to less visible roles in the organization. Yet, on the eve of World War II, the branch's efforts, though consistent, were nonetheless ineffectual, since police brutality continued. The NAACP was not alone. No black social justice organization in the city made much headway during these years. Like the Baltimore NAACP, the *Afro-American* consistently supported the anti-brutality cause. Not only did brutality and anti-brutality activism regularly appear in the paper's news articles and on its editorial page, the *Afro-American*'s stated core values, "What the AFRO Stands For," prominently included "colored policemen, policewomen and firemen."[20]

While the City-Wide Young People's Forum did not take up the cause with the same vim and vigor (or notoriety) as in its "Buy Where You Can Work" campaign or anti-lynching projects, it did attempt to address police brutality. In 1936 the Forum organized a petition drive aimed at compelling Maryland governor Harry W. Nice to appoint a police commissioner willing to hire officers "without regard to race or color." Other community institutions and organizations were pulled into the petition effort, planned as a house-to-house canvass for citizen signatures.[21]

The petition effort addressed the fact that police captains and commissioners, mayors and city councils, governors, and the federal government had all turned a deaf ear to police brutality, particularly as it involved black Americans. It was not until 1936, in *Brown v. Mississippi*, that the U.S. Supreme Court outlawed third-degree interrogation—"the police thought nothing of beating confessions out of prisoners"—perhaps the most institutionalized mode of police brutality. In Baltimore, a 1931 *Afro* op-ed noted the use of a sixteen-hour third-degree session in the Euel Lee interrogation in rural Maryland (see chapter 2) and asserted, "One wonders whether there is any difference between the lawlessness of the police and the lawlessness of the mob." Given the ineffectiveness of struggles against police brutality in Baltimore through the interwar years, it is perhaps surprising that two cases of police brutality—one mild, the other deadly—would spark comprehensive campaigns in the 1940s.[22]

A few weeks after Carl Murphy's arrest, Japanese fighter planes from the other side of the world destroyed the U.S. Naval Base at Pearl Harbor, Hawaii. Given the democratic themes underpinning the subsequent call to war, blacks saw an opportunity "to persuade, compel, embarrass and shame" the federal government and the nation's liberal forces into challenging the conservative guardians of racial inequality, a formidable task since, according to a survey, most white Americans believed that blacks were satisfied with their status and that they enjoyed all the opportunities they desired (or at least deserved). More than 50 percent of whites outside of the South believed that there should be segregation in schools, restaurants, and neighborhoods. A majority of whites nationwide believed that blacks would not be treated any better after the war than before and that black Americans' inferior status in society resulted from their own personal shortcomings more than any white initiative.[23]

The home front war began with a tragically familiar refrain. On the night of February 1, 1942, as on most others, West Baltimore's Pennsylvania Avenue teemed with people. Louis Armstrong opened a limited engagement at the Royal Theater that night, and good times were to be had all around. Just after midnight soldiers and their lady friends attempted to hail a jitney (unlicensed taxi) for a ride to an Eastside nightclub. Officer Edward Bender stood nearby, and witnesses saw him stop the group from getting into the car and order them instead to hail a legitimate cab. As the jitney pulled away and the group began to cross Pennsylvania Avenue on foot, one of the soldiers, Private Thomas Broadus, offered a few words to Bender. Based on what happened next, we can surmise that Bender did not like being sassed. While accounts vary slightly, all point to Bender as the aggressor, instigating a tussle that quickly took both men to the ground. The fight seemed to last long enough to attract a sizable crowd. At some point Broadus realized that things were unlikely to turn out well for him. He broke free from Bender and fled on foot southward down Pennsylvania, turning west along Pitcher Street. He did not get far. Officer Bender drew his service revolver and fired twice into the soldier's back. Broadus fell.[24]

Only twenty-six years old that night he came to blows with Officer Bender, Private Broadus was a Pittsburgher, hailing from the Perry South neighborhood in that city's Northside District. His parents, John and Estelle Broadus, lived there on Charles Street, the heart of black Pittsburgh at the time, which had a beat of its own not unlike Baltimore's Pennsylvania Avenue. The army had drafted Private Broadus in 1941 and then stationed him and his 1322nd Service Unit at Fort George G. Meade, in rural Anne Arundel County, Maryland, just about halfway between Baltimore and Washington. For decades black soldiers at Fort Meade had enjoyed spending leave time in the black communities of both cities. A family man, Private Broadus had a wife and four children—two sets of twins—back home in Pittsburgh. After being shot on the night of February 1, 1942, he was rushed to Provident Hospital, the "Negro" hospital, on Division Street, just around the corner from where he fell, but he was pronounced dead within minutes of arrival. Days later, his hometown *Pittsburgh Courier* printed a photograph of his wife, with babies in her lap, reading the *Afro's* coverage of her husband's final moments. Edward Bender, the same officer who had gunned down Charles Parker two years earlier, had now taken a second black life.[25]

A Baltimore City Criminal Court grand jury investigated Bender's killing of Broadus and formally arraigned the policeman on murder charges. But, in an unexpected turn, the grand jury reconsidered the case and dismissed all charges without explanation a few days later. Police Commissioner Stanton used this exoneration as grounds for his decision not to discipline Bender, who was simply transferred to another beat. Less than six weeks after fatally shooting a uniformed American soldier in the back, Officer Bender resumed his duties.

On the night that Edward Bender killed Thomas Broadus, two bystanders surrounded the officer, pounced on him, and landed several blows before others could restrain them. A few weeks later, another police officer attempted to arrest a black soldier early one Sunday morning on Pennsylvania Avenue, but, before the officer could draw his gun, two other soldiers knocked him to the ground and "soundly thrashed" him. As he struggled to his feet, the soldiers further humiliated him by relieving the cop of his cap and nightstick and then running off into the darkness. "Citizens have become aroused to the point that they have taken matters into their own hands," the *Afro* wrote. "This may be forewarning." A history of violence and abuse by the police department had produced this "smoldering powder keg" at the heart of the black community.[26]

City and state officials were unwilling to even acknowledge this situation. Lillie Jackson, president of the Baltimore NAACP, wrote to Maryland governor Herbert O'Conor, appealing for state intervention, but he did not respond. Carl Murphy then saw a tremendous opportunity. If the governor would not come to Baltimore to aid Maryland citizens, he later wrote, then "the mountain [was] coming to Muhammad." Murphy spurred the local NAACP to sponsor a "citizens' movement," and planning began immediately for a demonstration in Annapolis, the state capital. This and other issues galvanized a mass coalition of blacks in the city. "Instead of rioting, we marched," Juanita Jackson Mitchell later remembered. "I think we would have had a riot, if we hadn't had a march." Support for the effort was broad-based and even included whites.[27]

Over 150 civic, religious, fraternal, social service, and labor organizations in the city formed an umbrella group, the Citizens' Committee for Justice (CCJ). From the first, the CCJ stated its aims of addressing not only police brutality but also broader concerns: lack of equality and black opportunity. Carl Murphy chaired the CCJ, which presented a multiracial face. A number of its member groups (labor unions, most prominently) held racially integrated memberships, but this did not really amount to an interracial effort. The point of the CCJ work remained equality, and leaders such as Murphy saw that this could only be had through greater self-determination as flowed from full participation in government. The CCJ and its most important member organizations were black-led, black community–oriented, and nationalist in outlook.[28]

CCJ leaders planned not so much a protest demonstration as a meeting with state leaders, including the governor, in Annapolis. They expected simply to be heard but believed that their clearly stated grievances would command redress. They set the date, Friday, April 24, 1942, and would meet the governor that afternoon at two in the statehouse. CCJ organizers held a rally the night before. Many people who otherwise supported the goals of the effort but could not take the next day off from work to participate in the march crowded the streets around Sharp Street Church in West Baltimore, which vibrated with the energy that would send marchers off the next morning.[29]

By midmorning the next day, more than a dozen chartered buses, hundreds of private automobiles, and several train cars of the Baltimore and Annapolis Railroad carried protesters the twenty-five miles south by southeast to the state capital. The caravan made quite a spectacle, and as it passed through small towns and farm country along the route, black and white farmers at work in their fields took notice. Nobody "in fifty years [could] recall an occasion like this," the *Afro* reported. Governor O'Conor would later admit that he had no idea the delegation would be so large.[30]

Arriving at Annapolis by two, two thousand "serious, quiet, and resolute" Baltimoreans crowded into every available space of both chambers of the state capitol for the two-hour hearing. CCJ chairman Murphy presided, and several speakers each took up parts of the planks composing the protest platform. Police brutality received repeated and extended comment. Lillie Jackson spoke plainly and directly to the governor: "This meeting is the direct result of your refusal to answer the letters of the NAACP asking for a conference on police killings in Baltimore." Veteran attorney Linwood Koger, the former president of the Baltimore NAACP who had used his tenure as a vocal advocate for police reforms, said that the appointment of a black police magistrate would "put community behind the law and [eliminate] the persecution complex." He stated flatly that any real progress on police reform had to start with the immediate dismissal of Commissioner Stanton, who had tolerated ten shooting deaths of black citizens by his officers. The CCJ presented a petition signed by thirty-four hundred people calling for Stanton's removal. Juanita Mitchell added that the march was "born of desperation" over the frequency of such incidents and the lack of response, much less redress. The marchers also directed Mayor Howard Jackson to appoint more black police officers. Only five then existed in Baltimore for a black population of greater than 150,000 — and none wore a uniform. "Our people are being taught that policemen do not move among them to protect them and to uphold the law," Rev. E. W. White commented. "It is producing a damning psychology which in the end must lead to disaster."[31]

Beyond law enforcement, the absence of black representation on governing commissions and boards—especially the school board—received extended comment. The demonstrators urged Mayor Jackson to appoint blacks to one or all of the three vacancies on the Baltimore Board of School Commissioners. The body that governed a student population that was nearly one-third black had not a single black representative. Two thousand copies of a pamphlet outlining the full ccj platform, *Speed Morale for War Work in Maryland: A Partnership Is One For All, All For One*, were printed and distributed in advance.[32]

In a thirty-minute response, Governor O'Conor, who said he appreciated the "firsthand knowledge of the problem" he received from the presenters, nonetheless declined to state specifically what measures of redress, if any, would be taken. He would only declare his intention to appoint an investigative commission to study the problem. "Other matters," however, "would have to be taken up gradually." Perhaps the protesters expected little more from the governor. After the governor spoke, the group rose and spontaneously broke into song. "My country 'tis of thee," they sang, "sweet land of liberty." "They sang one verse and then the second," and this was no show for the governor, Murphy noted in the *Afro*, "they knew the words." Indeed, "Nobody who heard them sing, 'From every mountainside let freedom ring,'" Carl Murphy observed, "will ever forget it."[33]

The messages of the march were buttressed by a deluge of notes, letters, telegrams, and phone calls visited upon Governor O'Conor in the weeks surrounding the event. Walter White stressed to O'Conor the NAACP's support for an anti-brutality campaign in view of the "long continued police brutality in Baltimore City directed at Negro Citizens." Editorials in the *Afro-American*, the Baltimore *Sun*, and other newspapers kept the march's purpose fresh in people's minds during the weeks that followed. Commenting on the war-spawned flood of patriotic appeals, Elmer Henderson wrote to the *Sun* shortly after the march, "Men may be moved by slogans but they will not die for slogans unless they are given content and reality."[34]

Not in attendance at the Annapolis hearings, Baltimore native Thurgood Marshall, now based in New York, looked somewhat cynically on the prospect for progress following the march. "If Governor O'Conor were worth a dime," he believed, the protesters' efforts would get results. Fearing O'Conor was not, however, Marshall suggested, "The only way we will get any action out of him is by constantly hammering away."[35]

## The Demystifying Witness of the Workspace

Black migrants arriving in Baltimore had been urged by their relatives to leave the rural and small-town South. They came by bus, by train, by car, and on foot. They came to escape from the "hedged-in" experience of rural southern life for blacks. They came because their kids could stay in school for entire terms, and they came for political freedom, as black voting was always more possible in the urban South than in rural areas. But mainly, they came in search of greater job varieties and higher wages. A man from Granite Quarry, North Carolina, was enticed to Baltimore by his brother who had preceded him, and the brother continually wrote home of the great and wide opportunities at his job site, the Bethlehem Steel plant. Another North Carolinian—a seventeen-year-old kid from Tarboro—came to Baltimore for better wages and a better chance to support his infirm father. Possessing only a seventh-grade education, he was ecstatic over the prospect of earning as much as seventy-five cents per hour in the shipyards. If the jobs blacks could get in Baltimore seemed lesser than what whites could get, they nonetheless far surpassed anything the rural South offered. "I like Baltimore already," the young man from Tarboro admitted to the *Afro* shortly after arriving.[36]

It was a transformational time in Maryland. During the 1940s, the proportion of black Marylanders residing in Baltimore jumped from 59 percent to 75 percent, and blacks represented one out of every four of the city's residents. What was more, while many of these newcomers were natives of other states (Virginia, the Carolinas, Kentucky, and Tennessee most visibly), most had come from rural Maryland, and the proportion of blacks in each of the state's rural counties had correspondingly declined. As a corollary, Baltimore blacks went from comprising 7 percent of the city's industrial workers in 1940 to 17 percent 1945, "a proportion that never declined," as George Callcott notes, through the remainder of the century.[37]

This employment represented not just a gain but also a reversal. An early 1942 survey of Baltimore's ten largest firms showed no blacks at all employed above the unskilled level. "Only a few" even held even janitorial positions. World War II offered an opportunity for blacks to work to capacity and begin reaping the benefits of a fairer and more open job market. Between August 1941 and September 1943 more than 15,000 blacks registered for work with the United States Employment Service (USES)—12,000 men and 3,500 women. USES was frank with employers, making black employment a condition for renewing federal contracts at a number of Baltimore firms, including Glenn L. Martin and Bethlehem Steel. In September 1942, 137 war plants and industries

**TABLE 3.** Employment Status of the Baltimore Population by Race and Sex, 1940

| Race and Sex | Population 14 years and older | Total in labor force | % of pop. 14 years and older | % employed (excluding public emergency work) | % employed in public emergency work | % seeking work | % experienced workers seeking work | % new workers seeking work |
|---|---|---|---|---|---|---|---|---|
| **MALE AND FEMALE** | | | | | | | | |
| White | 563,227 | 308,554 | 54.8 | 91.4 | 1.2 | 7.4 | 6.0 | 1.4 |
| Black | 126,760 | 79,532 | 62.7 | 83.2 | 4.6 | 12.3 | 10.0 | 2.2 |
| Other | 448 | 331 | 73.9 | 92.7 | 2.4 | 4.8 | 4.5 | 0.3 |
| **MALE** | | | | | | | | |
| White | 276,120 | 222,970 | 80.8 | 91.4 | 1.3 | 7.3 | 6.2 | 1.1 |
| Black | 61,453 | 48,947 | 79.6 | 80.2 | 6.6 | 13.2 | 11.1 | 2.1 |
| Other | 378 | 314 | 83.1 | 93.0 | 2.2 | 4.8 | 4.8 | — |
| **FEMALE** | | | | | | | | |
| White | 287,107 | 85,584 | 29.8 | 91.3 | 0.9 | 7.9 | 5.7 | 2.2 |
| Black | 65,307 | 30,585 | 46.8 | 87.9 | 1.3 | 10.8 | 8.3 | 2.5 |
| Other | 70 | 17 | — | — | — | — | — | — |

U.S. Department of Commerce, Bureau of Census, Sixteenth Census of the United States: 1940.

reported to the War Manpower Commission (WMC) that 19,895 (11 percent) of the 218,799 workers were black. The next year the numbers had risen to 32,908 and 239,474, respectively, to 14 percent.[38]

Taking up the cause of the war pressed blacks and whites together on the home front in the urban South, and if blacks had been unknown to whites, the shared workspaces changed that. This new proximity allowed whites to see black ambition, skill, and determination, and it confirmed for them that blacks were coming and were unafraid.

Thrown in together, it was hard for blacks to see whites as superior or to see their advantages as deserving. They seemed like regular folk, and thus all the privileges segregation afforded them seemed unfair. Responding to the challenges of the Depression had brought out the best in many white workers, and they too admitted the unfairness of racial inequity—the pseudoscientific justifications had fallen away. Still, enough of them remained clannish and conniving. For blacks, working with whites on job sites, just as working for whites in their homes, revealed them for what they were, human beings, flesh and blood—not always worse than blacks but certainly no better. If in any place or at any time there had been a mystique to whiteness, that mystique was gone.

At the end of the day, most black women "day workers," as Elizabeth Clark-Lewis presents them, went home to their families and communities. The next day, they would do it all again, cooking and cleaning—perhaps with a different family. Many day workers maintained multiple clients. Whatever whites purported to be in Baltimore's public spaces, these black women, in an age-old tradition, knew who white people were at home, knew who they were in truth. Against the shifting demographics of the city and the new opportunities to challenge racism that some jurists and politicians seemed to be accommodating, white superiority complexes proved increasingly difficult to maintain.[39]

Workplace integration did not happen overnight. Answering a call for men to work in April 1942, for example, around the time of the March on Annapolis, black and white job seekers sent by USES presented themselves to the Bethlehem Steel Fairfield Shipyards just south of the Baltimore city limits. The whites got jobs, and the company sent the black applicants home. The same scenario and the same result were repeated at Bendix Radio Corporation just north of the city. Western Electric, Crown Cork and Seal Company, Koppers Company, and most white-run businesses in town were known for similar racist hiring policies. Walter Sondheim Jr., Maryland director for USES, admitted at one point that the agency experienced "difficulty" placing qualified black applicants in important positions. In spite of the need and applicants' skills, employers were reluctant to hire blacks and frequently said as much when filtering calls for labor through USES. The *Afro-American* kept photos and images of black women willingly taking up street-cleaning assignments in the city as near-desperate cries went out from the WMC for women to fill vital defense jobs. White women were being hired but not black women. *Afro* reporters even posed as job seekers to get a firsthand appreciation for the run-around blacks received, and they likened what they discovered to Hitler's "master race" ideology. War industry employers often claimed that white workers (and potential workers) were broadly resistant to working with blacks.[40]

Whites in the city, unsurprisingly, generally resented black migrants. Native white Baltimoreans even resented most *white* migrants, especially those coming from nearby Appalachia, whom they pejoratively called "hillbillies." (Blacks used this term too.) White resistance was strong enough for a time to stave off black aspirations for war work. The Baltimore Urban League made a study of black access to local employment opportunities in American Federation of Labor (AFL) organizations. It found most avenues for economic self-betterment were closed for blacks. Local unions of sheet metal workers, plumbers, and asbestos workers had no black members and were unwilling to accept blacks as members, apprentices, or helpers, even returning black veterans. The same went for the boilermakers, steamfitters, carpenters, electrical workers, glaziers, and lead burners (solderers and welders). Racial discrimination in the carpenters' union varied by local. While Local 101 totally denied black members, Local 544 had sixty-nine blacks. Others, like the Bricklayers Local 1, had no black members and would not accept black members, but would accept black veterans into apprenticeships, provided the black vets found master craftsmen who would accept them in the role. Of the twenty AFL affiliates polled by the Urban League, the Hod Carriers and Laborers Local 194 had the greatest number of black members (thirteen hundred), but since theirs was an unskilled pursuit, apprenticeships were not at issue. Only the Iron Workers Local 16, Carpenters Local 544, and Roofers Local 80 had sizeable black memberships and were open to other blacks for apprenticeships.[41]

After President Roosevelt's executive order in the summer 1941 and the March on Annapolis in the spring of 1942, opportunities began to emerge. The City of Baltimore, for example, began to accept blacks into positions that, while largely menial, had nonetheless previously been closed to them. Likewise, as mentioned, the WMC began to threaten private employers with the loss of lucrative defense contracts if hiring discrimination was not curbed. Thus, the Glenn L. Martin Company and Bethlehem Steel, two of the largest beneficiaries of defense contracts, began to crack their doors open to blacks for the first time. Though changes in institutional control and wider access came much more slowly, they too began before war's end. For their part, blacks only pushed harder.[42]

Meanwhile, Carl Murphy's *Afro* did all it could to lure more black folk to the city and into the war industries. "There are still plenty of good jobs with high wages left in Baltimore and anybody coming here is certain to find employment," the paper reported. "To insure unity, utilize all available human resources in war industry and the armed forces," the *Afro* advised. This democracy in practice—this "second emancipation" of black Americans—would further resonate well with the millions of people of color in Africa, Asia, and South America, demonstrating emphatically that America's war effort was not a fight "to maintain white supremacy." Indeed, as Murphy would remind readers, "We have to fight segregation before we can get to Hitler." But the tension proved constant between blacks seeking more and better employment opportunities, white workers seeking exclusivity on the jobsite, and employers seeking whatever peace would protect productivity and the bottom line. Employment discrimination against blacks proved almost nonexistent in the unskilled labor class and most pronounced in the white-collar world—to the near total exclusion of blacks. This seemed often as much the wish of white employers as their white employees, and, in the case of retailers, their white customers were also a factor.[43]

In spite of all the talk since the 1930s, white protectionism remained a big obstacle for black workers when it came to unions and union jobs. Although it was a workers' market, with jobs for all, many white workers perceived competition and sought to keep their advantage. Whiteness would continue to function as a job qualification and a conduit for economic and cultural status. Personal and community identities continued to be built around whiteness.[44]

Once employed, wartime blacks did not face the same challenges in joining the unions as they had earlier, but power in the union still rested with the majority white rank and file. And the whiteness of rank-and-file workers was actually expanded, as even more rural southern white migrant workers than blacks piled into the industrial labor force of wartime Baltimore, influencing white working-class culture. This promised to make the racial compromises sought by blacks more difficult to reach.

White migrants found themselves competing for hegemony with local whites to shape whiteness in the city during the war years. Attracted by Bethlehem Steel at Sparrows Point, Glenn L. Martin, and the area's other large employers, wartime white migrants to Baltimore came typically from smallish southern towns in Virginia, the Carolinas, West Virginia, Kentucky, and Tennessee. These whites settled largely in South Baltimore. Despite initial tensions between locals and migrants, common ground for all whites in the city was soon identified, as many shared a working-class consciousness laden with racial identity, deriving economic and material benefit from mere whiteness.[45]

The fact of the national emergency did not dampen whites' protectionist tendencies on the work site. The Baltimore Chesapeake and Potomac Telephone Company (C&P) advertised that it did not have enough good applicants to fill positions but at the same time resisted hiring blacks for fear of white client and employee reprisal. A civic pressure group called the Total War Employment Committee (TWEC), led by black activist physician J. E. T. Camper, protested to the governor and others. The liberal and interracial Union for Democratic Action (UDA), also spoke out against discriminatory employment practices. Camper's group also launched similar protest campaigns against an artificial labor shortage at the Baltimore Transit Company (BTC), which had a whites-only hiring policy for drivers, although passenger seating was not segregated. While the BTC would keep blacks out of the bus driver's seat for several years more, C&P offered a limited concession in spring 1943 when it renovated the old Immaculate Conception Building on Division Street for the training of black workers. No black would be trained as switchboard operator, however, which was still reserved as a "white" job.[46]

While employers would continue, with some justification, to blame undemocratic policies on white clients and consumers, the most troublesome expression of job discrimination against black workers was the "hate strike." In notable instances white workers walked off their jobs in mass protest against the mere presence of black workers or the absence of worksite segregation, which threatened to close the social distance constructed between them and black workers. Many of the explosive scenarios during the tumultuous summer of

**TABLE 4.** Baltimore Firms Employing One or More Blacks by 1954

| Occupation level | Before World War II (percent) | During World War II (percent) | After World War II (percent) | By 1954 (percent) |
|---|---|---|---|---|
| Non-managerial professionals | 1.6 | 1.2 | 1.8 | 1.8 |
| Managers and supervisors | 2.0 | 2.3 | 2.5 | 2.3 |
| Clerical workers | 6.0 | 6.7 | 8.9 | 8.4 |
| Sales workers | 1.6 | 1.9 | 4.3 | 3.8 |
| Foremen | 9.6 | 11.4 | 10.0 | 9.5 |
| Skilled workers | 17.9 | 18.5 | 19.4 | 18.7 |
| Semi-skilled workers | 41.4 | 43.3 | 45.8 | 45.8 |
| Service workers | 47.8 | 48.8 | 52.7 | 52.2 |
| Laborers | 58.2 | 59.0 | 53.9 | 53.2 |

Number of firms reporting: 251 before World War II, 254 during World War II, 391 after World War II, and 391 by 1954. It should be noted that 1954 was marked by a mild recession. Also, since a firm likely employed blacks in more than one category, percentage totals may exceed 100 percent. See Sidney Hollander Foundation, Toward Equality, 64.

1943, including the bloody Detroit Riot, stemmed from hate strikes and other anti-black reaction on the part of white workers, who claimed in more than one case that racial integration put them at risk of communicable disease from "unclean" blacks. Detroit represented all-too-common perspectives of white workers across the nation.[47]

On October 5, 1943, white members of Baltimore's Point Breeze Employees Association (PBEA) called a strike vote. The PBEA was an independent union for workers at Western Electric, a manufacturer of signal corps equipment with a plant in southeastern Baltimore, where the Patapsco River meets Colgate Creek. The Western Electric plant had few black employees prior to 1941. In the course of the subsequent two years, however, the number of blacks employed at Point Breeze had risen from 2 percent of the total to 29 percent. Before the war, working-class whites exercised near-hereditary prerogatives over black competitors in the job market, and during the war these blue-collar whites came to believe that labor leaders and federal policy makers were moving against them. By the fall of 1943, some blacks had earned promotions, some whites earned less than some blacks, and some whites had to answer to black bosses.[48]

These developments occurred during an infusion of rural white migrants and threatened to push Baltimore workplace standards toward those of the rural South. Blacks resisted, of course, seeking to expand their opportunities and break down the barriers that designated jobs as "white" or "black." For their part, employers generally played one group off of the other. When pressed, owners sided with the more numerous white workers, restricting blacks to the jobs whites did not want due to low wages or because they were supposedly undignified. As the circumstances of World War II and the immediate postwar years "tended to quicken the pace of black demands," they brought a nearly symmetrical intensification of white pushback. Indeed, white reaction to blacks and their demand of equality constituted the point of conflict in the industrial union movement.[49]

To that point at the Baltimore Western Electric plant, city code accommodated Jim Crow. Blacks and whites had separate lavatory facilities, for example. These facilities desegregated, however, in February 1942, after Roosevelt's executive order. For more than a year, few whites complained—at least formally. Yet desegregated toilets somehow pushed them to act, and some whites argued that Baltimore was a southern city and that southern white prerogatives had not been respected. Those pushing to strike couched their positions in the old language of contagion and quarantine: "Just because our forefathers a hundred years ago, gave these poor colored people diseases are they supposed to spread it among us now?" Although less than half of the

Western Electric plant workers bothered to participate in the October 1943 strike vote, by a count of 1,802 to 1,174 those voting determined that the union would walk out pending the outcome of a formal grievance hearing requested before the War Labor Board (WLB). Unconvinced that Jim Crow toilets protected innocent whites from black venereal disease, however, the WLB ruled against the PBEA. With this rebuff, the strike went forward.[50]

Outwardly, the company resisted the resumption of segregated facilities, citing the expense and worker time necessary for setup. Western Electric also claimed that segregation violated FDR's executive order. However, accusations circulated that the washroom situation represented only a straw argument and that the union, the PBEA, was actually a puppet of the company. Supposedly Western Electric hoped to drive a wedge between white and black workers over the issue, holding itself up as a paragon of moral virtue yet preventing the interracial cooperation necessary to organize a truly representative union, one affiliated with the Congress of Industrial Organizations (CIO).[51]

Many of the strikers, especially the younger whites, had only recently migrated to the city from the rural South. As one historian contends, rural southern whites proved more adamant about preserving separate, superior public spaces for whites, including better toilets. And so, while all 1,700 black employees reported to work, as did most of the older whites (presumably natives or at least longtime residents of the city), almost 4,000 whites were convinced, cajoled, or intimidated to stay away from their jobs at Western Electric while their country's war raged on. Concern over the potential spread of anti-black sentiment reached Governor O'Conor's desk in Annapolis. He was warned, particularly, that white employees at the Eastern Aircraft plant in Baltimore had expressed sympathy with strikers at nearby Western Electric.[52]

Throughout these war years, black blue-collar workers had been answering white rebuffs with their own shows of strength. At Sparrows Point, for example, a fistfight had broken out between two crane operators, one black, one white. By all reports, the white worker had instigated the fracas. When management suspended only the black employee, twelve other black crane operators walked off their jobs in a show of solidarity and filed a complaint with their union's grievance committee. Similarly, more than a week's worth of personnel hours was lost at the Bethlehem Steel plant at Sparrows Point—"Beth Steel" in the local parlance—when hundreds of whites walked off the job to protest blacks being admitted to riveting training courses. During the course of the war, both black and whites in the yards staged strikes and retaliated against strikes, organized walkouts and counter-walkouts. In the context of war materials production, with the industrial worksite as public theater, urban southern blacks demonstrated that traditional white tactics would not intimidate them. In response to the strong black showing and the politics of the moment, new allies in the federal government would step forward, giving blacks recourse they had not enjoyed before. Thereafter, appeal to the higher power of Uncle Sam no longer seemed as pointless as it had only a few years earlier.[53]

Black working-class opposition to Jim Crow came in many forms, and mass protest, especially on the job site, may have been the least if it. The significance of personal demeanor should not be underestimated. There is little evidence, for example, that native black Baltimoreans routinely offered the "hat-in-hand" interpersonal deference whites had come to expect in the rural South—what Laurie Green describes in mid-twentieth-century Memphis as "the plantation mentality." The way blacks carried themselves in interracial settings established expectations. These expectations, further, applied to whites and to nonnative blacks alike. "I didn't like the idea [of] a lot of these [black] guys who came up from the [rural] South more or less getting on their knees to white men," one African American former shipping clerk at Bethlehem Steel later remembered. "They'd say something to him, and first thing you know he'd, 'Yes sir, captain so-and-so.'" Many urban blacks despised that behavior. The vulnerabilities of rural and small-town life may have demanded such indignity and undue self-deprecation in homage to white power, but the big city—even in the South—did not. "I felt like hitting him upside the head," the shipping clerk recalled.[54]

Overall, throughout the Western Electric hate strike of 1943, Baltimore blacks consistently demonstrated that they would not be intimidated. Indeed, not only did blacks demonstrate willingness to respond to threats against their economic momentum, they also expected support in this effort from their allies, new as well as old. J. E. T. Camper, for example, led a delegation to Washington, D.C., in hopes of forcing the U.S. Fair Employment Practices Commission (FEPC) to send in the military to restore production. Some pushed Governor O'Conor to act against desegregation as the only way to "relieve this situation so pregnant with the possibilities of race riots and lynchings." The governor claimed no legal authority in the matter, deferring to the federal government. Recognizing the possibility of violence, Baltimore mayor Theodore Roosevelt McKeldin stationed about three hundred city policemen at the plant. After five days, however, with the strikers still out, President Franklin Roosevelt sent the U.S. Army from nearby Fort Meade. Picketing ceased almost immediately. By the first week in January, in fact, the Western Electric strike had all but petered out.[55]

## Door to Door, Bell to Bell

The 1940s would represent a political opportunity for African Americans in the urban South. Black electoral power had been suppressed across the South around the turn of the century as a means to protect racial segregation laws from black voter backlash. Still, in states such as Georgia, where blacks had been overwhelmingly disfranchised by legislation, a small core of Atlanta blacks managed to keep voting despite limited impact. Memphis blacks also kept voting despite Tennessee's efforts to disfranchise them. In that city, however, they voted mainly at the behest of machine bosses like Edward H. Crump, who paid poll taxes for large blocks of voters but only for the faithful. Maryland blacks, of course, had staved off formal disfranchisement (see chapter 1). However, as Baltimore too was a city with a political machine, black political impact there had been stunted time and again by racist gerrymandering and other machinations since the turn of the twentieth century.[56]

A number of factors shifted during the 1940s to improve the political prospects for blacks in the South, including those in Baltimore. Across the South, for example, the U.S. Supreme Court ruling in *Smith v. Allwright* (1944) eliminated the whites-only party primary election, a principal method of disfranchising blacks since before the turn of the century. State-level actions across much of the South discarded other tools of disfranchisement (like poll taxes) over the subsequent decade. The opportunity for Baltimore blacks came with the retirement of William E. "Boss" Curran, who had controlled the city machine since the 1920s. Curran's exit created a power vacuum in Baltimore that was never fully filled by another politician. In his place, only district- and ward-level powers emerged. Thus, as Baltimore's black population continued to surge, there seemed an opportunity to finally build a true electoral constituency. Thereafter, as Carl Murphy and others surely surmised, blacks might not only speak truth to power, they might make demands to power under penalty of Election Day reprisals.[57]

Behind urban black activism on the wartime labor front in the South was blacks' sense of electoral transformations. Blacks in Baltimore continued to draw national resources to support their local social justice agendas, and the tactic of litigation would never be abandoned, but electoral power was quickly revealing another path toward equality. Everyday Baltimoreans began to learn how to manipulate political circumstances locally and nationally, and via the ballot and other political pressure on elected officials they would produce some long-sought transformations.

The March on Annapolis had served as an early foray into this. Carl Murphy's instincts to "wait and see" before litigating for access to war work (training and employment), and the subtext of his description of the marchers as sober, rational, and middle class, meant to convey to Governor O'Conor that the citizens assembled were informed voters. They read the *Afro*, they supported politicians who held their best interests, and they opposed those who did not. The fall of 1942 would be a gubernatorial election season. That fact perhaps partly explained the willingness of the incumbent Democrat governor, who otherwise ignored black citizens, to allow the marchers an audience in April. "No demands were made," Murphy later said, and perhaps little was expected of O'Conor. The March on Annapolis represented public theater of a sort, the speaking of truth to power. Murphy's confidant Thurgood Marshall had said as much—O'Conor was not worth a dime in his estimation. He advised that while the march was important (for black people themselves, if no one other), blacks in the struggle had to keep hammering away if they hoped to effect the change they sought. By "hammering away," Marshall meant litigation. Murphy and others agreed, of course, but also paid attention to electoral opportunities. At city and state levels in 1942, black candidates appeared on both Democratic and Republican tickets. In the Democratic primary, with a light voter turnout, three black candidates for the state legislature lost to white opponents by an average of more than four to one. On the GOP side, however, former NAACP branch president Linwood Koger, a candidate for state senate from the Fourth District, defeated his challenger, who was white. Koger and the Republicans lost in the 1942 general election a few weeks later, however.[58]

Meanwhile, from his base in Harlem, New York pastor and politician Adam Clayton Powell Jr. formulated an electoral philosophy for blacks, to be applied locally and beyond. A staunch and vocal advocate of African American civil rights, Powell in 1941 became the first African American elected to the New York City Council and would be sent to Congress from Harlem (another New York black first) in 1944. Powell made frequent appearances in Baltimore during the 1940s, including as the keynote speaker at the mass rally on the eve of the 1942 March on Annapolis. He was received with considerable enthusiasm. Despite his good standing as a member of the Democrat Party, in his addresses to large urban audiences during this period Powell often described a "swing vote" strategy. "I always liked the guy who was nationally a Democrat, locally a Republican, theoretically a Socialist, but practically a Communist," Powell would say. Advocating that blacks dismiss party considerations as needed and support candidates most willing to promote legislative agendas in support of black causes, Powell saw this as the best way for large urban electorates to "make candidates more accountable, parties less conservative and voters, particularly black voters, more influential." Such a sentiment enjoyed wide appeal during the war, including in Baltimore.[59]

While the city's black leaders had consistently advocated voting, broadscale voter registration had not been part of any organization's basic program. But, hoping in part to finally address the state's Declaration of Intentions Act, a voter suppression tactic passed in 1902, black voter registration became an extension of the March on Annapolis. Aimed at stunting the impact of migrants coming into the city, the law required citizens to register their intention to vote in primary elections one year prior to the right being granted. "It is impossible to be a citizen without voting," activists insisted. "We can only share and expect to share in the management of our government when we vote," Rev. A. J. Payne, the activist pastor of Baltimore's Enon Baptist Church, told the *Afro*. Juanita Jackson Mitchell, who worked closely with Carl Murphy in leading the March on Annapolis, directed a "Votes for Victory" campaign for the Baltimore NAACP beginning in 1943.[60]

That year presented opportunities for the growing black electorate in Baltimore to experiment with the swing vote strategy Powell and others promoted, as the ambitious Republican Theodore Roosevelt McKeldin ran for mayor. Previously McKeldin had lost a mayoral election to Howard Jackson (in 1939). McKeldin had also lost a close race in the 1942 gubernatorial election to the incumbent O'Conor. As he had shown strongly, part of his 1943 mayoral campaign calculus was to retain the strong support he had received from the city's black voters the preceding year.

The Baltimore NAACP turned to the city's pulpits to preach "the voting gospel." This represented a solid tradition in Baltimore's enduring black struggle for equality. Baltimore black clergy had been in the forefront of social justice activism since the 1870s, when Harvey Johnson and those following him promoted the civil rights struggle through their Mutual United Brotherhood of Liberty. Around the turn of the century there were those like William Alexander and George F. Bragg, who used the power of the press to support the struggle. In the 1910s and 1920s this activism visibility and leadership continued, with Garnett R. Waller (Maryland Niagara), Abraham Lincoln Gaines (Baltimore NAACP), and James R. L. Diggs (Baltimore UNIA) as prominent examples of activist clergy. The Depression years were no exception, and during World War II black clergy and congregants were still stepping up to address social justice.

Most visibly, by these years, black churches worked with the Baltimore NAACP, and the leadership of Lillie Jackson, president of the Baltimore branch since 1935, was key in the expansion of the partnership. A deeply spiritual woman for whom service to others was an extension of her faith, Jackson early and often sought to tap the community resources of Baltimore's black churches. She went to churches for financial support and volunteers, but she kept the churches close to her work for the branch. For a long time one of the branch's main meeting places was Sharp Street Methodist Church on Dolphin Street in West Baltimore. She kept Baltimore black clergy heavily involved in leadership of the branch. In the early 1940s, for example, as David Mibolsky notes, clergy were everywhere in her organization: "eight out of fourteen vice presidents . . . , six of fourteen committee chairpersons, and eighteen of sixty executive committee members." Rev. John L. Tilley served as chairman of the Votes for Victory effort. Making no appeals on behalf of a particular party or candidate, the NAACP branch put out a general call for blacks to become first-class citizens.[61]

"No person knows the meaning of real citizenship who refuses to use the ballot," preached A. J. Payne to his congregation at Enon Baptist. Cedric Mills, who had followed the venerable George Bragg to the pulpit of St. James Episcopal Church upon his passing in 1940, spoke more bluntly. "Put up, or shut up," he admonished those in his congregation who complained about the wrongs of Jim Crow Baltimore. At another church, a committee of volunteers formed and went door to door, canvassing every member and former member and helping people get to the courthouse in time to register if they hadn't. Clergy were recruited from neighborhoods across the city, trained, and supported in order to conduct similar efforts. Rev. Lillian Thompson, a South Baltimore minister, gave many hours to the Votes for Victory effort. She served as an NAACP guide and personally escorted would-be voters to the courthouse. Over the course of the effort, city officials staffing Room 25 at the courthouse on Calvert Street would arrive for work in the morning to find a line of people whom the NAACP had brought to register. As Beatrice Martin, a volunteer with the NAACP effort, told the *Afro*, "Many of the people were wearing the happiest smile of their lifetime" when they left the election office, green voting card in hand. In 1943 Votes for Victory registered over nine thousand new voters.[62]

Though they would wholeheartedly support Democrat Franklin Roosevelt's fourth presidential bid the following year, blacks voted overwhelmingly for the Republican McKeldin in the 1943 mayoral election, and they did so despite the *Afro*'s endorsement of his opponent, incumbent Howard Jackson. Jackson was an opportunist and political chameleon on race-related issues. In his first stint as mayor (1923–1927), Jackson had formed a Committee on Segregation to *preserve* Jim Crow. During the 1930s and 1940s (when he served three consecutive four-year terms, 1931–1943), along with many other urban Democrats in the South, he hoped to be seen by black voters as at least moderate on race. Jackson appeared at select black functions, received black community leaders at City Hall, and even took out a membership with the local NAACP. But blacks saw through him—"he was an enemy," one leader recalled. Too often, when it mattered on issues of police brutality, black representation to the school board, public housing, and the like, Mayor Jackson took no political risks, preferring to stall and stonewall.[63]

In 1943 Theodore McKeldin was elected mayor, and he would not have won without the support of black Baltimoreans. In recognition of this support, not long after McKeldin was sworn in, Police Commissioner Stanton was "retired." The Annapolis marchers had demanded Stanton's dismissal because time and again he had refused to address anti-black brutality on his force. And, when the next vacancy emerged on the Baltimore school board, in 1944, Mayor McKeldin appointed an African American to serve on that body for the first time.[64]

Despite what they regarded as an improvement in the mayor's office, blacks realized that much work remained. Voter registration was one thing, but maximizing voter turnout proved more challenging. Carl Murphy believed, for example, that an opportunity was missed in 1943. Fewer than four in ten registered black voters in the Fourth District cast ballots that year. That minority had overwhelmingly voted for McKeldin and for three black Republican candidates to the city council: Marse Callaway, W. A. C. Hughes Jr., and J. Leslie Jones. Many whites had also supported McKeldin, of course, but this support had not extended to the black candidates. Quick calculus told Carl Murphy that since the black candidates' white opponents had won while averaging ten thousand votes each, if but half of the black registered voters had cast ballots (presumably along racial lines), all three black candidates would have been elected. "The defeat . . . is not a reflection on [the candidates]," Murphy lamented, "but on the colored community which allowed an unusual opportunity to slip through its fingers."[65]

The Baltimore NAACP nonetheless saw voter registration as important, and it repeated the campaign the following year, no doubt bolstered by the national office's new emphasis on voter registration across the South in the wake of its victory in *Smith v. Allwright*. The Supreme Court decision in the Texas case outlawing all-white primaries effectively returned the franchise to countless blacks in a number of other southern states. Baltimore continued to swell with migrants seeking war work. Thousands of blacks were among them. "It might be well to begin now an intensive door-to-door drive to get newcomers registered and prepared to vote," Carl Murphy observed in the wake of the 1943 municipal elections. Murphy pushed for them to invest in the well-being of the city and the ongoing black struggle for equality there by "register[ing] at the polls their desire for equal and equitable share in the city government." Rights-based claims and black electoral power were emerging.[66]

With talk of politics and racial progress, the living room of William and Victorine Adams had become a very busy place. Victorine Quille Adams had married William Lloyd Adams in 1935, and neither had been particularly active in politics save for William's involvement with municipal golf course equalization begun in the mid-1930s. Victorine, an alumna of Douglass High School and Morgan College, had been a Baltimore teacher for more than a decade. By the mid-1940s, however, she owned an upscale women's clothing store and haberdashery, the Charm Centre, at 1811 Pennsylvania Avenue. With Victorine born in Baltimore (1911) and William born in North Carolina (1914), the Adamses were among the most visible examples of city natives and migrants who were together shaping black Baltimore's destiny.[67]

At some point earlier in the decade, Victorine Adams had heard Adam Clayton Powell Jr. speak about his swing vote strategy, and it had resonated with her. In 1946 Adams gave structure to her growing interest in politics when she organized the[Colored Women's Democratic Coordinating Committee of Maryland (CWDCC)}Despite "Democratic" in its name, the CWDCC held allegiance to the black electorate more than to any political party. "We wanted to get some black representation but the Democratic Party wasn't supporting black candidates then," Adams later recalled. Thus, the advocacy group was not simply concerned with voter registration activities but also with mobilizing the black electorate on Election Day—"getting out the vote to elect people who looked like me," Adams would recall—and with better performances by black candidates.[68]

As evidenced above by Juanita Jackson Mitchell and Rev. Lillian Thompson, Baltimore's black women played leading roles in voter registration, voter education, and voter mobilization. In this they followed a tradition. In the history of blacks in the urban South to that point, the black woman as community organizer—for religious, educational, and moral causes, and for workers' rights and social justice—was almost a stock figure. As Jeanne Theoharis demonstrates, in the smaller southern city of Montgomery, Alabama, Rosa Parks was at the same time, the mid-1940s, holding Voters' League meetings in her small apartment, "exhorting her fellow Montgomerians to register despite the enormous poll taxes and unfair registration tests." In Baltimore, not only was Juanita Mitchell a central figure, but, as Prudence Cumberbatch reveals, her mother (Lillie Jackson, president of the local NAACP chapter) and her sister Virginia Jackson Kiah were fully involved in the voter registration project too. What was more, in the voter registration effort of the Baltimore NAACP and in the organization Victorine Adams constructed, there was vertical integration of black women, from street-level mobilizers to leaders and strategists.[69]

Much of the CWDCC's mobilization efforts, voter education, and outreach activities took place at the Charm Centre. During the day Adams outfitted debutantes in the latest and finest fashions and taught classes in etiquette and the social graces. In the evenings, however, her shop became a forum, a training ground for would-be voters, and a school for developing their political acumen. This too was in the tradition of the struggle—churches, fraternal halls, theaters, nightclubs, schools, office spaces, private residences, and retail outlets all served dual roles as sites of mobilization and community education for social justice causes. The CWDCC staffed voting precincts, handed out sample ballots, taught people to use the voting machines, and lobbied for legislation. Manifesting the aims of the 1942 March on Annapolis "to meet politics with politics," as the *Afro* put it, Victorine Adams's group carried its program "door to door, bell to bell, housewife to housewife." She arranged for designated "Voter Registration Days" in churches, when ministers used their sermons and church bulletins to advocate voting. Adams and her organizers used radio broadcasts from Pennsylvania Avenue's Club Casino to advocate for voter registration. "Don't Be a Slacker!" a CWDCC ad in the *Afro-American* admonished. "Exercise your authority by registering and voting to eliminate racial discrimination." By 1946 the Fourth District had twenty-three thousand black Republicans and sixty-five hundred black Democrats. Two years later, after voter registration drives in 1948, there were twenty-five thousand Republicans and ninety-three hundred Democrats.[70]

◎ ◎ ◎

Throughout this period the equalization agenda of activists in Baltimore's black struggle would continually meet the obstructionism of white liberals. While a majority of black Baltimore activists of the late 1930s and early 1940s were guided by a pragmatist black nationalist approach to resistance, white liberals more often than not sided with those seeking ways to maintain segregation. Peaceable "race relations" was their aim. In considering "the Negro problem" they proved most amenable to slow, incremental change, if any. Such individuals were not unique to Baltimore. The most obvious result of the March on Annapolis was the formation of a biracial commission to study and report on problems impacting Maryland blacks. Efforts to create such a body were underway shortly after U.S. entry into the war. White liberal views are apparent in the words of Marie Bauernschmidt, founder of a group called the Public School Association. "The fact is apparent," she wrote to Mayor Jackson in March 1942, "that the complaints of many of our Negro citizens are so justifiable that unless the situation about which they complain is studied and relieved there may be created a type of trouble in our State which both groups of citizens would have cause to regret."[71]

Although the idea for the commission came from Baltimore, Governor O'Conor wanted to exercise authority over who its members would be. Thus, the Commission to Study Problems Affecting the Negro Population, chaired by Maryland Drydock Company president Joseph P. Healy (thus known as the Healy Commission), was created as a state-level entity. With more than half the state's population in Baltimore, this decision promised to be a problem for the mayor's office. Further, while Rev. Harold Bosley spoke some truth with his contention that "the large majority of thinking white people" approved fair-play measures, there was a strong and often vocal element of the city that felt otherwise. "Discouragement of negro demands, enforcement of the Jim Crow laws, and more white police," wrote one Victor Schminke to Mayor McKeldin, "will do more—negro psychology being what it is—to promote [and] to induce orderly and ultimately amicable racial relations than all the pro-negro bi-racial commissions."[72]

On May 18, 1942, Governor O'Conor appointed the commission. Five blacks were appointed along with thirteen whites. The Healy Commission began its work soon after, meeting on May 27, 1942, with O'Conor, Mayor Jackson, Marie Bauernschmidt, and Carl Murphy also present. First and foremost on the agenda was to study the problems plaguing blacks and report findings to the governor. The Healy Commission's report, published March 23, 1943, amplified the problems and remedies outlined by the Annapolis marchers a year earlier—prompting an *Afro* editorial cartoonist to sum it up with a cartoon captioned "Right Back in their Laps."[73]

The commission recommended, in part, hiring of uniformed black police officers, appointment of blacks to the government bodies (especially the Board of School Commissioners), and greater access to government employment when the war ended. The Healy Commission recommended that the state's two training facilities for black teachers, Maryland State Teachers College at Bowie (Prince George's County) and Coppin College (in the city of Baltimore), be funded to levels appropriate to achieve the accreditation that neither had ever held. The report also called for increased state funding of the recently acquired Morgan State College, aimed at increasing Morgan's teacher training, improving its liberal arts programs, and instituting graduate and professional programs at some point in the future. The commission also called for increased pressure on local employers to act without racial and ethnic discrimination in hiring.

The Healy Commission report also recommended that administrative and fiscal attention be given to housing conditions and residential opportunities for blacks in Baltimore. Many agreed that this area needed immediate attention—"it is at the root of many of the stresses which arise between the white and colored races," the Baltimore *Sun* opined. Wartime immigration from rural areas placed unimaginable strain on the city's already congested black neighborhoods. Expansion of the black spaces in the city had traditionally met with resistance. Thus these "island cities," as the *Sun* described the contained black neighborhoods, were staggering under the weight of the population increases. The Healy Commission suggested that additional staff be hired to allow the Baltimore City Health Department to make a thorough survey of what was habitable and oversee any necessary rehabilitation, and said that new housing be built as needed and wherever appropriate. Finally, the commission called for a reopening of the case against Baltimore patrolman Edward Bender. As the *Afro* expressed it, reopening the Bender case would "give the colored people assurance that there is not one kind of justice for them and another for white people." Any such assurance, however, given the community's history with the city's police during the war, would be hard won.[74]

Some black members of the commission, particularly those aligned with the mainstream of the community-based struggle, felt stuck in the old paternalism that white southerners had seemingly always applied to "the Negro problem." With blacks comprising only five of the eighteen members, the Healy Commission seemed yet one more example of putting the brakes on substantive change, and they remained broadly distrustful of interracialism.

Even after its report was published, the Healy Commission continued the work of assessing the nature and problems of race relations and advising the governor on appropriate, remedial courses of action. Tensions among the commissioners were high. One particularly contentious issue involved the nature of employment racism in Baltimore and, by inference, the nature of the solution required—namely the role of federal oversight. Chairman Healy and members Albert Hutzler and Frank Ober attempted to stave off an investigation of Baltimore industry by the U.S. FEPC. Lillie Jackson and J. E. T. Camper took them to task for it.[75]

Two of the other black commissioners, however, were later remembered as amenable to white reservations about the need for FEPC involvement. Overly deferential in the eyes of at least one of his black peers, Bishop Monroe H. Davis of Bethel A.M.E. Church, for example, reportedly averred "that we colored people [are] satisfied to do domestic work," and thus, in his eyes, an FEPC investigation was unnecessary. According to Commissioner Camper, Davis feared that if the FEPC became involved, it would cause hard feelings between otherwise liberal members of both races. Recalled as similarly obeisant, black realtor Willard Allen expressed concerned about white backlash—"he wanted to be on very good friendship with white people," Camper thought. In turn, whites on the commission castigated black commissioners who did not go along with the white majority as some did, perceiving that all the black members were (or ought to have been) like-minded.[76]

Again, blacks had been down this road before. "Interracial commissions" and other officially appointed bodies to study "the Negro problem" had been around for two decades. Few had ever affected action. Whenever they had, any momentum quickly died in the politicking of policy making. Thus, while bodies of this nature experienced periodic turnover by design, black members would also sometimes resign in protest. In the case of the Healy Commission, Cedric Mills of St. James Protestant Episcopal Church resigned, saying that the commission was in his opinion a farce. J. E. T. Camper became convinced that Chairman Healy and most of the white members "had no intention of trying to solve any of the problems of the Negro people or bring any justice to the people." Camper even alleged that Chairman Healy tried to purchase his support through promises of influence. "I'll make you the black governor of Maryland," Healy supposedly told Camper. "No Negro can have a job from the State . . . that doesn't have to come by you." Camper rejected the bait in the clearest terms his dignified mind could muster: "I would rather shoot craps up and down Pennsylvania Avenue than to accept any such thing like that," he told Healy. In the end, Camper and Lillie Jackson did not resign but rather were simply not reappointed when their respective terms concluded.[77]

The Healy Commission continued its work for the next several years, but its existence did nothing to dissuade community activism. In fact, the subtleties separating politics and actual policy began to be understood and better manipulated by black leaders during this time, the war years. For more than a decade, Carl Murphy and others had pursued another way forward, forcing the government to acknowledge the sham of Jim Crow largely through litigation and decisions by the liberalizing courts. Separate had never been equal, and in that, they insisted, it was against the law. Exploiting this to effect desegregation had proven at least tenable for delivering the remedy of equality. But desegregation had not yet been pursued simply for the sake of desegregation.

# PART II

World War II proved a transformative time for the enduring black struggle for equality. The transformations indicated shifts outside the black community, however. While blacks had immediately resisted Jim Crow as it emerged around the turn of the century, the nature of that resistance had always reflected southern blacks' evolving perceptions of what was possible. The political realities of the region demanded resistance to Jim Crow that was undergirded by black counter-narratives to white supremacy. Although these counter-narratives were indeed constructed, and while local activists in southern cities affiliated with national social justice organizations, the black struggle in the South in these decades was a solitary struggle, theirs and theirs only.

The Great Depression and New Deal years saw ideological divisions widen among white Americans. The most pronounced fissures appeared in race relations, class, and political ideology. Into at least the first decade of the post–World War II years, urban southern blacks found that they could push the liberal forces in white America—and even to some degree in the South itself—further to the left than had been possible a decade before. Blacks could do this by instigating confrontations between white liberal forces and forces of status quo conservatism. In the postwar years (but not before) the black struggle could also instigate confrontations between white federal authorities and white locals in contests that served black goals. In the postwar environment everyday black folk, in their roles as citizens, parents, home buyers, and students, understood that opportunities existed for them to personally instigate confrontations with whites—in downtowns, in public parks, in neighborhoods, and at schools.

# CHAPTER 4

# "A Conspicuous Absurdity"

## Confronting Jim Crow Housing and Recreation, 1941–1955

Blacks in Baltimore and elsewhere in the postwar urban South continually sought weaknesses in Jim Crow and pressed until it yielded approximations of equality. This was especially true by the 1940s in the struggle for access to residential, recreational, and commercial spaces. By the end of the 1940s, working-class and middle-class black home buyers would breach the boundaries of the traditional black West Baltimore community. Met by white sneers, occasional minor violence, and ultimately white flight, blacks were undeterred and kept coming. New areas to live required new places to play, and many black Baltimoreans' first forays into social justice activism came as they worked to ensure that their children had public places to play. Likewise, black families—often led by women in their roles as wives, mothers, and homemakers—ventured to the unwelcoming downtown seeking to meet their material needs. Before long there was competition for their consumer dollars among white-owned businesses, and these black families would exact ever-greater measures of equality and customer service through these years.

For everyday black people in the urban South, assertion of personal dignity was the only consistently available response to Jim Crow's barriers and social expectations of black deference, though the self-respect it represented was begrudgingly noted by whites, if at all. The challenges blacks faced in finding decent homes are indicative. In cities like Baltimore, claiming personal living space and accessing neighborhoods' public facilities (the likes of parks and libraries) functioned as forms of resistance to Jim Crow. To push for a better home was to seek transcendence, an act of defiance, and Carl Murphy and the *Afro* aided rebels in this regard. The *Afro* listed the homes for sale in racially contested areas of the city, encouraging black families to buy and move in. The paper also gave an annual "Clean Block" award, a friendly contest of community pride and beautification. And Murphy himself, through his volunteerism and charitable giving to social justice organizations, supported litigation making its way through the court system in the postwar years that it was hoped would open even more housing stock to black buyers.

The Healy Commission's report had recommended that attention be given to the housing conditions, identifying it as the root of racial tension in the city. After the New Deal years and the New Deal progressive culture, a significant segment of the community sought public policy solutions to housing shortages and other housing needs. The war emergency, with its increased black rural–urban migration, heightened the need and accelerated the timetable. The housing policy emerging from the Roosevelt and Truman administrations "implied a right to decent living conditions for U.S. citizens," historian Rhonda Williams writes. But in southern cities like Baltimore, the questions of how and where to house war industry workers was complicated by racial segregation.[1]

As the war began, the scarcity of habitable housing open to black occupancy was appalling. Of all units available to blacks, 99.8 percent were deemed occupied. The Citizens' Planning and Housing Association, an advocacy group, considered that a normally functioning housing market needed to have at least 4 percent of its housing unoccupied and available. Though white occupancy rates were also near capacity, the units open to them were at least habitable. For blacks, less than 1 percent of the available units were so classified. The median monthly rent for the units in this survey was approximately thirty-five dollars for three-room units (on average). Approximately 80 percent of the units featured the standard facilities—heating, gas or electric lighting, running water, flush toilet, and bath or shower units. Each wartime newcomer further exacerbated the deficiency. "No new homes are being built for them, no vacant homes are available for them," observed the Healy Commission. "They must share accommodations with those who already live in these densely populated and segregated areas." In space that *was* available, occupancy tripled and even quadrupled. Ultimately, facing a critical need for production workers and housing for them, local white politicians and the federal government clashed in ways that black activists understood they might exploit. The degree to which confrontation might be instigated proved key.[2]

During the wartime 1940s and into the decade that followed, the strategy of equalization persisted on many black activist fronts in Baltimore. But unexpected opportunities presented themselves as new federal policies and transformational court decisions took effect. Blacks responded with a strategic shift: equalization when necessary, desegregation when possible. While organized activism remained central to the movement, the impact of everyday blacks, through their pursuit of everyday needs—decent housing, for example—changed the dynamic of the struggle. Where the advent of public housing raised old questions of who would live where, causing politicians to waffle, developments in the private market proved more explosive. In the process of asserting their dignity, blacks would remake their city by remapping their demographic footprint upon it. White supremacy still won out locally more than it did not, but Baltimore was being changed forever. Blacks began to erase long-maintained residential boundaries, and they concomitantly called for expanded access to educational, recreational, and other shared public space.[3]

Public housing initiatives increased during the war. As noted, the New Deal culture had made new housing strategies possible, and blacks were ready to exploit rifts between local officials and the federal government to help things along. Such a strategy was not unknown, but time and again since the late nineteenth century the courts, Congress, and White House had failed them. The New Deal, however, indicated real change, and so wartime public housing in Baltimore began to be built. The emergence of the federal government in this role and the capacity of black activists to ensure that it happened became a transformative element of the struggle. "The previously private sphere of home," as Rhonda Williams argues, "had become public and political space."[4]

## Better Homes through Better Living

A few years earlier, in 1936, Greenville, Tennessee, native Aretta Hurd married Louis Gross, a migrant from rural Pumphrey, Maryland. With few other options in overpopulated West Baltimore, Aretta and Louis first lived with Louis's sister, Harriet (who had come to the city a few years earlier) on West Franklin Street. As the Poe Homes opened, however, Aretta, her husband, and their two children (they would eventually have seven) comprised one of the first families in the new structures on Baltimore's Westside.[5]

The Grosses were a typical West Baltimore working-class family. Hardworking and nurturing, Aretta spent most of the 1940s and early 1950s as a homemaker (she sought employment outside the house when her youngest children became school aged). During World War II Louis had served as a fireman in the navy, but most of his working life (forty-seven years) would be spent as a longshoreman with the United Fruit Company at the Inner Harbor docks on Light Street. He worked mainly on the boats bringing bananas into Baltimore and frequently brought fruit home from work with him, sharing it with his neighbors (often replete with tropical snakes and bugs), so that Poe folk took to calling him Banana Man. In his spare time, Louis is known to have been a mechanic and a semipro athlete (boxing and football), and he was said to have been a numbers runner for Baltimore's William Adams—"We used to sit at the table sometimes and count the money," remembers his daughter. According to Carolyn Gross Collins, people of different economic levels lived in Poe Homes and nearby residences along Saratoga Street, Lexington Street, and Fremont Avenue. The neighborhood as a whole was nurturing and community minded: "People protected you down there."[6]

Blacks had been housed in "hand-me-down," deteriorated, former white residences. As J. D. Steele, chairman of the Commission on City Plan, would concede, "we know without going into details that the colored people generally take what the white people discard in the way of housing." "Houses that should have been torn down a generation or more ago, houses that were obsolete and unsanitary even then," argued the Citizens' Planning and Housing Association (CPHA), "are still lived in by colored families." City officials and the housing market would be made to respond to the problem, but, to be sure, the responses were laden with racism.[7]

Thanks to a powerful real estate lobby, housing codes in Baltimore had never truly been enforced before the war years. As much as any other factor, this allowed low-rent housing communities to devolve into slums. Among the nation's seven largest cities in 1940, Baltimore had the highest percentage of homes without a private flush toilet (15.4 percent), with outside toilets (11.5 percent), without a bath or shower (11.2 percent), in need of major repairs (9.2 percent), and overcrowded (3.4 percent). The first modern attack on the city's worst slums began in 1939 when authorities demolished a notorious area known as St. John's Court for violations of the building code. Earlier prosecutions for housing violations had often met with failure. "Cases . . . were often postponed, dismissed or delayed," a study found, while the cases that actually went to trial received only trivial attention as magistrates often seemed "disconcerted to find, among thieves and vagrants brought to court, [the likes of] a prominent citizen charged with failure to remove a yard toilet."[8]

Support for reform grew. Housing advocates like the CPHA had always pushed for greater enforcement of existing laws—indeed, the CPHA's founding had been a direct response to the poor quality and shaky operation of the Baltimore Housing Authority (BHA). The CPHA, seen by many in the day as a militant organization, stepped up the pressure on City Hall to do something. The result was a 1941 ordinance that resulted in the first housing inspector assigned to the Health Department for the purpose of rooting out those contributing to slum development. The new ordinance held slum conditions as crimes against the community and subjected owners—and tenants—to sanctions.[9]

A slum-clearance program followed, along with the inauguration of public housing. In only a few years, the BHA "evacuated" twenty-five-hundred black families but built only slightly more than twenty-four-hundred living units for black families. There were practically no habitable rental vacancies available to blacks and no new construction by private builders for black buyers, and restrictive covenants kept down the sale of used housing to blacks. Indeed, new housing construction for black occupancy of any kind, public or private, was grossly offset by the wartime influx of blacks to the city. "The greatest single need in Baltimore's entire housing problem is relief of the extreme density and excessive overcrowding suffered by the Negro population," the Baltimore Urban League insisted. "This means more living space." The BUL recommended that new private and public units be planned and made available to black occupants and that existing housing in white neighborhoods be open to them too.[10]

Still, Baltimore's public housing program would be hampered from the start by realtors and their allies in government (even on the BHA) and by a white public that stigmatized public housing as inferior and contrarily considered it as "a government 'handout' in ways that federal mortgage loan guarantees [to whites] were not." There were rumors of surveillance of tenants, curfews, prison-like "lights out" orders at a specific time each night, restrictive visiting hours, and firm standards of interior decoration. With that, public housing construction proceeded slowly. After several years authorities had barely even managed to house those dislodged by slum clearance. Still, as Williams notes, "For African-Americans, public housing, rather than private home purchases, provided the most unfettered government route to better housing opportunities."[11]

Groups like the CPHA that viewed public housing as integral in the fight against housing shortages, slum conditions, and general blight worked tirelessly to convey to the public the facts of public housing programs, sometimes holding seminars that included walk-through models. Public housing's saboteurs thus lost their greatest weapon in the battle for public opinion—misinformation—and public housing programs gained their greatest ally in the battle for legitimacy, public demand.[12]

Under a joint venture with the U.S. Housing Authority in the fall of 1939, construction of the city's first "low-rent" public housing project began (an attempt four years earlier having fallen to racial politics). In an area approximately one mile west of downtown—a neighborhood where the famous nineteenth-century poet resided for a time—280 substandard "slum" dwellings covering 7.5 acres were demolished to make way for the Edgar Allan Poe Homes. Segregation was the rule. Only black tenants would be accepted in the Poe Homes, which opened in September 1940. But the Poe Homes represented the first major housing development of any kind in the city's history built for original black occupancy. Pragmatist nationalist black activists understood, as Williams has observed, that "building public housing often meant accepting an expanded urban segregation—even if reluctantly." Much of the push aimed at assuring a fair number of units for blacks.[13]

Initially it was intended that the Poe Homes would replace dilapidated homes razed in the neighborhood, housing neighborhood residents instead of relocating them. However, the high density of population in the to-be-razed housing made relocation a necessary corollary to the project. Indeed, due to the neighborhood's 97 percent occupancy rate prior to demolition, the BHA conceded at the time, "the housing shortage for low-rent units throughout the city has made relocation of tenants a serious problem." As the nation was drawn into combat after Pearl Harbor, public housing initiatives in Baltimore continued under the stipulation that their primary, short-term use be to house war workers pouring into the city. Income limits were waived as most of the early low-rent projects—Poe Homes, Clarence Perkins Homes, Gilmor Homes, Somerset Court, and O'Donnell Heights—were reclassified to meet war needs. When the war ended, these complexes were returned to their originally intended low-rent housing use.[14]

How and where to house workers who migrated to Baltimore for war industry jobs represented a major concern. In a nearly pejorative way, longtime residents of the city viewed all of these workers—black as well as white—as temporary residents. Black migrants especially found a very difficult situation upon arrival. Overall, during the war years, the city's population grew from roughly 860,500 to nearly 962,000. Yet, by 1943, blacks occupied fewer houses than they had ten years earlier. "This condition results from the incomplete public housing program," the CPHA's Frances Morton argued, "and the fact that the Negro has not been able to expand into new areas because of various restrictive agreements entered into by owners of property in white neighborhoods." Morton and her cohorts found almost no housing open to blacks. As noted, a normally functioning housing market needed at least 4 percent of its housing to be habitable and available, but racial discrimination saw blacks eligible to compete for not more than 0.2 percent of all units available, despite their ability to pay. Regarding the units ostensibly available, serious questions of habitability abounded. According to the federal government, less than 1 percent of the scant units available to blacks were habitable. Each wartime newcomer to the city exacerbated this deficiency. "No new homes are being built for them . . . no vacant homes are available for them," officials observed. "They must share accommodations with those who already live in these densely populated and segregated areas."[15]

Across the city, Baltimore's two hundred thousand blacks comprised 20 percent of the population but occupied less than 2 percent of the residential area, approximately four square miles. Of these, at the start of the war, more than twenty-six thousand "black" homes were deemed substandard—"of a physical standard which will necessitate their early replacement or reconditioning." Meanwhile, slumlords profited as demand steadily increased, in part due to the ongoing slum clearance program. The *Afro*'s annual Clean Block Contest suffered for willing participants for a time, ironically. Rumor circulated that landlords had raised rents after renters themselves made material improvements to their properties while participating in the contest.[16]

A wartime study of population density in a single community—an area of thirty-seven square blocks bounded by Pennsylvania Avenue, Laurens Street, Mount Street, and North Avenue—revealed what blacks were made to endure. Sampling 833 of 1,673 structures in the neighborhood, which housed 5,036 of its 9,342 total population, 97 percent reported no vacancies whatsoever. In fact of all the structures in the area, only twenty-six vacant rooms could be found.[17] The structures included were detached houses as well as a mix of three- and four-story row houses, one- or two-story residential spaces above stores, and a few single-story retail structures with living space in the rear. Of these 833 structures, 566 (68 percent) lacked coal- or oil-heating furnaces, with only individual stoves heating them. Ten others had no known heating equipment whatsoever. At least 159 had no bathing facilities, and barely half (438) had private, indoor toilets, with the rest having shared indoor toilets (226), outside toilets (163), or no toilets whatsoever (6).[18]

Cases revealed at the time include a four-room residence on Paca Street with fifteen residents, some sleeping on a bed in the kitchen. On Hamburg Street, two adults and two children shared one bed in a poorly lit, rat-infested dwelling with inadequate water service. A mother and her eight children shared a single residence with another family. The place seemed all but falling down around them: the defective chimney caused fires, the roof leaked, the sink clogged, and the toilet overflowed. The basement filled with water due to burst pipes. In all, authorities estimated that at least 26 percent of Baltimore's residences were substandard—with limited or lacking toilet facilities, insufficient heating, and crowded living space. Given this already bad situation, in-migration promised intensification of the problem. The burden was not shared evenly across the city, as more black people competed for less black living space. A survey by the U.S. Census Bureau, for example, revealed that overcrowding (defined as dwelling units housing more than one and one-half persons per room) had been decreasing among whites since the beginning of the war, while increasing for blacks. Yet, as Rhonda Williams argues, "as war workers and citizens in the crucible of the world democracy, black people, like their white counterparts, felt entitled to specific freedoms and rights. Decent housing was one of them."[19]

In early 1943, the Federal Public Housing Authority (FPHA) launched an initiative to build two thousand units in Baltimore. In the short term, these units were to house war workers. After peace, however, they were to be converted to much-needed low-rent public housing. The FPHA appropriated $8 million for the project. By summer, however, as local racial politics came to bear, little had been done. Begun during the final months of Democrat Howard Jackson's administration, things came to a head during the early weeks of Republican Theodore McKeldin's mayorship. McKeldin directed the Commission on City Plan to recommend a site for the FPHA housing development. He also appointed an "Interracial Committee for the Study and Solution of the Negro Housing Problem" to do the same task. Both bodies recommended a site in East Baltimore, near Herring Run. McKeldin forwarded the recommendation to FPHA.[20]

Local whites raised a stink, embroiling the mayor, governor, and the FPHA in a protracted struggle that disguised white territorial protectionism as a debate over states' rights vis-à-vis federal authority. Governor O'Conor was inundated with telegrams and letters from East Baltimoreans and their supporters. But newly elected Mayor McKeldin most strongly felt the brunt of white backlash. "I along with several thousand others in this community voted for you," wrote one East Baltimore man, "but we seem to have made a mistake, which will be corrected at the next election, unless something is done to keep this negro housing out of our community." "I am wondering," he asked the mayor, "how you would like to have them move into your neighborhood, and have your wife and children mingle with them." The proposed housing unit was in an undeveloped, quasi-industrial district, with no houses, black or white, in the immediate vicinity, but whites still felt it was close enough to qualify as an invasion of their turf. "I fear that trouble of the most serious proportions may result. . . . Remember Detroit?," another wrote, referencing that summer's major race riot. "There are only my sister and I . . . so we have to consider our physical well-being," wrote one Greenhill Avenue resident concerned over the proposed black "colony."[21]

The white Ladies' Harford Road Democratic Association implored Mayor McKeldin to "safeguard our community and our homes, by protecting them from invasion." "If it is a social experiment being tried all over the country," wrote the association's president, "please preserve us from this trial." Some even offered the traditional "hand-me-down" housing solution, suggesting that once the new public homes were built at Herring Run, somewhat near a historical white community, they should be turned over to the white public housing residents of Latrobe Homes, an older community that was in a neighborhood rapidly turning from white to black. "I imagine the white residents at times feel out of place here, the same as the Negro would at Herring Run." Casting the proposed Herring Run construction as a threat to whiteness, political opponents of the project pandered to the racism of white working-class crowds, referring to the target in-migrating group as "the scum of the colored race" and "shiftless, ignorant and totally undesirable." Others suggested building on the open space in the existing black community, the parks and squares—"no longer beauty spots in our City, evidencing lack of appreciation by the surrounding population."[22]

Through much of the summer of 1943, no one—not McKeldin, the city council, or the federal government—would take the blame. In public, before whites, McKeldin demurred. "These homes are not being built by the city nor the state of Maryland but by the federal government," he said, "and the final responsibility rests with the federal government." He assured a white audience hostile to public housing, "I am as much opposed to in-migrant colored people coming here as you are." The Baltimore NAACP, Citizens' Planning and Housing Association, Baltimore Urban League, and others chided authorities for playing politics in the face of such great need. "We are not asking any favors, we are not asking mercy," Lillie Jackson reminded the mayor, "we are only insisting upon justice."[23]

In spite of any personal duplicity, McKeldin found himself in a no-win situation once the state's legislators got the FPHA to assist with strong-arming the mayor. Some blacks, like *Afro* columnist and Republican pundit Marse S. Calloway, realized McKeldin's predicament. If others saw his difficulty too, in the end many blacks, who had helped elect McKeldin, felt that he had sold them out. "We have now sufficiently recovered from shock and disappointment to write you," Randall Tyus of the Baltimore NAACP confessed in a letter. "Your oratorical ability caused a lot of us to have great faith in you and expect a real demonstration of courage." But they had been left with nothing but "grave disappointment over the resulting happenings," Tyus said. McKeldin did not reply.[24]

By November 1943, anti–Herring Run forces had succeeded in forcing the federal government to abandon the site. In the racial politics and failure to lead, blacks lost nearly 600 desperately needed housing units. Instead of one complex to house nearly 1,200 black families permanently, a plan for multisite development of largely temporary war housing units was put into play. The FPHA identified four sites: Turner's Station on Dundalk Avenue (200–300 units), Sparrow's Point (400), Holabird Avenue (400), and Cherry Hill (600–700). All but the homes to be built at Cherry Hill were to be demolished at the end of the war.[25]

Meanwhile, by this time, the midwar years, the BHA, which oversaw operation of public housing projects, had a tenant population of greater than twenty thousand. Of these, fifteen were war work migrants to the city who had arrived relatively overnight and in need of shelter in a tight housing market. The BHA managed eight thousand houses on a total of more than five hundred acres, including twenty-one hundred units on fifty acres for black housing. Housing projects and their tenants were to be "integrated into the surrounding neighborhood." The facilities of the projects were made accessible to the entire community. While the Edgar Allan Poe Homes in West Baltimore had a high percentage of working-class and working middle-class folks, according to early residents, as noted above, people of different economic levels could be found throughout Poe and in the neighborhood around it.[26]

"Pleasant environment is an important factor in forming the right mental pattern for good citizenship," postulated the BHA when assessing its wartime performance and formulating its postwar plan. "Good environment for children means good homes as well as good schools." Keeping in mind its motto, "better homes through better living," BHA administered its communities in many areas with an eye toward empowering tenants to help themselves, especially regarding recreational, educational, health-related, and civic activities. Generally there were two categories of services undertaken on behalf of BHA community members: those initiated by the various municipal agencies and those initiated by tenant organizations. Many projects had tenant organizations and tenant councils to promote the enjoyment of health, welfare, education, and recreation, and to share the privileges and responsibilities of community life. Adult education opportunities were created in the Edgar Allan Poe Homes community beginning in late 1945 in conjunction with Morgan State College. Lecturers addressed such topics as "The Negro Citizen of Baltimore—His Duties and Responsibilities," "Trade Unionism and the Labor Movement," "Some Contributions of the Negro to American Culture," "Food and Nutrition," and "The Release of Atomic Energy—How It Affects the Average Citizens."[27]

Some projects were designed to complement existing city recreational facilities and, where necessary, serve the wider neighborhood (where nothing else was available). Various committees and clubs were begun. These clubs initiated programs (recreational ones, for example), took on certain civic responsibilities, and engaged in fund-raising toward short-term financial aid to tenants in need.[28]

For a large part of the city's black population, relief from the traditional congestion, pestilence, and unhealthiness of neighborhoods would be provided only through successful implementation of public housing initiatives. Against the backdrop of the city's sordid, racist history with regard to housing, as Williams observes, "public housing would offer [black Baltimoreans] a way out, a chance, and a possible strategy for obtaining adequate, affordable, and sanitary housing and respectable neighborhoods."[29]

Through the war years, building programs slowed but continued steadily, so much so that the Baltimore Housing Authority pronounced its public housing initiatives a success at war's end. "There has been time for the novelty to wear off, time for the brass work to tarnish, shrubbery to become ragged, garbage and trash to overflow containers into the streets and playgrounds," an industry periodical announced. "This has not happened. . . . Within this time, these projects have become a tradition in the city." "They are known for their cleanliness, their order, their beauty," the article continued. "It is almost as though each one realized that in being one of the pioneer tenants of low-rent public housing a great responsibility had been placed upon him—the responsibility to make public housing such an unqualified success that homes such as his would become available to others."[30]

## They Flew, They Flew!

Throughout the history of Baltimore, blacks had pushed against the artificial and arbitrary boundaries that whites hoped to define as the black space. Crossing such boundaries when and where they could, in search of what they needed—more than what they had—blacks were conscious of the urban pioneering they had thus collectively undertaken. In the years following World War II, blacks in Baltimore began to breach the major western boundary of black West Baltimore, Fulton Avenue, which had held since the 1890s. As noted above, wartime black migrants had swelled the Westside beyond capacity. As with construction of public housing, black home buyers sought to breach the white enclaves.[31]

Whites' primary weapon against black home buyers was the restrictive covenant. Working-class and middle-class blacks had challenged the constitutionality of these nefarious instruments since broad use of them began in the 1920s. W. A. C. Hughes Jr., attorney for the Baltimore NAACP, had taken a restrictive covenant case, *Meade v. Dennistone*, to the state appellate level. He argued that state enforcement of restrictive covenants was tantamount to state action and thus state violation of the Fourteenth Amendment. He lost, and want of money to go further left the matter there. By the postwar years, however, restrictive covenant cases were being tried all across the nation. Previously, lower courts (like Maryland's in *Meade*) were rejecting these cases. The U.S. Supreme Court had danced around the issue in *Corrigan v. Buckley* (1927), in which it attempted to distinguish between state discrimination enforced by the government's apparatus and personal discrimination enforced by the government's apparatus, and had been reluctant to consider restrictive covenants again. The court refused certiorari more than a dozen times on such cases through the following decade.[32]

Meanwhile, if the federal courts were silent, the Federal Housing Authority was not, and it became the most vocal and powerful advocate in favor of racially restrictive covenants. The FHA had a penchant for reinforcing the racist notion that mixed-race neighborhoods made for lower property values and that all-black neighborhoods were not mortgageable due to poor valuation—at least not by the conventional market. This function of the federal government had been inherited from the New Deal and the Home Owners' Loan Corporation days. So too had the federal government's most infamous housing valuation practice—redlining. Maps of every major city in the nation were color coded. Red outlines or shading demarked majority black communities, and conventional financing for home purchases was next to impossible for anyone living there. Thus, as Rhonda Williams points out, a new tool of racism and white supremacy was institutionalized: "While the government subsidized mortgages for white people, black people were more likely to benefit from government largesse in the form of conventional public housing."[33]

By the time the Supreme Court considered restrictive covenants again, however, everybody sensed something of a change. "Probably at no other time in our history," the *Afro* observed in May 1948, "[have] there been in the various courts of the land so many cases involving the rights and privileges which so frequently have been denied to members of minority groups." Citing the national implications of a potential defeat of restrictive covenants, the *Afro* proffered, "The court's opinion in the case therefore, is of greater moment than in any previous pleadings that have come before it." Three covenant cases from St. Louis, Detroit, and Washington, D.C., combined to be heard together in *Shelley v. Kraemer*. In its decision, the court indirectly validated the argument put forth by W. A. C. Hughes Jr. a decade earlier in *Meade v. Dennistone*. "These are not cases, as has been suggested, in which the States have merely abstained from action, leaving private individuals free to impose such discriminations as they see fit," the high court found. "Rather, these are cases in which the States have made available to such individuals the full coercive power of government to deny to petitioners, on the grounds of race or color, the enjoyment of property rights in premises which petitioners are willing and financially able to acquire and which the grantors are willing to sell." For the justices, the difference between judicial enforcement and nonenforcement of the restrictive covenants was "the difference to petitioners between being denied rights of property available to other members of the community and being accorded full enjoyment of those rights on an equal footing."[34]

A rather ordinary revolution on its face, *Shelley* nonetheless delivered a fundamental shift in the availability of housing for blacks, most immediately in the urban South. The decision was widely hailed in black and liberal circles, where it was said that "the right of minorities to live decently has been upheld." Many wasted no time in making their intention known that they would continue to push against artificial barriers. Some even called upon elected officials to "enforce" *Shelley* with the same vigor that restrictive covenants had once been upheld and to take "the spirit of this decision" in addressing Jim Crow education, recreation, and employment opportunities. Coupled with wartime advances in employment, *Shelley* opened new housing opportunities for black middle-class folk, which in turn relieved some of the congested housing in black enclaves like West Baltimore.[35]

The scarcity of housing for Baltimore blacks—a circumstance created and maintained through restrictive covenants for more than a generation—had been a continuing feature of life in the city. *Shelley* promised powerful relief, however. Working- and middle-class blacks began to find opportunities in communities where there had been none before, and neighborhoods they moved to became contested terrains as communities transitioned. With blacks coming in, whites held their own for a time before inevitably feeling compelled to move away. It was not uncommon for a neighborhood that was all-white except for an island of black families living on a single block to become a wholly black neighborhood within a year or two. What had been only an occasional phenomenon of racial housing transition evident before the war gave way to whites' all-out residential abandonment in the face of the "Negro invasion" after the war.

Perhaps even more than the landmark decision yet to come in *Brown v. Board of Education of Topeka* (1954), the striking down of restrictive covenants offered immediate relief to a great number of blacks in Baltimore. Certainly, in the short run, more blacks voluntarily took advantage of *Shelley* than would take advantage of *Brown*. During the postwar years, middle-class white flight to the suburbs combined with rural in-migration of poor people, especially blacks, to shift the demographic balance in Baltimore. "It would be fatuous to deny that the increasing ratio of colored to white [in the city] does not impose

**TABLE 5.** Attitudes of Baltimore Realty Industry toward Minority Clients around 1953

| Type of service and qualifications | % of responses regarding blacks | % of responses regarding Jews | % of responses regarding others |
|---|---|---|---|
| **SALES** | | | |
| "Will sell to the group in any section of the city, if they are the same economic and social class as the neighbors" | 17.8 | 54.3 | 63.0 |
| "Will sell only in areas occupied by some of the group" | 57.8 | 28.3 | 24.0 |
| "Will not sell to them at all" | 24.4 | 17.4 | 13.0 |
| **FINANCING** | | | |
| "Will finance the group in any section of the city, if they are the same economic and social class as the neighbors" | 60.9 | 68.6 | 72.6 |
| "Will finance only in areas occupied by some of the group" | 30.4 | 19.6 | 17.6 |
| "Will not finance them at all" | 8.7 | 11.8 | 9.8 |
| **RENTALS** | | | |
| "Will rent to them in any section of the city" | 16.1 | 47.0 | 58.3 |
| "Will rent only in certain sections" | 58.1 | 32.4 | 22.3 |
| "Will not do rentals at all with the group" | 25.8 | 20.6 | 19.4 |

Maryland Commission on Interracial Problems and Relations, An American City in Transition: The Baltimore Community Self-Survey of Inter-Group Relations (Baltimore, 1955), 58, table 3.

new obligations and new problems on the municipality," the Baltimore *Sun* observed. By 1950, one in four Baltimore residents was black.[36]

During the postwar 1940s and into the early 1950s, the impact of *Shelley* may have been limited, but the impact was nonetheless significant for those able to take advantage of it. The Supreme Court's ruling against restrictive covenants offered Baltimore's African Americans greater access to the private housing market than at any time in the city's history. That access would be plagued by continued discrimination and usurious financing, but it was an improvement over the total exclusion from the market that African Americans had known since the rise of Jim Crow at the turn of the century. Working-class and middle-class African Americans went to great lengths to improve their individual housing situations, reflecting something of the pragmatist nationalism with which Baltimoreans had traditionally engaged the struggle for quality. For blacks in the city the existing racial makeup of a neighborhood was not an important consideration, and white reaction was of little consequence. For new black homeowners, moving in was a time of excitement and optimism. White neighbors would either accept them or leave. In either case, the new black homeowners believed that their families were better off than they had been before moving.[37]

The housing supply in all of Baltimore numbered 277,880 units by the end of the 1940s, having gained 30.6 percent during the decade. Of the total 1950 units, blacks occupied approximately 52,176 or 18.8 percent. However, sixty percent of the total black population in 1950 was packed into twenty of Baltimore's 248 census tracts, each with a black occupancy rate between 75 and 100 percent. The U.S. Supreme Court's 1948 decision in *Shelley v. Kraemer* would contribute greatly to the shift in where blacks lived in Baltimore, however. Census data suggests that the neighborhoods surrounding Easterwood Park, for example, just south of the parkway, saw tremendous turnover in the postwar years, only to be accelerated by *Shelley*. The total population for the neighborhoods surrounding Easterwood Park remained fairly stable during the 1930s (averaging 22,500 individuals). The white population for the Easterwood Park area showed stability and modest growth during the 1930s but had diminished by 1950, and on some blocks whites all but disappeared. Countering this was an explosion of blacks in that neighborhood during the same period. Thanks to wartime immigration, jobs that afforded improved purchasing power, and the death of restrictive covenants the black population had increased 560 percent. Notably the change was accomplished largely through home sales as opposed to rentals.[38]

In 1948 war veteran McAllister Tyler purchased his first house, at 2224 Presstman Street (which runs perpendicular from Bentalou Street, the eastern boundary of Easterwood Park). Earlier that year a black family had "invaded" the 1400 block of West Fayette (several blocks to the southeast) and had their house vandalized for their trouble. Yet fear of unfriendly or even violent white reactions did not sway black Baltimoreans from attempting to improve their housing circumstances. Many like Tyler registered their protest against Jim Crow by simply moving in.

Intolerant white reactions didn't go much beyond vandalism, perhaps because so many blacks made it known that they would not be intimidated. Carnell Simmons was one who had established that.[39] Carnell Simmons was a clean-cut, solidly built man. Born around 1920, he arrived in Baltimore in 1946, but his people were back in North Carolina. Intelligent, the "slow talking" Simmons served his country before coming to Baltimore, fighting in the U.S. Army with the storied Twenty-fifth U.S. Infantry Regiment as a machine gunner. He served more than a year in the Pacific Theater of World War II. In the fall 1947, Simmons and his wife Naomi were expecting a child. She was six months pregnant. They arranged housing via another black couple, James and Josephine Williams, who invested in real estate and owned several properties besides their own residence on North Calhoun Street. The Williamses had a son, James Jr., who was away at Howard University Medical School in Washington.[40]

The Williamses rented to Carnell and Naomi Simmons one of the three properties they owned on the 700 block of West Fayette Street, near Lexington Market, on the western edge of downtown Baltimore. One of Carnell's brothers lived a few blocks around the corner on Vine Street. The building at 713 West Fayette was substantial, with fourteen rooms and four baths. The Williamses had divided it into apartments, one on each of its three floors. Along with the Simmons family, Mr. and Mrs. William Brown and their two teenage children also took up residence in the building.[41]

On Friday evening, October 10, 1947, after leaving his job at a scrap metal plant, Carnell Simmons began moving his family into their new home. The Browns were also moving in that day. As the young black people worked, a small crowd gathered of their pensive new neighbors—white "hillbillies," as the *Afro* later describe them. "With solemn angry looks on their faces, they stood in small groups mumbling among themselves." Early in the evening, around 6:00 p.m., after the moving was done and the tenants were all inside, a gun was fired, and a bullet shattered the first-floor front window and embedded itself into a doorway. By the time those inside the house looked out, no one was in sight. Several hours later, however, second-floor windows shattered as two more bullets came into the house, one of which barely missed Naomi. Again no culprit could be found.[42]

Much later that night, Naomi smelled smoke and saw flames. Barefoot and in sleepwear, she dashed down the stairs and ran into a stranger in the vestibule. The man attempted to force Naomi back inside, but she pushed past him and ran down West Fayette Street to a nearby lunchroom. One of the Brown children tried to follow her out, but the man pushed the teenager back inside, closing the door behind him so he could not escape the burning house. The boy, William Brown Jr., ran back upstairs to where the others were.[43]

Next down the stairs was Carnell Simmons. "When I went to the door and couldn't get out," he told the *Afro*. "I returned to the middle room where someone handed me a revolver." Simmons stepped out into the hallway and fired two shots. "All I could see was the head and shoulders of the man," he said, "so I cut loose." The former army machine gunner put a bullet through the forehead of the man attempting to burn the house down with its occupants still inside. The man was later identified as Joseph M. Mayo, white. The forty-nine-year old hailed from Quincy, Massachusetts, a white working-class suburb on the southern outskirts of Boston.[44]

Hearing the shots and seeing the flames, police officers from the nearby Pine Street Station alerted the fire department and rushed to the scene where they found Mayo slumped to the floor in the vestibule. The officers surely had some sense of the nature of what had transpired—they were familiar with the whites of the block and would describe them to the *Afro* as having caused "quite some trouble among themselves in recent years." Nonetheless, the white policemen arrested all the blacks in the burning house.[45]

The 700 block of West Fayette Street was part of a neighborhood trying to hold back the advancing tide of change. Located in an old section of the city, racial transition was taking place all around it. If the 700 block was still mostly white in the fall of 1947, the 800 block was not, and neither were the cross streets, Vine to the north and Fairmont to the south. The many taverns in the neighborhood carried the cultural trappings of the "hillbilly" white residents, but they also did side-door or backdoor business with the area's increasingly numerous blacks.[46]

Ultimately only Carnell Simmons was charged with the shooting death of Mayo. Even before his hearing, Simmons confessed to the *Afro* that he did not feel badly about what had happened and would "do the same thing over again if necessary." Simmons was released on bail, and within two weeks a Baltimore judge exonerated him. As he stood before the magistrate, "clad in a neat pin-striped brown suit and matching tie, calmly . . . without evidencing undo fear," he heard his exoneration pronounced. In the magistrate's view, "the court must recognize the right of a man to defend his home."[47]

Simmons had set an example, and not just for working-class blacks. He likely became something of an urban legend too. Through his act of self-defense Simmons made an impression on the postwar housing transition. White would-be terrorists had been put on notice that rural-style racial intimidation might fatally backfire. Blacks simply had to invoke the memory of that day—in words or a gesture—to get the point across that they were moving in whether whites liked it or not.

A branch of the Koger family tree serves as another example. The youngest of ten children born to a former slave and his wife, Earl Koger came to Baltimore as a boy around 1920. His parents had owned a grocery store and a tavern back in their native Reidsville, North Carolina, a hamlet just over the Virginia border, north of Greensboro. All of the Koger children were instilled with a work ethic and a love for education. In Baltimore the Koger clan worked their way into the white-collar black middle class of professionals, entrepreneurs, and community leaders. The male Kogers established a reputation as race men and rebels. Earl's older brother, Azzie Briscoe Koger, became an accomplished attorney and amateur historian. Another brother was Linwood, the aforementioned attorney who served twice as president of the Baltimore NAACP. Earl established an insurance business and built a comfortable life for his family—a wife and four children—by midcentury. If there were any blacks prepared to make fullest use of *Shelley*, they were the Kogers.[48]

As he and his family moved to the contested terrain of a West Baltimore neighborhood along Harlem Avenue in the late 1940s, no more than a year after the Carnell Simmons self-defense shooting, Earl Koger was not blind to potential problems. Some whites still threw rocks occasionally, and white disgruntlement rarely resulted in more than words, but when Earl loaded his moving truck with his family's furniture he also brought along a friend's guns. As he unloaded the truck at his new home, 1911 Harlem Avenue, the army veteran stepped out in full view and held a rifle over his head—"with both hands," his daughter, Thelma, later recalled. His new and mainly white neighbors, all milling about, understood that he would not be intimidated. He was staying in his new home. Earl Koger then went back to the business of moving his family in. Later, as they completed their work, in case anyone had missed the earlier statement, Earl propped up several rifles in a front window for display (and, if needed, ready access). The point was made. "Nobody threw *anything* at our house!" his daughter recalled. By simply moving in, the Kogers represented eventually tens of thousands of black Baltimoreans determined to access better homes.[49]

By and large, the existing racial makeup of a neighborhood was not an important move-in consideration for blacks during the 1940s and 1950s. For most, including McAllister Tyler, white reaction was of little consequence. On the 2200 block of West Presstman Street to which he had moved: "Those [whites] that hadn't left were busy as all get out getting ready to leave." White neighbors hastily abandoned the block, but, Tyler remembers, "other than that there was no hassle, nor any problems." A few white neighbors were at least on speaking terms with Tyler before leaving, "[but] they didn't lose no time moving out." "When we moved in, we were the third black family in the neighborhood," Donna Tyler Hollie later recalled of the home her parents purchased in 1948. "Within less than a year, it was all-black. They flew. . . . They flew!" To seemingly add insult to injury for neighborhood whites, shortly after the Tylers' arrival, the Baltimore school board decided to build Carver Vocational High School for blacks at the intersection of Bentalou and Presstman.[50]

Dr. George Franklin Phillips moved his family to Bentalou Street in 1949 or 1950. The Phillips home, at 1505 Bentalou, sat across from Easterwood Park, near the site of the new Carver School, around the corner from the Tyler home on Presstman. As Dr. Franklin's daughter, Anastatia, remembers it, by the time they moved to the 1500 block of Bentalou, two or three black families had preceded them. In the beginning, neighborhood whites were not welcoming to their new black neighbors, and, as elsewhere, many began to move away. Some whites did not, however, and if they remained in the neighborhood long enough, they came around. One neighbor, a Mrs. Levy, was said to have been there "forever"—certainly long after the neighborhood's racial change. "She was a nice old lady," Anastatia Phillips would recall of her, and even occasionally brought the Phillips family homemade Jewish food.[51]

While *Shelley* was a catalyst, rapid racial turnover was not happenstance. Realtors preyed on deep-seated racism and white fears, using what was called "block-busting." In Baltimore, one company implicated in this was Goldseker Realty. With conventional financing options closed to nearly all blacks in the market, Goldseker's "rent-to-buy" program proved attractive. McAllister Tyler, for example, did not have enough for a down payment initially, so he took advantage of Goldseker's rent-to-buy option. Tyler paid rent on the Presstman Street house every month, with the understanding that Goldseker would place a portion of the rent in escrow, accumulating toward the necessary down payment. Once the amount had been reached, the rental agreement would convert to a mortgage.[52]

Goldseker's dual housing market approach seemed a "scheme" to some but a legitimate if unconventional opportunity to others. If some blacks appeared "duped" by it, many held otherwise. They understood the relative character of fairness as they attempted to do better for themselves. Most mortgage and lending agencies would contend that they did not discriminate against blacks per se; they discriminated against predominant black circumstances. As a Baltimore Urban League study proffered in 1952, "A new house is preferable to an old one, as is a new or very stable residential neighborhood to a deteriorating one." Blacks in Baltimore were historically restricted to old and dilapidated residential areas on the cusp of the downtown district. Very little new housing had ever been built for them.[53]

During the late 1940s and throughout the 1950s, Goldseker was believed by some to be encouraging white flight by selling homes to black "block-breakers" in previously all-white communities. "Are you ready to sell?" canvassers reportedly asked unsuspecting white homeowners. "You will be the only white family around here soon." Whites suddenly eager to leave often sold their homes at a loss to realtors, who then resold the homes at well above market value to black families faced with limited opportunities to purchase elsewhere. The compulsion of whites to leave neighborhoods when blacks arrived seems only to have been equaled by their fear that they could not stay. "If you don't do something about these negroes who are breaking block after block in West Baltimore," an anonymous person wrote to Mayor Thomas D'Alesandro in 1951, "I'm afraid we will have to take things into our own hands." "Suppose we can't sell, and don't want to live next to Negroes," the correspondent lamented. "What are we going to do?" Hoping that white privilege remained in effect, the writer implored the mayor, "Can you, will you, or don't you want to do anything about it? . . . If you can't God knows who can."[54]

Their property values would plummet, whites claimed, it would no longer be safe to walk the streets at night, and their daughters would inevitably give birth to brown grandchildren. Property values did fall—especially in the short run—but that was because the market in transitioning neighborhoods was flooded with houses for sale. With none wanting to be the last white family out, houses were to be had by white realtor speculators at bargain prices. These bargains were seldom passed on to black buyers, though. Even with so many homes on the market it never became a buyers' market for blacks; they always paid a premium.

Census data suggest that the mass white exodus from the Presstman and Bentalou Street neighborhood coincided with the black "invasion" in the wake of *Shelley* but also that whites were moving out faster than the blacks were moving in. Again, this accounts for depressed prices (drops in property values): there were likely too many houses on the market in any given area at one time. While more than twelve hundred blacks came to the area between 1930 and 1950, the overall population for the neighborhood registered a net loss of nearly the same number. Further, most blacks arrived during the 1940s, apparently simultaneous with nineteen hundred whites leaving. Thus, for every black moving in, two whites left.[55]

Blacks moving into previously whites-only neighborhoods in the wake of *Shelley* put a community's "stability" into question for lenders and mortgage underwriters. Likewise, white public opinion often caused mainstream lenders to avoid financing "block-breakers." Often mainstream banks and lenders flatly refused to finance homes in black neighborhoods—redlining—because their long-term value was difficult to predict, they would say. The justifications were not openly based on skin color, but the result was the same. Consequently, those coming into these destabilized neighborhoods—these "black" neighborhoods—had to deal with many characters aimed at exploiting their needs just short of usury (though, once the neighborhood began to "turn," others willingly jumped in).[56]

What is perhaps most impressive about this moment is that, even with the artificially inflated terms, blacks in Baltimore and across the urban South during the late 1940s and early 1950s took advantage of the opportunities and purchased homes. Redlining or not, blacks had never experienced or expected fairness when they pushed against Jim Crow. Opportunity cost blacks more, and they understood that. They certainly protested, working to eradicate discrimination, but never at a standstill, never in a holding pattern. They bought where they could buy, and they rented where they could rent.

"The major feature of this shift," a government study would later reveal, "[was] by way of breaking the boundary roughly indicated by Fulton Avenue on the West, North Avenue [in the north], Greenmount [east] and Down-town Baltimore [south/southeast], so that the current fringe centers around Gwynns Falls Park and Parkway." The centerpiece of the Gwynns Falls Park Community in postwar 1940s was the campus for one of Baltimore's elite white public institutions, Western High School for Girls. Over its twentieth-century history to that point, it seems blacks had chased Western all over the city. "We were seven and six, my sister and I, living at 1326 McCulloh Street," recalls Juanita Jackson Mitchell of life in the 1910s. "We sat on our front steps, watching the white girls in middy blouses and skirts going to the Western Female High School, a huge, block-long redbrick building in the 1300 block of McCulloh Street." Eventually more and more blacks joined the Jacksons on McCulloh and nearby streets. Out of a 21,014 total population in the neighborhoods surrounding the school in 1930, for example, whites numbered only 3,037.[57]

The pressure of black needs as they moved onto McCulloh and into the surrounding neighborhoods—and attendant white fears—saw Western and its white girls removed in 1929 to the safety of a solidly white middle-class and upper-middle-class neighborhood in the suburban developments of North-west Baltimore near Gwynns Falls Park, impregnable to blacks because of restrictive covenants. The old McCulloh Street campus was handed down to blacks to be used as Booker T. Washington Junior High. In the wake of *Shelley*, however, history would repeat itself. Barely twenty-five years later blacks had caught up to Western again, pushing from the south and east of the campus. White residents near the school were holding on, but just barely. "In our block which is opposite the Western High School, we are told there has been three or four houses sold to colored people," Edna Dixon Pierce, president of the Ladies of Charity of St. Gregory's notified the mayor. "These houses were bought by a jewish real estate dealer and then he in turn sells them to a colored dealer." "In all fairness to everyone," she complained, "I feel it is a great injustice to the folks in our block to have to move, some of them up in years and not really able." Though the neighborhoods surrounding Western's Gwynns Falls campus had a black population of no more than fifteen or so during the 1930s and most of the 1940s, after *Shelley* the black population exploded to better than thirty-three hundred. This trend was generally rep-resented in the neighborhoods to the immediate south and east of Western.[58]

Meanwhile, as blacks pushed their way into new neighborhoods, the ques-tion of access to neighborhood facilities, such as parks and schools, presented itself. The fight over schools would be somewhat protracted, as the practice of building a new facility for white students elsewhere and surrendering the old school building and grounds as a hand-me-down often staved off any battle to open whites-only schools to black students. Parks and other recreational facilities were a different matter. Indeed, before *Shelley*—before World War II, in fact—the inequities of recreational facilities were being challenged on legalistic grounds. Like everything else, the war years seemed to accelerate the pace, and the postwar era marked a period of greater transformation on this front.

## Personal and Present

When it opened during the Civil War, Druid Hill Park was Baltimore's premier idyllic escape from urban life, just beyond the city limits. By the mid-twentieth century, however, with residential neighborhoods now all around, the park played perhaps an even more important role as a place to enjoy fresh air and open space. Its first residential neighbors had been well-to-do whites. Now black households approached along its southern limits. Most of the park was open to all. Some features, however, like swimming pools and playgrounds, were Jim Crow. One day during the summer of 1944, seven black children from the neighborhood walked along the Madison Avenue border of the park and past the whites-only playground. They were heading to the fenced-in Jim Crow playground on Cloverdale Road, but they stopped just long enough for an *Afro* photographer to snap their picture as all seven stood looking with longing toward the whites-only playground entrance. Of the seven, some appeared toddlers of as young as two or three. Most seemed mesmerized, but one stared down with apparent melancholy. The children were outside looking in because that was all they could do. "Must Play as 'Colored' in the Park," the *Afro*'s headline read the next day. Just weeks before, a black man and U.S. Navy seaman, Edward Smith, had been arrested in Druid Hill Park for using the whites-only playground with his black kids. His case would only be dismissed, eventually, because he was shipping off to war. Carl Murphy was remaining in Baltimore, however. He was ready for a different sort of battle. Murphy announced in the *Afro* that his Legal Redress Committee for the Baltimore NAACP was actively seeking a test case for Jim Crow public park facilities.[59]

Nowhere did increasing black access to the private housing market have a more immediate impact than in the use of public recreational facilities. Most of the blacks concerned were working- and middle-class folks—those who could afford to buy a home—and thus it was this subset of black Baltimore that pioneered black access to the likes of Easterwood Park. Only a few blocks to the east of the park were some of the most congested black neighborhoods of the pre-war era. After the war, a combination of factors, including *Shelley*, saw the boundary of black residential space move westward, approaching Easterwood Park.

Marian Carroll and her husband, both educators in the public school system, purchased a home on the 2200 block of Presstman Street. They were neighbors of the Tylers, whose home was on the same block, and the Phillips family, who lived around the corner on Bentalou. Blacks were attracted to the area around the park because of the "modern, comfortable, compact homes with lawns, gardens, and garage space." The first wave of black families in the neighborhood included at least one *Afro* columnist and represented vocations ranging from factory worker, police officer, and realtor to the likes of teachers, construction company owners, physicians, and attorneys.[60]

The rapidity of the transition from white to black, accomplished in just a few years, outpaced any reconsideration of Jim Crow recreational facilities nearby. The Board of Recreation and Parks commissioners (the Baltimore Parks Board) still enforced regulations that barred what had become a majority of the residents around Easterwood Park from access to its most attractive features. Not surprisingly, that became a point of increasing contention. With each passing year, black neighborhood associations protested and petitioned against park segregation and the restricted use of the various facilities. As with other Jim Crow facilities around Baltimore, users of Easterwood feared that their children would be "arrested for swinging on swings" designated as whites-only even though few whites were around to use them. In South Baltimore repercussions had proven deadly: a black teenager was stabbed to death there by a white teen in a turf dispute over a park surrounded by a racially transitioning neighborhood. The Baltimore NAACP's Lillie Jackson, for one, pointed to the park board's indirect complicity in the tragedy by empowering whites to believe that a public park should be theirs alone in the first place.[61]

By 1950 blacks owned more than $30 million in real estate in the seven blocks surrounding Easterwood Park. A school survey conducted by the New Area Neighborhood Association (NANA), a body of the community's black homeowners, revealed that nearly two-thirds of the fourteen hundred school-age children in the area were black. Not only did blacks represent a majority of park visitors (despite the Jim Crow restrictions), black and white children played together regularly there. However, the only director on duty at the park worked with the handful of whites, to the exclusion of blacks. NANA took it upon itself to organize community committees to take up the slack and shoulder the duties of supervision and instruction in the park. The 1500 block of Bentalou and the 2200 block of Presstman both organized block clubs to perform these services.[62]

In this spirit, at midmorning on July 13, 1950, Earl Koger—who the year before had displayed rifles in the window of his newly purchased Harlem Street home—headed down to Easterwood Park, a few blocks south of his house, accompanied by his son, Earl Jr. The two were intent on playing a little baseball. They approached the office of Irvin Luckman, park director, to borrow equipment and to reserve use of the ball field. Luckman promptly denied Koger his request, saying that the park was designated for white Baltimoreans. Koger, a NANA officer, probably knew this would happen and was likely looking for a test case. Before Koger and NANA filed a suit, though, the Baltimore Parks Board was given an opportunity to address the situation.[63]

The board resolved to review its policy of segregation that year, realizing that something would have to give. A majority of board members had not agreed to desegregate, but they were searching for something more morally defensible, if not more equitable. One of them, Bernard Harris, was black. An esteemed doctor in the city, he would goad his conservative white colleagues, saying, "Segregation is expensive!" Harris and other black activists in the South believed that the transformations underway in the nation—as evidenced, for example, in the *Shelley* decision—made for new opportunities to press for actual equality under segregation or the destruction of segregation altogether. Thus, in his role on the park board, Harris would not allow his white colleagues to give black citizens short shrift any longer, not without a fight. If whites insisted on Jim Crow, they would have to pay for it.[64]

Throughout his tenure on the park board, Harris served as an unfailing advocate for fairness and equality for Baltimore blacks. He was unafraid to confront his colleagues when he believed them guilty of "dodging, side-stepping, [and] subterfuge." Harris's tactful militancy made them uncomfortable but often moved them to take the necessary steps to alleviate inequity.[65] In the case of Earl Koger's protest, however, Harris would be frustrated. A court case was averted, but not because the board desegregated Easterwood Park. By a four to one vote, Harris dissenting, the park was reassigned from whites to blacks effective December 1, 1950. In this way, whites in the urban South seemed to embrace equalization. This setup represented the last firebreak against desegregation.[66]

Pushing beyond the invisible but real boundaries of Jim Crow, blacks in Baltimore embarked on decentralizing commercial and social activity, away from the Westside. As they moved into new neighborhoods and faced decisions about where to shop for food and clothes, where to take the children to play ball and swim, and where to watch a movie, they continued to face barriers—and kept pushing against them. Everyday neighborhood folk became revolutionaries of a sort, but in some cases, perhaps, blacks suddenly found they had allies. White American voices for racial reform in the wake of

World War II became louder than at any time since the end of the Civil War. In 1946 President Harry Truman created the President's Commission on Civil Rights, charging it with making "very broad inquiry" into the government's role as guarantor of rights. Leaders of many labor and liberal organizations began or continued to advocate for racial reforms, in some cases as part of the emerging Cold War, working to reform (or exploit) the nation's most glaring contradiction: racial segregation.[67]

Begrudgingly, and never without a precipitating black demand, proponents of segregation began to concede on equalization. They did so only in hopes of preserving Jim Crow segregation. The important, if limited, black access to the private housing market during the 1950s after *Shelley* led to the Baltimore Parks Board being at the center of the local struggle for a time. Conceding the inequity of whites-only policies at majority-black Easterwood Park, the board (with one dissenter) hoped to preserve Jim Crow elsewhere in the city by flipping the park's designation from white to black. In blacks' view, this provided immediate relief without theoretically undermining their larger claim against segregation. Further, all involved understood the circumstantial nature of the decision: parks were largely neighborhood facilities. The board took firmer positions in maintaining the old ways at the city's regional facilities that drew people from around the city. The struggle for black access to municipal golf courses and municipal swimming pools and beaches illustrates this. So blacks accepted access within segregation at the neighborhood level but continued to press for desegregation of citywide facilities. This reflects the fact that the goal of black resistance locally was equality—which blacks interpreted as access—*not* interracialism (the desire to interact socially with whites).

Since the mid-1930s, black golfers had continually pressed the city for access to municipal facilities, and the premise of the *Murray v. Maryland* law school victory (see chapter 2), that separate had to be equal, was at the basis of the attempted integration of public fairways. Through its park board, Baltimore managed four public golf courses. The best of these were three eighteen-hole layouts: Mount Pleasant in the suburban northeastern part of the city, Clifton Park just north of downtown, and Forest Park in the city's plush westernmost suburbs. A fourth public golf course was Carroll Park, which sat in the semi-industrial southwestern part of the city called Pigtown. Smaller than the other public courses, with only nine holes, its fairways were shorter, and its "greens" were actually sand. "You had to putt on the sand—no such thing as a trap," one local remembered. Metal discs, not flags, marked the holes. "It was disgraceful."[68]

Inelegant, inadequate, ill placed, and ragged, this course was the only one available to the city's blacks. Baltimore was one of a number of southern cities

(Washington, Birmingham, Greensboro, Jacksonville, and St. Louis, among them) to operate Jim Crow municipal courses. But in Baltimore blacks didn't even have their substandard course seven days a week. They had to share Carroll Park with whites. Though few whites ever played Carroll Park, blacks could play there only three days a week ("and those days the least desirable from our standpoint," they complained). Blacks had won access to Carroll Park in 1934, and even then working-class whites (who did not even play the course but only lived in the neighborhood) protested loudly. The Monumental Golf Club, an organization started by some influential blacks in the city (including entrepreneur William L. Adams, Baltimore Urban League executive director Edward Shakespear Lewis, D. Arnett Murphy of the *Afro*'s Murphy family, and Henry Parks of the Parks Sausage family) pressed the city fruitlessly. Then came *Murray*. Subsequently Arnett Murphy sued the Baltimore Parks Board (*Murphy v. Durkee*) and won, and, for the duration of the war, black golfers enjoyed full and unfettered access to all the municipal courses. Having compared the course at Carroll Park with the whites-only courses, the court found that separate had not been equal. Until it could be made so, segregation had to be set aside. Wartime materials restrictions and labor needs meant that golf course renovations would have to wait, so black golfers played wherever, whenever, like everyone else.[69]

After the war, on the eve of the reopening of the now renovated and ostensibly equal Jim Crow course at Carroll Park, the black golfers' attorney Dallas F. Nicholas made a last effort appeal before the parks board, in hopes of continuing the integrated use of the city municipal courses. "It would be taking a step backwards," he contended. During the period of golf course integration, Nicholas pointed out, there had been no violence and little hostility or complaint, and the real estate market for neighborhoods near the golf courses had not collapsed. But most on the board would not hear it. The city had spent more than $50,000 lengthening Carroll Park's course by nearly one thousand yards, grass greens had replaced the sand ones, and traps and bunkers had been added. Board president Frank H. Durkee said he did not see how it would be feasible to toss the agreement aside and abolish segregation on the courses now.[70]

Black golfers refused to step backward, however. After the greenskeeper at whites-only Mount Pleasant refused Charles R. Law of the Monumental Golf Club entry upon the basis of the resegregation order, Law filed suit with federal court. In *Law v. Mayor and City Council of Baltimore*, the serendipitously named black golfer charged that the park board and the city failed to provide equal facilities to black and white golfers. He sought $5,000 in damages and an injunction against continuing segregated golf facilities. Instead of seeking pro bono assistance from the NAACP, Law retained veteran attorneys Charles Hamilton Houston and W. A. C. Hughes Jr. to represent him. Law's golf buddies put up the money. "We paid the fees ourselves," one would proudly recall. Others supported the cause by pressing Mayor D'Alesandro. "It [is] suggested that the Negroes of Baltimore would welcome a change in politics," one voter wrote Mayor D'Alesandro, "rather than suffer the humiliation and embarrassment which the Park Board seems to be so determined to impose upon us." Another asserted, "The Parks Board, which you have appointed, is a disgrace to the democratic way of life . . . the issue is clearly defined as Democracy versus Fascism."[71]

On June 18, 1948, despite the renovations, a circuit court ruled that the ill-placed, ill-planned, nine-hole course for blacks represented a blatant and undeniable violation of *Plessy*'s mandate. Judge W. Calvin Chestnut presented the Baltimore Parks Board with two options: open previously whites-only facilities to blacks and whites on a staggered schedule so as to provide equality within segregation or open the facilities on an unrestricted, desegregated basis. Citing fears of loss of revenue, new park board president Robert Garrett hoped to avoid a policy of open use. Not only would Carroll Park suffer without black patronage, which was certain to diminish in either case the judge laid out, it "might not be used at all," he stated. This was unwitting testimony to Carroll Park's lacking. All municipal courses where whites might encounter blacks would lose white patronage, Garrett believed. For ten days all courses operated without discrimination, pending action by the board. At last the board voted four to one (Harris again dissenting) to implement a staggered scheduled to preserve segregation. Blacks could play Mount Pleasant on Tuesdays, Clifton Park on Wednesdays, and Forest Park on Thursdays. Mondays, Fridays, Saturdays, and Sundays blacks could only play Carroll Park. All days at any given course not assigned for blacks were open to whites.[72]

The unintended impact of this new policy—quite humorous to many observers—was to place the burden of segregation squarely upon the shoulders of white golfers. Every Tuesday, Wednesday, and Thursday during golf season, white golfers crowded onto only two courses, while handfuls of black golfers made the rounds on all-but-empty fairways at whichever course was theirs for the day. By 1950, the sight of jam-packed courses of white golfers compared to a course scattered with a few foursomes of black golfers was "a conspicuous absurdity." "Some days there wouldn't be a[nother] person on the golf course," William Adams remembered. "We would go out there and have the whole golf course to ourselves." Seeing a lightly used golf course—some days totally unused—angered and frustrated whites barred on blacks' days. According to Adams, many of the whites thought, "My God, if there is any sport that blacks and whites could play together it would be on the golf course." At some point, the absurdity of the arrangement broke the park board's will. All municipal golf courses were opened on an unrestricted basis beginning July 10, 1951.[73]

◎ ◎ ◎

Jim Crow was dead on the public fairways, and in but a few years, using the same formula, black Baltimoreans gained equality through desegregation at other regional public recreation facilities, including municipal beaches and swimming pools. As with the golf courses, the Baltimore Parks Board pushed improvements to its Jim Crow facilities and then installed staggered schedules for blacks and whites before once more being made to concede defeat. With these precedents completed, the defeat of Jim Crow education in 1954 may have seemed inevitable. Black Baltimore's expansion into the public space followed their expanding residential footprint. While the latter owed much to the evolution of public housing and to successful litigation for access to the private markets (*Shelley*), its most important factor was the willingness of everyday black folk to assert their citizenship rights. Indeed, as the U.S. Fourth Circuit Court of Appeals observed when deciding combined municipal beaches and pools cases, "Liberty under law extends to the full range of conduct which the individual is free to pursue. . . . Rights secured by the Fourteenth Amendment are personal and present."[74]

Baltimore, ca. 1932. Maryland had been a slave state, though never seceding from the Union, and it did not abolish slavery until November 1864, nearly two years after the Emancipation Proclamation. Baltimore emerged from the slavery era as one of the largest cities in the South, with a substantial population of black urban natives and newcomers. Courtesy of the National Archives and Records Administration, Records of the Army Air Forces Group 18, 23940837.

West Biddle Street, 200 block, ca. 1920. Baltimore's black population grew considerably during the closing decades of the nineteenth century. A new black enclave emerged on the city's Westside. Early destinations, like this block, were quickly strained and then unable to meet the rising residential demand. Courtesy of the Maryland Historical Society, SVF.

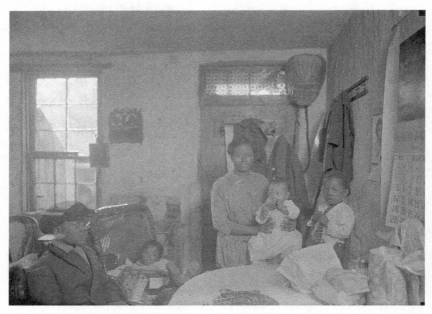

Alley House mother, ca. 1916. Blacks from all walks of life were migrating to Baltimore during this time. The overwhelming majority, like the natives they joined there, were working class. Like the woman shown here, turn-of-the-century black Baltimoreans performed menial labor and provided domestic service in white people's homes in order to feed their own families and care for themselves. Courtesy of the Maryland Historical Society, MC9451.

Light Street, looking north, ca. 1906: Baltimore's bustling Inner Harbor.
Courtesy of the Library of Congress, Prints & Photographs Division,
Detroit Publishing Company Collection.

Interior of Fennell's Pharmacy, Druid Hill Avenue and Biddle Street, ca. 1928. Some
black Baltimoreans in the early twentieth century achieved middle-class status
through professional and entrepreneurial pursuits. Such was the case with Joseph and
Estelle Fennell, proprietors of a pharmacy at 450 West Biddle Street, near Druid Hill
Avenue—"the Busy Corner." Courtesy of the Enoch Pratt Free Library, Maryland's
State Library Resource Center.

Children at play on Division Street, ca. 1934–1935. Public School 103 ("for Colored"), at 1315 Division Street, began as a school for whites in the 1870s prior to black migration to West Baltimore. Its conversion to a school for blacks by 1910 reflected the neighborhood change from white to black then underway. Future U.S. Supreme Court justice Thurgood Marshall, who lived on Division Street, attended PS 103 from 1914 to 1917. Courtesy of the Enoch Pratt Free Library, Maryland's State Library Resource Center.

Booker T. Washington Junior High School, ca. 1948. Formerly whites-only Western High School for Girls, this building was transferred to the city's black schools division in 1929 and renamed Booker T. Washington Junior High. It is seen here during a dismissal. Courtesy of the Paul Henderson Photograph Collection, Peale/Baltimore City Life Museum Photograph Collection, Maryland Historical Society, Baltimore, HEN.01.06-025.

Bethlehem-Fairfield shipyards, 1943. A booming job market drew still more southern and rural blacks to Baltimore industries during World War II. The "Beth Steel" shipyards were among the era's largest local employers. Racial segregation and discrimination still predominated, but blacks accessed more and better-paying jobs than ever before. Courtesy of the Library of Congress, Prints and Photographs Division, FSA/OWI Collection, LC-USW3-024140-C.

Workers hurrying to catch a bus, 1943. Young blacks traveled daily from West Baltimore residences to work in plants on the southeastern outskirts of the city. A photographer with the U.S. Office of War Information captured this couple heading to work in April 1943. Courtesy of the Library of Congress, Prints and Photographs Division, FSA/OWI Collection, LC-USW3-022015-E.

Baltimore branch NAACP baby contest winners, 1946. Even as racism showed its durability, expanded access to jobs afforded more and more working-class and middle-class blacks modest yet modern lifestyles unavailable in the rural worlds many had left behind. Here contestant mothers in the local NAACP's baby contest evince pride and optimism for their children's future. Courtesy of the Library of Congress, Prints and Photographs Division, Visual Materials from the NAACP Records, LC-USZ62-133185.

African American ministers and lawyers, ca. 1895–1900. Community building and nationalistic self-determination framed blacks' early resistance to Jim Crow's rise around the turn of the century. Here a number of black activists— including Rev. Harvey Johnson (*rear center, with muttonchops*), Harry Cummings (*first step, center*), and W. Ashbie Hawkins (*behind Cummings's right shoulder*)—pose to commemorate their alliance. Courtesy of the Harry Sythe Cummings Photograph Collection, Maryland Historical Society, PP240.004.

The NAACP's Thurgood Marshall (*left*) with client Donald Gaines Murray (*center*) and fellow attorney Charles Houston, ca. 1935. With a victory in *Murray v. Maryland*, the NAACP delivered the first returns on its pledge to open the University of Maryland to black students. The tactic that Houston would dub "suing Jim Crow out of the South" would be replicated in other states, culminating in 1954's *Brown v. Board of Education*. Courtesy of the *Afro American Newspapers* Archives and Research Center, Baltimore.

"Delegates to the 27th Annual NAACP Conference, Sharp Street Memorial M.E. Church Community House, Baltimore, June 29th to July 5th," 1936. The NAACP recruited Baltimore's Juanita Jackson (*first row, twelfth from left*), a pioneer in youth organizing. Also pictured here are Roy Wilkins (*second row, sixth from left*), Charles Houston (*second row, eighth from left*), Mary White Ovington (*second row, eleventh from left*), and Walter White (*second row, thirteenth from left*). Courtesy of the Library of Congress, Prints and Photographs Division, Visual Materials from the NAACP Records, LC-USZ62-130954.

Mason Albert Hawkins, PhD, professor of education at Morgan State College, Baltimore, undated. Mason A. Hawkins typified many of West Baltimore's activists during the Jim Crow era black struggle. A teacher, public school administrator, and ultimately college professor, Hawkins had a pragmatic approach to activism: he embraced the nationalist local Niagara Movement in the early years of the century, pragmatist local NAACP in the middle decades, and the interracialist local branch of Americans for Democratic Action toward the end of his life in the 1940s. Courtesy of the Enoch Pratt Free Library, Maryland's State Library Resource Center.

Picketers participating in Pennsylvania Avenue boycott, 1933. Led in part by Baltimore's City-Wide Young People's Forum, the action targeted hiring discrimination by West Baltimore employers and sought to convince them that all jobs in the all-black neighborhood should go to blacks (conceding for the time, perhaps, a continuing denial of jobs to blacks in all-white neighborhoods and downtown). Courtesy of the *Afro American Newspapers* Archives and Research Center, Baltimore.

Departing Baltimore for march on Annapolis, April 1942. More than two thousand Baltimore activists board buses for the state capital, where they would demand better access to opportunities and greater participation in government. Courtesy of the *Afro American Newspapers* Archives and Research Center, Baltimore.

NAACP meeting for voter registration campaign, Baltimore, ca. 1948. The Baltimore NAACP modeled voter registration drives in the region. Its 1943 effort, "Votes for Victory," demonstrated the growing power of the black vote and the strategic necessity of ongoing voter registration projects. Courtesy of the Paul Henderson Photograph Collection, Maryland Historical Society, Baltimore, HEN.00.A2-147.

Victorine Quille Adams, 1964. Black Baltimoreans like Victorine Adams, who owned the Charm Centre, turned enthusiastically toward electoral activism and politics by the late 1940s. Thanks to their efforts, black voting increased, black women became more empowered and better informed as a constituency, and black candidates began capturing seats in the state legislatures by the 1950s. Courtesy of the *Baltimore News American* Collection, Special Collections, University of Maryland Libraries, 1316.14.2.

Activist tennis players prepare to violate local laws against interracial play in Baltimore's Druid Hill Park, 1948. After World War II, a white-led interracialist project emerged alongside the pragmatist black struggle for equality, and the two often worked together, as in this case. Despite police orders to disperse, the tennis players sat down on the court and submitted to arrest. Courtesy of the *Afro American Newspapers* Archives and Research Center, Baltimore.

Visiting demonstrator Paul Robeson (*left*) and local activist J. E. T. Camper (*right*) picket Ford's Theatre for its Jim Crow policy, ca. 1948. The ongoing picket against the downtown theater, 1947–1952, was an important early interracialist project in Baltimore, and it garnered support from outside the city and region. Baltimore students, including whites, played a role in the campaign. Courtesy of the Paul Henderson Photograph Collection, Peale/Baltimore City Life Museum Collection of the Maryland Historical Society, Baltimore, HEN.00.A2-178.2.

White high school students rally at Baltimore City Hall against desegregation, autumn 1954. While some white students supported antisegregation efforts, many others demonstrated publicly against such developments. Those pictured here represent only some of those who had marched through the city streets most of that day. Courtesy of the *Baltimore News American* Collection, Special Collections, University of Maryland Libraries, OVER.2263.3.

Arkansas activist Daisy Bates addresses Morgan State College students, 1959. Many students at Baltimore colleges and universities became politically active in the 1950s, most prominently at historically black Morgan State. Their efforts of drew the attention of fellow activists across the South. Courtesy of the *Afro American Newspapers* Archives and Research Center, Baltimore.

Morgan State College students stage sit-in, ca. 1959. A range of student-led efforts—negotiation, picketing, and sit-ins—against segregated public accommodations near the Morgan campus began as early as 1953 and continued throughout the decade. Courtesy of the *Afro American Newspapers* Archives and Research Center, Baltimore.

CORE and other groups picket and sit in at the White Coffee Pot Restaurant, Mondawmin Mall, ca. 1958. Morgan students also collaborated with groups like Baltimore CORE, which organized successful protests against segregation of public spaces downtown and elsewhere in the city. Courtesy of the *Afro American Newspapers* Archives and Research Center, Baltimore.

Carl James Murphy, ca. 1957. From his *Afro-American* empire Carl Murphy (1889–1967) gave constant voice, leadership, and resources to Baltimore's enduring black struggle for equality. Murphy also worked with a number of social justice organizations—most prominently the NAACP. Courtesy of the *Baltimore News American* Collection, Special Collections, University of Maryland Libraries.

# CHAPTER 5

# Interracialists and the Struggle

## Getting Back Downtown, 1946–1959

Back in 1946, Joe Black, a pitcher with the Baltimore Elite Giants of the Negro National League, walked into the lobby of the York Hotel at the corner of Madison and Dolphin in West Baltimore. He was there to meet one of the York's guests, Jack Roosevelt Robinson. A former Negro Leaguer himself, Robinson was then in his first season with the Montreal Royals, a minor league affiliate of Major League Baseball's Brooklyn Dodgers. Robinson and his Montreal teammate, Johnny "Needle Nose" Wright, were the first African Americans on the Royals and, more significantly, poised to be the first in Major League Baseball. The Royals, Wright, and Robinson were in town to play their rivals, the Baltimore Orioles.[1]

Baseball was said to be the national pastime, but the major leagues played mainly in the Northeast. Only two southern cities had major league teams in the postwar years: Washington, D.C., had its Senators, and St Louis had the Cardinals and the Browns. To keep fresh talent available, each major league team affiliated with a number of minor league ("farm") teams. The highest minor leagues—those leading most directly to the major leagues—were stratified into classes: A, AA, and AAA, with "Triple A" being the highest of all. Baltimore, Louisville, and Kansas City were the only southern cities with Triple-A teams.

The Orioles played in the International League as the top farm team of Major League Baseball's Cleveland Indians. In 1947 and 1948, the Indians would add black players directly to its major league roster. Unlike the Dodgers with Robinson before them, neither of Cleveland's first black players, Larry Doby (1947) and Leroy "Satchel" Paige (1948), played a minor league season before joining the majors. While that was perhaps understandable in the case of Negro Leagues veteran Paige, Doby was young, with limited experience when he joined the Indians. Why would he not start in the minors like nearly every other Major leaguer? Doby would only play 29 of 154 games for the Indians in 1947. "Either the Orioles resisted the idea," baseball scholar James Bready surmises, "or Cleveland's owner Bill Veeck was put off by Baltimore's racism—or both."[2]

Backtracking to 1946, the Montreal Royals made three trips to Baltimore that year. On the first trip, at the start of a four-game series in April, Jack Robinson met Joe Black at the York Hotel, and then he and his teammates took the field on a frigid night before just twenty-five hundred spectators. The next day, better weather saw ten times as many fans jam into Municipal Stadium, half of them black. The scene was surreal. Baltimore-style Jim Crow segregated hotels, school buildings, and lunch counters, among other public spaces, but not seating in the stadium. Before 1950, admission tickets at old Municipal Stadium only entitled spectators to sit in a specified general section, in open bleacher-style seating rather than individually numbered seats (which came later). This meant that while one might select a general area for viewing the game, "[an actual] seat was where you found space." Fans of different teams and of different races found themselves side by side. With Montreal in town, black Baltimore supported the visiting team (or at least two of its players), while whites apparently seemed there in equal parts to cheer beloved Orioles and jeer that "nigger, son of a bitch" Robinson. The International League president had warned Montreal's management of the potential for "rioting and bloodshed" if Robinson played in Baltimore. There was no violence on this trip, however, only torrid verbal abuse. Through it all, Robinson answered racist jeers—"[You] oughta be behind a pair of mules!"—with superior play. In one spectacular moment, while whites booed, he stole home. Black folk loved it. At the end of another game, several Baltimore blacks rushed the field and attempted to carry him off on their shoulders triumphantly, even though he played for the visiting team.[3]

Some white fans almost started a riot on the Royals' second trip to Baltimore, in June. Several thugs stalked Robinson to the visitors' clubhouse door after a game. "Come out here, Robinson, you son of a bitch," one shouted. "We'll getcha!" Inexplicably no security detail was on hand despite constant death threats against Robinson that entire season. Three of his white teammates remained with him until well after midnight, when the rowdies were finally out of sight. Believing it safe, the four minor league baseball players quickly hopped on a streetcar together, only to part ways soon. The three whites went downtown to a whites-only hotel. Robinson went uptown, back to the York, where Jim Crow said he had to stay.[4]

Hotel segregation would be among the most stubborn bastions of Jim

Crow for postwar equality activists. Not until 1957 did the Baltimore Hotel Association begin to support the idea of limited concessions, at least to the black opponents of Baltimore's Orioles (professional baseball), Colts (pro football), and Bullets (pro basketball). Until that point, like Jack Robinson before them, black players stayed uptown while their white teammates stayed downtown. Along the way, however, as vulnerable as they were to economic intimidation from their respective organizations, a few players registered quiet protests. For example, at the start of the 1959 baseball season, a "Salute to the Orioles" luncheon was held at the otherwise segregated Emerson Hotel downtown. The Orioles' three black players—first baseman Bob Boyd and outfielders Willie Tasby (a rookie) and Lenny Green—were invited. After the luncheon, the Orioles would play the New York Yankees at Memorial Stadium, and the Yankees, including their lone black player, Elston Howard, were also invited to the festivities at the Emerson. The three Orioles, struck by the irony that, unlike their white teammates, they were not allowed to stay at the Emerson or almost any other downtown hotel, quietly boycotted, although Howard of the Yankees attended. Not until the decade closed did the Sheraton-Belvedere become the first of the major downtown hotels to end the ban on black guests. It opened both its guest rooms and dining facilities to blacks, but few others followed right away. About this time, a short-lived effort in the city council sponsored by Councilman William Dixon to force the issue via a public accommodations bill was defeated, leaving much left to do as the decade closed.[5]

## I Saw an American Flag in the Back of the Store

In the postwar years, Baltimore's black social justice activists organized on behalf of their right to shop downtown and access downtown spaces. During the war, in the wake of the 1942 March on Annapolis, blacks appointed to the investigative Governor's Commission on Problems Affecting the Negro Population had attempted to take up that matter, but the body's white leaders had resisted. "[It] was a matter of private business," the commission's chair, Joseph P. Healy, insisted. "Our responsibility was limited to the constitutional rights of the Negro, rather than to the private and personal affairs of [white business] people." Yet, with racial segregation pervasive, Baltimore's downtown district stood as a powerful symbol of dignity denied, and blacks had largely stayed away, preferring "their own" neighborhoods, including the Pennsylvania Avenue district, uptown. As part of a strategic shift, blacks and their allies began to stake out ground in downtown's public places. Without organizing, everyday folk pushed into Jim Crow's periphery, presenting themselves and their dollars to second-tier stores, five-and-dimes, and lunch counters.[6]

With more and more blacks migrating to Baltimore during and after the war, their commercial activity and purchasing power spilled beyond Pennsylvania Avenue. Indeed, by the late 1940s, retailers there had grown alarmed at "the gradual decrease of business along the Avenue." Downtown retailers were also alarmed, as the flight of middle-class white money to suburban shopping centers was already underway. Meanwhile, as residential space transitioned during the 1940s, so too did commercial space. Generally downtown retailers bowed to the will of their clientele. If white customers did not want to shop with blacks, their wishes generally prevailed as long as whites outnumbered blacks or outspent them. But as areas changed, and middle-class whites increasingly patronized suburban retailers, many downtown and center-city businesses previously hostile to blacks changed their policies (if not their hearts). Solvency demanded it.[7]

As with the housing market, white flight followed. Though resistant to black shoppers at first, white retailers eventually had to embrace their business, because generally whites were gone and never coming back. As the years passed, more and more whites fled Baltimore for the newness and whiteness of the suburbs. Many small white-owned businesses downtown or in transitioning residential areas understood and accepted this. During these years, blacks increasingly found open doors downtown (if not always welcoming arms), moving almost concentrically toward the city's retail epicenter at the intersection of Howard and Lexington Streets.

By the 1940s, this transition was most notable on the fringes of downtown. Lonzer Richburg, a South Carolina native, taught his Baltimore-born children to only patronize the shops away from downtown, where Jim Crow affronts were no longer as common. "I didn't even realize that you couldn't try on things downtown until I was much older," his daughter recalled. She never shopped downtown as a child: "He was very protective of us." Similarly, Esther Walton Redd refused to shop in the heart of downtown, preferring stores off the main strip or the smaller mom-and-pop stores of Pennsylvania Avenue, where you could sit down and have lunch while you were out. That was difficult if not impossible downtown because of the racial restrictions of the lunch counters at stores like W. F. Grant and Read's Drugstore. If Redd had a favorite, it was the old Schreiber's Brothers Market at the southwest corner of Lexington and Paca Streets, not only for its integration but also the fact that it reminded her of the farmers' market she had known years before, back home in Danville, Virginia. For Redd, who lived on the 900 block of Mason Street, Schreiber's was only a short trolley ride away.[8]

All these stores were located in or around the historic Lexington Market, the large open-air marketplace just west of center city. The market was on the fringe of downtown but just a block west of the huge department stores of Howard Street. By the 1940s, stores like Schreiber's were among a growing number of businesses in the downtown shopping district with predominantly if not exclusively black clienteles. On their trips downtown, the Tylers of Presstman Street, like the Redds, generally avoided stores that treated blacks as second-class customers. Respectively, the bigger retailers like Herman's, Goldenberg's, and Brager's ("Where All of Baltimore Shops and Saves!") were among the few department stores downtown that let blacks try on clothes by the mid-1940s. These stores had predominantly black clienteles.[9]

So it remained into the postwar years. The big retailers, including those along the city's famed Howard Street corridor, such as Hutzler's, Hecht's, May, and Hochschild-Kohn, did not treat black customers like they treated everyone else. Defending racism pragmatically, store managers cited white customers' preference for racial segregation. Some whites even disapproved of blacks in menial roles downtown. For example, after blacks were hired as stockers, janitors, elevator operators, and the like at Hochschild-Kohn, Walter Sondheim Jr., an executive with the retailer, reported that his store received overwhelmingly more letters of complaint than plaudits. White customers generally felt that "Negroes should not be allowed in the store on any condition." At Christmastime, even Santa Claus was segregated—there was no room on his knee for black children in the downtown department stores.[10]

Few issues were more contentious among members of the Healy Commission than the downtown department store situation. In this regard, the commission reflected conflicts in broader society. Commissioner Lillie Jackson of the local NAACP, for example, became a pariah to white liberals who argued for gradualism and resented her constant attack on department store segregation. The conflict revealed the paternalism with which many otherwise sincere white liberal elites approached social justice advocacy work in the postwar 1940s and 1950s, whether addressing race, gender, or class. Attacking the racist practices of downtown department stores in her public remarks, Jackson was sometime given to singling out Jewish retailers for pointed reproach—as she would contend that Jews, like fellow Healy commissioner Albert Hutzler, owned the largest stores and thus had the capacity to effect the greatest change. Jackson's often bombastic pronouncements were received by many as anti-Semitic rather than antiracist.

Jackson's most outspoken critic in this regard, Sidney Hollander, was neither a store owner nor a member of the Healy Commission (though he was related to Albert Hutzler by marriage). Hollander, however, had deep and meaningful connections to the local and national social justice communities. He was a board director for the Baltimore Urban League, the Baltimore branch of Americans for Democratic Action, and, at the national level, the NAACP. Hollander and Jackson sought the same thing, an end to Jim Crow in the stores, but Hollander rejected Jackson's approach and would not push his friend Hutzler as hard as Jackson would have preferred.[11]

The two had few direct or public encounters, and their relationship grew into a feud as blacks pushed against downtown department store segregation. Rather than meet with Jackson, Hollander only seemed willing to work with Jackson's superiors in the national NAACP. As Jackson and others of the Baltimore branch were no doubt aware, by the late 1940s Hollander was attempting to have his friend Walter White, head of the national NAACP, force Jackson out of the branch presidency. "I do wish the branch here might now have new leadership," Hollander confessed to White. Hollander met resistance, though, if not from Walter White himself, then from others on the national staff who valued Jackson's contribution to the branch (and recognized the waffling of the white department store owners). Frustrated when it became clear that his bid for her ouster would fail, Hollander flatly advised White that the wealthy white liberal community in Baltimore just wouldn't work with the local NAACP branch "as long as Mrs. Jackson [was] its fuehrer."[12]

At any rate the black members of the Healy Commission continued in their attempts to force the whites to address department store segregation sincerely, in spite of the chairman's repeated pronouncement that the problem "was for [blacks] to work out." Under persistent goading, Healy finally appointed a subcommittee on department stores. With members appointed by the governor, the Healy Commission experienced tensions related to questions of ultimate allegiance, tensions that many earlier interracial reform bodies had experienced. In Baltimore the fact that a number of the white commissioners had professional connections with downtown retailers increased tension at commission meetings.[13]

In the early spring of 1944, the Healy Commission subcommittee on department stores commissioned the Gallup Company to survey a cross-section of white Baltimoreans for their feelings on the matter. Assuring those polled that the commission had not yet taken a position, they were asked what type of merchandise blacks should be allowed to purchase, whether or not restroom facilities should be offered to black customers, whether or not changes in policy such as these would promote improved race relations, and whether or not whites would abandon stores that treated black customers equally. Upon review of the five hundred questionnaires involved, the subcommittee concluded, "The time is not ripe to go into the department store situation." With that, from the white commissioners' perspectives, the matter was "disposed of," and by resolution it was dropped for the foreseeable future."[14]

Organized leadership thus failing, everyday black people would persist on their own for a time. They pushed at inequitable policies with their wallets and their purses. Rather than deal with the segregated shopping of the finer stores in downtown Baltimore, many middle-class and professional blacks took the train to Philadelphia whenever they could, to shop in quality stores without discrimination. Others planned shopping sprees to New York, where they and their money were welcomed. According to the Baltimore Committee for Homefront Democracy (BCHD), this habit of shopping in Philadelphia and New York was increasingly common among the black middle class. Indeed, observers outside of the South wondered mockingly about the situation: "I don't see why [black] Baltimoreans put up with shopping in their hick town." The BCHD, an organization of well-connected, socially conscious white women, worked on this and other matters of racial tolerance during the war. The committee pushed other white women to validate the sacrifices made by blacks during the war (at home and abroad) by expressing their unhappiness with Jim Crow in the department stores.[15]

Most blacks had neither the time nor the inclination for shopping expeditions across the Mason-Dixon Line. Try as they might to avoid it, sometimes Baltimore black families had to go downtown. Parents developed methods, often subtle and unspoken, to protect their children's psyches. "No one ever told me 'you can't go to the bathroom when you go downtown,'" Lynda Hall remembered, but mothers insisted that their kids use the bathroom before leaving home. Joni Tyler spoke plainly to her daughter, Donna, who recalls, "We were not going to be able to go [once we get there]."[16]

Parents were creative and discreet. Selecting properly fitting clothes for growing youngsters could be a challenge since blacks weren't allowed to try on clothes at most stores, but black parents "did whatever they did to size them up." A common method for shoe shopping saw black parents make an outline of their children's feet while at home and then take those templates to shoe stores if shopping downtown was necessary. "You'd try [the shoe on later] and it'd always fit." Precision in such processes was imperative because downtown retailers did not accept returned items from black customers.[17]

As children matured and their worlds expanded, hard and frank lectures at home steeled them against white folks and their ugly ways. On necessary trips downtown, teens understood that certain stores did not welcome them, and so they did not even go in them. Far from being traumatized by this, they felt the stores were beneath them. Dignity and sense of self-worth instilled by parents and others shaped their perspectives. "I really didn't have a passion for going in them," Patricia Logan Welsh, recalls, "because I couldn't."[18]

Still, even the most savvy and prepared parents were sometimes surprised by Jim Crow affronts. They often grasped for words in attempting to explain Jim Crow. During the 1940s Juanita Jackson Mitchell took her eldest son, Clarence III, to a shoe store in the downtown shopping district. After browsing a short time, Juanita requested a certain pair of shoes from the clerk on duty. Before retrieving them, however, the clerk reminded her of store policy, "We can't let Negroes try on shoes." Though she probably knew better and likely even anticipated that response, the veteran freedom fighter became incensed. "This isn't Nazi Germany," she said to the clerk and then stalked out with her son, having purchased nothing. On the way out, the child said innocently, "You know, mama, I knew it wasn't Nazi Germany because I saw an American flag in the back of the store."[19]

Social justice advocacy groups struggled to address department store Jim Crow. For their part, sensing litigious plots afoot, stores acted with duplicity. For example, black activist J. E. T. Camper went to Stewart's, Hutzler's, and several other notorious establishments downtown to document discrimination in order to set up a test case for a lawsuit. Noted attorney Charles Hamilton Houston accompanied him. Perhaps the retailers had been warned in advance, though, since Camper was treated like a white customer. "Everyone permitted us to try on," he recalled in astonishment. "We bought stuff we didn't [even] want." But policy hadn't really changed: "After they found Houston was gone, they reverted back to the same procedures."[20]

## Let's Do Away with Walls

In the postwar 1940s, the mantle of interracialism and its relation to the black struggle for equality shifted from white moderate reformers to white radicals. This had really started at the beginning of the 1930s, when interracialist social justice advocacy began to assume a more radical posture. The South's most prominent interracialist outfit to that point, the gradualist Commission on Interracial Cooperation (CIC), was dominated by white academics and journalists and had almost no resonance with the masses in the South's big cities—particularly blacks. In Baltimore, the CIC branch had been absorbed in the Baltimore Urban League shortly after the latter's founding in 1924. Like the CIC, the BUL worked exclusively on easing the social and economic effects of Jim Crow instead of attacking segregation. Thus, at least until the mid-1930s, everyday blacks may have appreciated the BUL's basic program, but the league's reluctance to confront segregation likely tempered enthusiasm.[21]

The transformation of black perspectives on the veracity of white interracialists and the black struggle owed much to the work of members of the Communist Party USA during the Depression (see chapter 3). In service to the larger goal of broad-based labor organizing, Communists rightly divined that radical interracialism would place their program in the starkest relief against all other white-led efforts in addressing Jim Crow and thereby gain the trust of black workers and the black community. Holding white racism as a main antirevolutionary force in America, radical interracialism became a key tactic for party organizers. As part of the party's "Popular Front" strategy, Communists pursued their course through neighborhood organization and mass action. This included a program that encouraged breaking the southern taboo of interracial socialization between the sexes. According to baseball historian David Falkner, the first headway on integrating Major League Baseball came from the Communists in the 1930s. Blacks would have surely appreciated the attention given by white groups to this issue, but blacks themselves had been pressing against baseball's color line since the nineteenth century. More significant for them was the Communist goal of linking antifascism with their enduring struggle for equality in the South. In this way, for a time, Communists found favor.[22]

By the mid-1930s, the Communists' radical interracialist strategies were co-opted by liberal reformers. The Socialist Party of Maryland, for example, fielded an interracial ticket in 1934, running a black man, Clarence Mitchell, for the Maryland House of Delegates. Furthermore, key white Socialist voices like those of Broadus Mitchell and Naomi Riches came to serve in leadership of the Baltimore Urban League during the decade, recasting it as a protest organization.

The BUL began really pushing against Jim Crow, not simply to soften its effects as earlier. Pointing to the Baltimore NAACP's landmark victory in *Murray v. Maryland* (1935), Broadus Mitchell and Edward S. Lewis—the transformative executive director of the BUL hired in 1931—unsuccessfully conspired to break the color bar at Johns Hopkins University, where Jim Crow no doubt was an embarrassment to a number of local white interracialists for whom the school was employer or alma mater. After Mitchell failed to engineer Lewis's admission to Hopkins—"the regret of my life," he later said—he resigned his professorship at the university in protest and left Baltimore for good. Lewis kept up the cause, however, though less directly. With his help, Catherine Johnson Lane, passing as white, quietly entered a Hopkins graduate program. "Many of her classmates are still unaware [of her color]," the *Afro* reported months later.[23]

By end of the 1930s, as the war and the Nazi-Soviet Pact further eroded Left-liberal alliances, the most effective interracialist agenda was that of organized liberalism. In the urban South, and ultimately across the nation, white-led liberal organizations moved to separate their view of progress from that of the now-pariah Communists. Their vision for reform: continued interracialist and antisegregation advocacy.[24]

The Baltimore Interracial Fellowship (BIF), founded in 1942, sought social reeducation. Their approach was to lead by example through public demonstration of interracial activities. Its membership was small, consisting of the middle- and upper-middle-class whites and blacks associated more with Baltimore's colleges (Johns Hopkins, Goucher, and Morgan State) than with its churches or community organizations. With its motto, "Let's Do Away with Walls," BIF pledged through its constitution to "[build] a bridge of friendship and understanding across the barriers of race and religion, and through a program of action [help] to create together a community where prejudice and discrimination shall give way to opportunity and equality rights for all."[25]

Meanwhile, the Union for Democratic Action (UDA) also hoped to step forward in this way. The UDA emerged late in 1941 as an antifascist organization with two fronts, one domestic (lobbying) and one foreign. Overwhelmingly white and middle-class in membership, local chapters emerged in the South, to greater or lesser effect, including ones in the region's biggest cities: Washington, Miami, Louisville, New Orleans, St. Louis, Dallas, and Baltimore. Those drawn early to the upstart Baltimore UDA (BUDA) saw it as an organization—and saw postwar liberalism broadly—for its "dramatic potentialities." "The [Baltimore]UDA isn't the only liberal organization in these parts," its president and early driving force Sidney Hollander announced, "[but] it's the only liberal organization that's not limited to some specialized interest . . . and that doesn't pull its punches because some of the causes it sponsors run counter to local prejudices." During the war years, the Baltimore chapter (BUDA) blended anticommunism and antisegregation through its Inter-racial Affairs Committee, headed by the esteemed Mason A. Hawkins. A longtime educator and political activist in Baltimore, Hawkins had roots in the struggle dating to at least the Maryland Niagara Movement at the turn of the century. Now, four decades later, near the end of Hawkins's life, his committee in BUDA hoped to pull together a coalition with other local organizations for interracial advocacy.[26]

If Sidney Hollander and other local organizers had seen BUDA as an inherently interracialist organization "not as a gesture of goodwill but because they're equal partners with us in this enterprise," it commanded only token participation from the city's blacks (despite Hawkins) and working-class white people during its early years. Reaching across the lines of class as well as race proved a challenge for BUDA from its beginnings. BUDA's leaders attempted to build membership beyond solely "white-collar groups and the intelligentsia," concluding that "labor and Negroes should be our natural partners," but they also saw hazards in such alliances. "The closer our relationships get to the labor unions and the Negro organizations," Hollander told an audience in March 1947, "the less popular we'll be with some in the community on who[m] we have depended for part of our financial support." He continued, "Some of our not-too-convinced liberals have already indicated their displeasure at our low associates, which means that we'll have to look to other sources for the funds they've previously supplied."[27]

Anticipating growing postwar tension between liberals and "Commies" nationally, voices from within BUDA urged Hollander to attack radicalism directly—"we can't be subtle as we were during the war." An effort followed in Baltimore and throughout the national organization to effect "real coordination" of anticommunist liberals. Reinventing itself in this intense anticommunist climate, the UDA became Americans for Democratic Action (ADA) in 1947—"most felt . . . that the UDA would insure support from more new groups if it went forward under another name," Hollander said at the time. The ADA was "another strong forward thrust by the liberals," Hollander proclaimed, and its message let former radical allies understand that "communists and fascists would be 'invited out'" of the new organization. With its primary mission to drive communists out of the Democrat Party, the ADA nationally sustained no momentum on black social justice advocacy. For the strongest national ADA voices, there could be no compromise with communism. Thus, if necessary to build legislative coalitions for the strongest anticommunist agendas, "civil rights was an area in which to be flexible," Rossinow argues. "It was [only] a means to an end." In ADA branches in the urban South, however, where local politics and black votes carried greater weight, black social justice was on the agenda, and it resonated with community members. Indeed, electoral politics in the postwar South would prove to be the wellspring for a liberal interracialist agenda.[28]

Back at the turn of the century, shenanigans by white Democrats saw numerous attempts to disfranchise black voters, but the efforts were largely blunted by the combined efforts of local black organizations and allies nationally (among them a surreptitious Booker T. Washington). Literacy tests and poll taxes were denied, but one obstacle remained. From its creation in 1902 and despite near-annual attempts by blacks and their allies to repeal it, the Declaration of Intentions Act remained Maryland law into the postwar years. The law required would-be voters migrating to Maryland from elsewhere to declare their intentions for state citizenship a full year in advance of any election before being allowed to vote.[29]

As noted in chapter 3, black voter registration and voter education work were important parts of the struggle, especially after 1943 when the Baltimore NAACP inaugurated its "Votes for Victory" program, arguing that "we can only share and expect to share in the management of our government when we vote." Presenting themselves as candidates loyal to party structures and cultures, black Republicans and Democrats (and sometimes Socialists—members of the Socialist Party of America) watched on several occasions as whites supported the party's white candidates but not its black candidates. Black candidates had little success, but blacks as a voting bloc continued to matter. With "Votes for Victory," over several election cycles, civic-minded black citizens—from pastors and business owners to everyday community folk—participated in house-to-house canvassing. As already noted, the black vote in Baltimore proved critical in seating the next two mayors, Republican Theodore R. McKeldin (1943–1947) and Democrat Thomas D'Alesandro Jr. (1947–1959), and it became even more important thereafter. In return for their vote, blacks expected action on equality and civil rights. Thus, when the 1948 national Democrat Party platform included civil rights, it was answering these voters.[30]

## For Democracy Here and Elsewhere

The greatest testament to the growing electoral power of urban blacks across the nation was the leftward lurch of the Democrat Party in these years, especially on race. While their actions still lagged, Democrats nationally at least began to talk about race and civil rights and against Jim Crow and white supremacy. Under President Harry S. Truman's domestic agenda, black civil rights became a national policy issue again for the first time since Reconstruction. Late in 1946, for example, Truman established the President's Committee on Civil Rights (PCCR), with a fact-finding mandate toward "implement[ing] the guarantees of personal freedoms embodied in the Constitution" for all Americans. Later that summer Truman became the first U.S. president to address a gathering of the NAACP in a speech, given during its annual conference, from the steps of the Lincoln Memorial in Washington, broadcast worldwide on radio. Historian William Leuchtenburg notes that Truman "sent chills through the white South" when he declared: "We must make the Federal Government a friendly, vigilant defender of the rights of all Americans. And . . . I mean *all* Americans."[31]

At the end of 1947, the PCCR submitted its report, *To Secure These Rights*, which recommended a number of policy and legislative actions aimed at eradicating inequality and, with it, Jim Crow. Partly, these included expanding the civil rights investigative section of the U.S. Department of Justice, the passing of federal anti-lynching laws, the desegregation of the U.S. military, the outlawing of employment discrimination, and the banning of poll taxes. Drawing from this report, Truman used his January 1948 State of the Union Address to lay out a pro–civil rights vision for the nation, framing the new direction as a critical bulwark against the global spread of communism. Weeks later he formally asked Congress to pursue a legislative agenda to accomplish a number of long-sought civil rights reforms. In the summer of 1948, by executive order, Truman began the desegregation of the armed forces and the federal workforce.

Given these developments, white segregationist Democrats worked to oust Truman by denying him the party's nomination for reelection in 1948. When that did not happen, many of the staunchest segregationists bolted the party convention when it met in Philadelphia that summer. Weeks later, convening in Birmingham, the defectors formed the States' Rights, or "Dixiecrat," Party, proclaiming, "we stand for the segregation of the races." That fall the Dixiecrats ran South Carolina's Strom Thurmond for president. Meanwhile, the mainline Democrats not only nominated Truman for reelection but also continued the pro–civil rights direction he had begun two years earlier, approving a platform that presented Truman as a champion of civil rights and calling, in part, to guarantee to all Americans, regardless of race or color, full and equal rights in political participation, employment opportunity, and safety from violence. "The 1948 election," historian Glenda Gilmore observes, "became a referendum on civil rights and Communism." In a close election, the overwhelming black support for Truman secured his victory over the nearest challenger, Republican Thomas Dewey.[32]

Meanwhile the most radical interracialist outfit at work locally in Baltimore in the immediate postwar years was the Maryland chapter of the leftist Progressive Citizens of America (PCA), which coalesced around the 1948 presidential candidacy of Henry A. Wallace of the Progressive Party. Since the PCA was a social justice organization, antisegregation represented one of its core values, and its tactics included lobbying, electoral activism, and direct action (including willful civil disobedience in violation of Jim Crow laws). Simultaneously, however, the staunchly anti-Left ADA—a liberal organization formed expressly to purge communist influences from national life—endorsed the social justice agenda that would quickly become a mainstay of the postwar national Democratic platform. As black Baltimore activists and organizers assessed the opportunities each of these predominantly white groups represented, the PCA's direct-action tactics attracted more black supporters than the ADA's lobbying and voter education campaigns.

The PCA emerged in 1946 to challenge prevailing militarism in American life and advocate for an alternative course from that promised by the burgeoning Cold War. PCA activities promoted international peace, shared prosperity, and interracial democracy in America. Most publicly, racial desegregation was a hallmark of the PCA program. Twenty-five thousand members in chapters across nineteen states sprang up, actively seeking opportunities to demonstrate interracialism in everyday life, even in the South. By 1948, as noted, the PCA had come to be closely identified with Wallace, the Progressive Party candidate for president of the United States. Wallace had been a New Dealer, serving as FDR's Secretary of Agriculture (1933–1940) and then vice president in Roosevelt's third term (1944–1948). Wallace ran on a peace platform and spoke against the growing Cold War, calling for cooperation with the Soviet Union. Wallace also strongly condemned segregation in America. Locally, the organization affiliated with him and his party, the PCA, sought to publicly embarrass municipal governments like Baltimore's for their continued support of Jim Crow.

The black masses' enthusiasm for Wallace appeared high in Baltimore. During the election season, the fact that Wallace supporters were highly visible (instigating a number of public antisegregation demonstrations, as described in the following chapter) furthered black enthusiasm. On the Progressives' local ticket, J. E. T. Camper ran for Congress from the Fourth District. Few pundits, however, gave Wallace or the Progressive Party a chance. In the *Afro*, Carl Murphy dismissed Wallace (and the Socialist Party candidate, Norman Thomas, and the States' Rights, Dixiecrat candidate, Strom Thurmond) as "not serious."[33] Others went further, casting Wallace and the PCA as subversive. "We have no harsh words for [the Wallace campaign]," Sidney Hollander said, speaking in his role with the ADA, "but we intend to point out the sinister connection between those out front of the stage with those who pull the strings, chart the course, and write the script." "We refuse to accept their thesis," he continued, attributing positions to Wallace that he never put forward and regularly refuted, "that everything in America is wrong and everything in Russia, right." The ADA, more pointedly anticommunist than its UDA predecessor, presented itself as the alternative to broader (and Left-tolerant) groups like the Progressive Citizens of America. In this same spirit, the Baltimore *Sun* did all it could to dampen Wallace's impact, routinely referring to him as the "Progressive-Communist candidate" and defending the appellation when taken to task for its red-baiting.[34]

Election returns rewarded the skeptics. Nationally Wallace got only a million votes for president, fewer even than the upstart Dixiecrat ticket under South Carolina's racist Thurmond. Locally, however, the approximately 9,983 Wallace votes—almost all from Baltimore precincts—cost Harry Truman a victory in Maryland. (The Socialists and Dixiecrats together polled less than 4,500 votes, which would likely have otherwise gone to Democrats).[35]

Facing increased red-baiting in defense of segregation, radical interracialists in Baltimore were nonetheless energized by the late 1940s, and the momentum begun by PCA activists outlived the organization and was continued by other groups. New appetite for direct action among white liberal interracialist organizations served as a point of convergence with predominantly black groups already using such tactics. The campaign to desegregate Ford's Theatre in downtown Baltimore illustrates this time of transformation. It proved itself the entrée for radical interracialists in black Baltimore's enduing struggle throughout the 1950s.

Blacks had protested Jim Crow at downtown theaters since the late 1930s. During the war, for example, Baltimore's black community suffered a national embarrassment when a production of *Porgy and Bess* played Ford's Theatre on Fayette Street. World-renowned thespian Paul Robeson headed the cast. There was question at first as to whether the production would even keep its Baltimore engagement. Robeson had threatened a boycott rather than perform in front of an audience seated Jim Crow–style. Earlier in the year, *Othello*, also starring Robeson and tentatively scheduled to appear at Ford's Theatre, had been canceled due to antisegregation pressure from Robeson, the American Theatre Society (which sponsored the play), and the Theatre Guild (the play's New York–based producer). In the case of *Porgy and Bess*, however, contractual obligation likely led Robeson to not follow through with the threatened boycott.[36]

Beyond the drama of the threatened boycott, the *Porgy and Bess* production company was subjected to shabby treatment from Jim Crow hotels in the city. Many of the cast's northern members were unaccustomed to such treatment. As she attempted to hail a cab outside of the theater following a performance, Etta Moten, who was starring as Bess, was verbally assaulted by a local white woman who let loose with "a stream of epithets and vile language." When visiting the May Company department store, two other members of the cast were instructed that in order to shop they would need special permits issued to them by the store manager. Both cast members involved were from the Northeast and reportedly had never encountered such "absurd and rotten conditions."[37]

Another notable moment entailing Jim Crow accommodations downtown came in 1944, when First Lady Eleanor Roosevelt came to Baltimore in support of the local NAACP's "Votes to Victory" campaign. Intending to hold an event at the spacious Lyric Theatre, organizers were refused in their request for racially integrated seating there, so the event was held at Sharp Street Church in West Baltimore instead. A new campaign began in 1947, inspired by several developments. Baltimore's black social justice activists became aware of a growing willingness on the part of white actors, producers, and promoters—American and foreign—to support antisegregation demands. Also around this time, the Washington NAACP sought and received help from the Baltimore branch in protesting theater segregation. Throughout this era, local branches looked to each other for support rather than solely the national office.[38]

In support of Washingtonians' effort to desegregate that city's National Theatre, which was owned by Morris A. Mechanic, Baltimore activists set up picket lines in front of Mechanic's Baltimore playhouse—Ford's Theatre. Historically, Ford's not only barred blacks from floor seating but also from the first balcony just above the floor, sections that at least had favorable lines of sight. Blacks were restricted to the top balcony, "way up at the pit," as they called it (not to be confused with the pit up front in which musicians sit). "Blacks would purchase their tickets at the main ticket window along with whites and then they would have to come around the side, go in the alley and up the steps (climb all those steps) up to the pit of old Ford's Theater," Juanita Jackson Mitchell later recalled. "And there we were Jim Crow in those last few rows." As the Baltimore NAACP began to press the theater to alter its policies, they were joined by several organizations, including a number of interracialist ones. Six nights a week, plus two matinees, the Ford's picket line held. Adah Louise Killion Jenkins, a music teacher, critic, and sometime columnist for the *Afro*, chaired the umbrella organization coordinating the demonstrations, the Committee for Non-Segregation in Baltimore Theatres, and worked purposefully through the member organizations to provide the campaign's very visible interracial character.[39]

Sometimes dozens of picketers walked and stood in the front of the theater, often but a handful, and sometimes only one or two. But whatever the participation, the picket continued day after day. The managers of Ford's attempted to deflect culpability for the segregated policy, stating that they were only staying in line with industry policy in the city and that they would change when other theaters did so. The picket action represented blacks and whites, women and men, people from different generations and walks of life. Some of the most respected and influential Baltimoreans trod the pickets on the Fayette Street sidewalk in front of the theater. Robert Kaufman first heard of the activity from a fellow tenth grader at the Park School. "I'd been mouthing off about racial injustice for a long time," Kaufman later told the Baltimore *Evening Sun*, "but as a 16-year-old from a Jewish family, I'd never considered such a radical thing as picketing a theater." He continued, "But to back down was to demonstrate cowardice, so I joined my classmate. . . . Before long I'd advanced to captain of the picket line every Saturday afternoon."

The picketing was considered radical because the likes of judges, governors, and political leaders as well as socialites and business officials all attended Ford's Theatre. With so many powerful people attempting to cross the picket line daily, some feared that people who walked the line would lose jobs or suffer some other reprisal. Although the pickets turned many people away, some crossed the picket line, even those friendly to desegregation efforts, like Mayor McKeldin. Though McKeldin is often credited with being sincere in his support for reform, many blacks found him little more than a politician. As one who was there at the time recalls, "He was thinking about votes a lot of the times." In any case, McKeldin left many supporters very much disappointed.[40]

Jenkins was the driving force behind the day-to-day management of the pickets. On more than a few occasions she was the lone picketer. Liberal whites like Kaufman, Dan Atwood, and Kaufman's friend Larry Atkins were also active. In addition to picketing, Jenkins's group organized petition and letter-writing campaigns, hoping that moral pressure might sway theater owners and elected officials. Such activities may have been most successful early on in bringing playwrights, actors' organizations, and booking agencies on board, adding muscle to their demands. Activists in New York affiliated with the Congress of Racial Equality (CORE) and Students for Democratic Action (SDA, an affiliate of ADA) staged sympathy picketings against other venues in that city owned by Morris Mechanic. With picketing ultimately involving the Baltimore NAACP, the Baltimore Urban League, the Baltimore Interracial Fellowship, and CORE, as well as students from a number of the city's schools, especially Morgan State and Johns Hopkins, Ford's became a social justice battleground.[41]

Eventually, whether out of sympathy with the movement or desiring to avoid the embarrassment involved in crossing the picket line, the number of theatergoers patronizing Ford's productions began to decline. In its last year as a segregated playhouse, Ford's could book only three shows. By 1952, theater officials finally relented to protesters' demands. "The opening of Ford's Theatre to all citizens is a victory for democracy here and elsewhere," Adah Jenkins told the *Afro*. "It is proof, if such be needed, that we can be free if we wish to be and work with patience and persistence to that end." Weeks later, black and white theatergoers made their way into Ford's for the first time together, witnessing opening night for *The Merry Widow*.[42]

The effort to desegregate Ford's Theatre joined a growing list of demonstrations in the South after the late 1940s that transformed the enduring black struggle for equality. If public confrontation of Jim Crow by whites had been "radical" only a few years earlier, the move by liberals to claim the mantle of civil rights advocacy from leftists saw such activism become more main-stream. Regardless, the picketing of Ford's was something of a national cause célèbre in both liberal and leftist circles. Many actors protested and refused to play Ford's. More dramatically, activists from elsewhere came to town to join the line. Famously, Paul Robeson walked the picket line in 1948. He was in Baltimore for a political rally to benefit the Progressive Party's local and national campaign. The next year, Bayard Rustin, who had participated in the landmark Journey of Reconciliation during the spring of 1947 with the upstart radical interracialist organization CORE (a precursor to the Freedom Rides of 1961, now more widely known), walked the Ford's picket line on a visit to Baltimore.[43]

By the successful conclusion of the Ford's Theatre action in 1952, liberal interracialists were understandably stimulated and inspired toward further such actions. What was freshest here, at least for whites and interracialist organizations generally, was the consideration of direct action to challenge Jim Crow on the ground in the South. At a time when red-baiting was growing more vicious and ubiquitous throughout the South—when any critique of the "American way," especially condemnations of segregation, was politicized, potentially forcing whites further left than they desired—a great number of southern white liberals fell silent. All did not, however. By the 1950s, liberal interracialist organizations began to work on the ground in the urban South.[44]

In 1953, the year after the Ford's victory, CORE established a local branch in Baltimore. Unlike the PCA and ADA, whose main programs were political, CORE's organizational mission was the eradication of racial discrimination and inequality. Nationally as well as locally, CORE was by far the smallest interracialist outfit, similar to BIF in its membership profile: middle-class, educated whites and a few blacks, drawn largely from Baltimore college faculties and administrations.

As its affiliates had experienced success against discrimination in lunch counters in cities of the North and Midwest, the national CORE office had been sending out feelers to other organizations, seeking a sense of the situation on the ground in the South. Some evidence suggests that as much as a decade earlier, just as CORE was emerging, another activist group, the BIF, represented the city at a national gathering called by CORE. While BIF seems to have been sympathetic to CORE's efforts at interracial reform through nonviolent direct action and perhaps was inspired by CORE, it remained independent, making the Baltimore CORE later formed that organization's first formal establishment in the city.[45]

Reaching out to activists in Baltimore, George M. Houser, CORE's executive director, got a synopsis of the difficulties with public accommodations and service providers downtown. "The store managers pass the buck," Juanita Jackson Mitchell told Houser in 1952. "They say if the other managers will also take the more liberal attitude they will be happy to join in, but they cannot be the first." Not long after, Herbert C. Kelman, a Johns Hopkins affiliated psychiatrist only recently arrived in Baltimore, spearheaded an interest group that led to the formation of Baltimore's first CORE chapter. Kelman, who had earlier experience with CORE in New Jersey, put out a call to the ranks of Baltimoreans already familiar with the city's interracialist organizing. Attracted by CORE's mission to be "inter-racial in both character and intent," middle-class folk, labor organizers, high school and college students, professors, ministers, and others joined in pursuing equality for all Americans. National CORE's field representative, Wallace Nelson, spent more than a week in Baltimore helping the local chapter get chartered. It formally began on January 10, 1953, with about two dozen active members.[46]

Along with other challenges, interracial organizing became a problem of geography. Blacks and whites did not live in the same parts of town. Their cultural institutions were as separated by distance as they were by Jim Crow. The economies of midtown, where middle-class white liberals roamed, and those of uptown—West Baltimore—stood distinctly apart from each other. Baltimore CORE had to convince each community of the efficacy of interracialism. More practically, it had to establish an organizational identity grounded in one community or the other, which was critical to identifying organizational leadership, mobilizing support from the community, and applying leverage to targets of protest campaigns. There was also the matter of press coverage; the "white" papers (the *Sun*, *Evening Sun*, and *News-American*, principally) did not cover the black community, and the *Afro* did not cover whites. Meanwhile, the CORE approach had been used in Baltimore before: direct-action protest, quiet negotiation, and blacks and whites demonstrating together (picketing Ford's for example). Still, CORE set roots in Baltimore as a relatively new organization nationally and therefore was still very much outside of the main activist ranks. Baltimore CORE was clearly unconnected to the masses of black Baltimore. It was not in the black church, not on the streets or schools of the black community, and had no formal partnership with the Baltimore NAACP.

Among the founders of Baltimore CORE, the person with the most direct link to black Baltimore's institutions and its history of independent and interracial organization was Adah Jenkins. From an old Baltimore family, Jenkins moved among the ranks of social activists in the mode of Progressive reformers and the "respectability" crowd of the early century. She had long-standing relationships with those directing the local NAACP and the Baltimore Urban League, and her credentials as a radical interracialist dated at least to her hand in the founding of the Baltimore Interracial Fellowship in the early 1940s and her day-to-day management of pickets at Ford's Theatre. Thus, when CORE came to town in 1953, Jenkins was perhaps the most well placed of the local chapter's founding members to bridge old and new. The original group often met at the Jenkins home on Westwood Avenue near the intersection of North Avenue and Monroe Street. Of the other black founders and staffers—Bertha Johnson, Earl Jackson, McQuay Kiah, and Eugene Stanley—three of them, Jackson (School of Education), Kiah (Dean's Office), and Stanley (Education) connected the organization with the students and faculty at Morgan State College. The absence of other substantive links saw Baltimore CORE's early efforts go almost unnoticed in both the black community and the white one.[47]

The same might be said of national CORE, however. Formed in 1942 in Chicago by the impetus of northern-based radical Christian pacifist activists connected to the Fellowship of Reconciliation (FOR), the new organization was committed to effecting an interracial America through Gandhian nonviolent direct action. CORE sought to change attitudes and behavior by confrontation without compromise or hatred, and it wished to work in the South. Its first exclusively southern enterprise, the inspired Journey of Reconciliation in 1947, sought to test southern white compliance with the Supreme Court's ruling in *Morgan v. Virginia*, which invalidated segregation on interstate travel. The Journey of Reconciliation had been a qualified success (it had not tested compliance in the Deep South due to the certainty of white segregationist violence and likelihood of slipshod protection by local or federal law enforcement officials). Still, a number of leaders in the organization (including Bayard Rustin) pushed CORE to attempt to build a base of affiliates in the South.[48]

Not only had the campaign against Jim Crow at Ford's Theatre energized interracialist ranks and student activists in Baltimore, it also got the national CORE office enthusiastic about the potential for work there. By that point, CORE was already moving into the South. CORE held summer workshops on interracial nonviolent direct action in the region and established a few affiliates that engaged in direct action in their respective communities. Before Baltimore CORE, for example, CORE's Washington, D.C., affiliate staged successful sit-ins during the early 1950s at coffee shops, bus terminals, and movie theaters. Yet CORE's work in Washington encountered none but matter-of-fact commitments to nonviolence from black community folk. As historians August Meier and Elliott Rudwick note, Washington CORE's efforts in the fall of 1952 to inculcate local blacks with nonviolent direct-action methods (picketing against segregation at a public playground facility) went awry. When local whites attacked violently, a black observer fired his gun into the air to disperse them. Would-be activists drew clear distinctions between violent instigation and violent self-defense. "The incident became front-page news," Meier and Rudwick write, and the enhanced publicity increased pressure on city authorities, resulting in desegregation of the facility soon after. But Washington CORE's admonishment of local blacks for breaking from nonviolence, even in self-defense, "estranged them" from the black community. Support for interracialism was also tepid at best. Most of all, the black masses of the urban South would not long follow white leaders—which was still CORE's primary profile. As in Washington, this held true in CORE's other southern affiliate, St. Louis CORE. In Baltimore, however, the presence of strong black advocates among the interracialist ranks and the potential connection with a mass base of black activists—students at Morgan State College—proved vital to CORE's program in 1950s Baltimore.[49]

Around midday on a Thursday in early May 1953, Carl Murphy sent an *Afro-American* staff reporter downtown to Lexington Street in the heart of the city. There, amid the lunchtime bustle, the reporter saw what he had come hoping to see, something not witnessed in Baltimore in generations. For a couple of days a rumor had been circulating: some lunch counters had dropped the color line, and blacks and whites were sitting next to each other eating sandwiches, drinking coffee, and maybe even conversing. The reporter must have been excited to learn that the rumor was true. The next edition of the *Afro* confirmed: "Colored persons are now eating just as other citizens in Woolworth's Department store, 223 W. Lexington St., and Kresge's Department store, Park Ave. and Lexington St." This was big news and for more than the obvious reason.[50]

As late as 1950 only three restaurants outside of the black community served black patrons: the Homewood Friends Meeting House near Johns Hopkins University, Levering Hall on the Johns Hopkins campus, and the Savarin Restaurant in midtown's Pennsylvania Railroad Station. Deploying nonviolent direct action against lunch counter Jim Crow beginning in early 1953, Baltimore CORE sent teams of black and white activists to stores to confirm discrimination. This established, Baltimore CORE attempted to negotiate policy change. If negotiation failed, the discrimination was publicized via leaflet distribution. If this too failed to effect change, picketing and sit-ins aimed at disrupting business began.[51]

Baltimore's first lunch counter desegregation, at S. S. Kresge at Lexington and Park, came for the asking: appeal to Kresge's home office in Detroit brought immediate change. By the spring of 1953, campaigns had been deployed against all the Lexington Street lunch counters. With the campaign of more than local relevance in the estimation of Baltimore CORE, its activists drew from regional and national resources. For example, the sit-in at McCrory's on Lexington in Baltimore benefited from a concurrent action against a McCrory's in St. Louis. When the latter agreed to desegregate, the chain's national headquarters mandated desegregation of all of its stores. Likewise, while W. T. Grant's national managers seemed apathetic regarding the Baltimore struggle, a sympathy demonstration by New York CORE against the W. T. Grant store in Harlem, which itself practiced no discrimination, and an appeal to the company's board of directors and stockholders ended Jim Crow across the entire Grant chain by April 1954.[52]

These developments unfolded largely without note at the time. The mainstream white press in Baltimore, as in other southern cities, generally refused to cover race-related demonstrations, concerned about losing advertisers and claiming that coverage might spark violence. More puzzling, however, is the subdued coverage in the black press. Other than its scoop in May 1953 that blacks and whites were "sitting next to each other eating sandwiches," the *Afro-American* covered CORE's early 1950s downtown sit-ins with only passing interest. Writing soon after CORE began its downtown campaign, *Afro* columnist Buddy Lonesome (who would soon take up activism of his own), saw it as strange that more was not being made of CORE's triumphs. "Slowly and unheralded," he wrote, "a small interracial group is chipping at the deeply embedded rocks of bigotry and prejudice while most of us bask in the sublime indifference." Desegregation of lunch counters in the heart of downtown came in succession: S. S. Kresge and Woolworth's (May 1953), Schulte-United (1953), McCrory's (October 1953), W. T. Grant (May 1954), and Read's (January 1955). The hallmarks of this campaign—reaching back into the public accommodations activism of the 1940s—were nonviolent direct action, interregional cooperation, and interracial participation.[53]

The success of CORE's campaigns against Jim Crow lunch counters downtown, most of which were not locally owned, could not fully prepare it for the challenges yet to come toward the end of the decade. Moving to other public accommodations, Baltimore CORE found itself in protracted campaigns against obstinate, locally anchored white racist resistance, and these recalled the work done by other groups against Ford's Theatre. Two campaigns—against Gwynn Oak Amusement Park and the White Coffee Pot restaurant chain—tested Baltimore CORE and revealed the growing popularity of nonviolent direct action as well as its limits.

The Gwynn Oak project began in the spring of 1955, shortly after victory in the lunch counter campaign. Baltimore CORE deployed a picket line to coincide with the park's annual "All Nations Day" festival, a late summer celebration of global diversity and "good fellowship." For this the amusement park invited the formal participation of foreign embassies, consulates, and groups of local nationalities except Africans and those of African descent. The festivities featured a parade, folk dancing and music, ethnic cuisine, and demonstrations of foodways. Cultural exhibits were installed in the park's showplace Dixie Ballroom. Tens of thousands attended each year. Except for black maids in uniform caring for white children, blacks were excluded—by park policy. Arthur Price, former president of the Baltimore City Council, owned the park.[54]

Each year several dozen picketers marched at the entrance to the park as "an educational demonstration." As Adah Jenkins, Baltimore CORE's vice chair, told the Baltimore *Sun*, "We are working in the spirit of good will and nonviolence, [and] we are always ready to negotiate." Advance contact with the various embassies and consulates potentially participating in the festival informed them about undemocratic practices of the park. This ultimately saw a number of groups from Asia and Latin America decline participation by the late 1950s. Meanwhile, unaffiliated activists and other groups also lent support over the years. National CORE sent representatives. For one, LeRoy Carter, its field secretary, came to Baltimore to help. Since the launch of the Montgomery Bus Boycott in late 1955, CORE had been looking to support organic campaigns in the South, sending experts in nonviolent direct action to unfolding protest scenes. Before coming to Baltimore, for example, Carter had been on the ground in Montgomery, Orangeburg, and Tallahassee. Similarly during the late 1950s, James Peck of CORE's national office also occasionally participated in the Gwynn Oak Park campaign.[55]

After 1957, emboldened no doubt by news media showing white "massive resistance" and brutality across the South, whites in and out of uniform became increasingly verbally abusive and violent in Baltimore. On one occasion, private park security guards roughly ejected two nonviolent protesters who had slipped into the park unnoticed. White bystanders accosted the protesters and then beat them and ripped away their clothing. Police arrested not the assailants but the protesters. Unlike in the past, white journalists began to pay attention. Local white media had never been more than perfunctory in covering antiracist protests before, but after 1957—after a white newspaper and one of its columnists each took a Pulitzer Prize for coverage of the Little Rock, Arkansas, school desegregation "crisis"—white reporters and white racists in the South became two separate camps. Such was the case in Gwynn Oak Park, where a "no photography" policy was instituted. Reporters who persisted were thrown out along with protesters. During the late 1950s, the Gwynn Oak Park campaign was more of an annual event than an ongoing demonstration (although negotiation was attempted year-round).[56]

Baltimore CORE's major sustained effort in these years was its participation in a campaign aimed at desegregating the White Coffee Pot chain of restaurants in Baltimore. CORE participated in the White Coffee Pot campaign as part of an umbrella group, the United Citizens Committee for Human Rights (UCCHR). Chaired by Morgan State College professor Alexander J. Walker, the UCCHR was composed of representatives of thirty civic, fraternal, and neighborhood groups. None but CORE claimed to be pacifists and devoted to nonviolence. However, Walker pointedly spoke in the language of nonviolence brought into vogue by Martin Luther King in Montgomery. With concurrent demonstrations at various locations across the city, the White Coffee Pot campaign began in the fall of 1956 and was still ongoing after the Montgomery Bus Boycott was brought to a successful conclusion in December that year. "If colored people can walk for the right to ride the buses in Montgomery, Alabama, they can walk for the right to eat in restaurants in Baltimore, Maryland," the *Afro* reported one of a group of picketers declaring during a June 1958 protest. Others called for a Baltimore pastor to rise up and "emulate Rev. M. L. King, the messiah of the Montgomery bus boycott." A. J. Payne of Enon Baptist and Marcus Garvey Wood of New Providence Baptist shared UCCHR leadership duties with Professor Walker.[57]

The UCCHR primarily used nonviolent direct action, especially sit-ins, as well as picketing and leaflet distribution. The group was also grounded in the city's movement traditions. Whereas in the 1930s black Baltimore had been encouraged to "Buy Where You Can Work" (see chapter 2), in the 1950s protesters admonished, "Don't Eat Where You Can't Sit Down." However, keen to the publicity the black struggle was now receiving outside the black community, protest leaders and their supporters used the vocabulary of the day: "There's nothing wrong with our city that a few . . . passive resistance campaigns won't cure." Also similar to the activists in Montgomery, though certainly not in imitation, the UCCHR used local churches as staging grounds for its White Coffee Pot campaign. A White Coffee Pot restaurant at the newly opened Mondawmin Shopping Center was a special focus of the effort, and Mount Lebanon Baptist Church, a few blocks away, served as base camp for the demonstrators. The shopping center, ahead of its time in many design aspects, opened in October 1956. Of all its retailers and restaurants, only the White Coffee Pot was segregated.[58]

Mondawmin was built in West Baltimore on Gwynns Falls Parkway during a time of racial transition. Black families were arriving; whites felt compelled to flee to the suburbs. If some whites felt pushed around by the democratizing momentum of the postwar years, most blacks cared little. The sensibilities of white identity politics and the prerogatives taken in its name had seldom deterred urban southern blacks from pursuing opportunities for equality. Thus, as Mondawmin opened in what had become a predominantly black community, they would insist on fair treatment in their own neighborhood.[59]

Baltimore CORE played a peculiar role in the White Coffee Pot campaign. Because of its early association with nonviolent direct-action tactics, Baltimore CORE's impact in the city had been pronounced. However, as nonviolent resistance gained a higher profile with mass media coverage of Martin Luther King Jr. and his campaigns, Baltimore CORE's claim on nonviolence was reduced. Furthermore, as blacks nationwide approached nonviolent direct action more as a tactic than as a doctrine, they came to redefine it. The most pronounced result of this saw nonviolent direct-action campaigns become impatient. Traditionally, Baltimore CORE had deployed direct action as a last resort, only after an extended period of quiet, behind-the-scenes negotiation had failed to produce results. It was "a long drawn-out procedure," one activist remembered. Increasingly, however, Baltimore CORE witnessed impatience with this process from student groups who employed nonviolent tactics without any preliminaries. This happened not just in Baltimore but also across the South.[60]

By the late 1950s, certainly with regard to the White Coffee Pot campaign, even black adults were demanding action—nonviolent action, but action nonetheless. Negotiation seemed futile to many, as business owners seemed irrational and insincere. White business owners said that they were for desegregation but afraid that white patrons would abandon them. They even purported to welcome compelling legislation or a court ruling that would give them cover to make such a change. In the case of the White Coffee Pot, however, the fact still remained that it was the only business at Mondawmin that was segregated, and many other White Coffee Pot restaurants were located in all-black communities or communities clearly trending that way. Impatience with negotiation caused tension and even movement defections, as blacks and whites who were Baltimore CORE traditionalists split from those who were not. By the spring of 1957, Verda Welcome, for example, distanced herself from the UCCHR because she felt it did not faithfully adhere to the tried-and-true Baltimore CORE method—it had not allowed sufficient time for negotiation with White Coffee Pot owners before using direct action. The UCCHR, she complained, was too "radical."[61]

Equally demoralizing, perhaps, and not just to Baltimore CORE but to all the activists involved in the UCCHR, was the impossibility of organizing a community as large as Baltimore's into a united mass effort. Most blacks did not participate at all, whether out of philosophical disagreement or mere indifference. As tremendous as the Montgomery Bus Boycott had been as an example of grassroots action, most notable for its solidarity and its duration, it had been litigation (*Browder v. Gayle*) that had provided the decisive turn. The boycott may well have won out in the end, but it would likely have required a much longer time, with eventual success partial at best. As King himself came to understand during the late 1950s, there was much about the Montgomery effort that was simply not going to work elsewhere in the urban South, especially in the biggest cities. Montgomery's black community of approximately 50,000 was smallish when compared with black populations in other Jim Crow cities in the 1950s South: Louisville (70,075), Richmond (91,972), Birmingham (135,113), Memphis (184,320), Atlanta (186,464), St. Louis (214,377), New Orleans (233,514), Washington (411,737), and Baltimore (326,589). Having witnessed the Montgomery Bus Boycott firsthand, Rev. Fred Shuttlesworth, a Birmingham activist and early colleague of King, attempted to replicate the boycott program in Birmingham during the late 1950s. Among the obstacles that ultimately frustrated Shuttlesworth's effort was the size of black Birmingham compared with that of Montgomery. Scale mattered, and larger communities found it difficult if not impossible to reach the unanimity of opinion and purpose that had benefited King's bus boycott. As Baltimore CORE and the UCCHR came to lament, many Baltimore blacks crossed picket lines at White Coffee Pot restaurants. They walked past the sit-in activists, ordered food according to Jim Crow custom for takeout, and then went back to their lives without a word or apparent further consideration.[62]

◎ ◎ ◎

The first time Martin Luther King Jr. came to Baltimore he arrived with an entourage of white people. Over the week between Christmas and New Year's Eve in 1956 the college fraternity Omega Psi Phi honored King with one of its Citizen of the Year awards at a national convention hosted by Morgan State. By that time King had inspired black America with his work leading Alabama's Montgomery Improvement Association, whose mass boycott of Jim Crow buses had the week before reached its triumphant 381st day. In the glow of victory, the young King and his wife, Coretta, had become the celebrities of the cause perhaps even more so than Rosa Parks, the other most visible activist in the bus boycott. The *Afro-American* newspapers and *Ebony* magazine regularly covered the Kings, but so too did the *New York Times* and *Time* magazine. Black people had even seen the Kings on television.[63]

Taking a commercial flight from Montgomery for the event at Morgan State, the Kings landed at Washington National Airport, where they were met by friends who drove them the remaining thirty miles or so to Baltimore. The fraternity had planned a grand banquet for more than two thousand guests at Baltimore's Fifth Regiment Armory. At this event the beautiful twenty-nine-year-old Coretta Scott King appeared as a vision in royal red, as the press noted, with her street-length velvet dress tastefully complimenting her figure. As much or more for her talents as for her beauty, Coretta had played a strong and visible supporting role throughout 1956. Only weeks before the Baltimore engagement, in New York City, Coretta had displayed her considerable artistry as a singer at a benefit concert for the boycott, sharing the stage with an up-and-coming singer-activist, Harry Belafonte, and the iconic Duke Ellington, whose performance at the Newport Jazz Festival earlier that summer had already become legend. For all she was coming to do and represent, as she moved with her husband that evening in Baltimore, the press was clearly smitten, reporting on her hair—"a loose bob below her shoulders"—and looks. She made "an attractive matron," indeed.[64]

As they arrived at the gala, the Kings and their entourage met with still more acquaintances. With the exception of the Kings and Martin's colleague and mentor Bayard Rustin, everyone moving toward seats at the table of the guest of honor that evening was white. Attorney Harris Wofford and his wife were Washingtonians and, with Rustin, had met the Kings at the airport and ridden with them to Baltimore. Also at the table that night, having met King for the first time in the car ride that day, was New Yorker Stanley Levinson of the American Jewish Congress. The last members of the Kings' entourage were John and Margaret Neustadt. John Neustadt was on the staff at Johns Hopkins University Hospital. Several organizations and individuals at Hopkins had been following King's work in Montgomery and had been interested in bringing him to Baltimore to discuss movement tactics. Margaret Houghteling Neustadt (a second cousin to FDR) had been active in a variety of causes, including the Baltimore chapter of Americans for Democratic Action. Liberals all, and demonstrably committed to seeing the black struggle inspire a national movement toward broader social reform, the entourage must have nonetheless struck a chord with the event's other guests—the black guests—getting their first look at King. Some no doubt questioned the authenticity of their new Moses, accompanied as he was by an entourage of white people to a black frat's affair.[65]

In the late spring of 1958, King was back in Baltimore, having accepted an offer to deliver the commencement speech at Morgan State. Black Baptists in Baltimore were among the first to reach out in support of the young Alabama pastor when the television cameras thrust him onto the national scene. When Morgan State called, King had happily accepted the invitation. On that cool, clear spring day, some three thousand alumni, faculty, proud families, and well-wishing friends gathered to cheer on the graduates. With a glad hand and a broad smile, Maryland governor Theodore McKeldin personally conferred each undergraduate degree. For their part, college officials would confer honorary Doctor of Laws degrees on King and three others, including Walter Sondheim Jr., who had become head of the Baltimore school board. Taking his turn at the podium, the young Dr. King (twenty-nine at the time) rose to speak. That day King drew on ideas and used phrasings that would become famous in the years ahead. He spoke of new possibilities, new opportunities. "In a few years from now," he assured the graduates, "you will be able to sing with a new vim, 'My country, 'tis of thee, sweet land of liberty, of thee I sing; land where my fathers died, land of the pilgrims' pride.'" As the lyrics concluded, King beseeched, "From every mountainside, let freedom ring."

> Yes, let it ring from the prodigious hilltops of New Hampshire;
> Let it ring from the mighty mountains of New York;
> Let it ring from the heightening Alleghenys of Pennsylvania;
> Let it ring from the snowcapped Rockies of Colorado;
> Let it ring from the curvaceous slopes of California.

> But not only that, from every mountainside, let freedom ring!
> So let it ring from the Stone Mountain of Georgia;
> Let it ring from Look Out Mountain of Tennessee;
> Let it ring from every hill and mole hill of Mississippi;
> Let it ring from every mountain of Alabama;
> From every mountainside—let freedom ring!

> And when this happens, all men will be able to stand together, black men and white men, Jews and gentiles, Protestants and Catholics, and sing a new song— "Free at last, free at last, great God Almighty, we are free at last!"

Perhaps the earliest iteration of the words he would most famously speak five years later on the steps of the Lincoln Memorial at the 1963 March on Washington for Jobs and Freedom, these visions were not yet the stuff of his dreams. But on that June day in Baltimore, at the end of the 1950s, young Rev. King called them forth all the same.[66]

Still, if all welcomed the opportunity to end Jim Crow, many bristled at the patronizing tone of the integration culture that appeared to be rising in its place. Desegregation following the 1954 *Brown v. Board of Education* decision, a crowning achievement for some (see next chapter), was for others not much more than an overdue restoration of constitutional rights. In the minds of many, what developed distorted the true origins of the enduring black struggle. As historian Daryl Michael Scott notes, the ruling "subtly but effectively conveyed the plight of the [black] victim without censuring the [white] guilty." Missing from the indictments of *Brown* was the direct complaint against the intended inequality of Jim Crow segregation—generations burdened by hand-me-down schoolbooks, police brutality, gerrymandering, and economic violence. As such, in spite of the supposed advance implied by *Brown*, a separatist black nationalist critique drawn from long-held traditions found new voice and visibility in Baltimore, acquiring new currency. Its most charismatic personification would reach Baltimore two years later.[67]

In 1956 the Nation of Islam (NOI) opened Muhammad's Temple of Islam No. 6 at 1000 Pennsylvania Avenue in West Baltimore. Heading the Baltimore NOI was Isaiah X Edwards, later known as Isaiah Karriem, a colleague of the dynamic and highly visible Malcolm X (later el-hajj Malik el-Shabazz, or Malcolm Shabazz). At the time, concurrent with his role in the national organization, Malcolm X also headed the NOI Temple of Islam No. 4 in Washington, D.C., and more famously Temple No. 7 in Harlem. Like Martin Luther King Jr., Malcolm X visited Baltimore in 1958, in his case to help with fundraising activities for the Baltimore NOI. More than ten years earlier, in 1947, the founder of the NOI, Elijah Muhammad, had held a rally in West Baltimore's Harlem Park, and the NOI's profile had ascended rapidly during the 1950s along with that of Malcolm.[68]

As an alternative framework for nationalist activism, the NOI refrained from electoral politics almost completely. Yet it presented a specific counternarrative in the urban South under Jim Crow. Its black nationalist imprint and consistent rejection of Jim Crow's precepts spoke clearly about self-determination and black militancy. Indeed, from a secular perspective, the Black Muslims' personal comportment and dignified public demeanor no doubt struck respectability-conscious blacks favorably. Similarly, the fact that Muhammad's Temple of Islam No. 6 (like the larger NOI) strove for economic self-sufficiency as a community model was framed within the broader resistance to white supremacy. "We . . . are struggling to make our people economically independent of their oppressors," Isaiah X Edwards told the *Afro* in late 1959. This too won the Black Muslims admiration from much of the black Christian community, despite theological differences.[69]

# CHAPTER 6

# "This Beginning Will Awaken Others"

## Baltimore Students Activate for Desegregation, 1948–1959

Activism since the Depression and the war seemed to be bearing fruit. During the March on Annapolis in 1942, one of the issues pushed hardest by the delegates was the need for greater diversity on boards, commissions, and other bodies that set policy, outlined initiatives, and governed the city's institutions. Blacks believed that equality required greater representation in government. Representation on the Baltimore Board of School Commissioners, for example, "would make it possible for the Negroes to be treated on an equal basis as far as buildings and equipment" were concerned. Gaining representation on these governing bodies came in spurts. No sooner did the 1942 demonstration end than Baltimore mayor Howard Jackson filled vacancies on the school board with whites—he would argue, "without regard to political, racial, or religious consideration."[1]

Black votes sent Jackson out of the mayor's office later that year, however, and his successor, Theodore R. McKeldin, would in 1944 appoint George W. F. McMechen, the first black school board commissioner. Neither Commissioner McMechen nor administrators of the Colored Division of the Baltimore City Public Schools could do enough to bring true equality to the separate educational experiences, however. White students enjoyed a decided material advantage over blacks. In 1945, for example, whites outnumbered blacks in the Baltimore school population by more than two to one (74,482 to 31,446). The value of the collective public school physical plant, however (greater than $50 million), favored whites by nearly ten to one over black facilities. In secondary schools, in which whites outnumbered blacks nearly four to one (25,348 to 6,502), 39 percent of classes in black schools had fifty students or more (compared to only 27 percent of white classrooms with so many). And, whereas 64 percent of white classrooms with greater than forty students had no more than forty-four, only 38 percent of comparable black classrooms had as few.[2]

Some of the city's schools had names, but all of them were officially designated by numbers. The "colored" schools bore 100-series numbers. While whites-only schools operated facilities that fell short of being state-of-the-art, black schools routinely faced more challenges, including underfunding, overcrowding, antiquated buildings, and insufficient supplies, relying on hand-me-down, outdated materials and equipment. Even in the late 1940s, for example, School No. 115 on Merryman Lane near York Road was a campus of wooden buildings—"they were just like little houses," a former student recalled. Each room at School 115 had a potbelly coal stove for heating. Similarly lacking, the blacks-only elementary school at Gilmor and Presstman Streets, No. 108, had no cafeteria and no gymnasium. Students walked home for lunch every day, as did those attending School No. 104, Robert Brown Elliott (at Carey and School Streets).[3]

The crowded conditions were neither a mystery to the school board nor a particularly pressing matter. When parents expressed concern, they were counseled to be patient, to await the construction of new facilities for whites, after which blacks might occupy the discarded ones. "We shall have to do the best we can under crowded conditions," one superintendent said as late as 1952. Often the school board dismissed crowded conditions as a problem beyond their charge. "The problem of overcrowding is more one of neighborhood conditions than of racial segregation," preached the school board. "It *happens* that in Baltimore a greater proportion of our Negro citizens and their children live in congested neighborhoods." This view spoke pointedly to the disconnection between the white upper- and middle-class-dominated school board and the everyday poor and working people whose lives they attempted to shape. In the school commissioners' telling, those "congested neighborhoods" were mere coincidence or perhaps black preference.[4]

Material deficiencies aside, what black schools did enjoy in many cases, perhaps even to an advantage over many white students, were capable and concerned teachers. Teaching was one of only a handful of professional careers Jim Crow America allowed blacks. Because of this, many black teachers in Jim Crow schools in the urban South had greater training than their white counterparts, with a higher proportion holding advanced degrees. As with churches, schools were of signal importance to Jim Crowed black communities. Teachers were made to understand their charge: responsibility to the wider collective. "The teachers were so loving, so caring . . . they valued us," one later remembered, and for many students this caring offset "some really awful things about [material conditions]"—crammed classrooms, second-hand books, inadequate supplies, et cetera.[5]

Traditional education in most black schools came packaged along with equally necessary survival training for Jim Crow life. Teachers gave students the tools for success in a world of inequality and unfairness. "We were very conscious that the playing field wasn't level, but we never felt inferior . . . never," a former student recalled. "Our [teachers] told us constantly, we were just as good as anybody else." At the same time, teachers and mentors were honest about the ways of the Jim Crow world, advising black youngsters that they would likely have to work twice as hard as whites to succeed. Still, optimists like Frank Sorrell, principal at School No. 181, a junior high school, assured his students that "things [were] getting ready to change," and they had to study and be prepared to take best advantage. Public schools and the high value placed on education played a key role in the production of the black narrative that opposed false narratives about black people that underpinned Jim Crow and white supremacism. Schools were the black counter-narrative institutionalized and put into action. "I loved my school," an alumna of elementary schools in the Waverly and Walbrook communities remembers. "There were always things going on where you were given the opportunity to feel good about who you were."[6]

Family and community folk, of course, aided the educational experience, making up in certain ways for the deficiencies with which students coped. Though Baltimore was segregated, an abundance of free learning experiences were open to all children "if you could just get on a streetcar and get downtown." Some families supplemented formal education with regular trips to the Enoch Pratt Libraries' Children's Division, secondhand bookstores, and any number of cultural events. Some of Baltimore's open-air markets had an international flavor, and children might see live animals and hear foreign tongues spoken there. "Children had all kinds of ways of learning if parents had time to take them—just for a [ten-cent] trolley ride downtown and back." This extracurricular education was not merely pastime; it was a mandate of sorts for many. "It was understood that you were going to go to school, you were going to do your work, you weren't going to bring home any babies!" Because of that nurturing, attention, and expectation, many young black people knew that they were not second-class in any way. "We thought there was something wrong with [whites] because they didn't recognize what was going on with us," one remembered.[7]

Best efforts of teachers, parents, and community members notwithstanding, the congestion that had historically plagued Baltimore's redlined black community meant that its schools were constantly stretched to meet too great a demand with too few resources. The custodial staffs were limited, for example. "I remember being afraid to go to the bathroom in elementary school," one former student recalls. "There was always water on the floor, it was always filthy." At Booker T. Washington Junior High School "conditions were atrocious," remembers a former student. "The classrooms were packed, there were fights in the cafeteria all the time, [and] the hallways were crowded."[8]

Most impactful, there were never enough resources or supplies to go around. Students in some of the most congested neighborhoods went to school in shifts, a morning shift and an afternoon shift. In most schools, students shared textbooks—old, obsolete, textbooks deemed no longer fit for white students. No white student ever received a textbook that had been taken out of circulation at a black school. As a result, it was generally believed, the curriculum of black schools in Baltimore was about a year behind that of white counterparts. Hand-me-down books, hand-me-down buildings, overcrowded classrooms, staggered attendance schedules: all combined to see blacks schools get less work done in a year than white schools. As black children progressed upward through the grades, for many this resulted in an accumulated deficiency. Thus, while Jim Crow had never come to define black people, black culture, or the black community, everyone in West Baltimore understood that separate had never been equal, especially when it came to educational resources.[9]

### It Is Later Than You Think

"We [blacks] as Americans do not accept segregation," one activist clarified at the time, "but [it] is forced on us." While demanding at least equality in separation in the meantime, the ultimate goal was clear: "We are determined not to stop until segregation is no more." Since the initial enthusiasm of the March on Annapolis in 1942, the school board had failed to address inequities in black education. As the tenth anniversary of the march neared, black organizers and activists seemed colored with the mood of *Murray* as they demanded full implementation of separate-but-equal mandates. They would only acquiesce to "separate" if it could be shown to be equal. As such, once again, sights were set on the undeniable advantage that Baltimore's schools offered white over black, especially at the upper end of educational programs.[10]

As late as the war years, the Baltimore Board of School Commissioners continued to downplay black complaints of inequity between "colored" school curricula, facilities, resources, and support and those of whites. The board turned an especially deaf ear to the unique programs whites enjoyed exclusively. These included specialized vocational offerings, college preparatory training, and engineering courses. As Howell Baum demonstrates, the Baltimore NAACP understood the importance of specialized and vocational training to black progress in wartime and to earning capacities and the growth of the black middle class in the postwar years. Thus, access to education in highly sought disciplines became an issue of particular significance.[11]

The equalization strategy also necessarily brought attention to differences between black and white schools. Since the mid-1930s, NAACP lawyers had successfully shown inequality under Jim Crow—clear and indisputable violations of *Plessy*'s "equal" mandate for the maintenance of segregation—as in the watershed 1936 *Murray v. Maryland* case. As Nathan Margold, Charles Hamilton Houston, and others had predicted (see chapter 2), circumstantial desegregation was accomplished by focusing on this standard. Thus, it had been successfully argued before the courts that unique or circumstantial publicly supported opportunities (like law schools and municipal golf courses) were open to whites but fully excluded blacks with no reasonable expectation of duplication. In these cases, "separate" could not provide "equal," and therefore the constitutional standard could not be met. Equalization suits seeking circumstantial desegregation remedies provided the first legal victories over Jim Crow in Maryland, and throughout the South from the 1930s through the 1950s.

In the 1938 case *Missouri ex rel. Gaines v. Canada* (identical to its antecedent *Murray*, which only reached state appellate court), the U.S. Supreme Court held that where white students enjoyed access to public professional schools (a law school in this case), comparable in-state education had to be provided for blacks. By the postwar years, however, courts deliberated on whether hastily arranged measures to satisfy separate but equal met constitutional standards of equality. In *Sweatt*, the state of Texas had hurriedly set up a blacks-only law school when faced with desegregation suits against the whites-only University of Texas law school. Beyond the fact that a so-called law school existed for blacks (tangible equality), the court nonetheless found substantive problems regarding what could not be so hastily arranged: intangible equality—the intrinsic value of being taught by experienced practitioners, employment prospects that flow from professional relationships developed during training, perception of peers regarding quality of training, and other characteristics. These standards came to bear on the circumstantial desegregation being considered by the Baltimore schools.[12]

By the 1950s, black activists were seeing curricular differences in Jim Crow education systems as an exploitable vulnerability in the evolving white liberal political culture. Through letter writing, lobbying, and litigation, black activists worked to call attention to this inequity, as evidenced clearly in Baltimore's Polytechnic Institute for Boys. "Poly," as it was known, was a high school that offered a four-year advanced curriculum designed to prepare students for college entry and pursuit of an engineering education. This advanced curriculum was called the "A" course, and graduates of the program were generally certified and entered college as sophomores. The "A" course was a unique feature of Poly that distinguished it from other public schools in the city. Meeting certain academic criteria for entrance, any student could get a great engineering education at Poly. Any student, that is, who was also a white boy. For white girls, Western High School at least offered an "A" course in liberal arts, but there was nothing comparable in the city for black students.

The Ford's Theatre desegregation campaign during this time (see chapter 5) came as an epiphany of sorts to liberal, anticommunist white interracialists like those of the Baltimore chapter of Americans for Democratic Action (ADA). The organization had played no pronounced role in the campaign against Ford's, but individual members were inspired by it and looked to carry some of that momentum forward. Further, as leftists had been suspected of playing at least some role in the campaign against Jim Crow at Ford's, it was important to many in the local ADA that, in the name of liberals' effort to purge leftist influence from American life, their organization demonstrate concern for social justice and commitment to interracialist causes. White ADA members sought greater (if still limited) visibility for themselves working on domestic racism, and, as they did, blacks demanded action from them. More and more white liberal organizations began to advocate on behalf the black struggle. In this way, southern ADA chapters like Baltimore's had to run ahead of the national organization. Its partner in this work—for many obvious reasons—would be the Baltimore Urban League. The BUL and the Baltimore ADA had collaborated on previous initiatives.[13]

Under Edward Shakespear Lewis, its leader from 1931 to 1942, the BUL had taken a strong position as advocate and agitator, challenging discrimination in labor during the New Deal years. In the process, it had transformed itself from an advocacy and education entity into a standard bearer of reform interracialist activism. After 1950, the BUL came to be led by another visionary executive director, Furman L. Templeton. Templeton continued moving the BUL in an activist direction, with education and job training receiving priority. This shift to some degree reflected shifts among white liberals, who had always held influence with local Urban Leagues despite strong and apparently independent black directors.

Templeton reached out to white liberals generally (not all of whom appreciated his activist orientation) and the Baltimore ADA specifically. In the fall of 1951, addressing a Baltimore ADA gathering on "Baltimore's Minority Problem: What Is the ADA Doing and What Could It Do?," Templeton challenged the mainly white audience to "strik[e] out at race restrictions wherever they occur," as in the then-ongoing picket of Ford's Theatre. By the spring of 1952, the Baltimore ADA reported to its members that its Race Relations Committee had been "studying the problem of segregation in the public school system," and that "various approaches to the question [were being considered] together with a course of action." Templeton had planted a seed with the Baltimore ADA, and by the summer 1952 the seed had sprouted, and then a plan began to flower. At Templeton's instigation, Margret Neustadt, chair of the Race Relations Committee, spearheaded the formation of the Coordinated Committee on Poly Admission (CCPA), with hopes of gaining access for blacks to the benefits of a Poly education.[14]

It is important to note the traditions in Baltimore student activism from the interwar years and into the postwar years. Black student activists had always been visible. For example, most members of the City-Wide Young People's Forum in the 1930s had been twentysomethings like Juanita Jackson Mitchell, but some had been even younger. Likewise, in the search for test cases ultimately leading to *Murray v. Maryland*, a number of students at Morgan College—all in their late teens and early twenties—had stepped forward to participate. This student activism continued in the 1940s. For example, Harry A. Cole (future state senator and appellate judge) addressed the participants at the 1942 March on Annapolis when he was a student at Morgan. In 1947 a large body of Morgan students demonstrated at the statehouse against budgetary neglect of the school.[15]

High school students were also active, especially those embracing radical interracialist positions and involved in direct action. These students made lasting impressions and solid contributions to the enduring black struggle for equality. As might be guessed, a particular target of young people's activism was Jim Crow recreational facilities. As blacks slowly gained access to public spaces of Baltimore in the postwar years, student activist roles proved key. For example, in December 1947, young basketball players agreed to participate on an interracial basketball team in a campaign to increase public dialogue about Jim Crow. Organized by a white man affiliated with the local Progressive Citizens of America (PCA), Philip Boyer, the Fulton neighborhood team registered to compete in the Bureau of Recreation's Division of Amateur Sports League. In its first game, Boyer's team competed against an all-white squad. No one involved in the game or witnessing it objected to black players participating. Learning of the team's interracial composition after the fact, however, the Baltimore Parks Board suspended it, ordering an investigation. This became a minor controversy for several months and at least achieved its aim of increased public discourse regarding the future of Jim Crow in the city.[16]

A range of social justice groups, civic organizations, and private citizens took the park board to task, including the Baltimore CIO, the National Lawyers Guild, the Baltimore branch of the NAACP, and the Baltimore Interracial Fellowship. The Baltimore branch of Americans for Democratic Action flatly accused the board of protecting segregation so that political gain might be realized by exploiting racial tension. The Baltimore Urban League advised the board to be wary not to retard the "natural" and "willing" development of interracialism, especially in amateur sports. J. E. T. Camper, the black physician and activist, at this time a member of a local PCA affiliate, charged the board with duplicity, noting that it had never objected in the past to the mixed-race football teams which regularly played at the city's largest venue, Municipal Stadium on Thirty-Third Street.[17]

As the board ultimately had to answer to the mayor of Baltimore, Thomas D'Alesandro received criticism too. "I, as a member of the so-called 'majority,' [am] sick of the burdens heaped on our consciences by . . . the crimes and sins which other members of our so-called 'race' practice smugly and gratuitously and persistently against our fellow man," one citizen complained. Likewise, Alice Arrington, president of the Maryland League of Women's Clubs insisted to D'Alesandro, "This is not only a time when we must affirm our belief in democracy . . . we must [also] help see that it works."[18]

One problem in the emerging Cold War climate was the PCA's leftist bent. The board rejected the group out of hand for that reason alone. "We cannot," board chair Robert Garrett told the mayor, "cater to an element that knowingly or ignorantly is disloyal to this country." "There are many good proposals that suffer from bad sponsorship," D'Alesandro reminded Garrett. "The Board should neither allow [the PCA] to dictate a change in policy . . . nor should the Board feel driven to take the opposite position merely because this organization had interceded." In the end, the PCA's point had been made. The student activists had demonstrated their willingness to contribute to the struggle despite persecution.[19]

The following spring, in 1948, a project almost wholly of young people's making shed even brighter light on student activists. An interracial group of young people affiliated with the local chapter of the Young Progressives of America, the student organization of the PCA, joined with a group of black teens in a premeditated attack on the park board's segregated tennis facilities. Similar to what black golfers faced (see chapter 4), black tennis players were offered only poorly planned and badly maintained facilities. The Young Progressives of Maryland joined with the all-black Baltimore Tennis Association in a demonstration. As they notified the park board, the press, and the general public in advance, they would play together on the whites-only Druid Hill Park courts.[20]

Witnessed by hundreds, fifteen players of both races from nearby neighborhoods met at Druid Hill Park courts on July 11, 1948, and began to play. Ignoring orders to cease, desist, and disperse, the players simply sat down on the courts awaiting arrest. Onlookers expressed their distaste for the ludicrous display of governmental power—"Fascist! Gestapo!" several shouted. Ultimately the players were not charged with violating segregation laws but with refusing to obey an officer. Soon thereafter, fifteen hundred citizens assembled around the Northern District Police Station as the activists were booked inside. The action and arrest made national headlines. The trial for those arrested in the "Druid Hill Tennis Case" began in October 1948 and ended with seven convictions for disorderly conduct with intention to incite a riot. Mayor D'Alesandro publicly kept his cool, but behind-the-scenes conversations reveal that he did not appreciate the park board picking such poor fights. Added to these orchestrated postwar statements by young Baltimoreans calling for a move away from segregation must be added countless personal acts of defiance to Jim Crow committed by young people in parks, playgrounds, and other public spaces. Most would not consider themselves activists, of course. But the courage and fearlessness they exhibited would be important in activist campaigns in the 1950s.[21]

Student and parent activism would be key to postwar equalization efforts in schools, and many eagerly participated. Social proximity to whites was neither a goal nor incentive. Rather, the driving factors entailed curricula and a desire for greater access to resources and opportunities] By the spring of 1952, Coordinated Committee on Poly Admission recruitment of viable student candidates for Polytechnic High School began. Activists sought talented black male candidates who would press for admission to Poly and who would have the support of their families and the community, which was seen as being critical. Albert Hawkins Sr., a government worker, came home one day in 1952 to find his wife excited. Something truly wonderful had happened, she said. Before she could explain, the doorbell rang, and then two people were let in. There in the Hawkinses Walbrook Avenue home, the visitors explained that they were from the Baltimore Urban League and the Baltimore NAACP. They told the Hawkinses that according to school records, their son, Albert Jr., was smart enough to benefit from the best school in the city. Albert Sr. remembered later, "It was one of the proudest moments of my life."[22]

Though the local ADA and Baltimore Urban League had initiated the formation of the Coordinated Committee on Poly Admission (CCPA), others soon became involved. The Baltimore NAACP joined the CCPA soon after its formation, as did the Council for Human Rights and the Citizens Committee on Education. Juanita Jackson Mitchell had several other boys and their parents attend meetings at the NAACP office. As head of the Baltimore NAACP's legal committee, Carl Murphy also participated fully in the effort. Thurgood Marshall returned to Baltimore from the NAACP's New York offices to attend the meetings. William Clark Sr. and Susie Dowse Clark went to these meetings, and their sons, Carl and William Jr., were recruited. The Clarks were very open to the idea of their sons applying to Poly, as was Nathaniel Redd's mother, Esther Redd. Gene Giles's family got wind of the possible desegregation of Poly; his teachers and school administrators had chosen him based on scholastic ability, aptitude, personality, and how he handled himself. The Clark brothers and Gene Giles—friends who played pinochle together from time to time—were the only three students from Paul Lawrence Dunbar, the blacks-only high school in East Baltimore, to apply to Poly, and they were the only three who were about to be tenth graders. The others, from Booker T. Washington Junior High School, would apply as ninth graders.[23]

Student willingness notwithstanding, the Baltimore school board still had to be convinced to approve even this circumstantial desegregation. The black activist tactic was to first press liberal white board members to act on their behalf—to instigate policy confrontations between liberal whites and the conservative forces that maintained segregation. If this lobbying did not produce results, however, litigation would ensue. Of the school board's nine commissioners in 1952, one was black. Dr. Bernard M. Harris had come over from the parks board to hold what had become the "black seat" on the body. While the board conceded a fundamental inequality between black and white public schools in Baltimore, its white members generally feigned powerlessness to bring about deliberate corrective measures. Even though led by liberal idealists, the board moved haltingly when confronting the inequality of segregation. Their response had always been to investigate ways of building out the capacity of black Jim Crow schools, and even that was a dead end: no action would follow. In the end blacks inevitably had to continue going without, an outcome the white board members lamented "they [the board] had no choice but to live with."[24]

According to board member Walter Sondheim, by the time the CCPA was organized, white racial liberals on the school board had been in search of an opportunity to undermine the legitimacy of Jim Crow—to "breach the walls of segregation." However, any effort in this direction would be mediated by their unwillingness to challenge Jim Crow's legal underpinning. The white liberal commissioners only sought to "provide an opportunity *within* the law,"

Sondheim later said, "to move the school system forward to some extent." In spite of Commissioner Harris's prodding, this was certainly not an activist body. As such, while board leaders investigated the potential need for desegregation, they also directed that a plan be developed for one of the blacks-only schools to inaugurate an "A" course equivalent to Poly's.[25]

On September 2, 1952, with the school year scheduled to begin in a matter of days, the school board convened an intense public hearing on the matter, inviting certain groups to make a case for or against desegregation. Board president Roszel Thomsen reiterated throughout the session that whatever the personal feelings for or against, the consideration had to be purely procedural and legalistic. "The [board] has really very little discretion in the matter," he said. For Thomsen, "the only real question before the School Board is whether the proposed curriculum in one of the Negro schools which has been planned and set up by the [Department of Education] will be substantially equal to the Polytechnic 'A' course." If it was judged equal, segregation was to continue. If not, the black students were to be admitted to Poly.[26]

In the end, responding as the U.S. Supreme Court had in *Sweatt* (1950) when faced with hastily arranged educational programs at blacks-only schools as a measure to preserve racial segregation, Baltimore school commissioners determined that a parallel "A" course established in a matter of weeks at Douglass would not equal Poly's. Days later, fifteen black boys entered Baltimore Polytechnic Institute, enrolled in the "A" course: Leonard Cephas, Carl Clark, William E. Clark Jr., Milton Cornish Jr., Clarence Daly, Victor Dates, Elmer German, Gene A. Giles, Albert Hawkins Jr., Linwood Jones, Nathaniel Redd, Edward Savage, Everett Sherman, Robert Young, and Silas Young. Shortly after the semester began, having encountered only mild protests, several of the boys told Baltimore *Sun* reporters that their situation had become normal: "It's just like being in any other school."[27]

The admissions at Poly represented a breakthrough toward equality in secondary education. But unlike the similar *Murray* victory sixteen years earlier, the Poly victory was quickly tempered by the refusal of the Baltimore Board of School Commissioners to extend integration beyond that specific instance. These two developments—Poly admission of black students and the lack of transferability of this integration to other schools, much less system-wide— should not be disconnected. White liberals on the board were clearly uncomfortable with the idea of being seen as ushers of the end of Jim Crow education, and they quite pointedly resisted doing more than they already had.

Other Baltimore whites shared that perspective. Reporting and opinion in the mainstream white daily *Sun*, for example, poured water on the fire, pointing out that the Poly ruling merely exposed a loophole in the system.

"The provision of the City Code regarding segregation still stands," the paper opined. Despite such assurance, however, some citizens sharing their opinions with the *Sun* refused to deny the portent of the Poly admissions, and one cryptically admonished whites, "It is later than you think." Whites called on the mayor and the city council to demand respect for the segregation lest it be "thrown into the trash can." In the end, whether or not the liberal whites of the school board responded to the negative public discourse or to private pushback against their Poly decision, they clearly looked to tamp down the decision's impact. In that regard, Poly must be seen as an end rather than a beginning, representing the culmination of *Murray*'s legacy with regard to circumstantial desegregation as a viable resistance tool.[28]

A truer portent of the coming years emerging from the Poly decision received scant attention at the time from the black or white press. Within weeks of the Poly desegregation in September 1952, black students, parents, community organizers, and activists in the Gwynns Falls neighborhood pushed for access to two whites-only neighborhood schools, Western High School for Girls and Elementary School No. 60. The group was led by Martha Pulley, president of the Parkview Improvement Association. As theirs was a racially transitioning community, the activists claimed new proximity as rationale— an argument that had previously seen Easterwood Park redesignated for blacks in 1950. Yet Pulley's group also pointed to deficiencies in the material aspects of education resulting from chronic overcrowding in blacks-only schools. The group seems to have made no formal petition to the school board (perhaps after consultation with other activists), so it is not clear if it would have demanded desegregation as a remedy, allowing blacks and whites to attend them together, or if they would have accepted a redesignation of both schools from whites-only to blacks-only, as happened with Easterwood Park.[29]

For its part, the Baltimore NAACP also pressed school desegregation immediately upon the Poly ruling. Branch president Lillie Jackson requested permission from the school board to conduct a survey of the entire Baltimore public school system. Jackson asked to inspect records, plant facilities, and other measurable factors in hopes of demonstrating system-wide inequity, such that system-wide desegregation might be required. Denied that avenue, black activists persisted by identifying two new targets for circumstantial desegregation, the whites-only Mergenthaler Vocational High School of Printing and the "A" course program at the white Western High School for Girls. Among the city's vocational education schools—Edison (for white boys), Barton (for white girls), and Carver (for blacks)—Mergenthaler Vocational, or "Mervo" in the local parlance, was the only school with a linotype-printing program. Baltimore moved to update Mervo's facilities in the early 1950s, at the same time building a new and separate school for black students, Carver. However, Carver would open in West Baltimore, near Easterwood Park, without a linotype program. Meanwhile, Western represented the only public high school in Baltimore offering the advanced college prep "A" course" to female students. As noted, Western's "A" course focused on liberal arts. As with boys in Poly's engineering "A" course, girls completing the program at Western were generally accepted into college with sophomore status. Indeed, for college-bound young women in the city, "Western was *the* school." Thus, before the first desegregated school year at Poly had concluded, six black boys had sought permission from the Baltimore Board of School Commissioners to be admitted to the printing program at Mervo, and twenty-three black girls had declared their desire to pursue Western's "A" course.[30]

With Mervo and Western, as with Poly before, the white board members' primary inclination had been to attempt duplications of programs at black schools, even if in makeshift, hastily organized fashion, for the preservation of Jim Crow. Their duty to protect the right of black citizens to equal and high-quality education was only a secondary consideration. This was done despite the fact that the Supreme Court had already frowned upon such transparently insincere machinations. In this case the scrambling to make "equal" took place despite the fact that the board had admitted black boys to Poly only months before. The duplicity left some blacks incredulous. At a hearing where the quality of black schools was discussed, for example, Dwight Holmes, an activist and president emeritus of Morgan College, lamented aloud to the commissioners, "I ask you to give us a break! . . . You know as well as I do that [the black school facilities are not equal to the white]." Responding to the school board's deliberations on the matter, in his capacity as chair of the local NAACP's Legal Redress Committee, Carl Murphy spoke plainly to school leaders: if their ultimate intention was to deny, then the Baltimore NAACP wished the school system to formally turn the black students away as soon as possible so that court actions could be initiated. The applicants were, in fact, turned away. The programs at Carver and Mergenthaler were deemed to be equal enough, although no linotype training was offered at Carver. Regarding the "A" course, the white board members—including its self-professed liberals—expressed the opinion that a separate and equal program could be inaugurated at the blacks-only Frederick Douglass High School in time for the beginning of the 1953–1954 school year (only months away). From then, it would be built out incrementally. That too they deemed, would be equal enough. As Baum deduces, "Perhaps . . . white board members felt it would be politically difficult to give black petitioners everything they asked." Indeed, at least a few of the liberal commissioners felt as President Thomsen did, supporting the idea of letting the courts decide such matters. As Murphy had promised, suits were filed.[31]

Meanwhile, as the Baltimore combatants positioned themselves for a drawn out struggle, developments emerged nationally. Years earlier, in Topeka, Kansas, Oliver Brown had decided that his daughter was not receiving the public education to which she was entitled. His state disagreed with him. Across the Jim Crow South, people followed what became *Oliver Brown, et al. v. the Board of Education of Topeka, Kansas, et al.*, as it moved through the federal courts. Anticipating a ruling from the Supreme Court after final arguments in December 1953, a reporter for the Baltimore *Sun* put the obvious question directly to Baltimore mayor Thomas D'Alesandro: "If the Supreme Court outlaws segregation in the schools, would that mean that Baltimore Negroes would immediately begin using the same facilities as white children here?" D'Alesandro stated plainly that if desegregation was ordered, "it will be the duty and the responsibility of the Board of School Commissioners to carry out the mandate of the Supreme Court." The mystery was put to rest on May 17, 1954. With the Mervo and Western court cases still pending in Baltimore, the U.S. Supreme Court handed down its unanimous ruling in *Brown*: "In the field of public education the doctrine of 'separate but equal' has no place."[32]

## To Fare Ahead of Your Color Now

"Oh, baby! Oh baby!" Leonia exclaimed, "This is such a blessing. This is such a blessing!" Leonia Young, a teacher at Elmer A. Henderson Elementary, had just heard news over the radio of the *Brown* decision. It was May 17, 1954. She burst onto the front porch of her family home, ecstatic to share the "blessing" with her teenage niece, Lynda Hall. Leonia immediately appreciated the implications of access to better-funded schools for black students. The value of this access was not so much in the benefits of interracial exchange as in the material advantage that the public school system had always to that point afforded most white students. *Brown* could provide black students the opportunity for enrichment by materials that had not been previously available. The benefits of resources—the materials for learning—were the ultimate carrot enticing black parents and their children to be the "firsts"—the first black students at what had been whites-only schools. Most would wait and see. Was this opportunity real, or would white folks' ugliness reveal itself once again? As described above in the case of Poly, many of the first blacks entering previously whites-only schools were recruited to the task.[33]

*Brown* presented a great opportunity. In the near term, black students might be saved from the chronic material deficiency that had burdened previous generations. Going forward, presumptions of more equitable funding across the school system could mean alleviation of deficiencies altogether. Beyond that, the Supreme Court's ruling seemed a validation of the point of their enduring struggle for equality. That one of their own, Thurgood Marshall, had delivered the victory made the moment all the more gratifying. Not waiting for the school board to formally weigh in, Baltimore's black social justice community immediately began to plan for desegregation to start the ensuing school year. They would ask their children to be activists. While no one was dissuaded from transferring who wanted to do so, a concerted effort materialized to ensure that the most talented black students were among those first through the doors of formerly Jim Crow schools. Within days of the ruling, teachers shared news and background of the *Brown* case with students at Booker T. Washington Junior High. Several students were then ushered off to the counselor's office where they would be propositioned about being the first blacks in formerly whites-only schools. The school then reached out to parents, and conversations continued, family by family, around kitchen tables in West Baltimore.

From the earliest years of their resistance to Jim Crow education, pragmatic black nationalists worked to address the material deficiencies that segregation imposed on black students. Demonstrable qualitative and quantitative disparities existed in the public schools between black students and white students. Black school buildings were older, and facility maintenance allotments were inadequate. Black students' textbooks were shared and were discards from white schools, and student-teacher ratios were higher in blacks-only schools. These disparities amounted to violations of constitutional rights—Fourteenth Amendment guarantees of equal protection—the NAACP had argued. Since 1935 in Maryland with the *Murray* case, and at the Supreme Court three years later with *Gaines v. Missouri*, NAACP lawyers had sought equalization by what I have termed above "circumstantial desegregation." In case after case until 1950, by demonstrating disparities between what a state offered whites and what it offered blacks, the NAACP won desegregation suits across the South against colleges and professional and graduate schools. The constitutionality of segregated education categorically had not been challenged, however, nor had disparities between the races in Jim Crow grade schools and high schools. But by the summer of 1950, Thurgood Marshall and his team of lawyers had promised to do just that. Soon after, with a suit filed in South Carolina (*Briggs v. Elliott*), the first of five direct challenges to the constitutionality of Jim Crow education, ultimately combined upon reaching the U.S. Supreme Court as *Brown v. the Board of Education* (1954), had begun.[34]

Beyond simply demonstrating disparities in learning facilities along racial lines, the *Brown* cases pursued what Daryl Michael Scott dubbed the "intangible strategy." This approach built upon the last equalization decisions won by the NAACP. Leading to those earlier cases, two states had set up makeshift law school programs for blacks. Texas, for example, had set up a blacks-only law school in name only (providing scanty resources, facilities, and faculty) to avoid desegregation of its whites-only school. For the same purpose, Oklahoma officials admitted a black student to the previously whites-only law school but used partitioning and anterooms to effectively segregate that student from his white schoolmates within the law school itself. In each case, NAACP lawyers successfully argued that the use of race to deny black students the intangible benefits of legal education—prestige of faculty, networking with cohorts, reputation of the school, and similar characteristics—constituted violations of the Fourteenth Amendment.[35]

Now in the *Brown* cases (each of which concerned a primary or secondary school), the NAACP sought to reveal the intangible impacts of Jim Crow on children—that segregated schools fostered damage to black psyches—by incorporating the scholarship and expert witness testimony of social scientists, most importantly sociologists Kenneth Clark and Mamie Phipps Clark. Racial liberalism enjoyed a broad appeal with the postwar social science community, Scott explains. This led to the acceptance of the Clarks' theories, even in the absence of ample evidence in the literature supporting those theories. Other expert witnesses—few who had produced actual scholarship on the subject—lent their names and reputations to this line of argument against Jim Crow education.[36]

The "intangible" strategy and "damaged black psyche" argument were only part of the NAACP's case theory in *Brown*. In deciding for the plaintiffs, however, Chief Justice Earl Warren seized upon the damage theory, giving it a central place in his opinion. Explaining this, many scholars conclude that Warren considered the political implications; the defeat of Jim Crow could not be delivered as an accusation against southern whites. For a unanimous court he declared, "To separate [blacks] from others of similar age and qualification solely because of their race generates a feeling of inferiority as to their status in the community that may affect their hearts and minds in a way unlikely ever to be undone." Jim Crow education, he continued, "has a detrimental effect upon the colored children." He would not validate blacks' long-running demonstration of Jim Crow's moral bankruptcy or the material deficiencies foisted upon black students in the name of white supremacy. Indeed, Scott asserts, Warren's opinion "must be read as solely a device to placate" southern white segregationists at the hour of their rebuke. Warren repudiated "separate but equal" without repudiating whites and their demand for segregation. "The basic dishonesty of *Plessy* was allowed to escape censure," Richard Kluger observes, as Warren ended Jim Crow schools without condemning their purpose or perpetrators. What was more, the chief justice provided white America's move to correct its unnamed racism with, as Scott phrases it, "a ring of moral righteousness." For Kluger too, "The court was clearly taking pains not to level a finger [of accusation] at the [white] South."[37]

Meanwhile, desegregation for blacks in Baltimore following the *Brown* decision would not so much be "therapeutic" for "damaged psyches" but rather remedial and reparative with regard to the material deficiencies Jim Crow had always imposed on black students in black schools. With *Brown* won, activist students in the mode of "first blacks" stepped forward to demonstrate that not only were they ready to compete academically with whites now but also that they had always been doing more with less.

The pitch to students and parents was framed in the language of race activism. Many adults regarded being a "first black" as a duty and service to the race. "We were told [essentially] that the weight of the whole thing was on our shoulders," Anastatia Phillips Benton later recalled. As Michael May, headed to Baltimore City College high school that fall, came to understand it, "They wanted people who were going to succeed." "Somebody had to go there and do this," Alfreda Hughes remembers; it was necessary, she and others were told. Keiffer Mitchell, who was not yet eligible for high school but would transfer to a previously whites-only junior high school, heard from his mother, Juanita Jackson Mitchell, "You are a freedom fighter." He had to make his contribution.[38]

Like Keiffer Mitchell, many of the students who would be among those "first blacks" quietly accepted the activist mantle and "freedom fighter" mission for more or less personal reasons. Alfreda Hughes was the youngest daughter of Baltimore NAACP attorney W. A. C. Hughes Jr. and participated in school desegregation as an extension of her father's work. Similarly, reflecting upon the responsibility borne by her great-grandfather, Edward David Bland, a Reconstruction era senator in Virginia, Ann Todd Jealous understood that "if we went to this white school, and if we did well, it would make things easier for black people . . . [if] we messed up, then it would not." Her would-be Western classmate Carol St. Clair likewise hailed from a prominent black family. There was a high school in Dorchester County, Maryland, named for one of her ancestors, and her grandfather had been a city councilman there for fifty years. With this in mind, even while also realizing that desegregating Western "might not be fun," Carol St. Clair determined to take up the cause for equality at Western High School, which had moved to Centre Street in downtown Baltimore.[39]

Despite courage by young "first blacks", their families were not blind to the potential risk. "I was selfish," Mamie Bland Todd, Ann's mother, remembered. "I didn't have but one child; I didn't want her to be hurt." Like other parents, Mamie's concern was not so much for her daughter's physical safety. Rather, she feared that Ann would be treated poorly by resentful white teachers and administrators, something the girl had never experienced in any of her earlier schools. School was a place of nurture, not combat. Because of these same misgivings, many black parents flatly refused to subject their children to what was broadly recognized as "the experiment" of desegregation—at least in that first year. The lingering and historical distrust of white folks' aptitude for fairness toward blacks gnawed at them. Juanita and Clarence Mitchell, for example—in their dual capacities as parents and representatives of the NAACP, tried to recruit other students from the blacks-only Booker T. Washington Junior High School to be first blacks at historically white schools in the fall of 1954. Not only did they fail more often than not, upon making an appeal to a Parent-Teacher Association meeting they "were hooted down."[40]

A few months earlier the white liberals of the Baltimore school board had resisted desegregating the city's public schools, but with the sanction of the federal government via *Brown* it wasted little time in doing so. Meanwhile the state government in Annapolis—the State Board of Education and the Maryland attorney general—advised jurisdictions not to "jump the gun" by desegregating immediately. Like most of the South, Maryland counties hesitated or even pledged obstruction.[41]

Support for Baltimore's decision to move forward with desegregation immediately poured in from across the state and around the country, but so too did criticism. Walter Sondheim, who had become board president earlier that year, found himself subject to criticism. He received hate mail, and someone burned a cross on his lawn. The Baltimore City Council also criticized Sondheim and the school board for moving too fast, contending that the city was not ready. "Nonsense," said the *Afro*, "of course, we're ready."[42]

Traditionally, with a few exceptions, Baltimore's public school students were racially segregated but not districted. In this system, referred to as "freedom of choice" and "open enrollment," the intent was that no children would be forced to attend a school their parents did not choose for them. This practice continued after *Brown*. The school board simply removed the racial restrictions on transfers, envisioning a desegregated school system but not necessarily a truly integrated one. The compulsion for separation would not yet be replaced by compulsion for proximity.[43]

As the summer of 1954 progressed and the first day of desegregated schools loomed, most of the black girls who would begin at Western were not afraid, some because of disposition or because they were determined to be fearless, others because they did not know better. For Ann Todd, with no previous interaction with white peers, desegregation "was really like going to a different country . . . impossible to anticipate." Among the youngest of Western's "first blacks," Anastatia Phillips and Lynda Hall lacked the maturity to fully appreciate the historic moment. "I was a kid, [and kids are] fearless," Hall later remembered. The two were also best friends, and Hall would recall, "We figured we had each other." "Whatcha gonna wear?" was the most pressing question as the first day neared, Phillips noted. "Our concern was looking good," she remembered, "making sure that the crinolines were right!"[44]

Public school enrollment in 1954–1955 was largest to that point in Baltimore history. Though press reports vary, the total number of transfers creating desegregated classrooms in Baltimore following *Brown* was perhaps a few hundred, but these affected about six hundred classes in nearly thirty public schools. In Baltimore, as noted, the racial makeup of some neighborhoods was rapidly changing in this period. At the beginning of desegregation, many black families in these neighborhoods lived closest to an elementary school from which their children had earlier been barred. Now that these schools were open to them, most chose to enroll their children in them, mostly as a matter of convenience but also as a claim to neighborhood resources. A decision to travel a greater distance to another school likely was made only if the nearest school was deemed materially inadequate. With the fewer junior and senior high schools, however, it was necessary to send kids farther from home. Choosing to attend previously whites-only schools required black students to travel through potentially unwelcoming neighborhoods. For those evaluating the prospects of this choice, material benefits to be gained often seemed insufficient to make up for this downside, particularly when the school being considered was not one of the four elite public high schools, Poly, Western, City, and Eastern.

At any rate, the first year of desegregation in Baltimore amounted in many schools to not much more than a trickle. Among elementary schools, for example, Sir Robert Eden School (No. 20) in East Baltimore enrolled approximately 90 blacks among 936 students. Margaret Brent School (No. 53) on St. Paul in midtown added no more than 35 blacks to its enrollment of 1,007. The Arlington School, in the northwest suburbs (No. 234) gained only about 16 out of a total enrollment of 1,750. Only in a few instances, such as Oliver Cromwell School (No. 74) just north of downtown did black enrollment even come close to matching that of white students (275 black, 375 white). The formerly all-white junior high schools and high schools reached similar enrollment ratios to those of the elementary schools. Two previously blacks-only schools,

Booker T. Washington Junior High in West Baltimore and Harvey Johnson Junior High in South Baltimore, near the Inner Harbor, gained one white student each. Among the formerly all-white high schools, Western, the girls' school, enrolled the highest number of blacks, twenty-three.[45]

Parents and community folk supported their young people as they could. Keiffer Mitchell's first day as one of only eight blacks out of twenty-one hundred students at Gwynns Falls Junior High School in the Edmondson Village section of West Baltimore was fraught with intimidation and anxiety. The neighborhood had been perceived as a paradise for white-collar and blue-collar whites, safely beyond black residential reach, just a few years before. The impending desegregation swelled fears of a "Negro invasion." As Keiffer approached the school that first day, a mob of whites cursed and jeered him. He had taken public transit that first day, but the next day and every school day for six weeks after, his father drove him to school. With the boy safely at school, the elder Mitchell staged a one-man counter-demonstration. "I Am an American, Too," proclaimed his picket sign as he marched back and forth in front of the school.[46]

At Western, Anastatia Phillips's father drove a group of girls to the school's downtown campus on the first day of classes. There was no demonstration when the girls arrived. They knew that they weren't wanted, they later recalled, but no ugliness seems to have occurred that day. Midway through the morning, five girls were called down to the building's entrance. The offices of the *Afro-American* were just up the block at Eutaw Street, and a photographer had walked down to record the historic occasion.[47]

The "rather humdrum" response (in the *Sun*'s description) that the new black students at Western met that day pretty much represented the first desegregated school year in Baltimore, but Keiffer Mitchell's experience showed portent too. As the Baltimore *Sun* cautioned editorially, "To say that opening day went smoothly is not to say there will be no cases of friction in the weeks ahead." The second day of school entailed some of this friction, though few in the classrooms knew of it. As Kenneth Durr writes, "School integration gave rise to a number of white supremacist, anti-integration organizations." In Baltimore seven parents and six students, aided by the Maryland Petition Committee (MPC) and the National Association for the Advancement of White People (NAAWP) filed a petition for mandamus, contending that Baltimore law required segregation, not only of students but faculty too. Former Baltimore resident Bryant Bowles led the NAAWP. Some thirty-four hundred Baltimoreans signed a petition supporting the NAAWP stance.[48]

That failing, the MPC, NAAWP, the Baltimore Association for States' Rights (BASR), and other white nationalist Citizens' Council organizations in the

South began a resistance campaign against school desegregation immediately after desegregation began in the fall of 1954. In symmetry with the black struggle, the working-class white resistance to desegregation in these years used direct action. By and large, the MPC, NAAWP, BASR, and the like were not composed of the southern business and economic elites more commonly associated with white Citizens' Councils. Rather, they attracted white nationalists, "the more militant white supremacists," Clive Webb writes, "who made less pretense of operating within the democratic political process." Kenneth Durr notes Baltimore's Wilma Longmire, for example, a white working-class immigrant from Tennessee who parlayed her frustration over racial desegregation in schools into a leadership role with the white nationalist movement.[49]

Over the next several years a racist and white nationalist reaction played out, often organized but seldom violent. For example, the MPC lobbied the Maryland legislature for a bill to "provide assistance to those Negroes who wish to return to Africa." Another proposed measure would have allowed whites to access public funds for private education, and still another would have given the white people of Maryland "the right to initiate legislation by a referendum," in all likelihood with the thought that this might foster resumption of unadulterated white supremacy.[50]

Since the MPC, NAAWP, BASR, and the like were not demonstrably violent or engaged in illegal activities, the FBI headquarters pointedly reminded its field offices that "no [formal] investigations of [them] should be conducted." That said, the bureau stated that it was also "imperative" that field offices maintain close scrutiny of such organizations and their members. Informants within these groups, including those in Baltimore and throughout Maryland, were routinely employed by the FBI. By the spring of 1958, however, informants made it known to the FBI that the BASR, for one, was "not very active" — "they only meet once in a while, and the reason for lack of meetings and inactivity is that no one is taking interest in the group." "In Baltimore, extremist [whites] . . . were usually on the scene when racial conflict arose," Durr writes, "although rarely did they carry much influence among other whites." Work in rural Maryland Citizens' Councils continued more robustly, however.[51]

Meanwhile, in school classrooms and hallways, whatever animosities existed went largely unspoken. Western High School offers several examples of adjustments to desegregation. New black students there later recalled that their reception by some teachers had been "cold and chilly." This scenario had concerned Mamie Todd back in the spring as she had contemplated her daughter Ann's prospective transfer. "I don't know why some people don't stay where they're wanted," one English teacher announced rhetorically to her students in class one day. Other teachers were said to have marked roll books with black stars to designate black students. However, one teacher's iniquitous evaluation of black students provided an opportunity for a community intervention of sorts. This teacher, a French teacher, who seated the black students in the rear, along the back wall of the classroom, and withheld conversational civility from them, also discriminated in grading the girls' papers, holding black students to an unfairly demanding standard. "By October, all of us were doing poorly," Lynda Hall later recalled. Among those victimized by this teacher was Alfreda Hughes, whose mother, Blanche Dogan Hughes, had been a French teacher herself. "My mother came up to the school and confronted her," Hughes would remember. "[The teacher] turned red as a beet, and didn't know what to say . . . she had never been confronted by a black person." The teacher quit before the year was out. Minor though it was, this sort of victory could be sustaining for a black girl in a largely white school in the era following *Brown*.[52]

Western was not wholly hostile, however. In the case of the youngest white girls at Western—those who shared classes with the new black students who entered as ninth and tenth graders—the ignorance of youth reduced tense moments to few. "I can't remember any of the white girls being nasty to me," one of the blacks at Western would recall. Many white girls there were eventually cordial to their new schoolmates, at least in the classroom, though "once we [all] got out into the hall," Anastatia Phillips recalled, "they wouldn't speak to you, [and] if you were out in the street, they would not speak to you." Certainly desegregation fed the curiosities about race that some white Americans harbored. And this curiosity sometimes morphed into perversity—as when in the shower stalls after a gym class the black girls were uncomfortably ogled by their white classmates. "They thought we had tails," Anastatia recalled, "that's why they were staring, they were looking for our tails . . . that just floored me." Often these new students were the first blacks that the white girls had ever known, and they were certainly their first black peers. The only other blacks they had encountered with any regularity were the women who cleaned their homes. Some white girls at Western hailed from working-class families, but even many working-class white mothers seemed to have availed themselves of black "help."[53]

As for the faculty at Western, it had its share of liberals, and at least one white liberal activist taught at Western in these years. Dr. Una Corbett, an English teacher, was visible and active in many civic and social justice causes. In fact, during that first semester of desegregation, Corbett possibly escorted some of the young women at Western a few blocks down Howard Street from their Centre Street campus to the intersection of Lexington Street. There students observed the sit-in campaigns against Read's Drug Store then being executed by the Baltimore branch of CORE (see chapter 5). What is certain about Corbett's activism is that she was a leader of the Baltimore chapter of Americans for Democratic Action when that group worked with the Baltimore Urban League and the local NAACP to get qualified black boys admitted to the "A" Course program at Baltimore Polytechnic in 1952. Two years later she had black students in her own class at Western.[54]

During the first days of the school year, as she introduced her course to students, Corbett acknowledged the raised hand of one of the new black students, Lynda Hall. Hall had a question based on her previous experience as a student in Baltimore's Jim Crow blacks-only schools: "Which day of the week do we pass our book in?" Corbett did not understand at first, and the white students looked around at each other puzzled and amused by what seemed black naïveté. Not intimidated, Hall clarified her question: "How long during the week do we keep the book, and when do we turn it in so the other class gets a book?" After a few more awkward moments, Corbett realized what her new student meant. "Oh!" Corbett exclaimed. "Why, no . . . you keep your book all the time." The power of the historical moment struck Corbett then and there. Flushing, she turned quickly to the blackboard, her back to her class. When she finally turned to face her class again she had tears in her eyes. Gathering herself nonetheless, Corbett explained the nature of Lynda's question to the white students, and said of the black girls who had transferred from Booker T. Washington, "[They] have landed here [at Western], just as you have landed here, [and] without having a book all the time." Linda and the other blacks were gratified at Corbett's acknowledgment. Later in the day, the black teenagers eased any lingering tensions with humor. "What could be easier?" they teased. "We get to keep the book all the time!"[55]

For most of the students involved in desegregating Baltimore schools during the first week of the 1954–1955 school year, a quiet beginning soon gave way to mass demonstration by pro-segregation whites. As noted, a far-right white nationalist backlash had been organizing in the wake of *Brown* across the South, a campaign some called "massive resistance," but towns as far north as Milford, Delaware, population approximately fifty-two hundred in 1950, saw the likes of boycotts and school shutdowns. On Thursday, September 30, 1954, and continuing each school day through the middle of the following week, whites picketed and marched at a number of schools around Baltimore. That first day, a Baltimore *News-American* photographer captured a line of marching, picketing parents outside of School No. 34, in a largely white working-class South Baltimore neighborhood. They directed their anger not only at black interlopers but also at the elite and empowered institutions that had seemed to conspire against them in overturning segregation.

Mainly women, their signs declared "Segregation Is Our Heritage." Other scattered incidents that day and the next saw whites protest and act belligerently. At Southern High School on Federal Hill, Friday, October 1, 1954, a crowd amassed as protests and walk-out strikes by white students developed.[56]

On Monday, October 4, 1954, a throng of white protesters met students arriving at Mergenthaler Vocational Technical High School on Hillen Road a few blocks south of Morgan State College. They handed out literature, gave impromptu speeches, and urged white students to join them in a march through the city. As the mass moved down Hillen Road, turning west on Thirty-Third Street, it stopped at the campuses of Baltimore City College for Boys, and Eastern Senior High School for Girls, which sat contiguously on the south side of Thirty-Third, across from Memorial Stadium. The demonstrators attempted to intimidate black students (and many whites) as they were getting off municipal buses and heading into school. Michael May was one of those students, and he recalls that he had been enjoying his time at his new school—"until I got off of that bus [that day]." The Castle on the Hill, as City's campus was known, overlooked Thirty-Third Street several hundred yards below. A long and winding walk led from the street to the front doors of the school. The entire way was lined on both sides by "chanting, hissing, ugly, sign-carrying white people," May recalls. "They were hating me all the way up the path." His way was not impeded, no one attempted to assault him, but the intimidation quickened his pace. "I don't remember anything from the time I got off the bus to the time I got into the school . . . I was terrified." The four hundred or so demonstrators then went back down the hill and turned southward. Reaching downtown, they stopped to recruit at Western. Black parents of Western girls, learning of this, responded with added caution over the next several days. "I remember Daddy put that gun in his pocket because he didn't know what we were going to confront," Alfreda Hughes would recall. "Those were men [not kids] that were . . . [threatening] to beat us with baseball bats." "Daddy" was NAACP attorney W. A. C. Hughes Jr. "It was like Mississippi," Alfreda said.[57]

Receiving few converts at Western, the mass next moved toward City Hall, where they called for Mayor D'Alesandro (who was not in the building), before continuing toward the heart of the previous Friday's mass demonstration, South Baltimore. There they rallied for several hours at Southern High School. More than anywhere since the beginning of the impromptu march at Mervo, neighborhood whites in South Baltimore joined the protesters in the streets. They made their sentiments on desegregation clear with signs reading: "We don't want no Sapphires in Southern High School."[58]

Unlike the elite high schools that drew students citywide (Western, Poly,

Eastern, and City), Southern predominantly served its surrounding neighborhood. By the mid-twentieth century, that community was a working-class, hardscrabble bastion of white migrants to Baltimore from Appalachia, the Carolinas, rural Maryland, and other parts of the Mountain South. As one person recalled, "Those people didn't mind getting out there and brawling." Indeed, to students in other schools and in other parts of the city, Southern and its neighborhood, South Baltimore, seemed "another ilk . . . kind of a rough, hillbilly, white part of town." The working-class white rural migrant community there had "long bristled under the condescension of outsiders," Durr writes. The black and white middle class and the elites among these "outsiders" looked to South Baltimore's white working class and saw "bumpkins." That the anti-desegregation demonstration on October 4, 1954, would make its most pronounced statements at Southern High surprised no one. "What would you expect down there with those hillbillies?" one black mother explained.[59]

Meanwhile, news media, clergy, politicians, and others outside those identifying as liberals ridiculed white working-class Baltimore, questioning their patriotism in the Cold War context and seeing nothing in their complaint against desegregation but "fodder" for communists. The working-class white protesters in South Baltimore were accused of being pawns of outside agents (a charge black activists would have sympathized with). Only white nationalist organizers responded to the protests with encouragement. They too were excommunicated from the realm of the rational. As Clive Webb writes, "The members of these [white nationalist] organizations [we]re usually dismissed as uneducated, marginal members of society who suffered from some form of clinical psychosis."[60]

Shortly after the protests against desegregation, a coalition of interracialist opposition to it materialized in the form of the Coordinating Council for Civic Unity (CCCU), a representative body of nineteen organizations. Meeting with members of the school board and law enforcement agencies, the CCCU sought to punish the disruptive forces by enforcement of the truancy code and laws governing inappropriate behavior on school property. Fearing not only truancy and juvenile delinquency but also violent mob action and possibly even race riots, the CCCU requested that Police Commissioner Beverly Ober exhaust all legal means to dissuade the demonstrators from intimidating schoolchildren and disrupting the school day with on-campus demonstrations. Ober went on television to issue fair warning to all contemplating protest demonstrations. In no uncertain terms, Ober let it be known that the law would be enforced, and, if necessary, arrests would be made and offenders prosecuted. "Picketing and assemblies in the neighborhood of our various public schools . . . *will* cease tomorrow, or the police will take appropriate action." Many credited Ober with quelling the situation before it could get out of hand. "The firmness shown by the police force of Baltimore," community leaders acknowledged, "led to a rapid abatement of tensions."[61]

If these days appear mild compared to what came later in the 1950s—in Little Rock and Birmingham—it is important to note that black activists' tactic of instigating conflicts between whites over racism and white supremacy had materialized effectively. The government, which had given Jim Crow whatever strength it possessed, seemed—at least, in the eyes of white working-class protesters—to have switched sides. Indeed, the ability to summon the municipal police force *in defense* of the black struggle marked a turn. Black activists found, nonetheless, that they were asked to be patient as the state responded—and meanwhile white nationalism reemerged and white supremacy remained in place. "You are a very lucky nigger your address is Balto Md," Mary Smith assured the local Urban League's Furman Templeton in the weeks following *Brown*. "The white people have done plenty to help your race," the self-identified migrant woman lamented, "and you are to fare [too far] ahead of your color now."[62]

Thus, if at the beginning of the 1954 school year the black student integrators had thought perhaps that Jim Crow had been surrendered, the white protest of late September and early October disabused them. In its wake, many came to see that to maintain the courage of their convictions, to not be intimidated, might serve the cause of the race and not just their personal well-being. They had helped instigate confrontations between forces ordinarily and otherwise beyond black control, and they refused to be denied what so many had struggled before them to attain. A few generations earlier, as Jim Crow was being constructed, southern whites had been united—wealthy and poor, native and migrant, American-born and foreign-born—against blacks. But in the wake of *Brown v. Board of Education*, as part of the enduring black struggle for equality, with which young people had always played an important role, urban southern blacks had pitted white Baltimore against itself.

"I'm not enthusiastically happy, Thurgood, but I'm happy," Carl Murphy remarked after reading news of the Supreme Court's 1955 school desegregation implementation decree, known as *Brown II*, and its dubious "with all deliberate speed" mandate. From black vantages, school desegregation was supposed to be corrective, representing the most likely and effective path toward addressing the material disadvantage that Jim Crow had foisted upon black students. For those pioneering newly "black" neighborhoods, school deseg-regation was about making nearby schools truly neighborhood institutions. But to those engaged in the local struggle, Baltimore school desegregation was not "therapeutic."[63]

According to Baum, just before *Brown*, some of the local NAACP attorneys made half-hearted references to the black psychological "damage" theory and remedy during the school board hearings over the potential circumstantial desegregation of Mergenthaler Vocational and Western High School. If so, perhaps they were only pushing the national NAACP Legal Defense Fund's new line. Beyond this, there is no sense (and certainly no consensus) that everyday black Baltimoreans or blacks anywhere in the urban South felt their children were inferior or psychologically damaged by Jim Crow. Conversa-tions around Baltimore desegregation in 1954 give clues that the opposite was truer. Many parents sending their children into previously whites-only schools feared the potentially negative psychological impact of *greater* prox-imity to white resentment and persecution.[64]

In attempting to uncover what motivated urban southern blacks in school desegregation, it is best to set aside the portion of Chief Justice Warren's opin-ion that asserted, "Segregation of white and colored children in public schools has a detrimental effect *upon the colored children.*" Taking black Baltimoreans at their word, they sent their children into previously whites-only schools because they knew that their children's continued separation in schools, in a society still dominated by white supremacy, would never provide material equality. Until *Brown*, black children under Jim Crow had always been asked to do more with less. The "blessing" of *Brown*, then, was that a new, hopeful day had finally come.[65]

For most of the 1950s, even before *Brown*, the population of Baltimore city public schools grew. Additional black students enrolled, and they comprised more than eight out of every ten new students between 1950 and 1958. What was more, white student enrollment in Baltimore public schools began to de-cline by 1957. By the end of the decade, one out of every four black children in the city's public schools attended a school that had been whites-only before desegregation. Fifteen of those formerly whites-only elementary schools and two junior high schools were predominantly black by the end of the 1950s. In eight of these, black students made up 90 percent of the student population. All of this occurred because of residential racial turnover in the surrounding neighborhoods. Racial turnover can be seen not only as deeply influencing the course of school desegregation but even more so as a broader push for access to more space. By the end of the 1950s, black activists—prominently including young people—turned toward downtown again.[66]

## Sit Down Wins!

As early as 1953, Morgan State College student activists launched an extended nonviolent direct-action program under the auspices of their own campus-based organizations. They would call their tactic "passive resistance," as was common in the press before and after the Montgomery Bus Boycott, and principally they targeted public accommodations near their campus. In coming to this approach, the Morgan activists had been at least indirectly influenced by activists on the college's faculty associated with an emerging local chapter of the Congress of Racial Equality (CORE). The activists of CORE not only used nonviolent direct-action tactics and passive resistance doctrine, they were even more deeply committed to effecting desegregation: radical interracial change in America. The Morgan student activists, however, were not radical interracialists, nor was their nonviolence anything more than a tactic adopted out of practical considerations. Instead, as with much of the black struggle in the 1950s, sensing the fatal vulnerabilities of Jim Crow in the South, nonviolent direct action for the Morgan students served their radical rights-consciousness, allowing them to be proactive and direct in confronting the immorality of segregation. They were not averse to interracialism. In fact, they worked with white adults of the local CORE and with white student activists from other Baltimore campuses, particularly Johns Hopkins. Hopkins activists were generally affiliated with that campus's chapter of the Students for Democratic Action (SDA), a liberal anticommunist organization noted earlier whose parent group was the Americans for Democratic Action (ADA). Notably, because of this—and like their counterparts at Morgan—the Hopkins students' nonviolent direct action can also be seen as tactical rather than doctrinal. It served the SDA/ADA Cold War program, which in part sought to take the mantle of interracialist advocacy from the Left. For Morgan, though, even if interracialism represented a welcome by-product of their struggle, it was not the goal. The goal for Morgan students was the same as that of the larger black urban South since the beginning of Jim Crow resistance generations earlier: equality.

Student activism and campus-based organizing across the United States had a minor but visible tradition by the mid-twentieth century, generally tracking the themes and issues of student activism nationally. From the 1920s into the 1950s, reform and radical groups such as the American Youth Congress, the Socialist Youth League, the Young Communist League, NAACP Youth Council, Young Progressives of America, and Students for Democratic Action were venues for the activism of smallish numbers (perhaps thousands) of politicized young people. Not all schools were represented by such organizing. Levels of activism on college campuses reflected specific contexts and concerns, like the tolerance or intolerance of school administration, links to the broader world of activists, and setting (e.g., rural versus urban). Generally, the South—even the urban South—proved the greatest challenge for the radical groups. Radicals' influence fluctuated there, and radical strength on campuses came primarily during the Depression, though even then, it was said, "with much turnover" in membership. In the postwar 1940s, an anticommunist labor-liberal alliance generally replaced the previous Left-liberal one in strength and influence. The frenzied anticommunism on Capitol Hill in the House Un-American Activities Committee (HUAC) was replicated at every level of government nationwide. Reform groups emerging at this time, even on campus, reflected this turn, in part by having to be more circumspect and defensive.[67]

After 1948 the SDA worked toward desegregation at the same time it embraced anticommunism. The SDA's programs of civic education and legislative lobbying mirrored those of the ADA. However, the students often seemed more willing than the adult group to consider direct action not only to effect change but also to bring wider awareness to issues, particularly segregation.[68]

In early 1950s Baltimore, concurrent with the success of desegregating Ford's Theatre downtown, local SDA spokespeople were "investigating several possibilities" for taking up race relations projects. The SDA organized two chapters in Baltimore, one on the campus of Johns Hopkins University (JHUSDA) and the other a sort of catchall "Baltimore City" chapter (BCSDA). The latter came about mainly because of the inability to establish sustainable stand-alone chapters at other campuses, with Morgan State students exhibiting only "slight interest" in SDA and a Goucher College chapter amounting to little more than an unfulfilled dream after several years. Though the SDA was based on campuses, its role in the ADA was geared toward the ADA's anticommunist crusade. With very little concern for campus-based issues, the SDA struggled to demonstrate relevance to students.[69]

Even at Hopkins, the group's continued existence was tenuous. Although the Hopkins faculty was said to be "overwhelmingly liberal" and included the likes of C. Vann Woodward, who at the JHUSDA's behest lectured from time to time on the history of the South and segregation, organizers ultimately admitted that well into the 1950s the student body was "overwhelmingly conservative." In the wake of *Brown*, in fact, a number of Hopkins SDA members defected to the campus Republican Club. As a result, the BCSDA more than the JHUSDA worked off campus, largely in the general public. In the fall of 1954, for example, as the Baltimore public schools underwent the South's earliest implementation of *Brown*, the BCSDA executed an advocacy campaign, distributing buttons to high school students proclaiming "Democracy Begins in the Schools." Later, the JHUSDA participated in a broad fund-raising campaign in support of the Montgomery Bus Boycott. In the 1950s, however, as frenzied anticommunism grew by way of Senator Joseph McCarthy and a hyperactive HUAC, all but the most fervent liberal voices in the South would fall silent for several years. SDA membership and causes reflected this trend.[70]

Meanwhile, on black college campuses the principal entity organizing student activism and connecting it across regions was the NAACP, through its Youth Councils and College Chapters division. Begun in the mid-1930s, when the NAACP recruited Baltimore's Juanita Jackson to serve as the division's first director and principal architect, the Youth Councils and College division worked in chapters across the South throughout the 1940s and 1950s. By then, under the Washingtonian Ruby Hurley, the division deployed direct-action campaigns against Jim Crow public accommodations in large and small cities throughout the South and elsewhere, including Washington, Dallas, Louisville, Little Rock, Wichita, and Oklahoma City. It should be noted that NAACP legal experts such as Thurgood Marshall attempted to put a damper on direct action. Marshall and others lacked faith in direct action's efficacy and feared that students would be arrested for violating Jim Crow and then left to rot in jail, to bankrupt the NAACP through bail and litigation costs, or worse. (Marshall himself had experienced a harrowing brush with a pursuing lynch mob in Columbia, Tennessee, in 1946.) With Marshall's extensive experience, he believed direct action would gain little to show in the end.[71]

The NAACP's Youth Councils and College Chapters work emerged in the context of a broader effort by various organizations to mobilize American young people of all races and ranks toward effecting greater equality—not just in the nation but also internationally. Theologians like Mordecai W. Johnson, Vernon Johns, and Howard Thurman preached a radicalized Christian theory that resonated widely in the 1940s and 1950s. In the context of an emerging antiradical Cold War climate, the radical Christian message was especially useful for a time. It gave black student reformers the necessary theoretical ground to engage Left and liberal forces while remaining ideologically nonaligned. Inspired by *Brown*, the success of the Montgomery Bus Boycott, and the Christian example of the young Martin Luther King Jr. (himself deeply influenced by the likes of Johnson, Johns, and Thurman), black students pushed hard against Jim Crow throughout the 1950s. Few whites outside of the South, however, seemed to notice.[72]

During midcentury, Morgan's student body like those across the nation grew significantly. Among others, returning veterans of World War II and later Korea brought both maturity and militancy to the campus. As such, these years found black students organizing to claim their right to public space. Morgan students, for example, were visible and consistent from the beginning in the picketing of Ford's Theatre (1947–1952). On campus in these years, the students' Social Action Committee (SAC) became politicized, if not radicalized. Likewise, students were active immediately off campus in working for black access to public accommodations in the Northwood community.[73]

Back in 1919, the school's fifty-second year of existence, Morgan College had relocated to the then-rustic area later developed as Northwood. From that point forward, whites in the area behaved horribly. Verbal harassment and physical intimidation were commonplace. "They were very unfriendly, unpleasant, and made no secret about it," one student recalled. While blacks had experienced mainly frustration then, by the early 1950s they pressed more successfully for greater access to public accommodations in the neighborhood.[74]

In early 1953, students organized direct action against a lunch counter operated by the locally owned Read's Drug Store chain, two blocks west of the campus along Cold Spring Lane at Loch Raven Boulevard. Like many lunch counters in the city—and across the South—Read's served black customers only on a take-out basis. Blacks could not sit in the restaurant like other paying customers to enjoy a meal or talk with friends. One afternoon, Douglas Sands, a Morgan freshman, was literally pulled from his bed in Baldwin Hall and impressed into service by Freddie Randolph and Moses McDaniel, two upperclassmen organizers, to join the Read's sit-in. Sands, who had come to Morgan from rural western Maryland, had grown up watching his community folk subjected to the racist proclivities of small-town white people. He found his participation in direct action against Read's to be "liberating." "I began to realize . . . that I had come upon a time and place where I'd be able to respond to all the harassment that I saw my parents taking, all the denial I'd seen them going through," Sands recalled. "Carrying some of their wounds helps you to understand how people [became] so bitter, living separated as we did." Meanwhile, Read's held out in spite of student sit-ins.[75]

Despite Read's intransigence, Sands and his schoolmates were energized. By the following year, protest campaigns and direct action had shifted to other establishments in Northwood. Originally opened in the 1930s, Northwood Shopping Center had been remodeled and expanded beginning in 1949, gaining attractive amenities such as a movie theater and "one of the nation's most modern department stores." The revamping of Northwood Shopping Center, which lasted until the mid-1950s, brought benefits to everyone, including the Morgan community (the first municipal bus route reached the Morgan campus by 1955 as a result of the shopping center). Still, racism and Jim Crow were also in evidence. The shopping center built a seven-foot-high wall along the Hillen Road boundary it shared with the Morgan campus.[76]

Meanwhile, Sands grew into leadership on campus and among the community of student activists. A Committee of 100 was organized among students from the various Christian denominations on campus, and Sands was elected chairman. Sands spent most days juggling his studies and recruiting picketers. He arranged his class schedule so that he could lead demonstrations. And as had been the case in the 1930s and 1940s, a number of faculty and staff supported and encouraged student activism. McQuay Kiah, Morgan's assistant dean of men, was present at the earliest demonstrations. "He went the [first] night that I went," Sands recalled. The timing of the event and Kiah's involvement suggest that one of the initial activities of Baltimore CORE after its formation was the organization and perhaps training of a Morgan student contingent. As white student participants were regularly mentioned in press coverage, one may also conclude that some CORE-like organizing, however fleeting, took place on the campus of Johns Hopkins as well. Baltimore CORE was in its infancy still, having formed only months before, in January 1953, but found willing members on the faculty and staff at Morgan, such as Kiah. These were adults who had experience in interracialist activism thanks to projects like the picketing of Ford's Theatre in 1947–1952, and the teachers among them, in turn, engaged their students in the tenet of nonviolence. In the year leading up to CORE's organization, for general training purposes, would-be local leaders had requested a supply of literature from the national organization, including copies of CORE *Techniques and Restaurant Discrimination* and *What Is CORE*. By the late 1950s, little by little, Morgan students came to collectively appreciate nonviolent direct action as a useful tool for desegregation.[77]

More significant to students than Kiah, perhaps, was the presence of three members of the Morgan Political Science Department. According to their students, professors Alexander J. Walker, Robert Gill, and G. James Fleming "taught [direct action] in their classes . . . they'd teach you what you'd need to say." And they observed the demonstrations: "They were there watching the line." Indeed, activism was part of the culture of the college by the mid-1950s. It was one of the tasks that some professors put to their students. It was even something that students as a group expected of their leaders. Student government candidates included planks against Northwood racism in their campaign platforms: "That's my campaign pledge to you if you vote for me."[78]

Howard L. Cornish, director of the Morgan Christian Center, an independent entity on campus and just across Hillen Road from Northwood Shopping Center, also proved vital to the Northwood campaign throughout the 1950s.

A mathematics professor, Methodist minister, and Morgan alumnus, Cornish had a long history of activism, which began when he helped Juanita Jackson organize the City-Wide Young People's Forum in the early 1930s. A college chapter of the NAACP had existed at Morgan since the 1940s, and Cornish was its faculty advisor. He also allowed student activists to use the center as a base of operations. "We'd meet there during the day in between classes," Sands recalls, before beginning protests. Cornish would then keep the Christian Center open late into the night until demonstrations had ended.[79]

Student activists had the support of key faculty and staff at Morgan all along, and perhaps it was some of those faculty advisors who suggested the need for legal assistance in navigating the vagaries of Jim Crow law. That assistance would come from attorney Robert B. Watts, who embodied the Baltimore black struggle for equality. Watts was a Baltimore native, Morgan alum, and World War II veteran who had followed Donald Murray's lead through the University of Maryland School of Law (Class of 1949). He provided pro bono legal aid to the Social Action Committee. Help in this regard by the end of the 1950s also came from Juanita Jackson Mitchell—now an activist attorney, having earned a law degree in midlife in order to be of more service to the struggle.[80]

In the fall of 1954, with negotiations at a stalemate, Morgan students had returned to sit-ins and picketing at the Northwood Read's lunch counter. Of all the lunch counter chains in Baltimore at the time, Read's was the largest and the only locally owned chain. *Brown* was then being implemented across the city to the trepidation of many whites. Read's owners felt obliged to placate local white sensibilities and moved much more slowly than its competitors, many of whom had dropped Jim Crow over the preceding twelve months. As Read's held out, the national office of CORE, through its official organ, *CORE-lator*, issued an appeal for letter writing in support of desegregation of the chain.[81]

Pressure on Read's increased in early 1955. Thirty or more students began a continual sit-in at the Northwood Read's during the first week of January. The Northwood Read's began to show signs of weakness when, for example, a black waitress gave in to the demonstrators and served them against company policy. She was transferred to another location, and the company outwardly appeared unmoved.[82]

Meanwhile, a group of Morgan students commuting to campus through downtown staged an impromptu sit-in at another Read's location. "We wanted to sit down, unload our books, and get something hot to drink," a participant later admitted. "That's it." At any rate, responding to the culminating pressures and the futility of its position, the next day, Thursday, January 20, 1955—

mere hours after other Morgan students had concluded that day's sit-in at the Northwood store—Read's announced a new policy. "Our sympathy has been with the cause and we have sought to work out a solution which would be fair and could be accomplished with the least amount of discord," the company president's official statement claimed. That solution was to drop Jim Crow in all thirty-seven of its stores with lunch counters and to do so immediately. "Now Serves All," the *Afro-American* trumpeted. Even Baltimore CORE's activists, who had been negotiating behind the scenes while sit-ins were in progress, expressed surprise at the suddenness of the announcement.[83]

Later that year, in August 1955, the murder of Emmett Louis Till in Money, Mississippi, reverberated across the country. Then, that following winter, direct action against segregated buses in Montgomery, Alabama, inspired the students. In the meantime, Douglas Sands became president of Morgan's Student Government Association. On assuming this post, Sands penned an open letter to Northwood whites, made copies, and distributed it. "I took it to every house in the neighborhood," he recalled, "all the houses I could go to." Hoping to push student response to segregation beyond simple demonstration, Sands's letter was also an attempt to educate and to state the purpose of the student movement. The *Afro* excerpted the letter. "I believe that Baltimore must yield one day to the challenge of democracy and Christianity," Sands declared. "Mere admittance to a theatre means far less to us than the perpetuation of a democratic heritage. However, we feel that this beginning will awaken others just as it has stimulated us." Soon thereafter, reflecting his sense of the times, Sands changed the name of the Social Action Committee to "Political Action Committee," "to be more deliberate in how we challenge." Morgan's president, Martin David Jenkins, publicly disconnected the activism of students and faculty from the official policy of the public university. However he also made it clear that as citizens those students and teachers had every right to protest. Many of the mass meetings would take place on campus with little notice or fuss from the administration.[84]

Meanwhile, Dean Kiah and others connected with both Morgan and Baltimore CORE were joined by faculty members such as political scientists Robert Gill and Alexander Walker, who were familiar with direct-action methods though not formally members of CORE. These men prepared the Morgan students for activism—"they taught it in the classes," one former student recalled—and then observed the direct action on-site as it unfolded. Other Morgan faculty worked with students to conduct behind-the-scenes negotiation with segregators before direct action commenced. To reiterate CORE's method: those who could be persuaded to drop Jim Crow without sit-ins and pickets were given ample chance to do so. By that method, Morgan's Eugene

Stanley, a professor of education, and a contingent of students had negotiated for the desegregation of the lunch counter at the Northwood Kresge's in 1953. Direct action was never needed in that campaign.[85]

Gene Stanley was perhaps unique among members of early Baltimore CORE, black or white, as his involvement with CORE went back to the parent organization's beginnings. A Georgia native, Stanley had been active with an early CORE affiliate in Ohio, the Vanguard League, in the early 1940s, which probably served as his introduction to CORE. Soon thereafter he worked for a time on CORE's national staff as treasurer, a post he left to join the faculty of the North Carolina Agricultural and Technical College (NC A&T) in Greensboro as an assistant professor and dean of men. Maintaining his CORE connections, Stanley was one of the sixteen activists to participate in the historic Journey of Reconciliation in 1947, which no doubt portended his activism in Baltimore. As they stopped in various places along the way, Stanley and his CORE colleagues found the most enthusiastic reception for their nonviolent direct action among southern black audiences, especially college students. At any rate, for his role in the Journey of Reconciliation, Stanley lost his job at NC A&T, though it could have been worse. At a stop near Greensboro, North Carolina, where white thugs gathered to intimidate the activists, Stanley had attempted to calm things down but then narrowly escaped a beating, fleeing with the other activists. A few years later, Stanley arrived at Morgan.[86]

The impact of sharing such experiences with Morgan students can easily be imagined, and Stanley perhaps inspired young people like Freddie Randolph. In its coverage of the Northwood Read's campaign, the *Afro* mentioned a Morgan chapter of CORE, with Randolph as its head. Perhaps a CORE chapter had been started at the school but proved unsustainable or unnecessary, given the willing activism of student groups already active there. Across the South, CORE student chapters were short lived, to the consternation of national CORE leaders. In fact, only a few years later, CORE's headquarters in New York lamented the Morgan students' independence and propensity to adopt direct-action techniques "pioneered by CORE" but otherwise remain separate from CORE. In the end, CORE leaders consoled themselves, supposing that "Morgan students are typical of the active students all over the country— they prefer to be independent." They preferred, at least, to be independent of nonstudent leadership.[87]

In the fall 1955, after the Read's victory the previous semester, Morgan's Political Action Committee took up direct-action campaigns against other entities at the Northwood Shopping Center: the restaurant of the Hecht's department store, the Arundel Ice Cream Company restaurant, and the movie theater. The movie theater was the first target. While the students had used the sit-in tactic elsewhere, they dubbed their movie theater demonstration a "stand-in": on rotating shifts, some students remained in line at the ticket window while others marched in front of the theater with picket signs.

Morgan students were reportedly joined from time to time in their 1950s protest against segregation at Northwood by white students from the Johns Hopkins University chapter of Students for Democratic Action. In the Northwood Theatre campaign, for example, Morgan activists reached out to Hopkins students, advertising their intentions in the Hopkins student newsletter. Three hundred students participated in the picketing and "stand-in" actions at the theater—250 from Morgan and 50 from Hopkins. "One time, we had a line that stretched from [the shopping center] all the way to Holmes Hall," a student recalled—fully half a mile.[88]

Still, if Morgan students appreciated the support, they were also willing to remind the white students that the fullest service they might render was to combat the racism in their own communities, on their own campuses, that gave Jim Crow its strength. They were not calling for separate efforts—"we could meet once in a while to compare notes"—but emphasizing where the real work to end racism needed to be done. These sentiments and expressions spoke to the Morgan student activists' self-confidence and independence.[89]

Despite the allure of "action," negotiation was still part of the repertoire, if not necessarily the long and drawn out approach many believed Baltimore CORE required. Talks occurred, and demonstrations abated. When talks stalled or broke down, the demonstrations resumed. As protest campaigns tended to follow the academic semesters—fall and spring—by strategy or their good fortune, theater owners stonewalled long enough, until the end of spring semester, that subsequent protest was minimized as students left campus for summer break. Only a sporadic and skeletal campaign was maintained during the summer. This became a formulaic delaying tactic.

If the students wished to remain focused on Northwood because of its proximity to campus and because it was in their community, they nonetheless appreciated citywide and ultimately national connections with the wider black struggle. To increase pressure on the white owners of the Northwood movie theater to negotiate, the students deployed concurrent pickets at two of the owners' other theaters, the Eden and the Dunbar, both away from campus, just east of downtown. (Neither had Jim Crow policies; both were in long-established black neighborhoods.) Even this did not bring the Northwood theater into line, however.[90]

The Northwood movie theater stand-ins would be protracted—eight years until ultimate victory (1963). Opening the Rooftop Dining Room required still longer. Meanwhile, after a sustained sit-in campaign at the Northwood

Arundel Ice Cream Shop, in March 1959 students gained victory, which they savored and celebrated. The white press hardly noticed, while Baltimore's *Afro-American* was splashed with headlines, "Sit Down Wins!" Participation in resistance projects became a tradition for class after class of Morgan undergraduates in the 1950s.[91]

◉ ◉ ◉

By the end of the 1950s, with the student's Political Action Committee having morphed into a new group, the Civic Interest Group, or CIG (pronounced *Sig*), Baltimore activists were recognized across the community, and encouragement came from all corners of the black struggle across the South. For example, through the intervention of the Baltimore NAACP and others, when nationally recognized activists came to town, many stopped at Morgan to address the CIG students, who had instituted mass meetings by then to disseminate information and sustain morale and participation. In this way, they continued building their own activist profile.

Through the closing years of the decade, the group received words of wisdom and encouragement from athlete-turned-activist Jack Robinson. Bayard Rustin, a veteran activist and advisor to the Southern Christian Leadership Conference also addressed a CIG meeting. When Daisy Bates of the Arkansas NAACP, dynamic and charismatic leader of school desegregation activists in Little Rock, addressed the Morgan group she said, "I am proud of you because you are on the right track. You have a right at an early age to decide what type of world to live in." But perhaps it was the legendary labor organizer A. Philip Randolph—still the most important figure in the national black struggle at that time—whose words proved most instructive and most prophetic.[92] In 1957, at least partly in response to sit-ins, white supremacist business interests and pro-segregation forces had lobbied the Maryland legislature to strengthen trespass laws, raising the possibility of arrest and incarceration for sit-in participants. Visiting Morgan in early spring 1959, Randolph admonished the young activists, "If you have to go to jail, you ought to be willing to go to jail for your rights." "Somebody must bear the cross," he told them. "No liberty, no human justice, no decency have ever been won without sacrifice." As with the black Baltimoreans who had come before, through these students Randolph addressed—and those that followed—the black struggle for equality endured.[93]

# "We Were Fighting against White Supremacy"

## The Struggle at the End of the Fifties

Black attorney Harry Sythe Cummings won a seat on the Baltimore City Council in 1890, and subsequently blacks held frequent if not consistent positions among the city's elected officials. With the steady growth of the black population and blacks as a proportion of the electorate, some gains were realized. For example, in 1956, after numerous failed attempts over the preceding years, the Baltimore City Council passed a fair employment practices law — known popularly as the "Baby FEPC." The law provided for a nine-member Equal Employment Opportunity Commission (EEOC), which would begin work in 1957, and charged the body to work toward the elimination of employment discrimination. Though the law and the commission would enjoy fairly wide-based community support, especially among blacks and liberals, it was provided with no enforcement power. The EEOC could do little more than take job applicants' complaints and hold intercessory public hearings. Furthermore in the eyes of blacks, questions of integrity remained. Of the nine members, Mayor D'Alesandro appointed only one person of color, Morgan State College political scientist G. James Fleming. The Baltimore FEPC quickly became a political entity, with the two top spots going to whites (including one holding only a high school diploma). Disgusted, the *Afro* called it "a travesty."[1]

State and federal electoral success completely eluded black candidates during this time. Population shifts and redistricting produced new opportunities by 1954, however. By the fall of that year, as attorney Bob Watts worked hard and pro bono providing legal defense for students engaged in nonviolent direct action near their Morgan State campus (see chapter 6), an old schoolmate of his from Morgan in the early 1940s, Harry Augustus Cole, was out campaigning again. What the NAACP began in 1943 with its Votes for Victory effort, and what Victorine Adams and others institutionalized as the Colored Women's Democratic Campaign Committee of Maryland (CWDCC) in 1946 in an effort to support sincere and useful white politicians, had quickly shifted to improving black candidates' election campaigns. By the 1950s, however, black population numbers in the Fourth District of Baltimore had finally begun to undermine the anti-black gerrymandering of previous decades, which had theretofore kept blacks from office. Behind the efforts of the CWDCC, black voters elected three black candidates to the state legislature in 1954. They sent thirty-three-year-old Republican Harry Cole to the Maryland Senate, and Republican Emory Cole (no relation) and Democrat Truly Hatchett became the first blacks elected to the House of Delegates in the same election.[2]

Harry Cole by then was an established lawyer, an assistant attorney general, and had twice before run for office on the Republican ticket.[3] A dozen years earlier, however, while enrolled at Morgan State, Cole had been the only student invited to address the gathering at the March on Annapolis in 1942. To that audience young Cole humbly "spoke for youth" then fighting in World War II for their country—"when we fight abroad we can really feel we have something to fight for." In 1954, thanks to the efforts of Victorine Adams and others, not only did Cole become the first African American elected to the Maryland Senate, he did so by defeating a white Democrat candidate backed by the powerful but declining political machine of Jack Pollack. The margin was the slimmest—thirty-seven votes—but the victory was real and appeared as a turning point in black political life in the city.[4]

In his freshman session of the legislature, Cole introduced a civil rights bill "providing for equal rights for all persons in certain places of public accommodation, resort or amusement," proposing to make "exclusion because of race, creed, color, national origin, or ancestry unlawful" and punishable by fine and or imprisonment. Emory Cole introduced an identical bill in the House of Delegates. The bill would have applied to inns, hotels, and taverns; places of health care, recreation, and relaxation; restaurants of all types; garages and public conveyances—including stations and terminals; bathhouses, boardwalks, beaches, theaters, music halls, skating rinks, public libraries, child-care facilities, and conceivably any place else except private concerns, which would remain free to discriminate. Despite Harry Cole's enthusiasm after the bill cleared the Senate Judiciary Committee, the full senate voted it back to committee a few weeks later under the premise of an unresolved legal question requiring further study. And there it died. At the start of the 1957 session, Cole pledged to push matters again. He introduced a number of bills in what the *Afro* described as "a frontal legislative attack on segregation," touching on matters related to discrimination in employment (hiring or union membership), public accommodations, recreation, and lending, among other areas. These efforts, however, likewise fell short.[5]

In the 1958 campaigns, all of those black legislators elected in 1954 were defeated, but all lost to black challengers. Harry Cole lost his state senate seat to J. Alvin Jones. While Cole had been quick to press civil rights legislation, Jones would hesitate. But two black women, Irma Dixon and Verda Welcome, were elected to seats in the House of Delegates. That year Victorine Adams had helped form another nonpartisan organization, the Womanpower Committee, to conduct voter registration. Women were solid leaders and good "old-fashioned" organizers who knew how to mobilize people for the cause. During the campaign, the work of black women in getting out the vote was acknowledged from several sources—"More power to women!" Carl Murphy cheered publically. In the end, different paths toward equality were evident in Baltimore and throughout the South by the close of the 1950s. Those connected to the more visible organizations of the struggle pushed for power, electoral power. As the NAACP's Clarence Mitchell proffered at the time, "When you have the ballot you don't need bullets."[6]

Meanwhile, for others, protest remained the path. Aubrey Edwards, head of the Civic Interest Group (CIG) at Morgan State by 1959 wrote to peer student groups at other black colleges in the South, encouraging them toward the type of activism he was participating in at Morgan. This stands as evidence that the Morgan students, like other elements traditionally in the Baltimore black struggle, realized that theirs was but one point on the larger map of black resistance in the South. In the Jim Crow South—the whole of the South— black was community. In the major cities of the South, black colleges and black college communities were key cultural hubs. Formal communication and informal word got around in ways scholars have yet fully to grasp. The *Afro-American*, a national newspaper by this point, had been carrying news of student activism from across the South throughout the era. Likewise, students came together and talked about their respective campus activism at sorority and fraternity conferences, NAACP youth meetings, religious and social occasions, and intercollegiate athletic events, and during summer breaks and Christmastime trips back home. The black South was truly a nation within by the mid-twentieth century, and its colleges and universities played a vital role beyond simply education.[7]

The confrontational style of direct action had always appealed to young people and college students in the South, especially the urban South. Thus, Morgan students moved in ways similar to other black students. While seldom dogmatic or doctrinaire, such tactics dated back to the beginnings of Jim Crow, becoming ever more acceptable and legitimate from the New Deal era on. Students at Morgan State College in Baltimore presented one example of those engaged in direct action against segregation. But the use of the sit-in tactic itself, which dated at Morgan to 1953, was by no means proprietary. Though springing from organic local circumstances that differed from place to place, students of the era employed direct action, often sit-ins, against segregated public accommodations. Students joined a young North Carolina pastor, Douglas Moore, for example, at a sit-in against Durham's Royal Ice Cream Parlor in June 1957. In July 1958, black student activists in Wichita, Kansas, led by the young future political scientist Ron Walters, executed a successful three-week sit-in against the Dockum Drug Store lunch counter. That same summer, a teacher and a group of high schoolers successfully sat-in at the lunch counter of Katz Drug Store in Oklahoma City.[8]

In programmatic fashion similar to student activism at Morgan, activists at Fisk University in Nashville took up direct-action tactics in the mid-1950s. As at Morgan, Fisk students were supported on several levels by campus faculty and staff in the development of their activism in these years. Aided by this, a Nashville CORE chapter emerged in 1955, thanks largely to Anna Holden, a southern white radical interracialist from Florida, who worked as a social scientist at Fisk. Under her guidance over the next three years, Nashville CORE—composed largely of black college students—engaged in a number of direct-action campaigns. Most prominently, the local CORE worked in 1957 on school desegregation, which had engendered violent white reaction in Nashville similar to the more famous Little Rock backlash. By the fall of 1959, Nashville students began sit-ins at downtown lunch counters.[9]

Again, black student activism throughout this period in Baltimore and at Morgan stood with examples from across the South. In Orangeburg, South Carolina, blacks staged a boycott in August 1955 as retaliation for local Citizens' Council racism. The effort was organized by veteran activist Modjeska Simkins and involved students at South Carolina State College. Likewise, in the late spring of 1956, black students from Xavier University in New Orleans were reportedly held in jail following an impromptu action that saw dozens of them willfully violate seating laws on Jim Crow city buses. Shortly thereafter, in Tallahassee, two young black women students of Florida Agricultural and Mechanical University (FAMU) refused to surrender seats on a city bus when ordered to do so by the white driver. Responding to the women's subsequent arrest, their fellow FAMU students initiated a boycott of buses near campus, and the protest spread to Tallahassee's broader black community in the following days. The Tallahassee effort coalesced into the formation of an umbrella group, the Inter-Civic Council, for the purpose of representing the boycotters and negotiating terms of settlement with white city officials and

Cities Transit, the company that operated the Tallahassee bus franchise. And in December 1956, students at Allen University in Columbia, South Carolina, determined to test that city's compliance with the U.S. Supreme Court's recent *Browder v. Gayle* decision, forbidding Jim Crow on municipal transit. Over the course of a week several groups of students acting under the auspices of the campus NAACP chapter boarded city buses, sitting conspicuously where previously they had not been allowed to sit.[10]

Why the Greensboro sit-ins of 1960 incited the white-oriented mainstream news cycle but not those before it, especially Baltimore's, remains for another work of scholarship. Here it serves only to note the historical context up to that moment. Even if whites had not noticed, blacks in Baltimore and elsewhere in the urban South had responded to Jim Crow since its construction at the end of the nineteenth century. Early on, against the indignities and brutalities of government-sanctioned white supremacy, blacks nurtured a counter-narrative vision for themselves. This counter-narrative placed high value on education, community, self-respect, and achievement. Urban black activists in the South also connected local efforts with emerging national organizations—but they did this without surrendering local agency over their struggles. As a result, from early in the resistance to Jim Crow, the national struggle was deeply informed by grassroots experiences like those in Baltimore. Finally, taking advantage of post–World War II developments around a resurgent liberalism in America, black organizations were in position to instigate ideological and political confrontations on behalf of the struggle pitting liberal white voices and governmental authorities against the conservatism that perpetuated Jim Crow.

During the Jim Crow years, urban South blacks most often pursued a pragmatist black nationalist course. Dynamics continually shifted, sometimes of the black community's doing (such as their continual migration to West Baltimore), sometimes because of external developments (like the wide-ranging interracialist influence after World War II). The pragmatist black nationalist approach allowed the enduring black struggle the fluidity necessary to meet the opportunities of any moment. Throughout the first half of the twentieth century, the goal in the black struggle—equality—remained in place. The resistance model included community organizing and agency, litigation, lobbying, electoral activism, and direct-action campaigns, but the movement also valued uplift entailing education and self-sufficiency and the collective impact of the individual black folk seeking equality. After the war an emerging Cold War agenda presented new opportunities, and blacks instigated conflicts between forces of white liberalism and white reaction to the benefit of their struggle.

In cities like Baltimore, where Jim Crow existed as a fact of law and where pervasive segregation culture regenerated itself, the size of the black population and its proportion of the overall population made for a milieu relatively unique to the urban South, certainly in the earlier decades of the twentieth century. Together these factors created specific resistance environments, and the conditions and forces of both segregation and the struggle against it reflected the specific political, social, and cultural economies of the urban South. Electoral activism, direct-action campaigns, collective commitment to nurturing the counter-narrative, and promotion of the legitimacy and authenticity of black institutional, organizational, and cultural life—all were in use against Jim Crow before anyone outside black communities took notice. These were underway before the enduring black struggle inspired a national civil rights movement.

Looking back from the vantage of 1966, the student activist Stokely Carmichael (later Kwame Ture) insisted, "We were never fighting for the right to integrate." Despite the therapeutic language of the *Brown* decision, the enduring black struggle was never about sitting next to white people. The struggle from which the movement emerged did not seek racial integration for its own sake or as a goal unto itself. "That does not begin to solve the problem," Carmichael insisted. The enduring black struggle was more essential and more fundamental. "We were fighting against white supremacy!" he insisted. Racial integration was one approach toward the enduring goal of equality. But integration was not racial equality, certainly not by 1966. Thus, in the name of "Black Power," Carmichael and his generational cohort worked to return the struggle to its central purpose.[11]

# NOTES

## INTRODUCTION. An Enduring Black Struggle for Equality in Baltimore

1. Earl Lewis, *In Their Own Interests*, 90.

2. *Afro-American*, April 5, 1947.

3. George H. Callcott, *Maryland and America*, 3; Skotnes, *New Deal for All?*; Rhonda Williams, *Politics of Public Housing*; Durr, *Behind the Backlash*; and Baum, *"Brown" in Baltimore*. Other important works of recent publication on Baltimore include Smith, *Here Lies Jim Crow*; Gibson, *Young Thurgood*; Sartain, *Borders of Equality*; Pietila, *Not in My Neighborhood*.

4. Silver and Moeser, *Separate City*, 124; Goldfield, "Urban Crusade," 183.

5. Douglass, "Narrative of the Life of Frederick Douglass." The phrase "ethos of urbanicity" borrows in part from Blaine Brownell's similar "urban ethos in the South" but only in the similarity of phrasing, not in its meaning. Brownell, *Urban Ethos in the South*.

6. Wade, *Slavery in the Cities*, 215; Franklin and Schweninger, *Runaway Slaves*, 124–48. See also Painter, *Exodusters*.

7. Ayers, *Promise of the New South*, 56.

8. Doyle, *New Men, New Cities*, 12.

9. Calculated from U.S. Census figures, 1900–1930, as cited in Lynch, *Black Urban Condition*, appendix A.

10. Adams, "Headed for Louisville," 408; Goldfield, "Urban Crusade," 185; Ayers, *Promise of the New South*, 68.

11. Ayers, *Promise of the New South*, 68; Rabinowitz, *Race Relations*, 333–39.

12. Du Bois, *Negro*, 108; Cell, *Highest Stage of White Supremacy*, 131–32; Rabinowitz, *Race Relations*, 330.

13. Cell, *Highest Stage of White Supremacy*, 119–122; Carrie Francis Jackson interview, December 12, 1979, 25–26.

14. Woodward, *Strange Career of Jim Crow*, 91; Kirby, *Darkness at the Dawning*, 25; Grantham, *Southern Progressivism*, 32; Ayers, *Promise of the New South*, 55–57, 67; Bayor, *Race and the Shaping*, 15–17.

15. Cell, *Highest Stage of White Supremacy*, x; Grantham, *Southern Progressivism*, 32; Woodward, *Strange Career of Jim Crow*, 91; Doyle, *New Men, New Cities*, 278–89.

16. Cha-Jua and Lang, "'Long Movement' as Vampire"; Eagles, "Toward New Histories," 815–48; Hall, "Long Civil Rights Movement," 1233–63; Joseph, "Black Power Movement."

17. See Scott, *Contempt and Pity*, especially chapters 1 and 2; Michelle Alexander, *New Jim Crow*, 197–98.

18. Juanita Jackson Mitchell interview, July 25, 1975.

19. Brown-Nagin, *Courage to Dissent*, 2.

20. Cumberbatch, "What 'the Cause' Needs"; Skotnes, *New Deal for All?*; Sartain, *Borders of Equality.*

21. Lang, *Grassroots at the Gateway*, 3–4.

22. Gilmore, *Defying Dixie*; Robin D. G. Kelley, *Hammer and Hoe*; Honey, *Southern Labor*; and Skotnes, *New Deal for All?*

23. Gilmore, *Defying Dixie*, 5–10; Dudziak, *Cold War Civil Rights*, 11. The Little Rock Nine were a cohort of African American students who enrolled at the formerly whites-only Central High School in Little Rock, Arkansas, during September 1957 in compliance with the U.S. Supreme Court's desegregation mandates following *Brown* (1954). Encouraged by defiant language from Arkansas governor Orval Faubus, mobs of angry whites demonstrated against the black students and threatened violence against them. President Dwight Eisenhower was forced to deploy National Guard troops to restore order and facilitate the school's desegregation. Print and broadcast media gave wide and extended coverage to the Little Rock development. See Grif Stockley, *Daisy Bates: Civil Rights Crusader from Arkansas* (Jackson: University Press of Mississippi, 2012).

24. Rossinow, *Visions of Progress*, 189.

25. Goldfield, "Urban Crusade," 184–85.

## CHAPTER 1. Jim Crowed

1. *New York Times*, June 10, 1889.

2. *Baltimore American*, June 1, 1889; *New York Times*, June 10, 1889; Bogen, "First Integration"; Brackett, *Notes on the Progress*, 77.

3. *New York Age*, November 1, 1890.

4. *New York Age*, February 13, 1892; *Afro-American*, March 5, 1904, March 17, 1904; Hale, *Making Whiteness*, 15–16, 21–22, 29–30; Logan, *Betrayal of the Negro*; Woodward, *Strange Career of Jim Crow*, 67–109; Brackett, *Notes on the Progress*, 63; Bogen, "Transformation of the Fourteenth Amendment," 1030; Freeman, "Harvey Johnson and Everett Waring," 16–17; Paul, "Shadow of Equality," 289.

5. *Afro-American*, March 5, 1904; Wade, *Slavery in the Cities*, 14. The most effective thesis on the historical and cultural underpinnings of the rise of segregation culture and whiteness from the end of the nineteenth century remains Hale's *Making Whiteness*.

6. Brackett, *Notes on the Progress*, 39; Karen Olson, "Old West Baltimore," 57; Silver and Moeser, *Separate City*, 4–5; Paul, "Shadow of Equality," 389.

7. Takaki, *Strangers from a Different Shore*, 246, 253–54; Adams, *Way up North in Louisville*, 7–9, 11.

8. R. L. Polk, *Baltimore City Directory, 1910* [hereafter *Polk Directory, 1910*]; *First Colored Professional, Clerical and Business Directory . . . 1916–17*; Sherry H. Olson, *Baltimore*, 234–35; Pietila, *Not in My Neighborhood*, 12.

9. Baltimore's black population in 1880 was 53,715, and in 1910 it was 84,749. Lynch, *Black Urban Condition*, appendix A; *Polk Directory, 1910*; *First Colored Professional, Clerical and Business Directory . . . 1916–17*; Sherry H. Olson, *Baltimore*, 234–35; Kemp, *Housing Conditions in Baltimore*, 16–19, 45–47; *Sanborn Fire Insurance Map from Baltimore, Maryland*, 1901–1902 vol. 2, 1901, sheets 138, 146, Library of Congress, Geography and Map Division; *Afro-American*, March 7, 1925.

10. Platt, *E. Franklin Frazier Reconsidered*, 16.

11. Thomas, "Public Education and Black Protest," 384. In 1875 the ratio of white schools to white students was 1:252, and the ratio of black schools to black students was

1:237. In that same year blacks constituted 11 percent of the student enrollment and received 8 percent of the school budget. See Paul, "Shadow of Equality," 117.

12. *Woods' Baltimore City Directory*, 1886, Internet Archive, https://archive.org/details/woodsbaltimoreci1886balt; Paul, "Shadow of Equality," 231, 234–25; Brackett, *Notes on the Progress*, 88–89; Freeman, "Harvey Johnson and Everett Waring," 41–42; Thomas, "Public Education and Black Protest," 386.

13. *New York Age*, February 20, 1892; Paul, "Shadow of Equality," 240–41; Sherry H. Olson, *Baltimore*, 187.

14. Paul, "Shadow of Equality," 108–16; Brackett, *Notes on the Progress*, 88–89; Freeman, "Harvey Johnson and Everett Waring," 41.

15. *Afro-American*, October 19, 1895.

16. Sherry H. Olson, *Baltimore*, 187; Paul, "Shadow of Equality," 240–41, 316–17.

17. Hale, *Making Whiteness*, 51; Litwack, *Trouble in Mind*, 182.

18. Earl Lewis, *In Their Own Interests*, 3

19. Sherry H. Olson, *Baltimore*, 161.

20. Michaeli, *Defender*. "The busy corner" reference comes from an ad campaign of Fennell's Pharmacy. Joseph S. Fennell, a black man occasionally mistaken for white, opened a pharmacy, soda fountain, and packaged goods establishment with his second wife, Estelle, at 450 West Biddle Street around 1910. A Maryland native, Fennell had been a waiter and caterer in Baltimore before opening his pharmacy. Evidence of their entrepreneurial success, the Fennells purchased a home on the desirable upper blocks of Druid Hill Avenue. See also R. L. Polk, *Baltimore City Directory*, 1912, 737, Internet Archive, https://archive.org/details/baltimorecitydir1912rlpo; *First Colored Professional, Clerical and Business Directory . . . 1916–17*.

21. Penn, *Afro-American Press*, 50–54; Buni, *Robert L. Vann*; Suggs, *P.B. Young, Newspaperman*; Gregory, *Southern Diaspora*, 125–26.

22. Farrar, *Baltimore Afro-American*, 1–3; "Rev. William Moncure Alexander"; *Afro-American*, August 19, 1916.

23. Farrar, *Baltimore Afro-American*, 1–3; Hein and Shattuck, *Episcopalians*, 171; Mills, "Bragg, George Freeman, Jr.," 95–96; Shattuck, *Episcopalians and Race*, 21–22.

24. *Afro-American*, April 29, 1893; Farrar, *Baltimore Afro-American*, 4–6.

25. *Afro-American*, July 2, 1955.

26. Boyd, "Race, Labor Market Disadvantage," 654–55.

27. Hunter, *To 'Joy My Freedom*, 57; Wang, "Race, Gender, and Laundry Work," 78–82, 97n105, 97n109; Boyd, "Race, Labor Market Disadvantage," 648. The Druid Laundry, the sole known black-owned commercial setup, had two locations on Druid Hill Avenue: No. 926 and No. 1634. See Clark-Lewis, *Living In, Living Out*; *First Colored Professional, Clerical and Business Directory . . . 1916–17*; R. L. Polk, *Directory of Baltimore*, 1920, 2329.

28. Boyd, "Race, Labor Market Disadvantage," 654–55; Dabel, *Respectable Woman*, 82; Wang, "Race, Gender, and Laundry Work," 78–82, 97n105, 97n109.

29. Johnson, "Negroes at Work in Baltimore," 13–14; Boyd, "Race, Labor Market Disadvantage," 654–55; Hunter, *To 'Joy My Freedom*, 56, 92–95; Sterling, *We Are Your Sisters*, 356–58.

30. *New York Age*, November 1, 1890.

31. Boyd, "Race, Labor Market Disadvantage," 654–55.

32. Wang, "Race, Gender, and Laundry Work," 67; Takaki, *Strangers from a Different Shore*, 13–14.

33. Takaki, *Strangers from a Different Shore*, 13–14 (italics in original); R. L. Polk, *Baltimore City Directory, 1901*, 1878–79.

34. Calculations based on data published in Charles S. Johnson, "Negroes at Work in Baltimore," 13–14.

35. *Afro-American*, January 27, 1912, February 17, 1912.

36. Bogen, "Precursors of Rosa Parks," 744.

37. *Sun* (Baltimore), July 4, 1904; *Afro-American*, July 2, 1904, July 9, 1904; Margaret Law Callcott, *Negro in Maryland Politics*, 115–33; Paul, "Shadow of Equality," 276.

38. In 1884 Rev. Johnson was arrested and fined after he inadvertently entered the "whites-only" section of a ferry operated by the Norfolk Ferry Company. The case was not decided until December 1891, when an all-white Virginia jury ruled in favor of the defendants, "rendering their verdict without leaving their seats." This disrespect, humiliation, and disappointment for Johnson, who so adamantly believed in the system of law, served as the catalyst for Johnson's nearly four decades of civil rights activism that followed. *New York Age*, December 19, 1891; Freeman, "Harvey Johnson and Everett Waring," 16–18. See also Blair L. M. Kelley, *Right to Ride*; Meier and Rudwick, "Boycott Movement."

39. Bogen, "Precursors of Rosa Parks," 737–39; Thomas, "Public Education and Black Protest," 386.

40. *New York Times*, December 25, 1910.

41. *Afro-American*, October 1, 1910.

42. *State v. Gurry*, 121 Md. 534 (Md. 1913); *Jackson v. State*, 132 Md. 311 (Md. 1918); *Afro-American*, October 12, 1912; Kluger, *Simple Justice*, 109; Power, "*Meade v. Dennistone*," 802.

43. *Afro-American*, May 11, 1907.

44. Ibid.; "Case Studies: Judge Lynch's Court: Mob Justice in Maryland during the Age of Jim Crow, 1860s–1930s," in *Legacy of Slavery in Maryland*, Maryland State Archives, accessed January 23, 2016, http://slavery.msa.maryland.gov/html/casestudies/judge_lynch.html.

45. Contemporaneous to these exercises of brutality, of course, were the racist urban pogroms that emerged with Jim Crow (e.g., in Wilmington, North Carolina, in 1898, Atlanta in 1906, and Washington, D.C., in 1919). Where lynchings and police brutality claimed black bodies, white riots were aimed at evidence of black achievement—in property as much as person. See Dray, *At the Hands*; Leonard N. Moore, *Black Rage in New Orleans*; Cecelski and Tyson, *Democracy Betrayed*; Mixon, *Atlanta Riot*; Constance McLaughlin Green, *Secret City*.

46. Kirby, *Darkness at the Dawning*, 25; Grantham, *Southern Progressivism*, 32; Chappell, *Inside Agitators*, xxiv; Adler, "Greatest Thrill," 7; "Criminal Injustice," in *Baltimore's Civil Rights Heritage*, last modified April 10, 2017, https://baltimoreheritage.github.io/civil-rights-heritage/criminal-injustice/.

47. Litwack, *Trouble in Mind*, 263–64.

48. *Afro-American*, October 17, 1925, June 7, 1918.

49. Litwack, *Trouble in Mind*, 264.

50. Gildea, *Longest Fight*, 26–27.

51. *Afro-American*, July 9, 1910; *New York Times*, July 5, 1910.

52. *Afro-American*, November 25, 1933.

53. *Sun* (Baltimore), August 2, 1875, July 24, 1884; *Afro-American*, June 7, 1918,

March 22, 1930, March 29, 1930; *Woods' Baltimore City Directory*, 1876, 893, Internet Archive, accessed July 8, 2017, https://archive.org/details/woodsbaltimoreci1876balt; "Before Freddie Gray: A History of Police Violence in Baltimore," *Historic Sprawl*, last modified April 24, 2015, https://historicsprawl.wordpress.com/2015/04/24/before-freddie-gray-a-history-of-police-violence-in-baltimore.

54. Officer Schuman shot Vannie Lee after Lee had killed another cop (whose loss the black press lamented). Lee was described in the black press as a "maniac" driven mad by earlier experiences with police brutality from other cops. "Police Brutalities," typescript, box B116, in "Police Brutality: State, Baltimore, Md., 1940–1942," Records of the National Association for the Advancement of Colored People, Manuscript Division, Library of Congress, Washington, D.C. [hereafter NAACP records]; *Afro-American*, August 15, 1924, July 10, 1926, July 3, 1926.

55. *Crisis*, May 1934, 147; Dittmer, *Black Georgia*, 138; Bayor, *Race and the Shaping*, 174.

56. Litwack, *Trouble in Mind*, 264; Bayor, *Race and the Shaping*, 175.

57. *Afro-American*, June 7, 1918.

58. Ibid.

59. Ibid.

60. *Afro-American*, November 25, 1921.

61. *Afro-American*, February 2, 1918, February 9, 1918; Adler, "Greatest Thrill," 4–5; Juan Williams, *Thurgood Marshall*, 35.

62. *Afro-American*, November 5, 1904, January 9, 1909; Adler, "Greatest Thrill," 5; "Criminal Injustice," in *Baltimore's Civil Rights Heritage*, https://baltimoreheritage.github.io/civil-rights-heritage/criminal-injustice.

63. *Ledger* (Baltimore), July 30, 1898; Greene, "Black Republicans," 206; McAdam, *Political Process and the Development*, 69.

64. Margaret Law Callcott, *Negro in Maryland Politics*, 99; *Afro-American*, November 2, 1901; Paul, "Shadow of Equality," 252.

65. Margaret Law Callcott, *Negro in Maryland Politics*, 126–27; *Afro-American*, March 13, 1904, January 16, 1904.

66. *Afro-American*, July 22, 1905, February 6, 1904, January 30, 1904.

67. *Afro-American*, October 17, 1925; Shawn Leigh Alexander, *Army of Lions*, 217–27; Fox, *Guardian of Boston*, 81–82.

68. Washington, *Booker T. Washington Papers*, 8:186, 380–81.

69. Ibid., 381; Washington, *Booker T. Washington Papers*, 2:73, 78–82.

70. Chesnutt, *Exemplary Citizen*, 1n2, 3; Washington, *Booker T. Washington Papers*, 2:82; *Afro-American*, May 11, 1907; Crooks, *Politics and Progress*, 66–67; Margaret Law Callcott, *Negro in Maryland Politics*, 115–16, 125–31; Paul, "Shadow of Equality," 276; *Afro-American*, May 11, 1907; McAdam, *Political Process and the Development*, 72.

71. Paul, "Shadow of Equality," 260.

72. *Afro-American*, July 22, 1905, February 6, 1904, January 30, 1904, July 2, 1904; Carle, *Defining the Struggle*, 2; Margaret Law Callcott, *Negro in Maryland Politics*, 133.

## CHAPTER 2. National Struggle, Local Agenda

1. Carle, *Defining the Struggle*, 103–21.

2. Silver and Moeser, *Separate City*, 124; Goldfield, "Urban Crusade," 183.

3. Moses, *Golden Age*, 204–5.

4. Bay, *White Image*, 200.

5. Johnson's essays were published in pamphlet form individually and later compiled as an anthology. See Harvey Johnson, *Nations from a New Point*, 138; Bay, *White Image*, 200.

6. *Afro-American*, September 3, 1910, September 24, 1910.

7. Rolinson, *Grassroots Garveyism*, 3.

8. Hill, *Marcus Garvey and Universal Negro Improvement Association Papers*, 1:317–38, 3:258–59; *Afro-American*, December 13, 1918; Martin, *Race First*, 11; William Moses, *Golden Age of Black Nationalism*, 29.

9. Hill, *Marcus Garvey and Universal Negro Improvement Association Papers*, 4:351–53; Martin, *Race First*, 364; Tolbert, "Outpost Garveyism," 250; *Afro-American*, February 28, 1919; *Negro World*, February 1, 1919.

10. Hill, *Marcus Garvey and Universal Negro Improvement Association Papers*, 1:318, 2:447, 2:452n1, 2:496, 3:258–59, 4:489–94, 5:653; *Afro-American*, October 22, 1920, October 26, 1923; Carle, *Defining the Struggle*, 193; Duster, *Crusade for Justice*, 375–82; Martin, *Race First*, 364; Rolinson, *Grassroots Garveyism*, 1. See also *First Colored Professional, Clerical and Business Directory of Baltimore City*, 8th–11th annual eds.

11. For women presidents of southern UNIA divisions, see Rolinson, *Grassroots Garveyism*, appendix G. Rolinson defines "the South" as the eleven states of the former Confederacy, however, so she excludes possible women presidents in Missouri, Kentucky, West Virginia, Delaware, Washington, D.C., and Maryland (explaining Hattie Johnson's absence). According to Tony Martin, each of the aforementioned non-Confederate southern states had multiple UNIA divisions. Two years earlier the Baltimore Branch of the NAACP installed a woman as president for the first time too, Lillian Lottier. Hill, *Marcus Garvey and Universal Negro Improvement Association Papers*, 2:447, 2:452n1, 2:496, 5:653; *Afro-American*, October 22, 1920, October 26, 1923; Sartain, *Borders of Equality*, 55–56; Martin, *Race First*, 361–73; Musgrove, *Rumor, Repression, and Racial Politics*, 12; Duster, *Crusade for Justice*, 375–82; Carle, *Defining the Struggle*, 193; Rolinson, *Grassroots Garveyism*, 3, 214–15. See also *First Colored Professional, Clerical and Business Directory of Baltimore City*, 8th–11th annual eds.

12. Hill, *Marcus Garvey and Universal Negro Improvement Association Papers*, 2:447, 2:452n1, 2:496; *Afro-American*, October 26, 1923; Rolinson, *Grassroots Garveyism*, 4.

13. Hill, *Marcus Garvey and Universal Negro Improvement Association Papers MGP*, 1:318; 3:258–59; 4:489–94; 5:653; Martin, *Race First*, 364; Rolinson, *Grassroots Garveyism*, 1; *Afro-American*, October 22, 1920; October 26, 1923; Duster, *Crusade for Justice*, 375–82; Carle, *Defining the Struggle*, 193.

14. Hill, *Marcus Garvey and Universal Negro Improvement Association Papers*, 5:183–84, 653; *Afro American*, October 26, 1923; Martin, *Race First*, 237–41.

15. *Afro American*, February 7, 1925.

16. Hill, *Marcus Garvey and Universal Negro Improvement Association Papers*, 5:183–84.

17. Rolinson, *Grassroots Garveyism*, 8; Moses, *Golden Age of Black Nationalism*, 264.

18. Moses, *Golden Age of Black Nationalism*, 262; Rolinson, *Grassroots Garveyism*, 18.

19. Sosna, *In Search of the Silent South*, 22; Kimberley Johnson, *Reforming Jim Crow*, 27–29; Scott, *Contempt and Pity*, 11–19, 40, 58–66; Robbins, *Sideline Activist*, 9, 31, 35–36.

20. Sosna, *In Search of the Silent South*, 1–19.

21. Brown, "Election of 1934"; *Afro-American*, January 23, 1926, January 21, 1927, May 14, 1927, February 9, 1929, May 7, 1931, December 17, 1932, December 17, 1938.

22. Sosna, *In Search of the Silent South*, 8–11, 20–41; Kimberley Johnson, *Reforming Jim Crow*, 24–30; Scott, *Contempt and Pity*, 2–7, 20, 26.

23. Pearson, "National Urban League," 524; Carey, "Helping Negro Workers," 24.

24. *Afro-American*, February 24, 1922; Pearson, "National Urban League," 524–30; Platt, *E. Franklin Frazier Reconsidered*, 70; Robbins, *Sideline Activist*, 43.

25. *Afro-American*, September 3, 1910.

26. *Afro-American*, February 10, 1906, ibid., January 27, 1912.

27. *Afro-American*, January 6, 1906; ibid., September 8, 1906.

28. *Afro-American*, May 4, 1907, February 10, 1906; Niagara Movement-Maryland Branch Annual Meeting Program, ca. February 1908, W. E. B. Du Bois Papers (MS 312), Special Collections and University Archives, University of Massachusetts Amherst Libraries, http://credo.library.umass.edu/view/full/mums312-b004-i191.

29. *Afro-American*, February 10, 1906; Niagara Movement-Maryland Branch Annual Meeting Program, ca. February 1908; Chalkley, "Circle Unbroken."

30. *Afro-American*, January 6, 1906, February 10, 1906, May 4, 1907, May 11, 1917.

31. *Afro-American*, February 29, 1908, March 12, 1910, August 5, 1911; Wolters, *Du Bois and His Rivals*, 69.

32. Thornbrough, "National Afro-American League"; *Afro-American*, March 16, 1912.

33. *Afro-American*, May 9, 1914.

34. *Afro-American*, February 28, 1967.

35. *Afro-American*, August 1, 1914; *Crisis* 8, no. 4 (August 1914), 168.

36. *Hart v. State* 100 Md. Reports 595 (1905); *State v. Jenkins*, 124 Md. (1914); *Afro-American*, March 5, 1904, March 17, 1904, July 2, 1904, July 9, 1904, August 23, 1918, August 30, 1918, February 14, 1919, March 7, 1919, March 7, 1919, March 25, 1921, April 1, 1921, May 25, 1923, April 25, 1925, July 29, 1933; correspondence from "L. A. L." [Lillian A. Lottier] *Opportunity* (Department of Research and Investigations, National Urban League, New York City) 2 (May 1924), 160; *Crisis* 17, no. 1 (November 1918), 37; Hershaw et al., "Notes," 211–13; Bogen, "Precursors of Rosa Parks," 750.

37. Bogen, "Precursors of Rosa Parks," 746–48, 750.

38. David Levering Lewis, *W. E. B. Du Bois: Biography*, 517–22; *Afro-American*, November 22, 1918.

39. Taylor, "*Afro-American*'s 'House of Murphy.'"

40. Murphy to Bagnall, November 20, 1930, NAACP records, group 1, series G, box 84, 1930; Bagnall to Murphy, November 22, 1930, Murphy to Walter White, November 22, 1930, and Walter White to Murphy, November 25, 1930, all NAACP records, group 1, series G, box 84, 1930; A. C. Clark to Bagnall, February 16, 1931, Bagnall to Murphy, June 5, 1931, Walter White to Murphy, November 10, 1931; and Murphy to White, November 12, 1931, all NAACP RECORDS, group 1, series G, box 85, 1931; Bagnall to Murphy, October 8, 1932, NAACP records, group 1, series G, box 85, 1932–1934; Carl Murphy to Walter White, October 12, 1932, White to Murphy, October 13, 1932, Bagnall to Bragg, November 4, 1932, Vashti T. Murphy to Bagnall, November 22, 1932, Bragg to Bagnall, November 1, 1932, and Bagnall to Vashti Murphy, November 23, 1932, all NAACP records, group 1, series G, box 85, 1932–1934.

41. How might we see Du Bois's impact and his ever-leftward momentum in these years for its impact on Murphy's thinking, and thus on the local NAACP and the trajectory of the Baltimore struggle? The records as they are currently known to me shed little light on this question, unfortunately. McConnell, *History of Morgan Park*, 26; Du Bois, "Negro Editors on Communism"; David Levering Lewis, *W. E. B. Du Bois: The Fight*, 299–300, 627–28.

42. Lewis, *W. E. B. Du Bois: The Fight*, 300.

43. "Twenty-Third Annual Conference of the N.A.A.C.P., Washington, D.C., May 17–22, 1932," LC-USZ62–111530 (b&w film copy neg. of left section) and LC-USZ62–111531 (b&w film copy neg. of right section), NAACP records; *Afro-American*, May 21, 1932, May 28, 1932; David Taft Terry, "'Tinged with Hostility': Competing Agendas and Social Justice Reform in Baltimore, 1931–1959" (presentation, Baltimore Historical Society, Baltimore History Evenings, Baltimore, June 19, 2014); Sullivan, *Lift Every Voice*, 155.

44. *Afro-American*, May 28, 1932; Lewis, *W. E. B. Du Bois: The Fight*, 300; Sullivan, *Lift Every Voice*, 155.

45. *Afro-American*, May 21, 1932; Kluger, *Simple Justice*, 132–35.

46. Kluger, *Simple Justice*, 136–37; McNeil, *Groundwork*, 114–17; Skotnes, *New Deal for All?*, 205 (italics in original).

47. Carl Murphy to Walter White, December 20, 1932, NAACP records, group 1, series G, box 85, 1932–1934; *Afro-American*, January 14, 1933; Sullivan, *Lift Every Voice*, 163.

48. *Afro-American*, September 1, 1934.

49. Ibid.; Bogen, "Transformation of the Fourteenth Amendment."

50. Gibson, *Young Thurgood*, 231.

51. Skotnes, *New Deal for All?*, 3; James H. Gilliam Sr. interview.

52. Cumberbatch, "What 'the Cause' Needs," 55.

53. Skotnes, *New Deal for All?*, 184–85.

54. My emphasis. See photograph of demonstration in Skotnes, *New Deal for All?*, 149.

55. *Afro-American*, January 6, 1934, January 10, 1931.

56. *Afro-American*, January 10, 1931.

57. *Afro-American*, September 16, 1933, October 7, 1933, October 14, 1933, October 21, 1933, December 16, 1933; Pacifico, "Don't Buy"; Skotnes, *New Deal for All?*, 144–45; Cumberbatch, "What 'the Cause' Needs," 51.

58. Karen Olson, "Old West Baltimore," 67–69; Pacifico, "Don't Buy," 66–88; Skotnes, *New Deal for All?*, 206; Sullivan, *Lift Every Voice*, 155; Bynum, *NAACP Youth in the Fight*, 1–22.

59. Gibson, *Young Thurgood*, 20; "Case Studies: Judge Lynch's Court: Mob Justice in Maryland during the Age of Jim Crow, 1860s–1930s," in *Legacy of Slavery in Maryland*, Maryland State Archives, accessed January 23, 2016, http://slavery.msa.maryland.gov /html/casestudies/judge_lynch.html; U.S. Census, 1930; Ifill, *On the Courthouse Lawn*.

60. Sullivan, *Lift Every Voice*, 105–10, 190–97.

61. Skotnes, *New Deal for All?*, 134–36; Bay, *White Image*, 202. Skotnes deals with the Left's role in the aftermath of the two lynchings and the Lee trial at length (see especially chapter 5, "The Lynching of George Armwood, 1933."). See also Carter, *Scottsboro*.

62. *Afro-American*, November 25, 1933; Skotnes, *New Deal for All?*, 134.

63. Carl Murphy to Walter White, December 20, 1932, NAACP RECORDS, group 1, series G, b. 85, 1932–1934; *Afro-American*, January 14, 1933.

64. Gibson, *Young Thurgood*, 232–35.

65. Ibid., 82–105; Kluger, *Simple Justice*, 173–94.

66. As early as 1920, the NAACP attempted to organize a chapter at Morgan College but was put off. Unnamed faculty saw an affiliation with such a group as the NAACP—radical by the day's standards—as "inadvisable." Jas. H. Carter to Catherine D. Lealtad, August 18, 1920, Asst. Dir. of Branches to Prof. E. A. Love, October 15, 1920, Asst. Dir. of Branches to President J. O. Spencer, January 21, 1921, Asst. Dir. of Branches to Love, Jan-

uary 21, 1921, Love to Lealtad, February 4, 1921, Spencer to Robert W. Bagnall, March 20, 1923, Milton R. Bransom to National Office—NAACP, October 13, 1936, all in NAACP RECORDS, group1, series G, b. 86, "Morgan College, Baltimore, Md., 1920–1936."

67. J. W. Haywood Jr., to Charles H. Houston, October 6, 1934, Thurgood Marshall to Houston, September 21, 1934, R. A. Pearson to Harold Arthur Seaborne, July 26, 1933, Pearson to Juanita Elizabeth Jackson, January 26, 1934, Pearson to William Walker Proctor, June 8, 1934, Pearson to Donald Gaines Murray, December 14, 1934, F. K. Hazzard to Wayman R. Coston, September 11, 1933, H. F. Cotterman to Coston, January 22, 1934, Cotterman to Juanita E. Jackson, February 21, 1934, Cotterman to William W. Proctor, August 4, 1934, C. O. Appleton to Jackson, September 7, 1934, Cotterman to Jackson, September 14, 1934, J. W. Haywood Jr., to Charles H. Houston, October 6, 1934, Thurgood Marshall to Houston, September 21, 1934, all in NAACP RECORDS, group1, series D, b. 93, "Cases Supported, Univ. of Md., 1933–1934"; Kluger, *Simple Justice*, 186.

68. Appleton to Jackson, September 7, 1934, NAACP RECORDS, group1, series D, b. 93, "Cases Supported, Univ. of Md., 1933–1934."

69. Juanita J. Mitchell and Virginia Jackson Kiah interview, January 10, 1976; *Afro-American*, June 12, 1926; Klarman, "Why Massive Resistance?," 29; Gibson, *Young Thurgood*, 241–42.

70. Kieffer J. Mitchell interview, September 6, 2001; Kluger, *Simple Justice*, 190.

71. Houston, "Don't Shout Too Soon," 79, 91; Skotnes, *New Deal for All?*, 204.

72. Thurgood Marshall to T. Henderson Kerr, January 17, 1936, group 1, box C85, "Thurgood Marshall, Univ. of Md., 1935–1936," NAACP RECORDS; *Missouri ex rel. Gaines v. Canada*, 305 U.S. 337 (1938).

73. "Minutes of the Morgan College Board of Trustees, May 25, 1932," *Morgan College (Minutes), 1924–1937*, series 362–63, Maryland State Archives, Annapolis; "Minutes of the Morgan College Board of Trustees, June 30, 1932," ibid.; *Sun* (Baltimore), September 8, 1929; *Afro-American*, January 25, 1936.

74. *Afro-American*, December 25, 1948.

75. Albert J. Mitchell, "The Question of State Ownership of Morgan College," typescript, Morris Ames Soper Collection, box 16, folder 2, Beulah Davis Special Collection, Earl S. Richardson Library, Morgan State University, Baltimore.

76. Maryland Commission on Higher Education of Negroes, *Report of the Commission on Higher Education of Negroes to the Governor and Legislature of Maryland, January 15, 1937* (Baltimore: The Commission, 1937), 29–32.

77. Ibid., 31–33.

78. "Morgan Minutes," September 16, 1939, Morris Ames Soper Collection, box 16, folder 2, Beulah Davis Special Collection, Earl S. Richardson Library, Morgan State University, Baltimore; *Afro-American*, January 7, 1939, June 3, 1939, September 30, 1939; Wilson, *History of Morgan State College*, 87.

### CHAPTER 3. "We Have to Fight Segregation before We Can Get to Hitler"

1. *Afro-American*, September 16, 1939.

2. *Afro-American*, February 28, 1967.

3. "Selma" to Walter Winchell, August 6, 1942; "Carl James Greenburg Murphy," File 100–63963, vol. 1; H. I. Bobbitt to Hoover, October 28, 1942; "Report of Special Agent [redacted], February 13, 1943, at Baltimore, Maryland," 42–43—all in Records of the U.S. Department of Justice, Federal Bureau of Investigation. Washington, D.C.

4. Baum, *"Brown" in Baltimore*, 42.

5. "Brief Summary of Conferences on Current Educational Problems of Negroes to Date," April 11, 1940, in Minutes of Citizens Committee on Current Educational Problems of Negroes in Baltimore, box 88, folder 8, Letters of Carl Murphy, Afro-American Newspaper Collection, Moorland-Spingarn Research Center, Howard University, Washington, D.C. [hereafter Letters of Carl Murphy]; Justine Taylor to Carl J. Murphy, January 16, 1940, ibid.; Murphy to Francis M. Wood, April 15, 1940, ibid.; Murphy to Edward S. Lewis, April 15, 1940, ibid.; Wood to Murphy, April 23, 1940, ibid.; Lewis to Murphy, April 23, 1940, ibid.; Carl Murphy to David Weglien, July 23, 1940, ibid.; Weglien to Murphy, July 29, 1940, ibid.; Citizens Committee on Current Educational Problems of Negroes in Baltimore to Mayor Howard W. Jackson, July 27, 1940, ibid.; Murphy to Bramble, July 29, 1940, ibid.; Murphy to John J. Seidel, September 27, 1940, ibid.; Seidel to Murphy, October 30, 1940, ibid.; Thurgood Marshall to W. A. C. Hughes Jr., February 24, 1941, ibid.; Joshua E. Maxwell to Thurgood Marshall, October 3, 1945, group 2, box G143, "Schools: Md., 1944–1955," NAACP records.

6. Carl Murphy to Robert Stanton, November 14, 1941, box 88, folder 3, Letters of Carl Murphy; Stanton to Murphy, November 14. 1941, ibid.; Carl Murphy to Harry O. Levin, January 9, 1942, ibid.; O'Conor to Lillie M. Jackson, May 10 1941, ibid.

7. Edward S. Lewis to Carl Murphy, May 19, 1941, box 88, folder 3, Letters of Carl Murphy; Lewis to Murphy, ibid.; Carl Murphy to Arthur Jones, October 15, 1941, ibid.; *Afro-American*, May 6, 1941, May 23, 1941, February 28, 1967.

8. Litwack, *Trouble in Mind*, 263–64; Fairclough, *Race and Democracy*, 34–35; David Taft Terry, "Police and Policing Culture in the Big City South under Jim Crow," lecture, "Race and Justice: History as Context" symposium, Morgan State University, October 20, 2014.

9. Litwack, *Trouble in Mind*, 263–64; Fairclough, *Race and Democracy*, 110. See also Robin D. G. Kelley, "We Are Not What We Seem," 75–112.

10. *Afro-American*, September 6, 1930, June 12, 1926, October 26, 1929, October 17, 1925, April 30, 1927.

11. Honey, *Southern Labor*, 49.

12. "Police Brutalities," typescript, box B116, "Police Brutality: State, Baltimore, Md., 1940–1942," NAACP RECORDS; *Afro-American*, March 22, 1930, March 29, 1930, March 29, 1930, September 6, 1930, September 30, 1939; Fairclough, *Race and Democracy*, 34–35.

13. *Afro-American*, December 11, 1937, December 18, 1937, July 16, 1938, July 23, 1938, August 6, 1938.

14. K'Meyer, *Civil Rights in the Gateway*, 6–7; Bayor, *Race and the Shaping*, 177–78.

15. Victor E. Schminke to Theodore R. McKeldin, May 7, 1945, series 22, box 259, file [T] 10, Records of the Mayor: Theodore R. McKeldin Administrative Files (first term), 1943–1947, Baltimore City Archives, RG 9 [hereafter McKeldin Files BCA]; *Afro-American*, October 26, 1929.

16. *Afro-American*, March 29, 1930.

17. Fairclough, *Race and Democracy*, 110.

18. *Afro-American*, March 29, 1930.

19. *Afro-American*, February 22, 1936; *Afro-American*, May 22, 1937; Skotnes, *New Deal for All?*, 238–40. The Washington NAACP made an issue of brutality in the 1930s, joined in the effort by the D.C. Council of the National Negro Congress. See Gellman, *Death Blow to Jim Crow*, 135–62.

20. Wm. N. Jones to Walter White, May 25, 1930, group 1, series G, box 84, "1930," NAACP RECORDS; Linwood G. Koger to Robert W. Bagnall, November 14, 1930, ibid.; Bagnall to Carl Murphy, November 18, 1930, ibid.; *Afro-American*, January 18, 1930, September 6, 1930.

21. *Afro-American*, February 22, 1936.

22. *Afro-American*, August 6, 1938, October 31, 1931; *Brown v. Mississippi*, 297 U.S. 278 (1936); Fairclough, *Race and Democracy*, 34–35; Jeffrey S. Adler, "Greatest Thrill."

23. Dalfiume, "Forgotten Years," 93–103.

24. Reconstruction of evidence compiled from eyewitness accounts found in "Negro Meeting of Protests, April 24, 1942," "General Files, 1940–1942," series S 1041, Records of the Governor, Maryland State Archives, Annapolis [hereafter Records of the Governor, MSA, 1940–1942].

25. *Afro-American*, February 3, 1942, February 10, 1942; *Pittsburgh Courier*, February 14, 1942.

26. *Afro-American*, March 7, 1942, February 7, 1942, April 14, 1942.

27. Carl Murphy to Walter White and Roy Wilkins, March 20, 1942, group 2, box C76, "Baltimore, Md., 1942," NAACP RECORDS; Leon A. Ransom to Carl Murphy, March 23, 1942, ibid.; Juanita J. Mitchell interview, December 9, 1976, 43–44; *Afro-American*, April 28, 1942, March 31, 1942.

28. Juanita J. Mitchell interview, December 9, 1976, 43.

29. John E. T. Camper interview, July 2, 1976, O.H. 8134, 21–22; *Afro-American*, April 7, 1942, April 14, 1942, April 28, 1942.

30. *Afro-American*, April 28, 1942.

31. Ibid.

32. *Speed Morale for War Work in Maryland: A Partnership Is One For All, All For One*, 3–7. A copy of this pamphlet can be found in "Negro Meeting of Protests, April 24, 1942," Records of the Governor, MSA, 1940–1942.

33. Thurgood Marshall to Carl Murphy, April 27, 1942, box 88, folder 7, Letters of Carl Murphy; *Afro-American*, May 2, 1942, April 28, 1942.

34. Walter F. White to Herbert R. O'Conor, April 23, 1942 (telegram), "Negro Meeting of Protests, April 24, 1942," Records of the Governor, MSA, 1940–1942; *Sun* (Baltimore), May 3, 1942.

35. Thurgood Marshall to Carl Murphy, April 27, 1942, box 88, folder 7, Letters of Carl Murphy; *Afro-American*, May 2, 1942.

36. *Afro-American*, December 11, 1943, January 8, 1944.

37. George H. Callcott, *Maryland and America*, 46.

38. *Afro-American*, December 11, 1943, December 18, 1943, May 29, 1943; George H. Callcott, *Maryland and America*, 45.

39. Clark-Lewis, *Living In, Living Out*, 147–49.

40. *Afro-American*, April 28, 1942, April 24, 1943, May 1, 1943, May 29, 1943, April 3, 1943, April 17, 1943.

41. "The Industrial Program of the Baltimore Urban League," [undated], ser. VI, "Field Research Department, 1916–63," sub-ser. D, "Field Research Materials," box 30, "1944–63, Baltimore Md.," "Maryland: Baltimore—Labor Unions, Res. Dept., 1949," Records of the National Urban League, Manuscripts Division, Library of Congress, Washington, D.C. [hereafter NUL records]; Durr, *Behind the Backlash*, 17

42. "The Industrial Program of the Baltimore Urban League," [undated], ser. VI,

"Field Research Department, 1916–63," sub-ser. D, "Field Research Materials," box 30, "1944–63, Baltimore Md.," folder "Maryland: Baltimore—Labor Unions, Res. Dept., 1949," NUL records.

43. *Afro-American*, December 11, 1943, December 18, 1943, May 29, 1943, May 30, 1942.

44. Robin D. G. Kelley, *Race Rebels*, 4–5; Earl Lewis, *In Their Own Interests*, 29.

45. Donna Tyler Hollie interview, March 3, 2001; Durr, *Behind the Backlash*, 311–12.

46. Camper to O'Conor, March 1, 1944, "Negro Problems, Commission to Study, 1944," Records of the Governor, MSA, 1940–1942; Sidney Hollander to Barron, [draft copy, n.d.], box 67, folder 10, Sidney Hollander Collection (1926–1972), MS 2044, Maryland Historical Society, Baltimore [hereafter, Hollander Collection; Lawrence W. Cramer to Sidney Hollander, Feb 1, 1943, ibid.; *Afro-American*, March 13, 1943.

47. Anderson, "Last Hired, First Fired," 84.

48. Durr, *Behind the Backlash*, 313.

49. Ibid., 312.

50. *Afro-American*, November 20, 1943, December 11, 1943, December 25, 1943.

51. Ibid., December 25, 1943.

52. *Afro-American*, December 18, 1943; Durr, *Behind the Backlash*, 313.

53. *Afro-American*, December 25, 1943.

54. McAllister Tyler interview, May 3, 1001; Robin D. G. Kelley, *Hammer and Hoe*, 4–7; Laurie B. Green, *Battling the Plantation Mentality*, 2–4.

55. "Memorandum for Governor O'Conor," December 14, 1943, folder "WEL–WES," Records of the Governor, MSA, 1940–1942; Arthur Stewart to O'Conor, December 14, 1943, ibid.; Thomas Jones, Secretary of State, to Arthur Stewart, December 20, 1943, ibid.; *Afro-American*, August 7, 1943, January 8, 1944.

56. George H. Callcott, *Maryland and America*, 4–10. Ronald Bayor and others demonstrate, for example, that from the time of disfranchisement in Georgia until the mid-1930s, blacks still represented 5–11 percent of total registered voters, mostly concentrated in large urban areas like Atlanta, where periodic registration efforts were led by social justice activists, including the local NAACP branch. See Bayor, *Race and the Shaping*, 15–20; Dittmer, *Black Georgia*, 102–3. On Memphis's Boss Crump and black voters, see Laurie B. Green, *Battling the Plantation Mentality*, 5–6; Honey, *Southern Labor*, 44–52.

57. George H. Callcott, *Maryland and America*, 4–10; Bayor, *Race and the Shaping*, 15–20; Honey, *Southern Labor*, 44–52.

58. Marshall to Murphy, April 27, 1942, box 88, folder 7, Letters of Carl Murphy; *Afro-American*, September 19, 1942, September 29, 1942; George H. Callcott, *Maryland and America*, 57.

59. Capeci, "From Different Liberal Perspectives," 163.

60. *Afro-American*, November 2, 1943; Durr, *Behind the Backlash*, 18–20.

61. *Afro-American*, May 8, 1943, January 15, 1944, November 2, 1943; Mibolsky, "Power from the Pulpit," 278; Sartain, *Borders of Equality*, 76–107.

62. *Afro-American*, May 8, 1943, January 15, 1944, November 2, 1943; Mibolsky, "Power from the Pulpit," 277–78.

63. *Afro-American*, June 12, 1943; Power, "Pyrrhic Victory," 277; Skotnes, *New Deal for All?*, 81, 85, 298.

64. George H. Callcott, *Maryland and America*, 149.

65. *Afro-American*, May 8, 1943.

66. Ibid.; George H. Callcott, *Maryland and America*, 149.

67. *Sun* (Baltimore), October 26, 1996; *Afro-American*, November 26, 1983.

68. *Sun* (Baltimore), October 26, 1996; *Sun*, May 4, 2001.

69. Theoharis, *Rebellious Life*, 21; Cumberbatch, "What 'the Cause' Needs," 62. See also Neverdon-Morton, *Afro-American Women in the South*; Ransby, *Ella Baker*.

70. *Afro-American*, May 15, 1949.

71. Marie Bauernschmidt to Howard W. Jackson, March 11, 1942, series 21, box 246, folder s5–74 (1), Records of the Mayor: Howard Jackson Administrative Files (Fourth Term), 1938–1942, Baltimore City Archives [hereafter Jackson Files BCA]. An important study on the evolution of racial liberalism remains Sosna, *In Search of the Silent South*.

72. Harry Allers to Howard W. Jackson, March 12, 1942, series 21, box 246, folder s5–74 (1), Jackson Files BCA; Herbert R. O'Conor to Howard W. Jackson, March 12, 1942, ibid.; Victor E. Schminke to Theodore R. McKeldin, May 7, 1945, series 22, box 259, file [T] 10, McKeldin Files BCA.

73. *Afro-American*, March 27, 1942.

74. Ibid., *Sun* (Baltimore), March 24, 1942.

75. Camper interview, 21.

76. Ibid.

77. Ibid., 20.

## CHAPTER 4. "A Conspicuous Absurdity"

1. *Sun* (Baltimore), March 24, 1942; Rhonda Williams, *Politics of Public Housing*, 6.

2. Citizens Planning and Housing Association, *Annual Report, 1941–1942*, "Housing—Baltimore (Envelope I)," vertical file, Maryland Room, Enoch Pratt Free Library, Baltimore, 5; Work Projects Administration, "Survey of Vacancies in Dwelling Units of Baltimore, Maryland," Memorandum, March 19, 1942, ibid.; Healy, *Report of the Governor's Commission*, 117.

3. *Sun* (Baltimore), March 24, 1942.

4. Rhonda Williams, *Politics of Public Housing*, 6.

5. Carolyn A. (Gross) Collins interview, April 26, 2001; Citizens Planning and Housing Association, "History of CPHA's Relations with the Mayor, the Baltimore Housing Authority Commissioners, and the FPHA," 2, Records of the Citizens' Planning and Housing Association, Special Collections Department, Lansdale Library, University of Baltimore, Baltimore [hereafter CPHA RECORDS]; Housing Authority of Baltimore City, "Fifteen Years of Public Housing," November 1952, vertical file, Maryland Room, Enoch Pratt Free Library, Baltimore.

6. Collins interview.

7. Citizens Planning and Housing Association of Baltimore, "Memorandum on Negro Housing in Metropolitan Baltimore," August 1944, CPHA RECORDS; J. D. Steele to Theodore R. McKeldin, August 19, 1943, box 253, file G1–48 (5), McKeldin Files BCA].

8. "Baltimore—First—and Worst," *Housing*, May 1946, 1; Housing Bureau, Baltimore City Health Department, "The Baltimore Plan of Housing Law Enforcement," May 1952, box 263, file 21, "Baltimore Plan (1)," "Records of the Mayor: D'Alesandro, Jr. Administrative Files (from three terms between May 1947–February 1959 filed as a group), Baltimore City Archives, RG 9, series 23 [hereafter D'Alesandro Files BCA].

9. Frances Morton Froelicher interview, October 18, 1977, 2; Housing Bureau, Baltimore City Health Department, "The Baltimore Plan of Housing Law Enforcement," May 1952, box 263, file 21, "Baltimore Plan (1)," D'Alesandro Files BCA.

10. Citizens Planning and Housing Association of Baltimore, "Memorandum on Negro Housing in Metropolitan Baltimore," August 1944, CPHA RECORDS; Baltimore Urban League to Alfred H. Fletcher, May 18, 1945, "Housing—Baltimore, Envelope 1," vertical file, Maryland Room, Enoch Pratt Free Library, Baltimore.

11. Citizens Planning and Housing Association, "History of CPHA's Relations with the Mayor, the Baltimore Housing Authority Commissioners, and the FPHA," CPHA RECORDS, 2; Housing Authority of Baltimore City, "Fifteen Years of Public Housing," November 1952, vertical file, Maryland Room, Enoch Pratt Free Library, Baltimore; Citizens Planning and Housing Association of Baltimore, "Memorandum on Negro Housing in Metropolitan Baltimore," August 1944, CPHA RECORDS; J. D. Steele to Theodore R. McKeldin, August 19, 1943, box 253, file G1–48 (5), McKeldin Files BCA; Rhonda Williams, *Politics of Public Housing*, 31, 37.

12. Citizens Planning and Housing Association, "History of CPHA's Relations with the Mayor, the Baltimore Housing Authority Commissioners, and the FPHA," CPHA RECORDS, 2; "Fifteen Years of Public Housing."

13. United States Housing Authority, Release No. 389, September 25, 1939, "Housing—Baltimore—Edgar Allen Poe Homes," vertical file, Maryland Room, Enoch Pratt Free Library, Baltimore; *Afro-American*, October 26, 1935; Rhonda Williams, *Politics of Public Housing*, 36.

14. "The Story of Public Housing," series 21, box 243, folder G1–74 (1), 31, Jackson Files BCA; "Fifteen Years of Public Housing."

15. "The Citizen Looks at Defense Housing in Baltimore," submitted by Frances H. Morton, President of the Citizens' Housing Council of Baltimore to the House Committee Investigating Defense Migration to Baltimore—July 1st and 2nd, 1941," "Housing—Baltimore, Envelope 1," vertical file, Maryland Room, Enoch Pratt Free Library, Baltimore; *Sun* (Baltimore), March 3, 1946; Work Projects Administration, "Survey of Vacancies in Dwelling Units of Baltimore, Maryland," Memorandum, March 19, 1942, "Housing—Baltimore (Envelope I)," vertical file, Maryland Room, Enoch Pratt Free Library, Baltimore; Healy, *Report of the Governor's Commission*, 117.

16. Citizens Housing and Planning Association, "Resolution," April 23, 1943, box 253, file G1–48 (4), McKeldin Files BCA; Cleveland Bealmear, Chairman of the Housing Authority of Baltimore City, "Postwar Housing Program for Baltimore: General Statement," January 1944, box 252, file G1–38 (2), McKeldin Files BCA; *Baltimore Real Estate News* 8, no. 9 (September 1940): 10–11.

17. Baltimore Civilian Mobilization Committee, "A Survey of Negro Housing Facilities in District 15—Community 1, Blocks 1 to 37 of the Baltimore Block Brigade," box 253, file G1–48 (4), 3, table ix, McKeldin Files BCA; *Afro-American*, January 1, 1944.

18. "Survey of Negro Housing Facilities in District 15," tables vi–viii.

19. Citizens Planning and Housing Association of Baltimore, "Memorandum on Negro Housing in Metropolitan Baltimore," August 1944, CPHA RECORDS; U.S. Bureau of Census, "Survey of Occupancy in Privately Owned Dwelling Units of Baltimore, Maryland," September 3, 1944, "Housing—Baltimore (Envelope I)," vertical file, Maryland Room, Enoch Pratt Free Library, Baltimore; Rhonda Williams, *Politics of Public Housing*, 9.

20. Citizens Committee on Housing for Negro War Workers to Francis A. Davis, et al., July 9, 1943, box 253, file G1–48 (5), McKeldin Files BCA; Oliver C. Winston to McKeldin, n.d., ibid.; Herbert Emmerich to McKeldin, n.d., ibid.; Francis A. Davis to The-

odore R. McKeldin, July 10, 1943, ibid.; John J. Lang to Theodore R. McKeldin, July 22, 1943, ibid.; McKeldin to Oliver C. Winston, July 23, 1943, ibid.; *Afro-American*, May 1, 1943; Meyer, *As Long as They Don't Move*, 72–74.

21. John W. Holmes to Theodore R. McKeldin, July 17, 1943, box 253, file G1–48 (3), McKeldin Files BCA; *Sun* (Baltimore), July 20, 1943; Meyer, *As Long as They Don't Move Next Door*, 73.

22. Julia Herling to Theodore McKeldin, July 27, 1943, box 253, file G1–48 (3), McKeldin Files_BCA; Cornelia Arnold to Theodore McKeldin, July 20, 1943, ibid.; Sarah V. Blanchard to Theodore McKeldin, August 13, 1943, ibid.

23. Lillie M. Jackson to Theodore R. McKeldin, September 27, 1943, box 253, file G1–48 (5), McKeldin Files BCA; *Afro-American*, August 28, 1943, July 24, 1943.

24. McKeldin to R. L. Cochran, August 16, 1943, box 253, file G1–48 (3), McKeldin Files_BCA; Randall L. Tyus to Theodore R. McKeldin, August 16, 1943, ibid.

25. *Afro-American*, November 6, 1943; Meyer, *As Long as They Don't Move*, 74–75.

26. Compiled from statistics in *Public Housing in Baltimore, 1941–1942*; "Fifteen Years of Public Housing"; Collins interview.

27. Housing Authority of Baltimore City, *Annual Report*, 1945, S1041–9626–3, "Baltimore City—General File, 1945," Records of the Governor (General Files), Maryland State Archives; *Afro-American*, January 18, 1947.

28. *Afro-American*, January 18, 1947

29. "Poe, McCulloh, Douglass," *Houses and Homes* 2, no. 1 (June 1945): 4; Rhonda Williams, *Politics of Public Housing*, 23.

30. "Poe, McCulloh, Douglass," *Houses and Homes* 2, no. 1 (June 1945): 4

31. Thelma Koger Parker interview, August 7, 2003.

32. *Meade v. Dennistone* 173 Md. 295 (1938); Kluger, *Simple Justice*, 247–55.

33. Kluger, *Simple Justice*, 247–55; Rhonda Williams, *Politics of Public Housing*, 6.

34. *Shelley v. Kraemer*, 334 U.S. 1 (1948); *Afro-American*, January 20, 1948; Kluger, *Simple Justice*, 247–55; Rhonda Williams, *Politics of Public Housing*, 6.

35. Parker interview; Anastatia Phillips Benton, interview, August 20, 2001; "Population: Maryland," in *Sixteenth Census of the United States: 1940* (Washington, D.C.: Bureau of the Census, 1941), tract 14–3; "Dwelling Units by Occupancy Status and Race of Occupants, by Census Tracts," in ibid.; John E. T. Camper and James Stewart Martin to Thomas D'Alesandro, May 3, 1948, box 282, file 156, D'Alesandro Files BCA.

36. *Afro-American*, November 9, 1948; *Sun* (Baltimore), February 28, 1952, October 10, 1951, February 28, 1952.

37. Tyler interview.

38. "Metropolitan Districts, Population and area," in *Census of the United States: 1930* (Washington, D.C.: Bureau of the Census, 1932); "Population: Maryland," in *Sixteenth Census of the United States: 1940*; "Census Tract Statistics: Baltimore, Maryland, and Adjacent Area, Selected Population and Housing Characteristics," in *Census of Population: 1950* (Washington, D.C.: Government Printing Office, 1952); Maryland Commission on Interracial Problems and Relations, *American City in Transition*, 45–46.

39. *Sun* (Baltimore), February 2, 1948.

40. *Afro-American*, October 18, 1947, October 25, 1947.

41. *Afro-American*, October 25, 1947.

42. Ibid.

43. Ibid.

44. *Afro-American*, October 25, 1947.

45. Ibid.

46. Ibid.

47. *Afro-American*, November 8, 1947; Durr, *Behind the Backlash*, 89–90.

48. Parker interview; *Sun* (Baltimore), July 14, 1995; Meyer, *As Long as They Don't Move*, 5.

49. Parker interview.

50. "Minutes of the Board of School Commissioners for Baltimore City (Executive Committee)," October 20–December 1, 1949, Records of the Department of Education, Baltimore City Archives, RG 31 series 1, "Board of School Commissioners," sub-series A, "Minutes" [hereafter BSC Minutes BCA], folio, "Exec. Session Minutes," 1949, 28–36; Hollie interview; Tyler interview.

51. Benton interview.

52. Anonymous to Thomas D'Alesandro Jr., December 3, 1951, box 282, file 156, D'Alesandro Files BCA; Hollie interview; Orser, *Blockbusting in Baltimore*, 96–97.

53. Baltimore Urban League, "An Inquiry into Loans for Negro Home Purchases in Baltimore," June 26, 1952, series 3, box 50, file "Baltimore, 1952–53," NUL records.

54. Anonymous to Thomas D'Alesandro Jr., December 3, 1951, box 282, file 156, D'Alesandro Files BCA; Orser, *Blockbusting in Baltimore*, 96–97.

55. The total population of census tract 15–3, the Tyler's Presstman Street neighborhood, over the period 1930–1950, declined as follows: 5,628 (1930), 5,489 (1940), 4,746 (1950). The black population of that tract over the period increased from zero in 1930 (when one nonwhite person who claimed to be neither white nor black was recorded) to 104 in 1940 and 1,248 in 1950. The white residents were recorded as follows: 5,627 (1930), 5,385 (1940), 3,498 (1950).

56. See Orser, *Blockbusting in Baltimore*.

57. *Census of the United States: 1930; Evening Sun* (Baltimore), May 17, 1979; Maryland Commission on Interracial Problems and Relations, *American City in Transition*, 46.

58. Edna Dixon Pierce, President of the Ladies of Charity of St. Gregory's to D'Alesandro, October 15, 1947 [received], box 282, file 156, D'Alesandro Files BCA; "Metropolitan Districts. Population and Area," in *Census of the United States: 1930* (Washington, D.C.: Bureau of the Census, 1932); "Population: Maryland," in *Sixteenth Census of the United States: 1940* (Washington, D.C.: Bureau of the Census, 1941); "Census Tract Statistics: Baltimore, Maryland, and Adjacent Area—Selected Population and Housing Characteristics," in *Census of Population: 1950* (Washington, D.C.: Government Printing Office, 1952).

59. *Afro-American*, July 15, 1944.

60. Tyler interview; Hollie interview; Benton interview; Board of Park Commissioners Meeting Minutes, Records of the Department of Recreation and Parks, 1865–Present, RG 51, Baltimore City Archives [hereafter BPC Minutes BCA], September 15, 1950, series 5, vol. 1946–1951, fol. 546.

61. Hollie interview; Juanita J. Mitchell interview, December 9, 1976, 34; *Afro-American*, November 19, 1949, October 8, 1949; *Sun* (Baltimore), November 17, 1949.

62. BPC Minutes BCA, September 15, 1950, series 5, vol. 1946–1951, fol. 548.

63. Ibid., fol. 546.

64. BPC Minutes BCA, July 14, 1950, series 5, vol. 1946–1951, fol. 529.

65. BPC Minutes BCA, March 1, 1949, series 5, vol. 1946–1951, fol. 302.

66. *Afro-American,* April 19, 1969; BPC Minutes BCA, May 10, 1949, series 5, vol. 1946–1951, fol. 328, 338.

67. Leuchtenburg, *White House Looks South,* 165.

68. Willie Adams, Interview by Charles Wagandt, August 4, 1977, Governor Theodore R. McKeldin–Dr. Lillie Mae Jackson Oral History Project, Oral History Collection, Maryland Historical Society, Baltimore, 10.

69. Adams interview, 7–8; *Afro-American,* August 18, 1934, August 25, 1934, September 22, 1934; Kirsch, "Municipal Golf and Civil Rights," 376–77; Wells, Buckley, and Boone, "Separate but Equal?," 157–59. For a more detailed description of the golf struggle of the mid-1930s through the mid-1940s, see Terry, "Tramping for Justice," 234–41.

70. BPC Minutes_BCA, June 5, 1945, series 5, vol. 1934–1946, fol. 508, 515; Adams interview, 11.

71. Leon J. Raymond, et al. to Thomas D'Alesandro Jr., June 13, 1951, box 282, file 156, D'Alesandro Files BCA; Lillie M. Jackson to D'Alesandro, July 24, 1948, box 276, file 93, ibid.; Adams interview, 9–10; *Afro-American,* December 27, 1947.

72. *Evening Sun* (Baltimore), June 18, 1948; BPC Minutes BCA, June 25, 1951, series 5, vol. 1951–1956, fol. 46; Adams interview, 9–10; *Afro-American,* June 19, 1948; *Evening Sun* (Baltimore), June 29, 1948.

73. BPC Minutes BCA, June 25, 1951, series 5, vol. 1951–1956, fol. 46; Adams interview, 9–10; Sidney Hollander Foundation, *Toward Equality,* 22.

74. *Lonesome et al. v. Maxwell et al., Dawson et al. v. Mayor & City Council of Baltimore et al., Isaacs et al. v. Mayor & City Council of Baltimore et al.* 123 F. Supp. 193 (1954); *Afro-American,* November 8, 1955.

**CHAPTER 5. Interracialists and the Struggle**

1. Wright would never play a regular season game in the major leagues. Riley, *Biographical Encyclopedia,* 883; Falkner, *Great Time Coming,* 139–41.

2. *Afro-American,* July 12, 1947; *New York Times,* July 4, 1947; Luke, *Integrating the Orioles,* 16–23; Bready, *Baseball in Baltimore,* 213; "1946 Minor League Baseball League Encyclopedia," *Baseball-Reference.com,* http://www.baseball-reference.com/minors/league.cgi?year=1946, accessed September 7, 2013; "1947 Cleveland Indians," *Baseball-Reference.com,* http://www.baseball-reference.com/teams/CLE/1947.shtml, accessed September 7, 2013.

3. Tygiel, *Baseball's Great Experiment,* 130–31; Luke, *Baltimore Elite Giants,* 101; Falkner, *Great Time Coming,* 136; Bready, *Baseball in Baltimore,* 212, 214.

4. *Afro-American,* August 3, 1946; Falkner, *Great Time Coming,* 139–40. An earlier version of this passage appeared as David Taft Terry, "Baseball, Hotdogs, Crackers, and Jack," *Baltimore Gaslight: Newsletter of the Baltimore City Historical Society* 13, no. 1 (Spring 2014): 8.

5. BPC Minutes BCA, April 25, 1945, fol. 508; *Afro-American,* August 3, 1946, April 18, 1959.

6. Healy, *Report of the Governor's Commission,* 133.

7. *Afro-American,* October 15, 1949; George H. Callcott, *Maryland and America,* 65–67.

8. Delores Richburg Harried, interview, March 3, 2001, Baltimore; Nathaniel Redd interview, April 2, 2001, Baltimore; Patricia Logan Welsh interview, March 5, 2001, Baltimore.

9. Hollie interview.

10. Memorandum on Baltimore Urban League meeting with Hochschild-Kohn & Co., November 1, 1949, series 6, "Field Research Department, 1916–63," sub-series D, "Field Research Materials," box 30, "1944–63, Baltimore Md.," file "Baltimore, Maryland Industrial Committee," NUL records; Mrs. Frances M. Jencks and Mrs. H. Milton Wagner to Gov. Herbert O'Conor, April 12, 1944, S1041, file "Negro Problems, Commission to Study—1944," Records of the Governor, MSA, 1942–1944; *Afro-American*, January 6, 1948; Sidney Hollander Foundation, *Toward Equality*, 22, 65.

11. Smith, *Here Lies Jim Crow*, 144–45.

12. Hollander to Walter White, August 22, 1947, group 2, box C 78NAACP records; Hollander to Walter White, September 18, 1947, box A 305, ibid.; David Taft Terry, "'Tinged with Hostility': Competing Agendas and Social Justice Reform in Baltimore, 1931–1959" (presentation, Baltimore Historical Society, Baltimore History Evenings, June 19, 2014).

13. Camper interview, 23.

14. *Afro-American*, March 25, 1944; Joseph P. Healy to Herbert O'Conor, April 25, 1944, S1041, file "Negro Problems, Commission to Study—1944," Records of the Governor, MSA, 1942–1944.

15. Mamie Bland Todd interview, November 18, 2001; Benton interview; Mrs. Frances M. Jencks and Mrs. H. Milton Wagner to Gov. Herbert O'Conor, April 12, 1944, S1041, "Negro Problems, Commission to Study—1944," Records of the Governor, MSA, 1942–1944; Memorandum on Baltimore Urban League meeting with Hochschild-Kohn & Co., November 1, 1949, series 6, "Field Research Department, 1916–63," sub-series D, "Field Research Materials," box 30, "1944–63, Baltimore Md.," files "Baltimore, Maryland Industrial Committee," NUL records; Mrs. Frances M. Jencks and Mrs. H. Milton Wagner to Gov. Herbert O'Conor, April 12, 1944, S1041, file "Negro Problems, Commission to Study—1944," Records of the Governor, MSA, 1942–1944; *Afro-American*, January 6, 1953.

16. Lynda Hall Gowie interview, August 18, 2001; Hollie interview.

17. Gowie interview; Collins interview; memorandum on Baltimore Urban League meeting with Hochschild-Kohn & Co., November 1, 1949, series 6, "Field Research Department, 1916–63," sub-series D, "Field Research Materials," box 30, "1944–63, Baltimore Md.," file "Baltimore, Maryland Industrial Committee," NUL records.

18. Welsh interview.

19. Clarence M. Mitchell Jr. interview, February 12, 1977, 34.

20. Camper interview, 35; Juanita J. Mitchell to George M. Houser, January 21, 195[2], in *Papers of the Congress of Racial Equality*, series 3, roll 8, no. 6.

21. *Afro-American*, October 15, 1938, December 3, 1938, December 10, 1938.

22. *Afro-American*, January 13, 1933, January 28, 1933, October 15, 1938; Skotnes, *New Deal for All?*, 64–68; Falkner, *Great Time Coming*, 95; Peterson, *Only the Ball Was White*.

23. Broadus Mitchell," August 14–15, 1977, http://docsouth.unc.edu/sohp/B-0024/menu.html; *New York Times*, April 30, 1988; *Afro-American*, January 13, 1940, February 14, 1942; Skotnes, *New Deal for All?*, 185, 191–93.

24. Edward Lewis to Sidney Hollander, June 26, 1940, box 7, folder 10, Hollander Collection; *Afro-American*, November 18, 1939.

25. See draft of BIF Constitution, circa 1942, Fellowship House (Philadelphia, Pa.) Records, series 7, box 78, Special Collection Research Center, Samuel L. Paley Library, Temple University, Philadelphia [hereafter Fellowship House Records].

26. Sidney Hollander to Dorothy Dare, February 11, 1942, box 67, folder 10, Hol-

lander Collection; "Third Anniversary of Baltimore Chapter, Union for Democratic Action Report and Introduction of Guest Speaker, Bruce Bliven—Baltimore, Md.," May 1, 1945, box 1, file 17, ibid.; *Baltimore U.D.A. Newsletter* 1, no. 2 (March 1, 1945), *Americans for Democratic Action Papers, 1932–1965* (Sanford, N.C.: Microfilming Corporation of America, 1979), [3]; *Afro-American*, February 8, 1947.

27. "A.D.A and the Liberal Movement," March 28, 1947, box 1, folder 18, Hollander Collection; Edna Walls to William Cochrane, September 20, 1945, box 67, folder 12, ibid.

28. Sidney Hollander, "Speech to Baltimore Chapter of UDA, announcing the formation of the Americans from Democratic Action," January 10, 1947, box 92, file 9, Hollander Collection; "Speech to Baltimore Chapter of UDA, announcing the formation of the Americans from Democratic Action," January 10, 1947, box 92, folder 9, ibid.; Rossinow, *Visions of Progress*, 189–90.

29. *Sun* (Baltimore), March 9, 1918, August 22, 1920; Margaret Law Callcott, *Negro in Maryland Politics*, 102–14; *Laws of Maryland* 476, chap. 133, 202–5.

30. *Afro-American*, November 2, 1943, November 12, 1938, November 12, 1938, October 6, 1934, March 18, 1944, March 20, 1945, March 26, 1946.

31. Leuchtenburg, *White House Looks South*, 165, 171–72. Ellipses and emphasis in original.

32. Gilmore, *Defying Dixie*, 417.

33. *Sun* (Baltimore), February 12, 1948, June 12, 1947, July 24, 1947, September 15, 1947, March 28, 1948, August 29, 1948; *Afro-American*, October 18, 1947, October 2, 1948.

34. "Speech to Baltimore Chapter of Americans for Democratic Action," March 5, 1948, box 92, file 11, Hollander Collection; Rossinow, *Visions of Progress*, 190; *Sun* (Baltimore), September 16, 1948, September 13, 1948.

35. Republican Dewey, who had shown strongly in 1944 against FDR, with 292,949 votes (48.15 percent) to Roosevelt's 315,490 (51.85 percent), losing by only 22,541 ballots, won the state in 1948 with 294,814 votes, less than a majority (49.4 percent).

36. *Afro-American*, June 19, 1943.

37. *Afro-American*, October 9, 1943, October 16, 1943.

38. Sartain, *Borders of Equality*, 65–69.

39. Mitchell and Kiah interview, 3; *Afro-American*, June 19, 1943, October 9, 1943, October 16, 1943; Cumberbatch, "What 'the Cause' Needs," 62; Smith, *Here Lies Jim Crow*, 153–54.

40. Camper interview, 23; Mitchell and Kiah interview, 4; *Afro-American*, July 15, 1944; *Evening Sun* (Baltimore), September 17, 1993.

41. Camper interview, 23; *Sun* (Baltimore), February 12, 1950.

42. Camper interview, 23; *Afro-American*, February 9, 1952; *Evening Sun* (Baltimore), September 17, 1993.

43. *Afro-American*, October 29, 1949, April 3, 1948; *Sun* (Baltimore), March 28, 1948.

44. Rossinow, *Visions of Progress*, 188–89.

45. Meier and Rudwick, *CORE*, 16–17.

46. Juanita J. Mitchell to George M. Houser, January 21, 195[2], in *Papers of the Congress of Racial Equality*, series 3, roll 8, no. 6; Elizabeth T. Meyer to George Houser, January 4, 1952, ibid.; Kelman, *Time to Speak*, 229–30; Herbert Kelman to George Houser, February 9, 1952, in *Papers of the Congress of Racial Equality*, series 3, roll 8, no. 6; Houser to CORE Groups, April 7, 1953, in *Papers of the Congress of Racial Equality*, series 3, roll 8, no. 6.

47. *Afro-American,* January 14, 1950; May 12, 1973.

48. Farmer, *Lay Bare the Heart,* 70; Meier and Rudwick, *CORE,* 4–39, 48, 76.

49. Meier and Rudwick, *CORE,* 45–46, 49–54; Jones, "Before Montgomery and Greensboro."

50. *Afro-American,* May 9, 1953.

51. Herbert Kelman to George Houser, May 19, 1953, in *Papers of the Congress of Racial Equality,* series 3, roll 8, no. 6.

52. Tom O'Leary to George Houser, November 10, 1953, in *Papers of the Congress of Racial Equality,* series 3, roll 8, no. 6; O'Leary to Houser, March 1, 1954, ibid.; O'Leary to Houser, November 10, 1953, ibid.; Houser to Herbert Kelman, December 4, 1953, ibid.; Houser to Kelman, December 17, 1953, ibid.; *Afro-American,* May 8, 1954.

53. O'Leary to Houser, November 10, 1953, in *Papers of the Congress of Racial Equality,* series 3, roll 8, no. 6; Houser to Kelman, December 4, 1953, ibid.; Houser to Kelman, December 17, 1953, ibid.; O'Leary to Houser, March 1, 1954, ibid.; *Afro-American,* August 1, 1953, May 9, 1953, August 20, 1960, May 8, 1954; *Sun* (Baltimore), January 30, 1992; Meier and Rudwick, *CORE,* 25, 34–35; *Lonesome v. Maxwell,* 123 F. Supp. 193 (D. Md. 1954).

54. *Sun* (Baltimore), September 5,1955; *Afro-American,* September 4, 1956; Wolcott, *Race, Riots, and Roller Coasters,* 183–84.

55. *Afro-American,* September 4, 1956; *Sun* (Baltimore), September 2, 1957, September 1, 1958; Arsenault, *Freedom Riders,* 44; Meier and Rudwick, *CORE,* 78, 83, 76.

56. *Sun* (Baltimore), September 1, 1958, September 7, 1959, September 8, 1959.

57. *Afro-American,* March 30, 1957, June 24, 1958.

58. *Afro-American,* December 29, 1956, January 19, 1957, February 23, 1957, April 11, 1959; Brugger, *Maryland,* 584.

59. Edna Dixon Pierce, President of the Ladies of Charity of St. Gregory's to D'Alesandro, October 15, 1947 [received], box 282, file 156, D'Alesandro Files: BCA; Hollie interview; *Evening Sun* (Baltimore), May 17, 1979.

60. Clarence Logan interview, March 11, 2011.

61. *Afro-American,* November 24, 1956, December 29, 1956, April 6, 1957.

62. *Afro-American,* October 18, 1958; Lynch, *Black Urban Condition,* 430–31; Manis, *Fire You Can't Put Out,* 192–93; Eskew, *But for Birmingham,* 144–46.

63. *Afro-American,* October 6, 1956.

64. *Afro-American,* October 6, 1956, January 1, 1957; Branch, *Parting the Waters,* 207–11; Garrow, *Bearing the Cross,* 83–84.

65. *Sun* (Baltimore), December 25, 2004, November 20, 1964.

66. *Afro-American,* June 8, 1958.

67. Scott, *Contempt and Pity,* 136.

68. *Sun* (Baltimore), December 1, 1992; Marable, *Malcolm X,* 105, 111; Amin, "From Mosque Six," 24–25.

69. *Afro-American,* November 21, 1959.

## CHAPTER 6. "This Beginning Will Awaken Others"

1. Dallas F. Nicholas to Howard W. Jackson, March 17, 1942, series 21, box 246, file s5–74 (2), Jackson Files BCA; McKeldin interview, April 6, 1971, 26, 43; *Sun* (Baltimore), May 29, 1942.

2. The population breakdown was as follows: in the elementary schools, 47,680 whites to 24,535 blacks; in the vocational schools, 454 whites to 409 blacks; in the junior highs,

14,919 whites to 4,596 blacks; and in the senior highs, 10,429 whites to 1,906 blacks. "Argument Used in Introducing Committee on Education to School Board Thursday, February 15," February 28, 1945, group 2, box G143, file "Schools: Md., 1944–1955," NAACP records.

3. Welsh interview; Hollie interview; Alfred Hughes interview, August 29, 2001.

4. W. H. Lemmel to Sylvia McKinney, November 21, 1952, series 23, box 297, files 258 (9), D'Alesandro Files BCA; BSC Minutes BCA, March 5, 1953 (Private Session), 15 (italics are mine).

5. Ann Todd Jealous interview, November 11, 2001.

6. Hollie interview; Welsh interview.

7. Benton interview; Hollie interview; Todd interview.

8. Jealous interview; Keiffer J. Mitchell interview.

9. *Sun* (Baltimore), February 16, 1945.

10. Ibid.

11. Baum, *"Brown" in Baltimore*, 42.

12. *Missouri ex rel. Gaines v. Canada*, 305 U.S. 337 (1938); *Sweatt v. Painter*, 339 U.S. 629 (1950).

13. Templeton, "Admission of Negro Boys," 22; O'Wesney, "Historical Study of the Progress," 58; Baum, *"Brown" in Baltimore*, 51.

14. Elizabeth T. Meyer to George Houser, January 4, 1952, in *Papers of the Congress of Racial Equality, 1941–1967*. Sanford, N.C.: Microfilming Corporation of America, 1980, series 3, roll 8, no. 6; *ADA News*, March 1952, September 1951, October 1951; *Sun* (Baltimore), September 26, 1951; Templeton, "Admission of Negro Boys," 22–29.

15. *Afro-American*, April 5, 1947.

16. Daniel Atwood to Rev. Roy Ross, February 4, 1948, box 276, file 93, D'Alesandro Files BCA; Robert Garrett to Thomas D'Alesandro, January 27, 1948, ibid.; D'Alesandro Jr. to Garrett, January 29, 1948, ibid.

17. BPC Minutes, January 6, 1948, series 5, vol. 1946–1951, folder 146; ibid., January 14, 1948, series 5, vol. 1946–1951, folder 149; ibid., May 4, 1948, series 5, vol. 1946–1951, folder 209; ibid., October 11, 1948, series 5, vol. 1946–1951, folder 254; *Afro-American*, December 7, 1947, January 10, 1948.

18. Maurice Braverman to D'Alesandro, February 9, 1948, D'Alesandro Files BCA, box 276, file 93; Alice B. Arrington to D'Alesandro, February 17, 1948, ibid.

19. Garrett to D'Alesandro, January 27, 1948, D'Alesandro Files BCA, box 276, file 93; D'Alesandro Jr. to Garrett, January 29, 1948, ibid.

20. "Racial Tennis Group to Face Grand Jury," *Evening Sun* (Baltimore), July 12, 1948.

21. Marjorie N. Everingham and Ben. C. Everingham to D'Alesandro, July 23, 1948, D'Alesandro Files BCA, box 276, file 93; *Afro-American*, November 20, 1948, October 23, 1948, November 4, 1948; *Evening Sun* (Baltimore), July 15, 1948, July 22, 1948, July 26, 1948, July 27, 1948, October 25, 1948, November 9, 1948.

22. *Sun* (Baltimore), November 27, 1988.

23. Gene A. Giles interview, March 31, 2001; *Sun* (Baltimore), May 25, 1952.

24. While no black had served on the school board until 1944, apparently the seats were doled out according to constituencies: a Jewish seat, a Catholic seat, a seat for the University of Maryland, a seat for Johns Hopkins, a black seat, and so on. See Baum, *"Brown" in Baltimore*, 51, 68.

25. Walter Sondheim Jr. interview, September 27, 1976, 2.

26. BSC Minutes BCA, September 2, 1952, 198; *Afro-American*, September 13, 1952.

27. *Sun* (Baltimore), September 3, 1952, September 4, 1952, September 20, 1952; Carl Clark interview; Giles interview; Redd interview.

28. *Sun* (Baltimore), September 4, 1952, September 7, 1952.

29. *Afro-American*, September 27, 1952; Baum, *"Brown" in Baltimore*, 58.

30. Lillie M. Jackson to William H. Lemmel, September 12, 1952, BSC Minutes BCA, September 18, 1952, 219; Gwinn Owens to the Board of School Commissioners, January 15, 1955, BSC Minutes BCA, February 3, 1955, 123; Hughes interview; *Shipley et al. v. the Board of School Commissioners* (1953).

31. BSC Minutes BCA, March 5, 1953, 14–15; Juanita J. Mitchell interview, July 25, 1975, 55–56; *Shipley et al. v. the Board of School Commissioners* (1953); Baum, *"Brown" in Baltimore*, 54–57, 62–63.

32. William Jabine II, to Mayor Thomas D'Alesandro Jr., December 28, 1953, series 23, box 297, folder 258, D'Alesandro Files BCA; Mayor Thomas D'Alesandro Jr. to William Jabine, II, December 29, 1953, ibid.; *Brown v. Board of Education*, 347 U.S. 483 (1954).

33. Gowie interview; Terry, "Dismantling Jim Crow," 10.

34. The *Brown* cases were *Gebhart v. Belton*, 33 Del. Ch. 144, 87 A.2d 862 (Del. Ch. 1952); *Davis v. County School Board of Prince Edward County*, 103 F. Supp. 337 (1952); *Briggs v. Elliott*, 98 F. Supp 529 (1951); *Brown v. Board of Education of Topeka*, 98 F. Supp. 797 (1951); and *Bolling v. Sharpe*, 347 U.S. 497 (1954).

35. *McLaurin v. Oklahoma State Regents*, 339 U.S. 637 (1950); *Sweatt v. Painter*, 339 U.S. 629 (1950); Scott, *Contempt and Pity*, 121.

36. Kluger, *Simple Justice, 321*; Scott, *Contempt and Pity*, 123–25.

37. *Brown v. Board of Education of Topeka*, 347 U.S. 483 (1954); Scott, 132–36; Kluger, *Simple Justice*, 703–5.

38. Benton interview; Michael May interview, November 18, 2001; Hughes interview; Keiffer J. Mitchell interview; Jealous interview; Todd interview.

39. Hughes interview; Jealous interview; Carol St. Clair interview, August 20, 2001; George H. Callcott, *Maryland and America*, 159.

40. Keiffer J. Mitchell interview; Todd interview.

41. Sondheim interview, 3–7; BSC Minutes BCA, May 20, 1954, 99; BSC Minutes BCA, June 3, 1954, 109–10; BSC Minutes BCA, June 10, 1954.

42. *Afro-American*, August 21, 1954.

43. BSC Minutes BCA, June 10, 1954; Baum, *"Brown" in Baltimore*, 71–72.

44. Jealous interview; St. Clair interview; Gowie interview; Benton interview.

45. *Afro-American*, September 11, 1954; *Sun* (Baltimore), September 8, 1954.

46. Keiffer J. Mitchell interview; *Afro American*, October 5, 1954; Durr, *Behind the Backlash*, 94; Orser, *Blockbusting in Baltimore*, 110–13.

47. Gowie interview; Benton interview; St. Clair interview; *Afro-American*, September 7, 1954.

48. *Sun* (Baltimore), September 8, 1954; Durr, *Behind the Backlash*, 95.

49. Webb, introduction to *Massive Resistance*, 15; Durr, *Behind the Backlash*, 95–96.

50. Memorandum, "Re: Citizens Councils, Baltimore Field Office," January 15, 1957, "FOIA: CitCouncils-Baltimore," *Internet Archive*, last accessed January 23, 2017, https://archive.org/stream/foia_CitCouncils-Baltimore.pdf/CitCouncils-Baltimore [hereafter FOIA: CitCouncils-Baltimore]; Memorandum, "Re: Citizens Councils, Baltimore Field Office," February 14, 1957, ibid.; Memorandum, "Re: Citizens Councils, Baltimore Field

Office," March 15, 1957, ibid.; Memorandum, "Re: Citizens Councils, Baltimore Field Office," April 12, 1957, ibid.

51. Memorandum, SAC [Special Agent in Charge], Baltimore to Director, [Federal Bureau of Investigation] (105-34237-3), July 24, 1957, FOIA: CitCouncils-Baltimore; Memorandum, Re: Citizens Councils and the Ku Klux Klan organizations (KKK), Baltimore Field Office, August 19, 1957, FOIA: CitCouncils-Baltimore; Memorandum, SAC, Atlanta to Director, FBI, December 13, 1956, FOIA: CitCouncils-Baltimore; Memorandum, Director, FBI (105-34237) to SAC, Baltimore (100-2 0067) Re: "Baltimore Letter Dated, 4/24/58," May 23, 1958, FOIA: CitCouncils-Baltimore; Durr, *Behind the Backlash*, 95–96.

52. Jealous interview; Gowie interview; Hughes interview.

53. Natalie Ann Forrest interview, February 2, 2002; Spintman interview; Hillman interview; Miller interview; Benton interview.

54. Forrest interview.

55. Gowie interview.

56. Baum, *"Brown" in Baltimore*, 84, 87–88; Durr, *Behind the Backlash*, 92–93, 95.

57. May interview; Hughes interview; *Afro American*, October 5, 1954.

58. *Afro American*, October 5, 1954. "Sapphire" was a racial slur and stereotype portraying black females as "rude, loud, malicious, stubborn, and overbearing." See "Sapphire Caricature."

59. Gowie interview; Hollie interview; May interview; Durr, *Behind the Backlash*, 93.

60. Durr, *Behind the Backlash*, 93–94; Webb, introduction to *Massive Resistance*, 15.

61. Italics are mine. *Sun* (Baltimore), October 5, 1954; Maryland Commission on Interracial Problems and Relations, *American City in Transition*, 12.

62. Mary Ida Smith to Furman Templeton, October 8, [1954], October 11, 1954, series 1, sub-series D, box 80, folder "Baltimore, Md. 17, 1953–1954," NUL RECORDS; Baum, *"Brown" in Baltimore*, 84.

63. *Brown II*, 349 U.S. 294 (1955); Kluger, *Simple Justice*, 747; Scott, 119–36.

64. Todd interview; Baum, *"Brown" in Baltimore*, 54, 59.

65. *Brown v. Board of Education of Topeka*, 347 U.S. 483 (1954); Gowie interview. My emphasis.

66. Baum, *"Brown" in Baltimore*, 49, 92–93.

67. Skotnes, *New Deal for All?*, 64–68, 47; Lorence, *Unemployed People's Movement*, 29–32; United States, Congress, House, Committee on Un-American Activities, *Investigation of Communist Activities in the New Orleans, La., Area*; Isserman, *If I Had a Hammer*, 58–59; Lang, "Black Power on the Ground," 71.

68. Altbach and Peterson, "Before Berkeley," 6–7.

69. Ibid., 9–10.

70. *SDA Bulletin*, December 1957, in *Americans for Democratic Action Papers, 1932–1965* (Sanford, N.C.: Microfilming Corporation of America, 1979), series 8, roll 128, no. 94, "Maryland, corr."; Phillip R. Hughes to Stanley Jaffe, December 1, 1954, ibid.; *Sun* (Baltimore), May 18, 1954, October 31, 1954; Altbach and Peterson, 9–12; Palumbos, "Student Involvement," 460.

71. Adams, *Way up North in Louisville*, 126–27; Bynum, *NAACP Youth and the Fight*, 34–41, 51–52, 61–62, 69–70, 84–87, 95–98; Juan Williams, *Thurgood Marshall*, 131–42.

72. Bynum, *NAACP Youth and the Fight*, 1, 39–40; Altbach and Peterson, "Before Berkeley," 4–6.

73. *Afro American*, November 27, 1948.

74. Doug Sands interview, June 23, 2014.

75. Ibid.

76. *Sun* (Baltimore), September 16, 1949, January 17, 1951, June 3, 1952, April 16, 1953, September, 23, 1954, October 8, 1955.

77. Logan interview; Sands interview; Herbert Kelman to George Houser, February 9, 1952, in *Papers of the Congress of Racial Equality, 1941–1967* (Sanford, N.C.: Microfilming Corporation of America, 1980), series 3, roll 8, no. 6.

78. Sands interview; Logan interview.

79. Sands interview; Aubrey Edwards interview, August 16, 2015; *Afro-American*, September 8, 1945.

80. Edwards interview; *Sun* (Baltimore), October 9, 1998.

81. Mary Schlossberg to George and Katie [Houser], November 25, 1953, *Papers of the Congress of Racial Equality, 1941–1967* (Sanford, N.C.: Microfilming Corporation of America, 1980), series 3, roll 8, no. 6; *CORE-lator*, no. 63 (October–November 1954), 1.

82. *CORE-lator*, no. 64 (February 1955), 1–2; *Afro-American*, January 22, 1955.

83. *Afro-American*, January 18, 1955; Cassie, "And Service For All."

84. Sands interview; Logan interview; *Afro-American*, May 14, 1955, May 17, 1955, May 24, 1955, May 28 1955, March 17, 1959.

85. Sands interview; Kiah to Houser, April 10, 1953, in *Papers of the Congress of Racial Equality, 1941–1967* (Sanford, N.C.: Microfilming Corporation of America, 1980), series 3, roll 8, no. 6; *Afro-American*, May 9, 1953.

86. *Afro-American*, April 26, 1947; Meier and Rudwick, *CORE*, 25, 34–35

87. Though giving substantial coverage to the Baltimore campaign, no mention of a "Morgan CORE" chapter appeared in *CORE-lator*, official organ of national CORE. *Afro-American*, January 22, 1955; Sands interview; Edwards interview.

88. Edwards interview; *Afro-American*, May 17, 1955.

89. Meier and Rudwick, *CORE*, 105–106; *SDA Bulletin*, October 1957; Ed Hirschmann to Phil [Hughes] March 26, 1956, *Americans for Democratic Action Papers, 1932–1965* (Sanford, N.C.: Microfilming Corporation of America, 1979), series 8, roll 128, no. 94; Theodore Palmer to Charlotte, October 31, 1956, ibid.

90. Edwards interview; *Afro-American*, May 17, 1955.

91. Logan interview; *Sun* (Baltimore), May 4, 1955; *Afro-American*, April 30, 1955, May 10, 1955, May 14, 1955, May 24, 1955, May 31, 1955, March 17, 1959, March 27, 1959; Palumbos, "Student Involvement," 455–56; Horn, "Integrating Baltimore," 95.

92. Edwards interview; *Afro-American*, March 28, 1959.

93. Maryland Criminal Trespass Statute, Code (1957), art. 27, sec. 577; *Afro-American*, April 4, 1959, March 17, 1959.

## CONCLUSION. "We Were Fighting against White Supremacy"

1. Sidney Hollander Foundation, *Toward Equality*, 38; *Afro American*, September 29, 1956, September 28, 1957; Greene, "Black Republicans."

2. *Afro American*, November 20, 1954, January 29, 1955. For a history of electoral activism and civil right groups, see Berg, *Ticket to Freedom*.

3. *Afro American*, March 13, 1943, June 17, 1950, May 23, 1953.

4. *Afro American*, April 28, 1942; *Sun* (Baltimore), February 23, 2007; George H. Callcott, *Maryland and America*, 139–41.

5. *Afro American*, April 2, 1955; *Sun* (Baltimore), March 10, 1955.

6. *Afro American*, September 20, 1958, January 17, 1959, March 7, 1959, November 21, 1959, February 8, 1958; *Sun* (Baltimore), January 11, 2006.

7. Edwards interview.

8. Morris, *Origins*, 192–94.

9. Meier and Rudwick, *CORE*, 74–75, 84–85; Morris, *Origins*, 135.

10. *Afro-American*, December 8, 1956, December 15, 1956; *New York Times*, March 20, 1956; Modjeska Simkins interview, July 28, 1976, http://docsouth.unc.edu/sohp/G0056₂ /G0056₂.html; Morris, *Origins*, 44, 82.

11. Stokely Carmichael quoted in "Stokely Carmichael, "Black Power (29 October 1966)," Voices of Democracy: The U.S. Oratory Project, accessed April 4, 2015, http:// voices-of-democracy.org/carmichael-black-power-speech-text; Joseph, *Waiting 'til the Midnight Hour*, 168; Scott, *Contempt and Pity*, 119–36; Kluger, *Simple Justice*, 315–45, 657–99.

# BIBLIOGRAPHY

## Manuscript Collections

Ella Baker Papers. Schomburg Research Center, New York Public Library, New York City.

Fellowship House (Philadelphia, Pa.) Records. Special Collection Research Center, Samuel L. Paley Library, Temple University, Philadelphia.

Letters of Carl Murphy. Afro-American Newspaper Collection, Moorland-Spingarn Research Center, Howard University, Washington, D.C.

Records of the Citizens' Planning and Housing Association. Special Collections Department, Lansdale Library, University of Baltimore.

Records of the National Association for the Advancement of Colored People. Manuscript Division, Library of Congress, Washington, D.C.

Records of the National Urban League. Manuscripts Division, Library of Congress, Washington, D.C.

Records of the Southern Christian Leadership Conference, 1954–1970. Martin Luther King, Jr., Center for Social Change Archives, Atlanta.

Sidney Hollander Collection (1926–1972). Special Collections, Maryland Historical Society, Baltimore.

W. E. B. Du Bois Papers, 1908–1979. Special Collections and University Archives, University of Massachusetts Amherst Libraries. http://credo.library.umass.edu/view/collection/mums312.

## Government Records Collections

### CITY OF BALTIMORE

Records of the Baltimore City Department of Education, 1830–Present. Baltimore City Archives.

Records of the Baltimore City Department of Recreation and Parks, 1946–Present. Baltimore City Archives.

Records of the Mayor: Howard Jackson Administrative Files (fourth term), 1938–1942. Baltimore City Archives.

Records of the Mayor: Theodore R. McKeldin Administrative Files (first term), 1943–1947. Baltimore City Archives.

Records of the Mayor: Thomas D'Alesandro Jr. Administrative Files (three terms between May 1947–February 1959, filed as a group). Baltimore City Archives.

### STATE OF MARYLAND

Morgan State College (Minutes), 1939–1967. Maryland State Archives, Annapolis.

Records of the Governor. Maryland State Archives, Annapolis.

UNITED STATES

Library of Congress. Geography and Maps Division.
Records of the U.S. Department of Justice, Federal Bureau of Investigation. Washington, D.C.

## Government Documents

Bureau of the Census. *Fifteenth Census of the United States, 1930: Population*. Washington, D.C.: Government Printing Office, 1943.
Bureau of the Census. *Sixteenth Census of the United States, 1940: Housing*. Washington, D.C.: Government Printing Office, 1943.
Bureau of the Census. *Sixteenth Census of the United States, 1940: Population*. Washington, D.C.: Government Printing Office, 1942.
Bureau of the Census. *Seventeenth Census of the United States, 1950: Housing*. Washington, D.C.: Government Printing Office, 1943.
Bureau of the Census. *Seventeenth Census of the United States, 1950: Population*. Washington, D.C.: Government Printing Office, 1942.
United States, Congress, House, Committee on Un-American Activities. *Investigation of Communist Activities in the New Orleans, La., Area: Hearings*. Washington, D.C.: Government Printing Office, 1957.

## Microforms

*Americans for Democratic Action Papers, 1932–1965*. Sanford, N.C.: Microfilming Corporation of America, 1979.
*Papers of the Congress of Racial Equality, 1941–1967*. Sanford, N.C.: Microfilming Corporation of America, 1980.

## Interviews

CONDUCTED BY AUTHOR

Benton, Anastatia Phillips. August 20, 2001, Baltimore.
Clark, Carl. March 17, 2001, via telephone.
Collins, Carolyn A. (Gross). April 26, 2001, Baltimore.
Edwards, Aubrey. August 16, 2015, via telephone.
Forrest, Natalie Ann. February 2, 2002, via telephone.
Giles, Gene A. March 31, 2001, Catonsville, Maryland.
Gowie, Lynda Hall. August 18, 2001, via telephone.
Harried, Delores Richburg. March 3, 2001, Baltimore.
Hillman, Rosalie Carter. February 3, 2002 via telephone.
Hollie, Donna Tyler. March 3, 2001, Baltimore.
Hughes, Alfreda. August 29, 2001, Columbia, Maryland.
Jealous, Ann Todd. November 11, 2001, via telephone.
Logan, Clarence. March 11, 2011, Baltimore.
May, Michael. November 18, 2001, via telephone.
Miller, Judy Berstein. February 3, 2002 via telephone.
Mitchell, Kieffer J. September 6, 2001, Baltimore.
Parker, Thelma Koger. August 7, 2003, Annapolis, Maryland.

Redd, Nathaniel. April 2, 2001, Baltimore.
St. Clair, Carol. August 20, 2001, Baltimore.
Sands, Doug. June 23, 2014, Cooksville, Maryland.
Spintman, Judith Goldstein. February 2, 2002, via telephone.
Todd, Mamie Bland. November 18, 2001, via telephone.
Tyler, McAllister. May 3, 2001, Baltimore.
Welsh, Patricia Logan. March 5, 2001, Baltimore.

## CONDUCTED BY OTHERS

Adams, Willie. Interview by Charles Wagandt. August 4, 1977. Governor Theodore R. McKeldin–Dr. Lillie Mae Jackson Oral History Project, Oral History Collection, Maryland Historical Society, Baltimore.

Baker, Ella. Interview by Eugene Walker. September 4, 1974. Southern Oral History Program Collection (4007), Southern Historical Collection, Wilson Library, University of North Carolina, Chapel Hill, North Carolina.

Blair, Ezell and Corene. Interview by William Chafe. March 13, 1972. William Henry Chafe Oral History Collection, Rare Book, Manuscript, and Special Collections Library, Duke University, Durham, North Carolina.

Camper, John E. T. Interview by Leroy Graham. July 2, 1976. Governor Theodore R. McKeldin–Dr. Lillie Mae Jackson Oral History Project, Oral History Collection, Maryland Historical Society, Baltimore.

Edmonds, Edwin. Interview by William Chafe. 1975. William Henry Chafe Oral History Collection, Rare Book, Manuscript, and Special Collections Library, Duke University, Durham, North Carolina.

Froelicher, Frances Morton. Interview by Barry Lanman. October 18, 1977. Governor Theodore R. McKeldin–Dr. Lillie Mae Jackson Oral History Project, Oral History Collection, Maryland Historical Society, Baltimore.

———. Interview by Alice Jewell. January 5, 1976. Oral History Collection, Maryland Historical Society, Baltimore.

Gilliam, James H., Sr. Veterans History Project, American Folklife Center, Library of Congress. http://memory.loc.gov/diglib/vhp/bib/48906.

Hudgens, Eula. Interview by William Chafe. December 17, 1974. William Henry Chafe Oral History Collection, Rare Book, Manuscript, and Special Collections Library, Duke University, Durham, North Carolina.

Jackson, Carrie Francis. Interview by Lucy Peebles. December 12, 1979. Baltimore Neighborhood Heritage Project, Lansdale Library, Special Collections, University of Baltimore.

McKeldin, Theodore R. Interview by Charles Wagandt. April 6, 1971. Oral History Collection, Maryland Historical Society, Baltimore.

McNeil, Joseph. Interview by William Chafe. 1978. William Henry Chafe Oral History Collection, Rare Book, Manuscript, and Special Collections Library, Duke University, Durham, North Carolina.

Mitchell, Broadus. Interview by Mary Frederickson. August 14–15, 1977. Southern Oral History Program Collection (4007), Southern Oral History Program Collection, Southern Historical Collection, Wilson Library, University of North Carolina, Chapel Hill.

Mitchell, Clarence M., Jr. Interview by Charles Wagandt. February 12, 1977. Governor Theodore R. McKeldin–Dr. Lillie Mae Jackson Oral History Project, Oral History Collection, Maryland Historical Society, Baltimore.

Mitchell, Juanita J. Interview by Charles Wagandt. July 25, 1975. Governor Theodore R. McKeldin–Dr. Lillie Mae Jackson Oral History Project, Oral History Collection, Maryland Historical Society, Baltimore.

———. Interview by Charles Wagandt. December 9, 1976. Governor Theodore R. McKeldin–Dr. Lillie Mae Jackson Oral History Project, Oral History Collection, Maryland Historical Society, Baltimore.

Mitchell, Juanita J., and Virginia Jackson Kiah. Interview by Charles Wagandt. January 10, 1976. Governor Theodore R. McKeldin–Dr. Lillie Mae Jackson Oral History Project, Oral History Collection, Maryland Historical Society, Baltimore.

Simkins, George. Interview by Karen Kruse Thomas. April 6, 1997. Southern Oral History Program Collection (4007), Southern Oral History Program Collection, Southern Historical Collection, Wilson Library, University of North Carolina, Chapel Hill.

Simkins, Modjeska. Interview by Jacqueline Hall. July 28, 1976. Southern Oral History Program Collection (4007), Southern Oral History Program Collection, Southern Historical Collection, Wilson Library, University of North Carolina, Chapel Hill.

Sondheim, Walter, Jr. Interview by Ellen Paul. September 27, 1976. Governor Theodore R. McKeldin–Dr. Lillie Mae Jackson Oral History Project, Oral History Collection, Maryland Historical Society, Baltimore.

### Website

*Baltimore's Civil Rights Heritage*. Last modified April 10, 2017, https://baltimoreheritage .github.io/civil-rights-heritage/criminal-injustice.

*Legacy of Slavery in Maryland*. Maryland State Archives. Accessed January 23, 2016. http://slavery.msa.maryland.gov/.

Library of Congress. "African American Perspectives: Pamphlets from the Daniel A. P. Murray Collection, 1818–1907." Accessed July 11, 2018. http://www.loc.gov/teachers /classroommaterials/connections/afam-perspectives.

### Books, Articles, Dissertations, and Theses

Adams, Luther. "'Headed for Louisville': Rethinking Rural to Urban Migration in the South, 1930–1950." *Journal of Social History* 40, no. 2 (Winter 2006): 407–30.

———. *Way up North in Louisville: African American Migration in the Urban South, 1930–1970*. Chapel Hill: University of North Carolina Press, 2010.

Adelson, Bruce. *Brushing Back Jim Crow: The Integration of Minor-League Baseball in the American South*. Charlottesville: University of Virginia Press, 1999.

Adler, Jeffrey S. "'The Greatest Thrill I Get Is When I Hear a Criminal Say, "Yes, I Did It"': Race and Third-degree in New Orleans, 1920–1945." *Law and History Review* 34, no. 1 (February 2016) 7–15.

Alexander, Michelle. *The New Jim Crow: Mass Incarceration in the Age of Colorblindness*. New York: New Press, 2012.

Alexander, Shawn Leigh. *An Army of Lions: The Civil Rights Struggle before the NAACP*. Philadelphia: University of Pennsylvania Press, 2011.

Altbach, Philip G., and Patti Peterson, "Before Berkeley: Historical Perspectives on American Student Activism." *Annals of the American Academy of Political and Social Science* 395 (1971): 1–14.

Amin, Dawan el-. "From Mosque Six to Masjid Al Haqq: A History of an African American Muslim Community in Baltimore, Maryland, 1956–1996. Master's thesis, Morgan State University, 2014.

Anderson, Karen Tucker. "Last Hired, First Fired: Black Women Workers during World War II." *Journal of American History* 69 (June 1982): 82–97.

Arsenault, Raymond. *Freedom Riders: 1961 and the Struggle for Racial Justice.* New York: Oxford University Press, 2011.

Ayers, Edward. *The Promise of the New South: Life after Reconstruction.* New York: Oxford University Press, 1992.

Baum, Howell S. *"Brown" in Baltimore: School Desegregation and the Limits of Liberalism.* Ithaca: Cornell University Press, 2010.

Bay, Mia. *The White Image in the Black Mind: African-American Ideas about White People, 1830–1925.* Oxford: Oxford University Press, 2000.

Bayor, Ronald H. *Race and the Shaping of Twentieth-Century Atlanta.* Chapel Hill: University of North Carolina Press, 1996.

"Before Freddie Gray: A History of Police Violence in Baltimore" *Historic Sprawl.* Last modified April 24, 2015. https://historicsprawl.wordpress.com/2015/04/24/before -freddie-gray-a-history-of-police-violence-in-baltimore.

Berg, Manfred. "Black Civil Rights and Liberal Anticommunism: The NAACP in the Early Cold War." *Journal of American History* 94 (June 2007): 75–96.

———. *"The Ticket to Freedom": The NAACP and the Struggle for Black Political Integration.* Gainesville: University of Florida Press, 2005.

Bogen, David S. "The First Integration of the University of Maryland School of Law." *Maryland Historical Magazine* 84 (Spring 1989): 39–49.

———. "Precursors of Rosa Parks: Maryland Transportation Cases between the Civil War and the Beginning of World War I." *Maryland Law Review* 63 (2004): 721–51.

———. "The Transformation of the Fourteenth Amendment: Reflections from the Admission of Maryland's First Black Lawyers." *Maryland Law Review* 44 (1985): 939–1046.

Boyd, Robert L. "Race, Labor Market Disadvantage, and Survivalist Entrepreneurship: Black Women in the Urban North during the Great Depression." *Sociological Forum* 15 (December 2000): 647–70.

Brackett, Jeffrey. *Notes on the Progress of the Colored People of Maryland since the War.* Baltimore: Publication Agency of the Johns Hopkins University, 1890.

Branch, Taylor. *Parting the Waters: America in the King Years, 1954–1963.* New York: Simon and Schuster, 1988.

Bready, James H. *Baseball in Baltimore: The First 100 Years.* Baltimore: Johns Hopkins University Press, 1998.

Bristol, Douglas W., Jr. *Knights of the Razor: Black Barbers in Slavery and Freedom.* Baltimore: Johns Hopkins University Press, 2010.

Brown, Dorothy. "The Election of 1934: The 'New Deal' in Maryland." *Maryland Historical Magazine* (1973): 405–21.

Brown-Nagin, Tomiko. *Courage to Dissent: Atlanta and the Long History of the Civil Rights Movement.* New York: Oxford University Press, 2011.

Brownell, Blaine A. *Urban Ethos in the South, 1920–30*. Baton Rouge: Louisiana State University Press, 1975.

Brugger, Robert J. *Maryland: A Middle Temperament, 1634–1980*. Baltimore: Johns Hopkins University Press, 1990.

Buni, Andrew. *Robert L. Vann of the* Pittsburgh Courier: *Politics and Black Journalism*. Pittsburgh: University of Pittsburgh Press, 1974.

Bynum, Thomas L. *NAACP Youth and the Fight for Black Freedom, 1936–1965*. 2013.

Callcott, George H. *Maryland and America, 1940 to 1980*. Baltimore: Johns Hopkins University Press, 1985.

Callcott, Margaret Law. *The Negro in Maryland Politics, 1870–1912*. (Baltimore: Johns Hopkins University Press, 1969.

Capeci, Dominic J. "From Different Liberal Perspectives: Fiorello H. La Guardia, Adam Clayton Powell, Jr., and Civil Rights in New York City, 1941–1943." *Journal of Negro History* 62 (April 1977): 160–73.

Carey, John R. "Helping Negro Workers to Purchase Homes." *Opportunity*, January 1924, 23.

Carle, Susan D. *Defining the Struggle: National Organizing for Racial Justice, 1880–1915*. New York: Oxford University Press, 2013.

Carmichael, Stokely. "Black Power (29 October 1966)." Voices of Democracy: The U.S. Oratory Project. Accessed April 4, 2015. http://voices-of-democracy.org/carmichael -black-power-speech-text.

Carson, Clayborne, ed. *Birth of a New Age, December 1955–December 1956*. Papers of Martin Luther King, Jr., vol. 3. Berkeley: University of California Press, 1997.

———. *Symbol of the Movement, January 1957–December 1958*. Papers of Martin Luther King, Jr., vol. 4. Berkeley: University of California Press, 2000.

Carter, Dan T. *Scottsboro: A Tragedy of the American South*. Baton Rouge: Louisiana State University Press, 1979.

Cassie, Ron. "And Service For All." *Baltimore Magazine*, January 2015. http://www .baltimoremagazine.net/2015/1/19/morgan-students-staged-reads-drugstore-sit-in -60-years-ago. Accessed July 4, 2015.

Cecelski, David S., and Timothy B. Tyson, eds. *Democracy Betrayed: The Wilmington Race Riot of 1898 and Its Legacy*. Chapel Hill: University of North Carolina Press, 1998.

Cell, John W. *The Highest Stage of White Supremacy: The Origins of Segregation in South Africa and the American South*. New York: Cambridge University Press, 1982.

Chafe, William. *Civilities and Civil Rights: Greensboro, North Carolina, and the Black Struggle for Freedom*. New York: Oxford University Press, 1980.

Cha-Jua, Sundiata Keita, and Clarence Lang. "The 'Long Movement' as Vampire: Temporal and Spatial Fallacies in Recent Black Freedom." *Journal of African American History* 92 (Spring 2007): 265–88.

Chalkley, Tom. "Circle Unbroken," *Baltimore City Paper*, June 18, 2003. https://web .archive.org/web/20071213091105/http://www.citypaper.com:80/news/story.asp?id =2328.

Chappell, David L. *Inside Agitators: White Southerners in the Civil Rights Movement*. Baltimore: Johns Hopkins University Press, 1994.

Chesnutt, Charles Waddell. *An Exemplary Citizen: Letters of Charles W. Chesnutt, 1906–1932*. Stanford: Stanford University Press, 2002.

Clark-Lewis, Elizabeth. *Living in, Living Out: African American Domestics and the Great Migration*. New York: Kodansha America, 1996.

Crooks, James B. *Politics and Progress: The Rise of Urban Progressivism in Baltimore, 1895 to 1911*. Baton Rouge: Louisiana State University Press, 1968.

Cumberbatch, Prudence. "What 'the Cause' Needs Is a 'Brainy and Energetic Woman': A Study of Female Charismatic Leadership in Baltimore." In *Want to Start a Revolution? Radical Women in the Black Freedom Struggle*, edited by Dayo F. Gore, Jeanne Theoharis, and Komozi Woodard, 47–70. New York: New York University Press, 2009.

Dabel, Jane E. *A Respectable Woman: The Public Roles of African American Women in 19th-Century New York*. New York: NYU Press, 2008.

Dalfiume, Richard M. "The 'Forgotten Years' of the Negro Revolution." *Journal of American History* 55 (June 1968): 90–106.

Dittmer, John. *Black Georgia in the Progressive Era, 1900–1920*. Urbana: University of Illinois Press, 1980.

Douglass, Frederick. *Narrative of the Life of Frederick Douglass, an American Slave*. Electronic ed. *Documenting the American South*. http://docsouth.unc.edu/neh /douglass/douglass.html.

Doyle, Don. *New Men, New Cities, New South*. Chapel Hill: University of North Carolina Press, 1985.

Dray, Philip. *At the Hands of Persons Unknown: The Lynching of Black America*. New York: Modern Library, 2007.

Du Bois, W. E. B. *The Negro*. New York: Holt, 1915.

———. "Negro Editors on Communism." *Crisis* 39 (April 1932), 118–23.

———. *The Souls of Black Folk*. Chicago: A. C. McClurg, 1903.

Dudziak, Mary L. *Cold War Civil Rights: Race and the Image of American Democracy*. Princeton: Princeton University Press, 2000.

Durr, Kenneth. *Behind the Backlash: White Working-Class Politics in Baltimore, 1940–1980*. Chapel Hill: University of North Carolina Press, 2007.

Duster, Alfreda M. *Crusade for Justice: The Autobiography of Ida B. Wells*. Chicago: University of Chicago Press, 1991.

Eagles, Charles W. "Toward New Histories of the Civil Rights Era." *Journal of Southern History* 66 (November 2000): 815–48.

Eskew, Glenn T. *But for Birmingham: The Local and National Movements in the Civil Rights Struggle*. Chapel Hill: University of North Carolina Press, 1997.

Fairclough, Adam. *Race and Democracy: The Civil Rights Struggle in Louisiana, 1915–1972*. Athens: University of Georgia Press, 1999.

Falkner, David. *Great Time Coming: The Life of Jackie Robinson, from Baseball to Birmingham*. New York: Simon & Schuster, 1995.

Farber, David, and Beth Bailey. *The Columbia Guide to America in the 1960s*. New York: Columbia University Press, 2001.

Farmer, James. *Lay Bare the Heart: An Autobiography of the Civil Rights Movement*. New York: Arbor House, 1985.

Farrar, Hayward. *The Baltimore Afro-American, 1892–1950*. Santa Barbara: Greenwood Publishing Group, 1998

*The First Colored Professional, Clerical and Business Directory of Baltimore City, 1916–17*. 4th annual ed. R. W. Coleman. Archives of Maryland Online. Maryland State Archives. http://aomol.msa.maryland.gov/000001/000496/html/index.html.

*The First Colored Professional, Clerical and Business Directory of Baltimore City,*
    *1920–21.* 8th annual ed. R. W. Coleman. Archives of Maryland Online. Maryland
    State Archives. http://aomol.msa.maryland.gov/000001/000500/html/index.html.
*The First Colored Professional, Clerical and Business Directory of Baltimore City,*
    *1921–22.* 9th annual ed. R. W. Coleman. Archives of Maryland Online. Maryland
    State Archives. http://aomol.msa.maryland.gov/000001/000501/html/index.html.
*The First Colored Professional, Clerical and Business Directory of Baltimore City,*
    *1922–23.* 10th annual ed. R. W. Coleman. Archives of Maryland Online. Maryland
    State Archives. http://aomol.msa.maryland.gov/000001/000502/html/index.html.
*The First Colored Professional, Clerical and Business Directory of Baltimore City,*
    *1923–24.* 11th annual ed. R. W. Coleman. Archives of Maryland Online. Maryland
    State Archives. http://aomol.msa.maryland.gov/000001/000503/html/index.html.
Foner, Philip S. "Address of Frederick Douglass at the Inauguration of Douglass Insti-
    tute, Baltimore, October 1, 1865." *Journal of Negro History* 54 (April 1969): 174–83.
Fox, Stephen R. *The Guardian of Boston: William Monroe Trotter.* New York: Atheneum
    Press, 1970.
Franklin, John Hope, and Loren Schweninger. *Runaway Slaves: Rebels on the Planta-
    tion.* New York: Oxford University Press, 1999.
Freeman, Elaine. "Harvey Johnson and Everett Waring." Master's thesis, Goucher
    College, 1968.
Garrow, David J. *Bearing the Cross: Martin Luther King, Jr., and the Southern Christian
    Leadership Conference.* New York: Vintage Press, 1988.
Gatewood, Willard B. *Aristocrats of Color: The Black Elite 1880–1920.* Bloomington:
    Indiana University Press, 1991.
Gellman, Erik. *Death Blow to Jim Crow: The National Negro Congress and the Rise of
    Militant Civil Rights.* Chapel Hill: University of North Carolina Press, 2012.
Gibson, Larry S. *Young Thurgood: The Making of the Supreme Court Justice.* Amherst,
    N.Y.: Prometheus Books, 2012.
Gildea, William. *The Longest Fight: In the Ring with Joe Gans, Boxing's First African
    American Champion.* New York: McMillan, 2012.
Gilmore, Glenda Elizabeth. *Defying Dixie: The Radical Roots of Civil Rights, 1919–1950.*
    New York: W. W. Norton, 2008.
Goldfield, David. "The Urban Crusade: Race, Culture and Power in the American
    South since 1945." *American Studies* 42 (1997): 181–95.
Grandage, Jon. "The Tallahassee Bus Boycott Begins (May 1956)." *Florida Memory Blog.*
    Posted May 26, 2013. https://www.floridamemory.com/blog/2013/05/26/tallahassee
    -bus-boycott.
Grantham, Dewey W. *Southern Progressivism: The Reconciliation of Progress and Tradi-
    tion.* Knoxville: University of Tennessee Press, 1983.
Green, Constance McLaughlin. *Secret City: A History of Race Relations in the Nation's
    Capital.* Princeton: Princeton University Press, 1967.
Green, Laurie B. *Battling the Plantation Mentality: Memphis and the Black Freedom
    Struggle.* Chapel Hill: University of North Carolina Press, 2007.
Greene, Suzanne Ellery. "Black Republicans on the Baltimore City Council, 1890–1931."
    *Maryland Historical Magazine* 74 (September 1979): 203–22.
Gregory, James N. *The Southern Diaspora: How the Great Migrations of Black and*

*White Southerners Transformed America*. Chapel Hill: University of North Carolina Press, 2005.

Hale, Grace Elizabeth. *Making Whiteness: The Culture of Segregation in the South, 1890–1940*. New York: Vintage Press, 1998.

Hall, Jacqueline Dowd. "The Long Civil Rights Movement and the Political Uses of the Past." *Journal of American History* 91(2005): 1233–63.

Hall, James C. *Mercy, Mercy Me: African-American Culture and the American Sixties*. New York: Oxford University Press, 2001.

Hamilton, Charles V. *Adam Clayton Powell, Jr.: The Political Biography of an American Dilemma*. New York: Collier Books, 1991.

Harlan, Louis. *Booker T. Washington: The Wizard of Tuskegee, 1901–1915*. New York: Oxford University Press, 1983.

Harris, Michael D. *Colored Pictures: Race and Visual Representation*. Chapel Hill: University of North Carolina Press, 2003.

Heale, M. J. "The Sixties as History: A Review of the Political Historiography." *Reviews in American History* 33 (2005): 133–52.

Healy, Joseph P. *Report of the Governor's Commission on Problems Affecting the Negro Population*. Annapolis: The Commission, 1943.

Hein, David, and Gardiner H. Shattuck Jr. *The Episcopalians*. New York: Church Publishing, 2004.

Hershaw, L. M., George A. Towns, J. R. Van Pelt, and Edward A. Arnold. "Notes." *Journal of Negro History* 19, no. 2 (April 1934): 211–13.

Hill, Robert A., ed. *The Marcus Garvey and Universal Negro Improvement Association Papers*. 9 vols. Berkeley: University of California Press, 1983–95.

Hill, Robert A., and Barbara Blair, eds. *Marcus Garvey: Life and Lessons*. Berkeley: University of California Press, 1987.

Hine, Darlene Clark. "Black Professionals and Race Consciousness: Origins of the Civil Rights Movement, 1890–1950." *Journal of American History* 89 (March 2003): 1279–94.

Honey, Michael K. *Southern Labor and Black Civil Rights: Organizing Memphis Workers*. Urbana: University of Illinois Press, 1993.

Horn, Vernon E. "Integrating Baltimore: Protest and Accommodation, 1945–1963." Master's thesis, University of Maryland, 1991.

Houston, Charles H. "Don't Shout Too Soon." *Crisis*, March 1936, 79, 91.

Hunter, Tera W. *To 'Joy My Freedom: Southern Black Women's Lives and Labors after the Civil War*. Cambridge: Harvard University Press, 1998.

Ifill, Sherrilyn A. *On the Courthouse Lawn: Confronting the Legacy of Lynching in the Twenty-First Century*. Boston: Beacon Press, 2007.

Isserman, Maurice. *If I Had a Hammer: The Death of the Old Left and the Birth of the New Left*. New York: Basic Books, 1987.

Johnson, Charles S. "Negroes at Work in Baltimore, Md." *Opportunity: Journal of Negro Life*, January 1923, 12.

Johnson, Harvey. *The Nations from a New Point of View*. N.p.: National Baptist Publishing Board, 1903.

Johnson, Kimberley. *Reforming Jim Crow: Southern Politics and the State in the Age before "Brown."* New York: Oxford, 2010.

Jolly, Kenneth S. *"By Our Own Strength": William Sherrill, the UNIA, and the Fight for African American Self-Determination in Detroit.* New York: Peter Lang, 2013.

Jones, Beverly W. "Before Montgomery and Greensboro: The Desegregation Movement in the District of Columbia, 1950–1953." *Phylon* 43 (1982): 144–54.

Joseph, Peniel E. "The Black Power Movement: A State of the Field." *Journal of American History* 96 (December 2009): 751–76.

———, ed. *Neighborhood Rebels: Black Power at the Local Level.* New York: Palgrave/MacMillan, 2010.

———. *Waiting 'til the Midnight Hour: A Narrative History of Black Power in America.* New York: Henry Holt, 2006.

Kahn, Ashley. *Kind of Blue: The Making of the Miles Davis Masterpiece.* New York: Da Capo, 2000.

Kazin, Michael. "Martin Luther King, Jr. and the Meanings of the 1960s." *American Historical Review* 114 (2009): 980–89.

Kelley, Blair L. M. *Right to Ride: Streetcar Boycotts and African American Citizenship in the Era of "Plessy v. Ferguson."* Chapel Hill: University of North Carolina Press, 2010.

Kelley, Robin D. G. *Hammer and Hoe: Alabama Communists during the Great Depression.* Chapel Hill: University of North Carolina Press, 1990.

———. "'We Are Not What We Seem': Rethinking Black Working-Class Opposition in the Jim Crow South." *Journal of American History,* 80 (1993): 75–112.

Kelman, Herbert C. *A Time to Speak: On human Values and Social Research.* San Francisco: Jossey-Bass, 1968.

Kemp, Janet E. *Housing Conditions in Baltimore: Report of a Special Committee of the Association for the Improvement of the Condition of the Poor and the Charity Organization Society.* Baltimore: Baltimore Association for the Improvement of the Condition of the Poor, 1907.

"Kenneth and Mamie Clark Doll." Brown v. Board of Education National Historic Site, Kansas. Accessed August 9, 2018. https://www.nps.gov/brvb/learn/historyculture/clarkdoll.htm.

Kern-Foxworth, Marilyn. *Aunt Jemima, Uncle Ben, and Rastus: Blacks in Advertising, Yesterday, Today, and Tomorrow.* Westport, Conn.: Greenwood, 1994.

Kirby, Jack Temple. *Darkness at the Dawning: Race and Reform in the Progressive South.* Philadelphia: J. B. Lippincott, 1972.

Kirsch, George B. "Municipal Golf and Civil Rights in the United States, 1910–1965." *Journal of African American History* 92 (2007): 371–91.

Klarman, Michael J. "Why Massive Resistance?" In *Massive Resistance: Southern Opposition to the Second Reconstruction,* edited by Clive Webb, 21–38. New York: Oxford University Press, 2005.

Kluger, Richard. *Simple Justice: The History of "Brown v. Board of Education" and Black America's Struggle for Equality.* New York: Vintage Books, 1977.

K'Meyer, Tracy E. *Civil Rights in the Gateway to the South: Louisville, Kentucky, 1945–1980.* Lexington: University of Kentucky Press, 2009.

Kousser, J. Morgan. *The Shaping of Southern Politics: Suffrage Restriction and the Establishment of the One-Party South.* New Haven: Yale University Press, 1974.

Lang, Clarence. "Black Power on the Ground: Continuity and Rupture in St. Louis." In *Neighborhood Rebels: Black Power at the Local Level,* edited by Peniel E. Joseph. New York: Palgrave/MacMillan, 2010.

———. *Grassroots at the Gateway: Class Politics and Black Freedom Struggle in St. Louis, 1936–1975*. Ann Arbor: University of Michigan Press, 2009.

Leuchtenburg, William E. *The White House Looks South: Franklin D. Roosevelt, Harry S. Truman, Lyndon B. Johnson*. Baton Rouge: Louisiana State University Press, 2005.

Lewis, David Levering. *W. E. B. Du Bois: Biography of a Race, 1868–1919*. New York: Henry Holt, 1993.

———. *W. E. B. Du Bois: The Fight for Equality and the American Century, 1919–1963*. New York: Henry Holt, 2000

Lewis, Earl. *In Their Own Interests: Race, Class, and Power in Twentieth-Century Norfolk, Virginia*. Berkeley: University of California Press, 1991.

Litwack, Leon F. *Trouble in Mind: Black Southerners in the Age of Jim Crow*. New York: Vintage Press, 1999.

Logan, Rayford. *Betrayal of the Negro: The Nadir*. New York: Collier Books, 1970.

Lorence, James J. *The Unemployed People's Movement: Leftists, Liberals, and Labor in Georgia, 1929–1941*. Athens: University of Georgia Press, 2011.

Luke, Bob. *The Baltimore Elite Giants: Sport and Society in the Age of Negro League Baseball*. Baltimore: Johns Hopkins University Press, 2009.

———. *Integrating the Orioles: Baseball and Race in Baltimore*. Jefferson, N.C.: McFarland, 2014.

Lynch, Hollis R. *The Black Urban Condition: A Documentary History, 1866–1971*. New York: Thomas Y. Crowell, 1973.

Manis, Andrew M. *A Fire You Can't Put Out: The Civil Rights Life of Birmingham's Reverend Fred Shuttlesworth*. Tuscaloosa: University of Alabama, 2001.

Marable, Manning. *Malcolm X: A Life of Reinvention*. New York: Penguin Press, 2011.

Martin, Tony. *Race First: The Ideological and Organizational Struggles of Marcus Garvey and the Universal Negro Improvement Association*. Dover, Mass.: Majority Press, 1976.

Marwick, Arthur. "The Cultural Revolution of the Long Sixties: Voices of Reaction, Protest, and Permeation." *International History Review* 27 (2005): 780–806.

Maryland Commission on Interracial Problems and Relations. *An American City in Transition: The Baltimore Community Self-Survey of Inter-Group Relations*. (Baltimore: The Commission, 1955).

McAdam, Doug. *Political Process and the Development of Black Insurgency 1930–1970*. Chicago: University of Chicago Press, 1999.

McCaskill, Barbara, and Caroline Gebhard, eds. *Post-Bellum, Pre-Harlem: African American Literature and Culture, 1877–1919*. New York: New York University Press, 2006.

McConnell, Roland C. *The History of Morgan Park: A Baltimore Neighborhood, 1917–1999*. Baltimore: Morgan Park Improvement Association, 2000.

McNeil, Genna Rae. *Groundwork: Charles Hamilton Houston and the Struggle for Civil Rights*. Philadelphia: University of Pennsylvania Press, 1983.

Meier, August, and Elliott Rudwick. "The Boycott Movement against Jim Crow Streetcars in the South, 1900–1906." *Journal of American History* 55, no. 4 (March 1969): 756–75.

———. *CORE: A Study in the Civil Rights Movement, 1942–1968*. New York: Oxford University Press, 1973.

Meyer, Stephen Grant. *As Long as They Don't Move Next Door: Segregation and Racial Conflict in American Neighborhoods*. Lanham, Md.: Rowman & Littlefield, 2000.

Mibolsky, David. "Power from the Pulpit: Baltimore's African-American Clergy, 1950–1970." *Maryland Historical Magazine* 89 (1994): 275–90.

Michaeli, Ethan. *The Defender: How the Legendary Black Newspaper Changed America*. New York: Houghton Mifflin Harcourt, 2016.

Mills, Frederick V. "Bragg, George Freeman, Jr." In *African American Lives*, edited by Henry Louis Gates and Evelyn Brooks Higginbotham, 95–96. New York: Oxford University Press, 2004.

Mixon, Gregory. *The Atlanta Riot: Race, Class, and Violence in a New South City*. Gainesville: University of Florida Press, 2004.

Moore, Leonard N. *Black Rage in New Orleans: Police Brutality and African American Activism from World War II to Hurricane Katrina*. Baton Rouge: Louisiana State University Press, 2010.

Moore, Winfred B., and Orville Vernon Burton, eds. *Toward the Meeting of the Waters: Currents in the Civil Rights Movement of South Carolina during the Twentieth Century*. Columbia: University of South Carolina Press, 2008.

Morris, Aldon D. *Origins of the Civil Rights Movement*. New York: Free Press, 1986.

Morton, Frances H. *A Social Study of Wards 5 and 10 in Baltimore, Maryland*. Baltimore: Baltimore Council of Social Agencies, 1937.

Moses, Wilson Jeremiah. *The Golden Age of Black Nationalism, 1850–1925*. New York: Oxford University Press, 1978.

Musgrove, G. Derek. *Rumor, Repression, and Racial Politics: How the Harassment of Black Elected Officials Shaped Post-Civil Rights America*. Athens: University of Georgia Press, 2012.

Neverdon-Morton, Cynthia. *Afro-American Women in the South and the Advancement of the Race, 1895–1925*. Knoxville: University of Tennessee Press, 1989.

———. "Black Housing Patterns in Baltimore City, 1885–1953." *Maryland Historian* 16 (1985): 25–39.

Nisenson, Eric. *Ascension: John Coltrane and His Quest*. New York: St. Martins Press, 1993.

Olson, Karen. "Old West Baltimore: Segregation, African American Culture, and the Struggle for Equality." In *The Baltimore Book: New Views of Local History*, edited by Elizabeth Fee, Linda Shopes, and Linda Zeidman. Philadelphia: Temple University Press, 1991.

Olson, Sherry H. *Baltimore: The Building of An American City*. Baltimore: Johns Hopkins University Press, 1980.

Orser, Edward. *Blockbusting in Baltimore: The Edmondson Village Story*. Lexington: University of Kentucky Press, 1994.

O'Wesney, Julia R. "Historical Study of the Progress of Racial Desegregation in the Public Schools of Baltimore, Maryland." EdD diss., University of Maryland, 1970.

Pacifico, Michele F. "'Don't Buy Where You Can't Work': The New Negro Alliance of Washington." *Washington History* 6, no. 1 (Spring–Summer 1994): 66–88.

Painter, Nell Irvin. *The Exodusters: Black Migration to Kansas after Reconstruction*. New York: Alfred A. Knopf, 1977.

Palumbos, Robert M. "Student Involvement in the Baltimore Civil Rights Movement, 1953–63." *Maryland Historical Magazine* 94 (Winter 1999): 449–92.

Patterson, Ted. *The Baltimore Orioles: Four Decades of Magic from 33rd Street to Camden Yards*. New York: Taylor Trade Publishing, 1994.

Paul, William George. "The Shadow of Equality: The Negro in Baltimore, 1864–1911." PhD diss., University of Wisconsin, 1974.

Pearson, Ralph. "The National Urban League Comes to Baltimore." *Maryland Historical Magazine* 72 (Winter 1977): 523–33.

Penn, I. Garland. *The Afro-American Press and Its Editors*. Springfield, Mass.: Willey, 1891.

Perman, Michael. *Struggle for Mastery: Disfranchisement in the South, 1888–1908*. Chapel Hill: University of North Carolina Press, 2001.

Peterson, Robert. *Only the Ball Was White: A History of Legendary Black Players and All-Black Professional Teams*. New York: Oxford Press, 1970.

Pietila, Antero. *Not in My Neighborhood: How Bigotry Shaped a Great American City*. Chicago: Ivan R. Dee, 2010.

Platt, Anthony M. *E. Franklin Frazier Reconsidered*. New Brunswick: Rutgers University Press, 1991.

Power, Garrett. "*Meade v. Dennistone*: The NAACP's Test Case to '. . . Sue Jim Crow Out of Maryland with the Fourteenth Amendment,'" *Maryland Law Review* 63, no. 4 (2004): 773–810.

———. "Pyrrhic Victory: Daniel Goldman's Defeat of Zoning in the Maryland Court of Appeals." *Maryland Historical Magazine* 82, no. 4 (Winter 1987): 275–87.

*Public Housing in Baltimore, 1941–1942*. Baltimore: Baltimore Housing Authority, 1943.

Rabinowitz, Howard. *Race Relations in the Urban South, 1865–1890*. New York: Oxford University Press, 1978.

Ransby, Barbara. *Ella Baker and the Black Freedom Movement: A Radical Democratic Vision*. Chapel Hill: University of North Carolina Press, 2005.

"Rev. William Moncure Alexander: First-Rate, Second-Tier Leadership." Maryland State Archives. Accessed August 2, 2005. http://msa.maryland.gov/msa/stagser/s1259/121/6050/html/26140000.html.

Riley, James A. *The Biographical Encyclopedia of the Negro Baseball Leagues*. New York: Carroll and Graf, 1994.

Robbins, Richard. *Sideline Activist: Charles S. Johnson and the Struggle for Civil Rights*. Jackson: University of Mississippi Press, 1996.

Roberts, Gene, and Hank Klibanoff. *The Race Beat: The Press, the Civil Rights Struggle, and the Awakening of a Nation*. New York: Vintage Press, 2007.

Rolinson, Mary G. *Grassroots Garveyism: The Universal Negro Improvement Association in the Rural South, 1920–1927*. Chapel Hill: University of North Carolina Press, 2007.

Rossinow, Doug. *Visions of Progress: the Left-Liberal Tradition in America*. Philadelphia: University of Pennsylvania Press, 2008.

Rowan, Carl T. *Dream Makers, Dream Breakers: The World of Justice Thurgood Marshall*. Boston: Little, Brown, 1993.

"The Sapphire Caricature." Jim Crow Museum of Racist Memorabilia. Accessed August 9, 2018. https://ferris.edu/HTMLS/news/jimcrow/antiblack/sapphire.htm.

Sartain, Lee. *Borders of Equality: The NAACP and the Baltimore Civil Rights Struggle, 1914–1970*. Jackson: University of Mississippi Press, 2013.

Scharf, John Thomas. *History of Baltimore City and County, from the Earliest Period to the Present Day: Including Biographical Sketches of Their Representative Men*. Baltimore: L. H. Everts, 1881.

Scott, Darryl M. *Contempt and Pity: Social Policy and the Image of the Damaged Black Psyche, 1880–1996*. Chapel Hill: University of North Carolina Press, 1997.

Shattuck, Gardiner H., Jr. *Episcopalians and Race: Civil War to Civil Rights*. Lexington: University of Kentucky Press, 2000.

Sidney Hollander Foundation. *Toward Equality, Baltimore's Progress Report: A Chronicle of Progress since World War II toward the Achievement of Equal Rights and Opportunities for Negroes in Maryland*. Baltimore: Sidney Hollander Foundation, 1960.

Silver, Christopher, and John Moeser. *The Separate City: Black Communities in the Urban South, 1940–1968*. Lexington: University of Kentucky Press, 1995.

Skotnes, Andor. "The Black Freedom Movement and the Workers' Movement in Baltimore, 1930–1939." PhD diss., Rutgers University, 1991.

———. *A New Deal for All? Race and Class Struggles in Depression-Era Baltimore*. Durham: Duke University Press, 2013.

Smith, C. Fraser. *Here Lies Jim Crow: Civil Rights in Maryland*. Baltimore: Johns Hopkins University Press, 2008.

Sosna, Morton. *In Search of the Silent South: White Southern Racial Liberalism, 1920–1950*. Madison: University of Wisconsin Press, 1972.

Sterling, Dorothy, ed. *We Are Your Sisters: Black Women in the Nineteenth Century*. New York: Norton, 1984.

Stockley, Grif. *Daisy Bates: Civil Rights Crusader from Arkansas*. Jackson: University Press of Mississippi, 2012.

Suggs, Henry Lewis. *P. B. Young, Newspaperman: Race, Politics, and Journalism in the New South, 1910–1962*. Charlottesville: University of Virginia Press, 1988.

Sullivan, Patricia. *Lift Every Voice: The NAACP and the Making of the Civil Rights Movement*. New York: New Press, 2010.

Takaki, Ronald. *Strangers from a Different Shore: A History of Asian-Americans*. New York: Penguin Books, 1989.

Taylor, Blaine. "The *Afro-American's* 'House of Murphy.'" *Baltimore*, December 1974, 16–23.

Templeton, Furman L. "The Admission of Negro Boys to the Baltimore Polytechnic Institute 'A' Course." *Journal of Negro Education* 23, no. 1 (Winter 1954): 22–29.

Terry, David Taft. "Dismantling Jim Crow: Baltimore's Challenge to Racial Segregation, 1935–1955." *Maryland Humanities*, Winter 2004, 10–14.

———. "Tramping for Justice: The Dismantling of Jim Crow in Baltimore, 1942–1954." PhD diss., Howard University, 2002.

Theoharis, Jeanne. *The Rebellious Life of Mrs. Rosa Parks*. Boston: Beacon Press, 2013.

Thomas, Bettye C. "Public Education and Black Protest in Baltimore, 1865–1900." *Maryland Historical Magazine* 71, no. 3 (Fall 1976): 381–91.

Thornbrough, Emma Lou. "The National Afro-American League, 1887–1908." *Journal of Southern History* 27, no. 4 (November 1961): 494–512.

Tolbert, Emory. "Outpost Garveyism and the UNIA Rank and File." *Journal of Black Studies* 5, no. 3 (March 1975): 233–53.

Tygiel, Jules. *Baseball's Great Experiment: Jackie Robinson and His Legacy*. Oxford, UK: Oxford University Press, 1997.

Wade, Richard. *Slavery in the Cities: The South, 1820–1860*. New York: Oxford University Press, 1964.

Wang, Joan S. "Race, Gender, and Laundry Work: The Roles of Chinese Laundrymen and American Women in the United States, 1850–1950." *Journal of American Ethnic History* 24, no. 1 (Fall 2004): 58–99.

Washington, Booker. *The Booker T. Washington Papers*. 14 vols. Edited by Louis Harlan. Urbana: University of Illinois Press, 1972–89.

Webb, Clive. Introduction to *Massive Resistance: Southern Opposition to the Second Reconstruction*, edited by Clive Webb, 3–20. New York: Oxford University Press, 2005.

Wells, James E., Geoffrey L. Buckley, and Christopher G. Boone. "Separate but Equal? Desegregating Baltimore's Golf Courses." *Geographical Review* 98, no. 2 (April 2008): 151–70.

Wiebe, Robert H. *The Search for Order, 1877–1920*. New York: Hill and Wang, 1966.

Wilkerson, Isabel. *The Warmth of Other Suns: The Epic Story of America's Great Migration*. Random House: New York, 2010.

Williams, Juan. *Thurgood Marshall: American Revolutionary*. New York: Times Books, 1998.

Williams, Rhonda. *The Politics of Public Housing: Black Women's Struggles against Urban Inequality*. New York: Oxford University Press, 2004.

Wilson, Edward N. *The History of Morgan State College: A Century of Purpose in Action, 1867–1967*. New York: Vantage Press, 1975.

Wolcott, Victoria W. *Race, Riots, and Roller Coasters: The Struggle over Segregated Recreation in America*. Philadelphia: University of Pennsylvania Press, 2012.

Wolff, Miles. *Lunch at the 5 and 10*. Rev. and expanded ed. Introduction by August Meier. Chicago: Ivan R. Dee, 1990.

Wolters, Raymond. *Du Bois and His Rivals*. Columbia: University of Missouri Press, 2003.

Woodward, C. Vann. *The Strange Career of Jim Crow*. 3rd rev. ed. New York: Oxford University Press, 1974.

# INDEX

Baltimore, Md. (*continued*)
Chinatown, 33; comparative demographics, 7, 50; and Douglass's boyhood, 5; examples of interracialism in, before Jim Crow era, 21; Great Baltimore Fire, 28; and Maryland attempts at black disfranchisement, 46, 47; and nation's first residential segregation laws, 36; and rise of white nationalist organizations, 196; and rural black migrants, 97, 101; and rural southern migrants, 22; and social justice activism among black clergy, 34; traditional interpretations of, 2; transformation of black struggle to mass mobilization in, 72, 74; and "urbanicity" versus "Border South" thesis, 4; as urban South, 15, 21; as "white man's city," 45; and white modes of antisegregation, 13. *See also* West Baltimore

Baltimore and Annapolis Short Line, 35
Baltimore and Ohio Railroad, 34
Baltimore Association for States Rights, 195, 196
Baltimore Board of School Commissioners, 136, 177, 179, 185, 186, 189; black representation on, 96, 176; challenges after desegregation at Poly, 188; desegregating after *Brown*, 193; Healy Commission recommendations for, 113; obstinacy of, 186; wartime vocational training equalization, 85
Baltimore City College, 24, 192; antidesegregation protestors at, 199; student experiences, 199
Baltimore City Council: Baltimore FEPC passed, 213; criticizes school board for desegregation, 193; enacts residential segregation ordinance, 36
Baltimore City Public Schools, 202, 204; Colored Division, 23, 25, 26, 176; desegregation after *Brown*, 193–195, 198; desegregation's impact on white enrollment, 202; Elementary School No. 60, 187; racial disparities in curriculum, 179, 180; transition to all black faculties, 26
Baltimore Committee for Homefront Democracy, 153
Baltimore Equal Employment Opportunity Commission, 213
Baltimore Hotel Association, 149
Baltimore Housing Authority, 122, 128; slum clearance, 123, 124; wartime programs, 128, 129

Baltimore Inter-racial Conference, 57; industrial study commissioned by, 58
Baltimore Interracial Fellowship, 13, 156; advocates desegregation of amateur sports, 183; comparison to CORE, 164; and Ford's Theatre campaign, 163; founding and mission, 156; Jenkins as a founder, 166
Baltimore Orioles, 147, 148; absence of black minor leaguers, 148; black players' quiet boycott of Jim Crow, 149; impacted by Jim Crow downtown, 149; play Robinson and Montreal Royals, 147, 148
Baltimore Police Department, hiring black officers, 89. *See also* anti–police brutality; police brutality
Baltimore Polytechnic Institute for Boys, 24, 181, 184, 186, 187; "A" course curriculum, 181; circumstantial desegregation, 186
Baltimore *Sun*, 169; anticipating school desegregation, 189; on changing demographics in Baltimore, 132; on desegregation at Poly, 186; discourages support for Wallace, 160; on March on Annapolis, 96; on school desegregation, 195; on wartime black in-migration, 114
Baltimore Tennis Association, 183
Baltimore Transit Company (BTC), 102
Baltimore Urban League (BUL), 58, 127, 151, 181, 184; advocates desegregation of amateur sports, 183; antisegregation projects with ADA, 181, 198; becoming protest organization, 155; and desegregation of Poly "A" Course, 184; and Ford's Theatre protest, 163; founded, 58; and interracialist work of Jenkins, 165; perceptions of, by everyday blacks, 154; on private housing market, 137; study of black employment, 100; on wartime housing, 123; white influence in, 62
Bates, Daisy, 212, 220n23
Bauernschmidt, Marie, 112; on Healy Commission, 113
Bender, Officer Edward, 94, 114; Broadus killing, 93, 94; Parker killing, 88. *See also* police brutality
Bethel AME Church, 55; and Bishop Davis of Healy Commission, 114; Garvey speaks at, 53
Bethlehem Steel, 99, 101; hiring discrimination, 99; and migrants from rural South, 97; opportunities open to blacks, 100; and racial ethos of black workers, 105; white protest of opportunities for blacks, 104

Cole, Emory, 214
Cole, Harry A., 182, 215; early political career, 213, 214; election, 214; proposed civil rights legislation, 214
Collins, Carolyn Gross, 122
Colored High School, 25
Colored Polytechnic Institute, 25
Columbia, S.C., 217
Commission on City Plan, 122, 126
Commission on Interracial Cooperation, 57, 154
Commission to Study Problems Affecting the Negro Population (Healy Commission), 113, 149, 151, 152; authorization, 113; composition and appointments, 113; conflict over consumer discrimination downtown, 151; Gallup poll on department store policies, 152; racial make-up of, 114; and racist policies at department stores, 152; recommendations on housing, 113; recommendations on police brutality, 114; report and recommendations, 113; on wartime housing, 120; work of commission, 114, 115
Committee for Non-Segregation in Baltimore Theatres, 162
Committee of Twelve for the Advancement of the Negro Race, 47
Committee on Segregation, 37
communists, 154, 155; C. J. Murphy on communism's appeal, 67; loss of antiracist mantle to liberals, 155; as radical antiracists, 14; support for Euel Lee, 14
Congress of Racial Equality (CORE), 164; attempted Morgan State College affiliate, 210; Nashville affiliate, 216; New York affiliate supports Baltimore CORE protests, 168; St. Louis affiliate, 167; support for Read's campaign, 208; Washington sit-ins, 166. See also CORE (Baltimore affiliate)
Coordinated Committee on Poly Admission, 182, 185
Corbett, Una, 197, 198; and ADA (Baltimore chapter), 198; and desegregation at Western High School, 198; and effort to desegregate Baltimore Polytechnic, 198; as liberal activist, 197
CORE (Baltimore affiliate), 165, 167, 168, 169, 171, 203, 207, 209; challenges to organizing, 165; downtown lunch counter, 167, 198; founding black members, 165; Gwynn Oak campaign, 168; interest in organizing Mor-

gan students, 207; limited Afro reporting, 168; limited connections to black community, 166; limits of organizing, 172; and members from Morgan faculty, 203, 207, 209, 210, 203; origins, 164, 207; social inter-racialism and nonviolent direct action tactics, 15; techniques of, with student activists, 171; White Coffee Pot campaign, 170, 171
Cornish, Howard L., 207
Cornish, Milton, Jr., 186
Cranston, Joseph Josiah "J. J.," 53–55
Cummings, Harry Sythe, 19; absence of segregation at commencement, 20; early professional life, 20, 46; graduates UM Law, 1890, 19; and national Republican politics, 47; and B. T. Washington's aid to SLM, 46

D'Alesandro, Thomas "Tommy," Jr.: administration criticized over PCA basketball team suspension, 183; appointment of Baltimore FEPC, 213; and black electorate, 158; chides Parks Commissioner Garrett, 183; on impending school desegregation, 189; and Parks Board, 145; and white fears of residential change, 137
Dallas, Tex., 205; UDA chapter, 156
Daly, Clarence, 186
Dates, Victor, 186
Declaration of Intention Act, 108, 157
Delta Sigma Theta, 63
desegregation, 15, 197, 202; anti-desegregation demonstrations, 200; as catalyst for "hate strikes" in defense industries, 105; circumstantial, 2, 180, 185, 186, 187; criticism of school, 193, 196–199; demographic impact on schools, 194, 202; nonviolent direct action tactics, 207; as strategic outcome of equalization campaign, 74, 120. See also lunch counter desegregation sit-in campaign
Diggs, James Robert Lincoln "J. R. L.," 54, 55, 60, 108
disfranchisement, 44, 45–49, 51, 106, 157
Dixon, Irma, 215
Dockum Drug Store (Wichita, Kans.) desegregation, 216
Donald G. Murray v. Raymond A. Pearson, et al., the University of Maryland, 77–79, 81, 144, 179; as abortive basis for desegregation of JHU, 155; and circumstantial desegregation at Poly, 187; and Forum, 182; immediate impacts of, 79–80; limits of impact, 83; as

Progressive Citizens of America (PCA), 160; Camper as member of, 183; emergence of, in Maryland, 159; and HAW campaign, 160; origins, 159; youth basketball team sponsored by, 182; YPA affiliates and tennis protest, 183

public housing, 123; wartime growth and difficulties, 121–129

Pulley, Martha, 187

Randolph, A. Philip, 212

Randolph, Freddie, 206, 210

Rankin, William D., 53, 54

Read's Drugstore, 150; Lexington Street, Baltimore, store, 168; sit-ins, 206, 208. See also lunch counter desegregation sit-in campaign

Redd, Esther, 150, 185

Redd, Nathaniel, 185, 186

reform interracialists, 51, 56–58

residential segregation ordinances (ca. 1910s), 36, 37, 62, 66

restrictive covenants, 37; and FHA, 130; impact on housing available to blacks, 123; *Meade v. Dennistone*, 129; *Shelley v. Kraemer*, 129–132

Richardson, Barney, 42

Richardson, Gloria St. Clair, 192

Richburg, Lonzer, 150

Richmond, Va., 42, 63, 84, 172; and black urbanization, 7; large black community in, 15; NUL chapter, 58

Robeson, Paul, 161, 164

Robinson, Jack Roosevelt, 148, 149, 155, 212; plays minor league Orioles in Baltimore, 147–148

Roosevelt, Theodore, 47, 108, 126

Round Bay Resort, 35

Royal Ice Cream Parlor (N.C.), 216

Royal Theater, 93

Rustin, Bayard, 164, 166, 173, 212

Sands, Douglas, 206, 207, 209

sassing, 41, 78, 86, 93; as pretext for white police brutality of black citizens, 88

Savage, Edward, 186

Savarin Restaurant, 167

Schreiber's Bros. Market, 150

Schulte-United, 168. See also lunch counter desegregation sit-in campaign

Scottsboro Boys Case, 73

SDA (Johns Hopkins University chapter), 203, 204, 205, 211

segregation, 11, 81, 93; defined, 9–10; everyday nature of, 34; reaction to imposition of, in press, 21; and southern white liberals, 112; and urban black life in South, 2; as white reaction to southern black urbanization, 1; and white solidarity, 2

separatist black nationalism, 51, 58, 175; and Harvey Johnson, 52; and reception by Baltimore blacks, 55; and UNIA, 53. See also pragmatist black nationalism

Sharp Street ME Church, 59, 95, 109, 161

*Shelley v. Kraemer*, 140; impact in Baltimore, 130–133; impact near Easterwood Park, 133; and neighbor racial transition, 137, 138; and recreational facilities, 143

Sheraton-Belvedere Hotel, 149

Sherman, Everett, 186

Simkins, Modjeska, 216

Simmons, Carnell, 135, 136; armed self-defense, 133–135

Simmons, Naomi, 133, 134

Simuels, Henry, 88, 90

Smith, Fulton, 41

*Smith v. Allwright*, 106, 110

Sondheim, Walter, Jr., 99, 151, 174, 193

South Carolina State College (Orangeburg), 216

Southern Christian Leadership Conference (SCLC), 212

Southern High School, 199

S. S. Kresge Co., 168. See also lunch counter desegregation sit-in campaign

Stanley, Eugene, 166, 209, 210; arrives at Morgan State College, 210; as a black founder of Baltimore CORE, 166; participation in Journey of Reconciliation, 210; work with CORE in 1940s, 210

Stanton, Robert, 87, 94, 95, 110

*State v. Jenkins*, 65

St. Clair, Carol, 192

Stevender, Robert, 41

Stewart's Department Store, 154

Stewart sisters (Martha, Lucy, Winnie, and Mary), 35

St. James Episcopal Church, 29, 109, 115

St. Louis, Mo., 13, 130, 144, 148, 172; and black urbanization, 7; Chinatown, 33; large black community in, 15; NUL chapter, 58; UDA chapter, 156

CPSIA information can be obtained
at www.ICGtesting.com
Printed in the USA
LVHW111537080719
623448LV00009B/175/P